SCHAUM'S OUTLINE OF

THEORY AND PROBLEMS

of

PROGRAMMING
WITH
FORTRAN 77

•

WILLIAM E. MAYO

Associate Professor
Department of Mechanics and Materials Science
Rutgers University

MARTIN CWIAKALA
Gemco

SCHAUM'S OUTLINE SERIES
McGRAW-HILL
New York   San Francisco   Washington, D.C.   Auckland   Bogotá   Caracas   Lisbon
London   Madrid   Mexico City   Milan   Montreal   New Delhi
San Juan   Singapore   Sydney   Tokyo   Toronto

WILLIAM E. MAYO is an Associate Professor in the Department of Mechanics and Materials Science at Rutgers University. He received his Ph. D. from Rutgers (1982) and has been a member of the Rutgers faculty since then. He served as a postdoctoral fellow at Bell Laboratories (1982-83) where he worked on semiconductor lasers. His primary interests are in computer simulation of materials-related processes such as solid state diffusion and deformation processing. Dr. Mayo is the author of several books and has published over 50 papers in refereed journals and conference proceedings.

MARTIN CWIAKALA received his Ph.D. from Rutgers University in 1988. After graduation, he taught courses in CAD/CAM and Computational Methods for Mechanical Engineers at Rutgers. During this period, Dr. Cwiakala also served as a CAD consultant. This included educational seminars, software development, teaching computer aided design, and beta testing of CAD commercial software packages. Dr. Cwiakala joined Gemco (General Machine Company of New Jersey) as a project engineer and quality control manager. His areas of expertise include developing CAD tools, software to create standard process and instrumentation diagrams (P&ID), automatic generation of main assembly drawings, and an automated proposal generation system. Dr. Cwiakala has published a number of papers on the topic of enhancing CAD capabilities. He is currently the engineering manager at Gemco.

Schaum's Outline of Theory and Problems of

PROGRAMMING WITH FORTRAN 77

18 19 20 DIG/DIG 17 16 15

ISBN 0-07-041155-7

Sponsoring Editor: John Aliano
Editing Supervisor: Patty Andrews
Production Supervisor: Louise Karam

Library of Congress Cataloging-in-Publication Data

Mayo, William E.
   Schaum's outline of theory and problems of programming with
  Fortran 77/William E. Mayo and Martin Cwiakala.
      p. cm. —— (Schaum's outline series)
     Includes index.
     ISBN 0-07-041155-7
     1. FORTRAN 77 (Computer program language) I. Cwiakala, Martin.
II. Title. III. Title: Programming with Fortran 77. IV. Series.
QA76.73.F25M3945 1995
005. 13'3——dc20   94-26460
                                     CIP

McGraw-Hill

A Division of The *McGraw-Hill* Companies

Preface

An Outline, however comprehensive, cannot substitute for a good textbook nor for practical experience in writing and running programs. But we do expect that this book will be a useful supplement and will demonstrate many of the points that a textbook does not have time to cover. There are problems here that will challenge anyone, even experienced Fortran programmers. Yet, there are a large number of problems that even a beginning programmer can handle. Our objective therefore, in putting this Outline together, is to make anyone, from novice through expert, a better programmer.

FORTRAN (Formula Translation) is the oldest, but still one of the most widely used, computer programming languages in the sciences and in engineering. Its continued success is due not only to its power and versatility in dealing with computationally intensive problems and the availability of a wide range of specialized mathematical and statistical library programs, but also to its efficiency and rapid program execution.

Introduced by IBM in the late 1950s, Fortran has gone through a number of revisions, with Fortran IV being the first standardized version issued in 1966 by the American National Standards Institute (ANSI). The version (Fortran 77) discussed in this text is more compatible with the principles of structured programming and features improved capabilities in manipulating nonnumeric data and in processing external files. A newer version (Fortran 90) with significant modifications and improvements is still not widely in use. For the moment at least, FORTRAN 77 remains the most commonly encountered implementation.

Within this Outline, the body of each chapter contains a number of worked examples and additional solved and supplementary problems appear at the end of the chapter. Where appropriate, we have included algorithms and flowcharts with each of the worked examples. Most of the solved and supplementary problems, however, contain only the final program. It is left to you to develop the algorithm/flowchart and match your solution to the program that we give.

At the end of each chapter, we present a section on debugging techniques. This is something that is usually minimized in many textbooks, and we feel very strongly that this is a serious oversight. Therefore, we stress throughout this Outline how to detect and remove bugs. More importantly, we present advice along the way that will help make your programs "bug proof," so that you won't have to spend so much time later in removing bugs.

We would like to express our thanks to Daniel Handal, who ran the programs listed in this Outline and checked them for bugs; and to Martin Cunningham, who proofread the text. May they both live long and prosper.

William E. Mayo
Martin Cwiakala

Dedicated to the memory of
Steven B. Shapiro

WEM

Contents

Chapter 1

Algorithm Development and Program Design

1.1 INTRODUCTION

Writing a computer program to solve a problem is a multistep process consisting of at least the four major elements shown in Fig. 1-1. Note that only one portion of this process (coding) focuses on the use of a specific programming language. The other three steps relate to the development of a *problem-solving approach*. Students often incorrectly assume that once they master a programming language they can solve almost any problem. This could not be further from the truth. In fact, most experienced programmers spend up to 90% of their time working on the logic of their programs, not on the coding. Therefore, it is crucial that you understand this process and develop good problem-solving skills before attempting to write any programs.

The first stage of developing a program is the most crucial. If you *define the problem* carefully, you will find that the remainder of the process will be greatly simplified. Conversely, if you fail to define the problem adequately, you will usually have great difficulties at later stages.

The second step in the program development process is the *generation of the algorithm*. An algorithm is a map or an outline to a problem solution. This outline shows the precise order in which the program will execute individual functions to arrive at the solution. As we will see very shortly, all problem solutions, no matter how complex, can be reduced to combinations of only three basic building blocks. How we use these basic building blocks to arrive at a problem solution

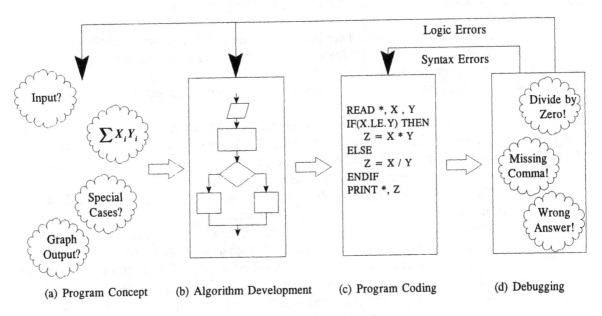

(a) Program Concept   (b) Algorithm Development   (c) Program Coding   (d) Debugging

Fig. 1-1 Stages of program development

1

will be discussed in great depth in later sections of this chapter. It should be emphasized here that the algorithm is *language independent*. This means that it does not depend on the details of the language. For example, a Fortran programmer can use an algorithm developed by a Pascal programmer though the two programmers do not speak each other's language. Thus, the process of developing algorithms can be taught even before we begin a discussion of Fortran.

The third step in the program development process is the *coding* or conversion of the algorithm into the desired programming language. The algorithm allows the programmer to visualize the path to a solution, but it is too imprecise to run intact on a computer. Accordingly, we need to convert the algorithm into a more structured device, *the source code*. The program will follow specific rules required by the specific language. Every programming language has its own set of rigid and somewhat artificial rules, called *syntax*. Nonetheless, you will find these rules easy to master, and subsequently the coding process will be almost automatic.

The final step in the programming process is *debugging*. Every program contains *bugs* that can range from simple mistakes in the language usage (syntax errors) up to complex flaws in the algorithm (logic errors). Removing syntax errors from your programs is usually very simple since the computer will give you *diagnostic messages* highlighting the problem. Logic errors, on the other hand, are much more difficult to remove since the computer will give you no clues. After all, the computer is simply executing your instructions. The computer cannot know what the answer is supposed to be and so you should not expect it to help you find the problem. Consequently, removal of logic errors is an *art* and you must develop techniques to correct these problems.

This chapter will focus on the first two steps in the program development process: defining the problem and writing the algorithm. How to convert the algorithm into a program and how to debug it will be the subject of Chapters 2 through 9.

1.2 BASIC PROGRAMMING TOOLS

You will find that you will need only three basic building blocks to develop a solution to a problem. These building blocks are independent of the language and can be used to develop a conceptual plan to tackle a problem. The three basic building blocks are:

- *Sequential executions*, where instructions are performed one after the other;
- *Branching operations*, where a decision is made to perform one block of instructions or another; and
- *Looping operations*, where a block of instructions is repeated.

Each of these basic blocks may have several slightly different versions, but they are still recognizable. For example, the branching operation usually chooses between two alternative blocks of instructions. But there are other forms of the branching operation that choose between three or more choices. Yet they are all branching operations.

Figure 1-2 illustrates the three basic building blocks, along with their corresponding *flowchart symbols*, which are standardized figures used to show specific programming instructions. By combining these symbols you can generate a map of the algorithm, which makes it much easier to visualize the solution to the problem. Just think of the flowchart as a road map.

The arrows in the list of flowchart symbols are examples of unconditional transfer. No testing is performed – instead, the control of the logic simply follows the arrows to the next instruction for execution. The parallelogram symbol is used to represent either input or output of data. You

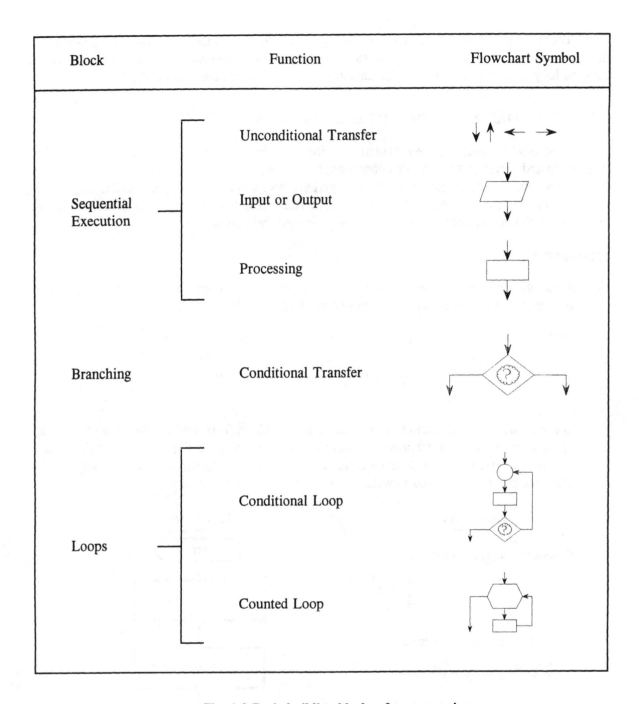

Block	Function	Flowchart Symbol
Sequential Execution	Unconditional Transfer	
	Input or Output	
	Processing	
Branching	Conditional Transfer	
Loops	Conditional Loop	
	Counted Loop	

Fig. 1-2 Basic building blocks of programming

can usually tell which function is intended by its context. Input is usually (but not always) used at the beginning of the program, while output is usually done at the end. So although the same symbol is shared by two different functions, there is usually no ambiguity. The final symbol in the sequential category is the rectangle to represent simple processing such as mathematical operations.

The branching operations contain only a single flowchart symbol (diamond shaped) in which a question is posed, and, depending on the output, control goes in one direction or the other.

There are two types of loops shown in Fig. 1–2. The first is the *conditional* loop where we do not know in advance how many times something is to be repeated. The second type is the *counted* loop where we do know in advance how many times to repeat the instructions.

1.3 SEQUENTIAL EXECUTION OF INSTRUCTIONS

Sequential instructions are executed one after the other. The computer begins with the first instruction and performs the indicated operation, then moves to the next instruction and so on. This kind of sequence is seen often in engineering and science, where the computer evaluates a series of equations and uses these results in subsequent equations. Unless the series of equations are evaluated in the correct order, the correct answer cannot be obtained.

EXAMPLE 1.1

Construct an algorithm and a flowchart to compute the weight w of a hollow sphere of diameter d, wall thickness t, and density ρ, using the following equations:

$$r_o = \frac{d}{2} \qquad\qquad r_i = \frac{d}{2} - t$$
$$v = \frac{4}{3}\pi\,(r_o^3 - r_i^3) \qquad w = \rho v$$

We start with the calculation of the outside and inside radii (r_o and r_i), based on the values of the diameter d and thickness t. From these, we next calculate the volume v of the hollow sphere. Finally, we calculate the weight, which is just the volume times the density, or ρv. Here are the algorithm and flowchart to perform these instructions:

Algorithm

Compute inner and outer radii by

$$r_o = \frac{d}{2} \qquad r_i = \frac{d}{2} - t$$

Compute volume of sphere by

$$v = \frac{4}{3}\pi\,(r_o^3 - r_i^3)$$

Compute weight of sphere by

$$w = \rho v$$

Flowchart

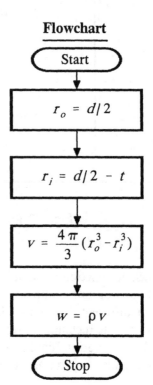

Note in this example that the order in which the computations are performed is important. If the radii r_o and r_i are not calculated first, then it is impossible to calculate correctly the volume and the weight. Notice also that the values of d, t, and ρ have never been entered, nor is the value of w ever printed out once the computations are complete. We will show you how to do that in the next example. Instead, focus on the sequence in which the four instructions above are done.

When we wrote the algorithm, we did not need to follow any rules about how to write it. Instead, we used *pseudocode*, which is a free form list of statements of the sequence of instructions to follow. When you write pseudocode, use any English-like form with which you feel comfortable. That way, it will be intuitive and relatively easy to construct. One word of caution though. Sloppy use of pseudocode may lead to algorithms that cannot be converted into full programs later on. The flowchart, on the other hand, is more formal and requires correct use of the symbols. Therefore, flowcharts may be slightly more difficult to construct. The advantage, however, is that flowcharts force you to use structures which exist in the Fortran language. Therefore, they are much easier to turn into source code than pseudocode.

The symbols that appear at the beginning and end of the above flowchart indicate convenient starting or end points for a process. You should include these in all your flowcharts to make it more convenient for other readers. One final point about this flowchart is that you can combine all the computations into one process box if you prefer. This will save some time.

EXAMPLE 1.2

Rewrite Example 1.1 to allow for input of the values of d, t, and ρ. Also, allow for output of the values of v and w.

Algorithm

Enter values for d, t and ρ
Compute inner and outer radii by

$$r_o = \frac{d}{2} \qquad r_i = \frac{d}{2} - t$$

Compute volume of sphere by

$$v = \frac{4}{3} \pi (r_o^3 - r_i^3)$$

Compute weight of sphere by

$$w = \rho v$$

Print out values of v and w

Flowchart

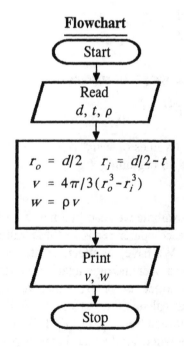

We have combined all the computations into <u>one</u> process box to simplify the flowchart. Also, we have used the same flowchart symbol (the parallelogram) for both input and output (I/O).

Usually, the context of the problem will indicate which function (input or output) is executed. As a result, we could have omitted the I/O instructions (Read and Print). But to avoid any confusion, we have included the input or output command.

The last sequential command is the *Unconditional Transfer*. In spite of its formidable name, this function is one of the simplest. It merely transfers control between points in a program. As we will see shortly, this command is implemented by the GO TO statement, which more clearly suggests its function. You may use this command to repeat a series of other instructions, for example, or this command may also be used to jump over another set of instructions.

EXAMPLE 1.3

Rewrite Example 1.1 and Example 1.2 to allow for repeated calculation of the weight of a hollow sphere of diameter d, wall thickness t, and density ρ. This time, however, allow for input of different values of d, t, and ρ before each calculation of w and v.

Algorithm	**Flowchart**

Enter values for d, t and ρ
Compute inner and outer radii by

$$r_o = \frac{d}{2} \qquad r_i = \frac{d}{2} - t$$

Compute volume of sphere by

$$v = \frac{4}{3} \pi \left(r_o^3 - r_i^3 \right)$$

Compute weight of sphere by

$$w = \rho v$$

Print out values of v and w
Go back to beginning

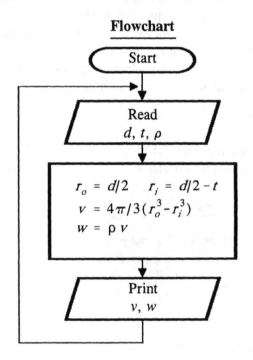

In this example we read in a new set of values for d, t, and ρ before each calculation. Only after the computer reads in these values will the new values of v and w be calculated and printed. We have, in effect, created a *loop*. The series of instructions to calculate v and w are reused over and over again, each time with a different set of input data. A very important point to notice, however, is that we have set up an *infinite loop*. There is no way to stop the repeated calculations except to pull the plug on the computer! Therefore, using the unconditional transfer (or GO TO) to construct a loop is generally <u>not</u> a good idea. In almost all cases where an unconditional loop seems useful, one of the other control structures (loops or branches) can be substituted, and in fact is preferred. We will these control structures in more detail in the next section.

1.4 BRANCHING OPERATIONS

With sequential instructions, the computer executes the instructions one after another. Note that there is no possibility of skipping over one instruction with sequential execution. Many times though, there is a need to allow *branching*. A branch is a point in a program where the computer will make a decision about which set of instructions to execute next. A simple analogy is a fork in a road. At the fork, a question is posed, and depending on the answer to that question we will go to either the right or to the left. Of course, the question must be formulated such that it has a simple answer that will allow us to make the proper decision.

In programming, we also have "forks" that allow us to decide which way to proceed. In Fortran, these branches allow a choice between two or more alternatives. The questions that we use to make the decision about which branch to take must be set up so that the answers can only be *yes* or *no*. This is sometimes a very restrictive requirement, but you will soon see the logic behind this requirement.

The flowchart symbol for branching graphically summarizes its operation. It consists of a diamond in which a question is asked. The question must be set up so that the only possible outcomes are *yes* or *no*. Then, depending on the answer, control flows in one direction or the other:

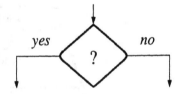

EXAMPLE 1.4

Construct an algorithm and flowchart to read two numbers and determine which is larger.

Algorithm

Enter values of *x* and *y*
Is *x* larger than *y*?
    If yes, print "*x* is larger"
    If no, print "*y* is larger"
End Branch

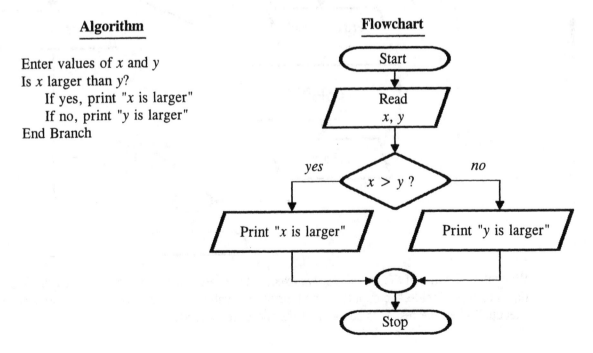

Note how we use the conditional transfer. If x is larger than y, then the block of instructions to the left is executed. In this case, there is only one instruction — a print statement saying that "x is larger". If however, y were larger than x, then the answer to the question would have been false, and the instruction to the right would be executed. Note that only <u>one</u> block of instructions is executed, not both! After one block or the other executes, the two paths merge (at the circle) and control transfers to the next sequential instruction.

The instructions within the branch could have been of any complexity. For example, we could have had several loops inside each block since we are not limited to just one instruction.

EXAMPLE 1.5

Construct an algorithm and flowchart to determine if a point (x, y) lies within a circle of radius, r, centered at the origin. Use the condition that if $(x^2 + y^2)^{1/2} < r$, then the point is within the circle. If the point lies within the circle, print out a message and the distance, z, of that point from the center of the circle.

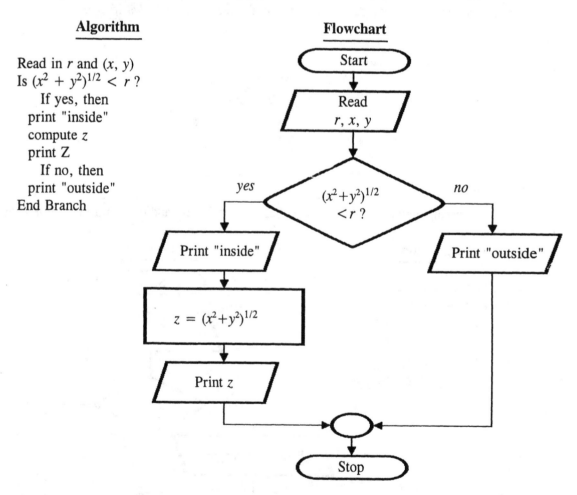

When the outcome of the test is yes, we execute the three instructions on the left side — print the message "inside," compute z, and print the value of z. But only one instruction is executed when the test is false — print the message "outside."

1.5 NESTING OF BRANCHING OPERATIONS

In the previous examples only two alternatives were possible, but there are many times when we need to choose between more than two alternatives. One solution to this dilemma is to *nest* (or embed) one transfer operation within another.

EXAMPLE 1.6

Construct an algorithm and flowchart to see if a number n is negative, positive, or zero.

Algorithm　　　　　　　　　　Flowchart

```
Read in n
Is n < 0?
    If yes, n is negative
  print "Negative"
    If no, is n = 0?
  If yes, n is zero
        print "Zero"
  If no, n is positive
        print "Positive"
        End Branch
End Branch
```

The easiest way to follow how this algorithm works is to substitute a number and trace through the steps. Let's try a value of $n = -5$. The first test is true, so control flows to the left where the next instruction is Print "Negative". This completes the process and control transfers to the end. Now, let's try $n = +5$. The first test is false, so control goes to the right, where a second test is performed to see if $n = 0$. Of course, the result of this is false, so control transfers to the right again, where the Print "Positive" instruction is found. Try the value of $n = 0$ yourself to make sure that you understand how this process works.

1.6 THE SELECT CASE STRUCTURE

A simpler way to handle multiple alternative problems is the *Select Case Structure*. It is not available on some Fortran 77 compilers, but it is now part of the Fortran 90 standard. So before you read this section, check to see if your compiler supports this feature.

The following diagram illustrates how the select case structure works. Several alternatives are offered, but only one can be executed — the one selected inside the diamond. After this set of

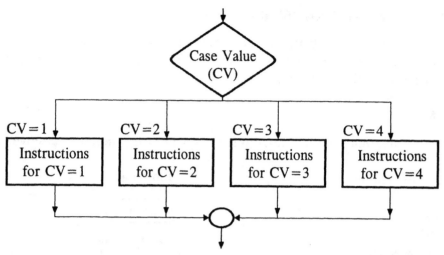

instructions executes, control transfers to the end of the structure. You may have as many alternatives as you wish (only 4 in this example though). The computer decides which set of instructions to execute by examining the value of the case value (CV). If CV=1 for example, the instructions listed under CV=1 will execute, and so on for the other possible values of CV.

EXAMPLE 1.7

Write an algorithm and flowchart to calculate the value of a based on the equations:

$$a = x \cdot y \cdot z \quad (when\ x = 1) \qquad a = x/z \quad (when\ x = 3)$$
$$a = x \cdot y/z \quad (when\ x = 5)$$

Algorithm

Read in values of x, y and z
Select Case (based on value of x)
   When X=1: $a = x \cdot y \cdot z$
   When X=3: $a = x/z$
   When X=5: $a = x \cdot y/z$
End Select Case
Print value of a

Flowchart

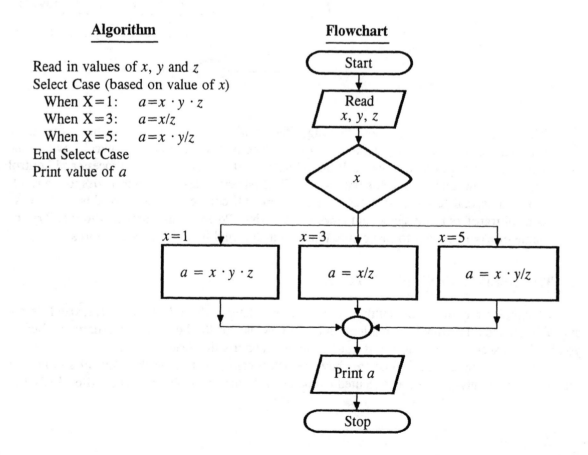

1.7 LOOPS

Loops are the third major type of control structure that we need to examine. There are two different types of loops, the *counted* loop and the *conditional* loop. As the names imply, a counted loop repeats a predetermined number of times while the conditional loop repeats until a condition is satisfied. The figures below (not the true flowchart symbols) schematically illustrate this:

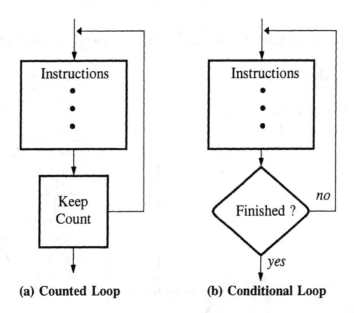

(a) Counted Loop   (b) Conditional Loop

The differences between these two structures are important. In the *counted loop*, a counter keeps track of the loop executions. Once the counter reaches a predetermined number, the loop terminates. The important point is that the limit for the number of loop executions is set <u>before</u> the loop begins and cannot be changed while the loop is running. The *conditional loop*, on the other hand, has no predetermined stopping point. Rather, each time through the loop the program performs a test to determine when to stop. Also, the quantity being used for the test can change (and in fact *must change*) while the loop executes.

The *counted loop* is the most widely used loop in computer programming. These loops execute for a predetermined number of iterations, and the variables controlling the loop cannot be altered once the loop begins to execute. Below is the flowchart symbol for this type of loop:

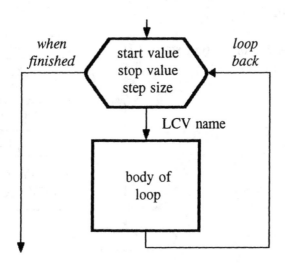

The hexagonal shape is the flowchart symbol for loop. Inside the hexagon are the start and stop values for the *loop control variable (LCV)* that the computer uses to control the loop. Also included is a step size from which the computer will determine how many times to execute the loop. Inside the loop is the *body*, which can consist of any number of instructions. When the loop finishes, control transfers to the first statement outside the loop.

EXAMPLE 1.8

Write an algorithm and flowchart to print out the numbers 1 to 100 and their squares.

Algorithm	**Flowchart**

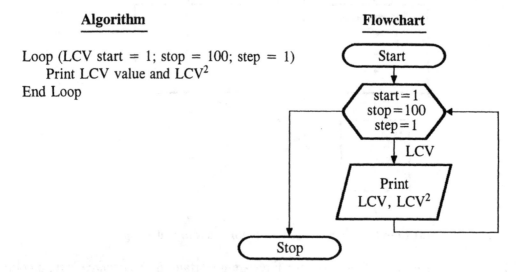

Loop (LCV start = 1; stop = 100; step = 1)
    Print LCV value and LCV^2
End Loop

In this example, the computer will begin with LCV=1, and then print out the value of the LCV (1) and its square (1). Since the loop is not yet finished, the loop will cycle with a new value of LCV = 2. This second value of the LCV is determined from the previous value plus the step size. So, in this example, the LCV will take on values 1, 2, 3, . . ., 100. Only when the LCV exceeds 100 will the loop stop.

EXAMPLE 1.9

Modify Example 1.8 to print out a list of only the even numbers and their squares.

Algorithm	**Flowchart**

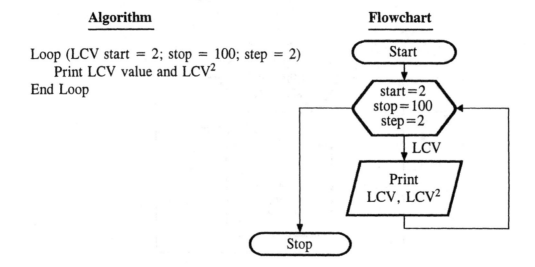

Loop (LCV start = 2; stop = 100; step = 2)
    Print LCV value and LCV^2
End Loop

In this case, we want the LCV to have the values LCV = 2, 4, 6, . . ., 100. So, we will modify the previous algorithm to start at a value of 2 and to have a step size of 2. This will give the desired sequence of LCV = 2, 4, 6,. . ., 100. When we start the loop, the LCV has an initial value of LCV=2, and its square, of course, is 4. The next value of the LCV is determined by adding the step size of 2 to the old value of the LCV. Thus, its new value is 4, and its square is 16. If you examine this example carefully, you will note that the number of loop iterations is given by:

$$Number\ of\ iterations\ =\ \frac{stop\ value\ -\ start\ value}{step\ size}\ +\ 1$$

This calculation is done for you by the computer. All you need to do is set up the start, stop, and step size values. One important point to understand about counted loops is that the LCV is under the control of the computer. You may *look* at its value and *use* it in calculations as we did in these two examples. But, you are not allowed to *change* its value.

One of the keys to using counted loops is that you <u>must</u> know in advance how many times the loop will execute. But many times this information is not available. Yet the problem may demand a loop. So, how can we handle this situation? The solution is the *conditional loop*, where the machine will check every time through the loop to see if it should repeat. In such a situation, there must be one or more variables to control the loop. In addition, this variable <u>must</u> change within the loop. This is the key difference between the two type of loops. In the counted loop, the programmer cannot change the control variable, but in the conditional loop, the programmer must change the control variable.

The most common type of conditional loop is termed the *while loop*. In this loop, a set of instructions is repeated while some condition is true. When this condition becomes false, the loop terminates. There is no specific flowchart symbol for the while loop. Instead, we will reuse the conditional flowchart symbol. In this use of the diamond, though, we will return to a point <u>before</u> the diamond:

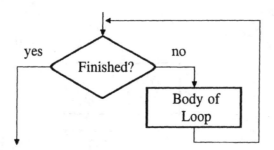

As with counted loops, the body of the loop may contain any number of instructions.

EXAMPLE 1.10

Construct an algorithm and a flowchart to read in a series of numbers and keep track of the running total and the number of data items. Stop reading in the numbers when one of them has a value of zero. Then compute the average of all the numbers and report it.

Since we do not know how many times to repeat the process, the best way to deal with this is to use a conditional loop. We will do the following when the number is nonzero:

- Read in a number and add it to the total
- Add one to the number of items.

Once the critical value (zero) is entered, we can then compute the average:

- Stop the loop
- Divide the total by (number of items − 1)
- Report the average.

When we are finished, we will have read in one data item too many. That's why we have to subtract 1 from the number of data items before computing the average.

Algorithm   **Flowchart**

Set SUM, COUNT to 0
Read in the first number, X
Add that number to SUM
Conditional Loop: (While X ≠ 0)
    Read in next value of X
    Add X to SUM
    Add 1 to COUNT
End Loop
AVG = SUM/(COUNT−1)
Print value of AVG and (COUNT−1)

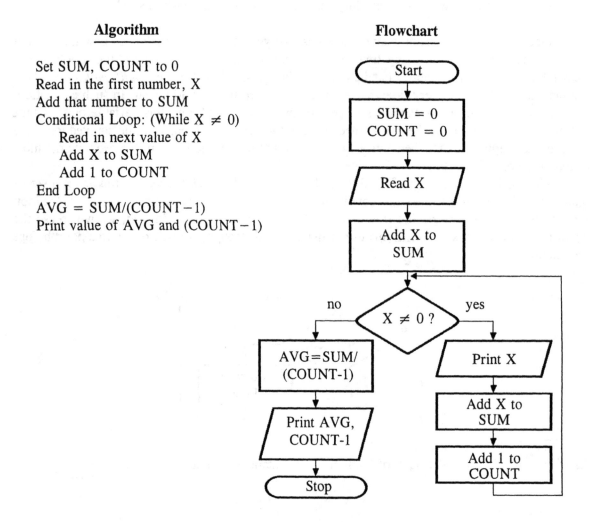

1.8 NESTED LOOPS

In Section 1.5, we showed you how to nest control structures. This can be done also with loops. You can place a counted loop within another counted loop, a conditional loop within another conditional loop, or a combination of different loops within each other.

EXAMPLE 1.11

Construct an algorithm and flowchart to create a 10 by 10 multiplication table such as $1 \times 1 = 1$, $1 \times 2 = 2$, and so forth. This problem is best solved by nesting two counted loops. One loop keeps the value of the first number constant, while the second loop changes the second number from one to ten.

Value of LCV1 in Outer Loop	Value of LCV2 in Inner Loop	Product (LCV1 × LCV2)
1	1	1
1	2	2
:	:	:
2	1	2
2	2	4
:	:	:
10	9	90
10	10	100

Algorithm

Loop (LCV1 start = 1; stop = 10; step = 1)
    Loop (LCV2 start = 1; stop = 10; step =1)
        Product = LCV1×LCV2
        Print LCV1, LCV2, and Product
    End Loop
End Loop

Flowchart

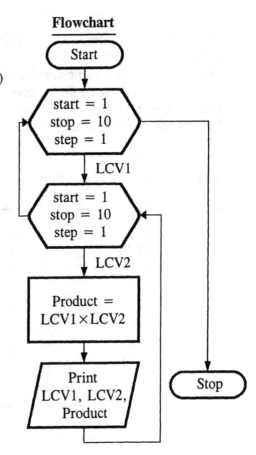

EXAMPLE 1.12

Construct an algorithm and a flowchart that accomplishes the following:

1. Reads in a series of <u>whole</u> numbers (integers), one at a time.
2. Determines how many digits are in each number.
3. Terminates the process when any of the numbers entered is less than zero.

First, let's consider how we determine the number of digits in a whole number. One way to do this is to continually divide the number by 10 until the number is less than or equal to 1. All you have to do then to determine the number of digits is to keep track of the number of divisions. Consider for example the number 123. Note that we do not know in advance how many such divisions we need. So this will require a conditional loop. Here is how the process proceeds:

Step	Number	Number of Divisions	Comments
1	123	0	*Starting value*
2	12.3	1	*First division*
3	1.23	2	*Second division*
4	0.123	3	*Stop, since number is less than 1.0*

Notice that the number of divisions (3 in this example) is the same as the number of digits in the starting number (123).

Once the analysis of the first number is completed, we will need to go back and get the next number and repeat the process. Note that this is a conditional loop, since we do not know how many numbers to analyze. For example, suppose we had the sequence of numbers 123, 17, and -10 to analyze. This is how the program should execute:

Step	Number	Number of Divisions	Comments
1	123	0	*Get the first number*
2	12.3	1	*Divide by 10 and continue*
3	1.23	2	*Divide by 10 and continue*
4	0.123	3	*Finished with first number*
5	17	0	*Get the second number*
6	1.7	1	*Divide by 10 and continue*
7	0.17	2	*Finished with second number*
8	-10	0	*Get third number*
9			*Stop since number less than zero*

Algorithm

Read in a number n
Conditional Loop: (While $n \geq 0$)
    Conditional Loop: (While $n \geq 1$)
        Divide n by 10
        Add 1 to dig (# of digits)
    End Loop
    Print value of dig
    Read in next value of n
    Set dig to zero
End Loop

Flowchart

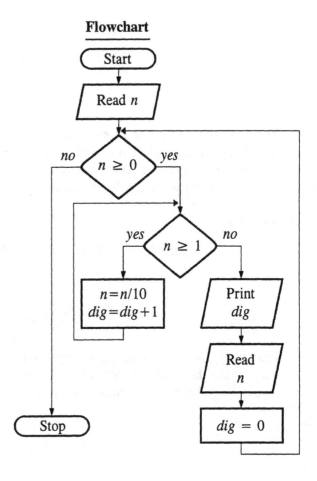

Note carefully how we used the variable n:

- First, we *initialize* the control variable to give it starting value.
- Next, we use this control variable to *test* whether to stop the loop or to continue.
- Finally, we *increment* the control variable and give it its next value.

1.9 PROCEDURES

An important element in all programming languages is the ability to break a single large program down into several smaller ones. By doing so, what may have started as a seemingly intractable problem becomes a solvable one. Thus, breaking the problem down into several smaller components (sometimes called *modules* or *procedures*) allows you to focus on a smaller, more manageable part that attempts to perform only a single well defined task.

By tackling one subproblem at a time, you can focus all our attention on that one problem. Also, the programming modules that you create can be reused. You may reuse them in the same program (with a different set of data for instance), or you may use the modules in another program. The easy way to do this is to store the module in a library that you or other programmers can use. Conversely, you may be able to gain access to libraries that others have written, thus reducing your workload. There are commercially produced libraries that often contain thousands of such modules and you will find these particularly useful.

The modularization process uses the following symbol:

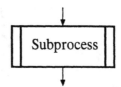

The *subprocess* refers to another set of instructions that describe the details. This is often called an *offpage* process, since it can be placed on another piece of paper. The main idea that you need to grasp here is that you don't want to be bogged down in details. You simply want to focus on the big picture and leave the details for later.

EXAMPLE 1.13

Construct an algorithm and a flowchart to evaluate the first ten terms of the infinite series:

$$a = \frac{1}{1!} + \frac{1}{2!} + \frac{1}{3!} + \cdots$$

where $n!$ is the factorial of n given by $(n)(n-1)(n-2) \ldots (3)(2)(1)$. We need a loop where we evaluate the terms one at a time. Since we know that we want ten terms, this loop will be a <u>counted</u> loop. It is convenient for us to use the LCV from this loop by noting that:

$$\textit{Value of individual term} = \frac{1}{LCV!}$$

The first time through the loop, LCV=1, and the first term is 1/1!. The second time through the loop, LCV=2, and the value of the term is 1/2!; and so forth for LCV=3 to 10.

Now, let's begin to work on the module to compute the factorial. All we have to do is take the value of the LCV and set up a counted loop (with a new LCV2 as its control variable which goes from 1 to LCV). Inside the body of this loop, we will multiply together all the values from 1 to LCV. As an example of how this works, let's assume LCV=3. This value is transferred to the module for computing the factorial, which then computes the product of all integers from 1 to LCV or 1 to 3. The value of the factorial is, of course, $1 \cdot 2 \cdot 3 = 6$. In a similar way, any other value of LCV that is transferred down will be used to compute $1 \cdot 2 \cdot \ldots \cdot$ LCV.

Algorithm

Main Program:

```
Loop (LCV=1 to 10, step=1)
    TERM = 1 / LCV!
    add TERM value to TOTAL
End Loop
Print TOTAL
```

Module for Factorial:

```
FACT=1
Loop (LCV2 =1 to LCV,  step=1)
    FACT = FACT × LCV2
End Loop
```

Flowchart

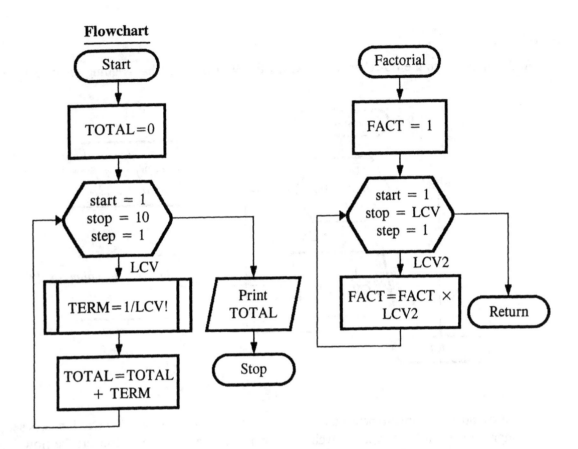

Once the module to compute the factorial is set up, we can use it as many times as needed without having to rewrite the code. In this example, we will use the module ten times, but each time we will send down a different value for which the factorial is to be computed. For example, when LCV=1 in the main part of the flowchart, the value of 1 is transferred to the module, where 1! is computed. The next time though, LCV=2 and so 2! is computed. Note that the loop within the factorial module has a variable limit. Thus, it will compute factorials of different numbers depending on the value of the LCV.

1.10 COMMENTS

There are many times when you want to add comments to your flowcharts to make it easier for others to understand what you are doing. This is done with a special flowchart symbol:

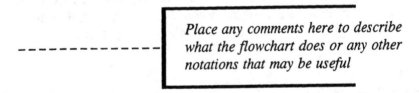

Comments greatly improve the readability of your flowcharts and programs. Not only will other people who read your flowcharts find them helpful, but you will find them useful yourself during debugging by reminding you what you were thinking when you first constructed the solution.

EXAMPLE 1.14

Add comments to the flowchart in EXAMPLE 1.9 to explain what is going on at each step.

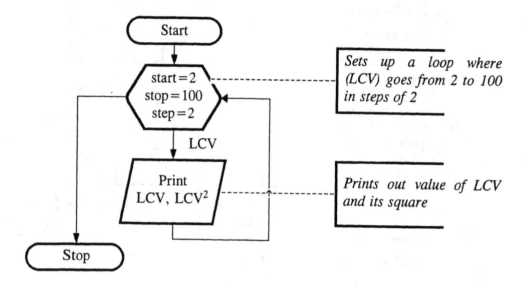

There are no rules for comment statements. Just place them liberally wherever it makes sense to improve the clarity of your flowcharts. Later on, when you go to convert the flowchart into a program, you should also place them in the program.

1.11 DEBUGGING TIPS

Debugging is the process of removing errors from your program. Bugs fall into two general categories — *syntax* and *logic* errors. Syntax errors are mistakes in the grammar of the computer language. These types of errors are easy to correct, and we will discuss them in the following chapters. Logic errors, on the other hand, are mistakes in the sequence of instructions that you have given the computer. For example, you might have given it the wrong instructions, or you may have had a loop execute too many times. In any case, the machine will carry out the instructions in the exact sequence that you told it. As far as the machine is concerned, there was no error!

Logic errors are most easily corrected at the algorithm/flowchart level by a process known as *tracing* where you can see where your logic deviates from what it is supposed to be. Then it should be a relatively simple matter to correct the logic. Tracing is done by making a list of each variable and keeping track of how each changes as you step through the algorithm. You can also trace the program, but it is preferable to do it at the logic forming stage.

EXAMPLE 1.15

The following flowchart is supposed to approximate the sum of the first 100 terms of the infinite series:

$$b = 1 + 1/2 + 1/4 + 1/8 + \ldots$$

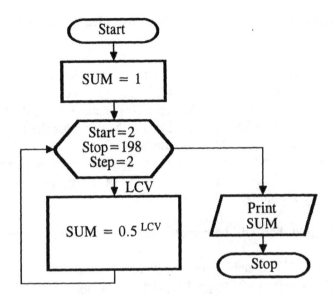

To find and correct the logic error, we must trace through the flowchart by hand. The way that the flowchart is supposed to work is to calculate one series term at a time and add it to the running total (SUM). Let's follow the variables as we step through the program:

Step	LCV	Term	Sum	Comments
1	–	–	1.0	*Initialization before loop*
2	2	1/4	1.25	*LCV = 2*
3	4	1/16	1.0625	*LCV = 4*

The error has already occurred, so there is no need to go further. Instead, it is time to find out what went wrong. We do this by listing what the values *should* have been:

Step	LCV	Term	Sum	Comments
1	–	–	1.0	*Initialization before loop*
2	2	1/2	1.5	*LCV = 2*
3	4	1/4	1.75	*LCV = 4*
4	6	1/8	1.875	*LCV = 6*

There are two problems with the proposed flowchart. See if you can find them before reading any further.

- Once a value of any individual term is calculated, it should be added to the approximation previously obtained. Thus, the value of SUM should increase after each term is calculated. Therefore, the statement inside the loop should read SUM=SUM+TERM, where TERM is the value for the current term and is added to the old value of SUM to get the new value.
- The mathematical expression for the individual term is correct (0.5^{LCV}), but the limits on the loop are incorrect. Instead of having LCV values of 2, 4, 6, . . ., 198, they should be 1, 2, 3, . . ., 99.

In summary, the flowchart will be correct when the following changes are made:

- $SUM = 0.5^{LCV}$ should change to $SUM = SUM + 0.5^{LCV}$.
- LCV limits (start=2, stop=198, step=2) changes to
  LCV limits (start=1, stop=99, step=1).

After implementing these changes, this is what the corrected flowchart will look like:

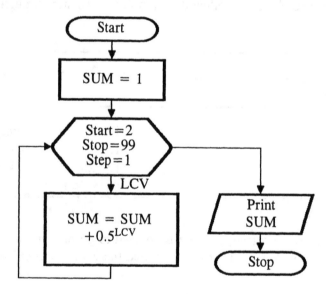

After you have made the changes in the program logic it is a good idea to trace through the new algorithm or flowchart to make sure that it now provides the correct answers. One final word about tracing is that only rarely do you need to trace through the program completely. Usually, only a few data points need to be evaluated before you see what the problem is. That is what we did here. After only a few passes through the loop we were able to find the deviation between the expected results and the actual results. Finally, note that you need to have some idea of the intermediate results before you can begin to find logic errors. In this example, for instance, we knew what the value of each term in the series had to be. This then made it possible to locate the error.

Solved Problems

1.1 Construct an algorithm and a flowchart to read in three values and assign them to the variables x, y, and z.

Algorithm   **Flowchart**

Read in x, y, and z

1.2 Construct an algorithm and a flowchart to print a prompt message to remind you which variables to enter. (A prompt is a message that contains instructions about what to do next.)

Algorithm   **Flowchart**

Print "Ready: Enter x, y, z"
Read in x, y, and z

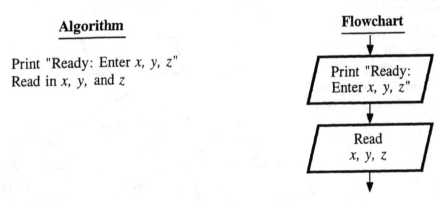

1.3 Construct an algorithm and a flowchart to read in x, y, and z and then compute the value of

$$u = x^{y^{z}}$$

Algorithm   **Flowchart**

Read in x, y, z
Compute u
Print u

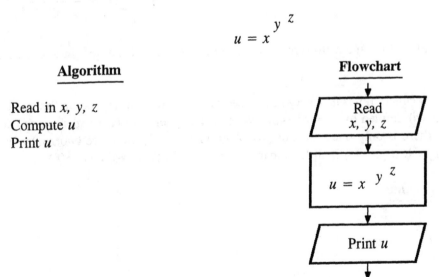

1.4 Construct an algorithm and a flowchart to determine if a whole number n is odd or even. (Hint: integer division produces no remainder. Thus $5/2 = 2$, if both numbers are integers.)

Algorithm

Is $n/2*2 = n$?
    If yes, Print "n is even"
    If no, Print "n is odd"
End Branch

Flowchart

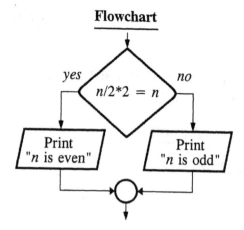

1.5   Construct an algorithm and a flowchart to determine if three whole numbers are all even.

Algorithm

Read i, j, and k
Is $i/2*2=i$ and $j/2*2=j$
and $k/2*2=k$ simultaneously?
    If yes, Print "All are even"
    If no, Print "Some are odd"
End Branch

Flowchart

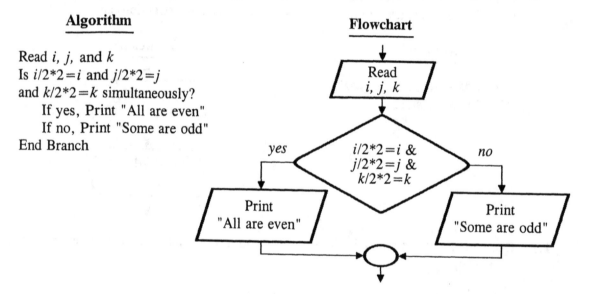

1.6   Construct an algorithm and a flowchart to calculate the roots of the quadratic equation:

$$ax^2 + bx + c = 0$$

Recall that this equation has *three* possible types of solutions that depend on the value of the *discriminant* (d) defined by $d = b^2 - 4ac$. When $d > 0$, there are two real roots (x_1 and x_2). When $d = 0$, there is only one real root (x_1). And when $d < 0$, there are two roots, but they are imaginary (Real part (r), and Imaginary parts (i_1 and i_2)). (Assume $a \neq 0$.)

Algorithm

Read a, b, c
Calculate $d = b^2 - 4ac$
Is $d \geq 0$?
    If yes, then
        Is $d > 0$?
            If yes, then

(Algorithm continues on next page)

$$x_1 = (-b + \sqrt{d})/2a$$
$$x_2 = (-b - \sqrt{d})/2a$$
If no, then
$$x = -b/2a$$
End Branch
If no, then
$$r = -b/2a$$
$$i_1 = + \sqrt{|d|}/2a$$
$$i_2 = - \sqrt{|d|}/2a$$
End Branch

Flowchart

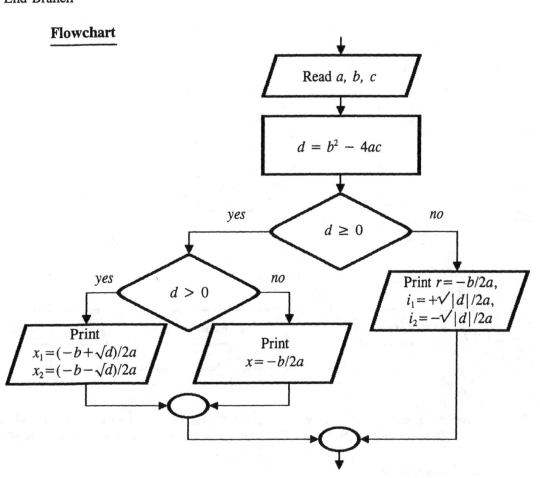

1.7 When we write a program, we often have the program ask questions which are answered "yes" or "no." People have a tendency, however, to answer the questions with things like yes, YES, y, Y, true, or True. A good program should consider how people are likely to answer such a question. Construct an algorithm and flowchart to read in an answer and print out one of three answers — "True," "False," or "Reenter," assuming that yes, YES, y, Y, true, True, t and T are valid equivalents to "True," and that no, No, n, N, false, False, f, and F are equivalent to "False." Any other answer would result in the "Reenter" message. (Hint: Although you could use several nested branching operations, it is better to use the select case structure.)

Algorithm

```
Read ANS
Case Select based on ANS
    If ANS = t, true, T, TRUE,
        y, yes, Y, or YES, then Print "True"
    If ANS = f, false, F, FALSE,
        n, no, N, or NO, then Print "False"
    All other cases, Print "Reenter"
End Case Select
```

Flowchart

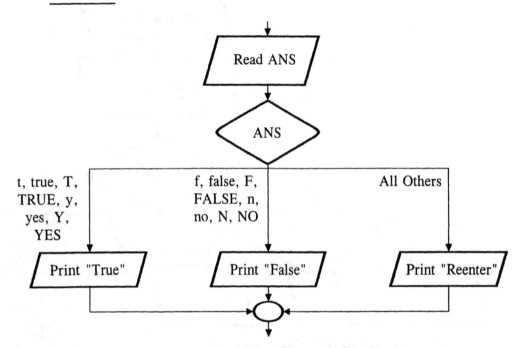

1.8 Construct an algorithm and flowchart to solve the quadratic equation using the Select Case structure. Refer to Solved Problem 1.6 for details about the three categories of possible roots.

Algorithm

```
Read a, b, c
Calculate d = b² − 4ac
Case Select based on d
    If d > 0, then
        x₁ = (−b + √d)/2a
        x₂ = (−b − √d)/2a
    If d = 0, then
        x = −b/2a
    If d < 0, then
```

$$\text{Calculate } d = b^2 - 4ac$$

$$x_1 = (-b + \sqrt{d})/2a$$
$$x_2 = (-b - \sqrt{d})/2a$$
$$x = -b/2a$$

(Algorithm continues on next page)

$$r = -b/2a$$
$$i_1 = + \sqrt{|d|}/2a$$
$$i_2 = - \sqrt{|d|}/2a$$

End Case Select

Flowchart

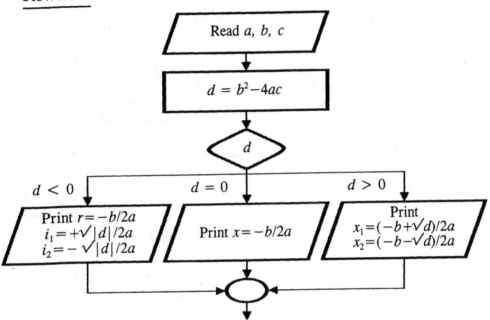

1.9 Construct an algorithm and flowchart to read in two integers i and j and find the sum of all integers between them.

Algorithm

Read i, j
$sum = 0$
Loop (LCV$= i+1$ to $j-1$, step $= 1$)
    $sum = sum + $ LCV
End Loop
Print SUM

Flowchart

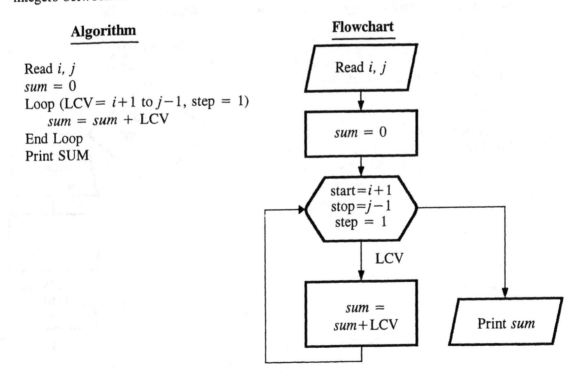

1.10 Construct an algorithm and a flowchart to calculate the values of y for values of $x = 1.0$ to 10.0 in increments of 0.01. The function for y is given by:

$$y = \frac{1}{x} - 4.3 \log(x) + x^4$$

Algorithm

Loop (LCV = 1.0 to 10.0, step = 0.01)
$$y = \frac{1}{LCV} - 4.3 \log(LCV) + LCV^4$$
    Print y
End Loop

Flowchart

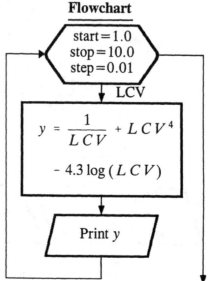

1.11 Construct an algorithm and a flowchart to read in values for a, b, and c and then print their sum. Stop this procedure if <u>any</u> value of a, b, and c is negative.

Algorithm

Conditional Loop: (While a, b, $c \geq 0$)
    Read a, b, c
    $sum = a+b+c$
    Print sum
End Loop

Flowchart

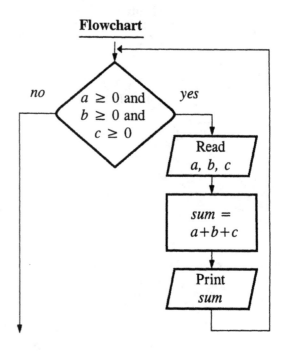

1.12 Construct an algorithm and a flowchart to compute an approximation to the series:

$$\frac{1}{1^3} + \frac{1}{2^3} + \frac{1}{3^3} + \frac{1}{4^3} + \cdots$$

This series continues indefinitely and it is impossible to complete the computation. Yet we can *estimate* the series value by carrying out the computation until a term in the series adds a negligible amount to the total sum of all the previous terms. The way that we will do this is by performing the computation until any term falls below a critical value (ϵ) that you read in. As an example, if we read in a value of $\epsilon = 0.005$ each term will be evaluated and added to the total until any individual term becomes smaller than 0.005 as shown below.

Term	Sum	Comments
$1/1^3$	1.0	*Term (1.000) > ϵ (0.005), so continue series*
$1/2^3$	1.125	*Term (0.125) > ϵ (0.005), so continue series*
$1/3^3$	1.162	*Term (0.037) > ϵ (0.005), so continue series*
$1/4^3$	1.178	*Term (0.016) > ϵ (0.005), so continue series*
$1/5^3$	1.186	*Term (0.008) > ϵ (0.005), so continue series*
$1/6^3$	1.191	*Term (0.0046) < ϵ (0.005), so stop*

Algorithm

Read ϵ
term = 1
sum = 1
count = 2
Loop: (While *term* $\geq$ ϵ)
   term = $1/count^3$
   sum = *sum* + *term*
   count = *count* + 1
End Loop
Print *sum*

Flowchart

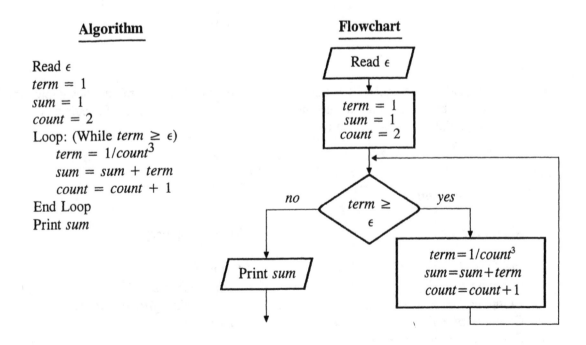

1.13 Construct an algorithm and flowchart to evaluate the following series for $n=3$ to $n=10$. For each value of n, evaluate n terms in the series. For example, if $n=4$ we will evaluate four terms in the series.

$$1 + \frac{1}{1^n} + \frac{1}{2^n} + \frac{1}{3^n} + \cdots$$

We will use the control variable (LCV1) from the first loop to set the upper limit on the second loop. For example, if LCV1 = 4, the inner loop will execute from LCV2 = 1 to 4.

Algorithm

```
Loop (start = 3, stop = 10)
   sum = 1
   Loop (start = 1, stop = LCV1)
      sum = sum + 1/LCV2^LCV1
   End Loop
   Print sum
End Loop
```

Flowchart

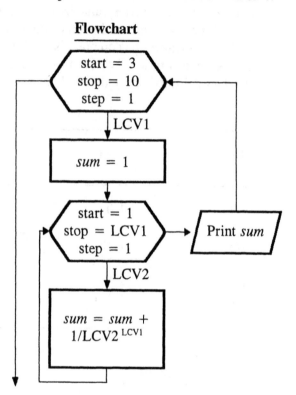

1.14 Construct an algorithm and a flowchart to compute the number of combinations c into which you can organize a class of n students into groups of i and $n-i$ using the formula below. Use a separate module to compute the factorial.

$$c = \frac{n!}{i!(n-i)!}$$

Algorithm

Main Program:

```
Read , n, i
Compute n!
Compute i!
Compute (n−i)!
Compute c = n!/i!/(n−i)!
Print c
```

Module for Factorial:

```
factorial = 1
Loop (LCV = 2 to VAL, step = 1)
     factorial = factorial × LCV
End Loop
```

Flowchart

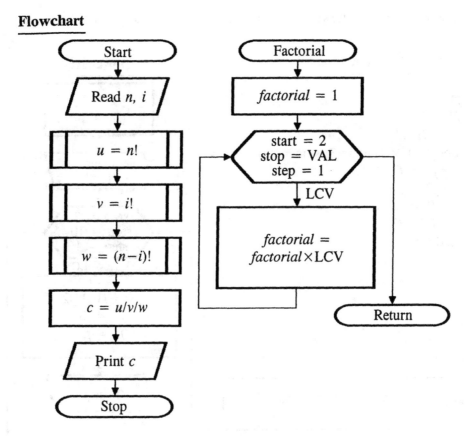

1.15 Construct an algorithm and flowchart of a module that switches two numbers *a* and *b*.

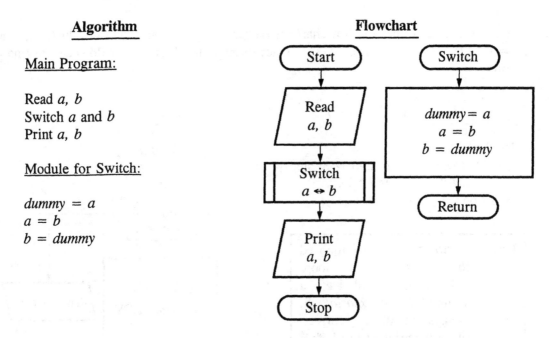

Algorithm

Main Program:

Read *a, b*
Switch *a* and *b*
Print *a, b*

Module for Switch:

$dummy = a$
$a = b$
$b = dummy$

Flowchart

Note the three statements in the module to switch two numbers. The only way to switch two numbers is to use a *dummy* variable to temporarily store one of the values.

1.16 Trace through the following flowchart (or algorithm) and predict the output.

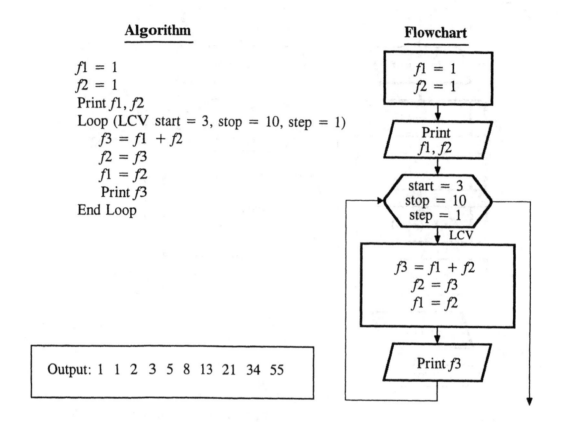

Algorithm

$f1 = 1$
$f2 = 1$
Print $f1, f2$
Loop (LCV start = 3, stop = 10, step = 1)
  $f3 = f1 + f2$
  $f2 = f3$
  $f1 = f2$
  Print $f3$
End Loop

Output: 1 1 2 3 5 8 13 21 34 55

Flowchart

1.17 The following algorithm and flowchart are flawed. They are supposed to evaluate $n!$, where $n! = (1)(2)(3) \ldots (n-2)(n-1)(n)$. Trace through the algorithm or flowchart to find the error(s).

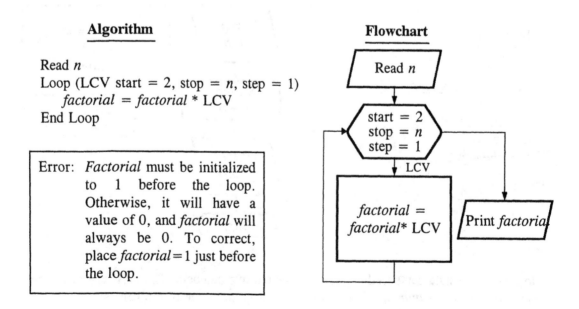

Algorithm

Read n
Loop (LCV start = 2, stop = n, step = 1)
  factorial = *factorial* * LCV
End Loop

Error: *Factorial* must be initialized to 1 before the loop. Otherwise, it will have a value of 0, and *factorial* will always be 0. To correct, place *factorial* = 1 just before the loop.

Flowchart

Supplementary Problems

1.18 Construct an algorithm and a flowchart to output the values of three variables, x, y, and z.

1.19 Construct an algorithm and a flowchart to show that for $a = 2.13$ and $b = 1.3$, the following trigonometric identity holds for the tangent function, tan (x).

$$\tan(a + b) = \frac{\tan(a) + \tan(b)}{1 - \tan(a)\tan(b)}$$

1.20 Construct an algorithm and a flowchart to calculate the apparent difference in ages between twins separated at birth. One is kept on earth while the other one is placed on a rocket ship traveling to the nearest star, Alpha Centauri, which is 4.8 light years away. Assume that the ship travels at 0.96 times the speed of light and that the trip takes 5 earth years. The age of the twin (to an earth observer) is given by

$$t_m = t_s \left[1 - \left(\frac{v}{c}\right)^2 \right]^{1/2}$$

where t_m = elapsed time measured on the moving object
         t_s = elapsed time measured on the earth
         v = velocity of the rocket
         c = speed of light.

1.21 Construct an algorithm and a flowchart to calculate the current I in a diode (an electrical device), at any applied voltage V if the diode characteristics are given by

$$I = I_0(e^{kV} - 1) \qquad for\ V \geq V_R$$
$$I = -I_0(e^{-kV} - 1) \qquad for\ V < V_R$$

where I_0, V_R, and k are constants.

1.22 Construct an algorithm and a flowchart to read in four whole numbers and determine how many of the numbers are equal to any of the other numbers in the group.

1.23 Construct an algorithm and a flowchart to issue grades to students. Use the following criteria:

if score is between 90 and 100, then grade = A
if score is between 89 and 80, then grade = B
if score is between 79 and 70, then grade = C
if score is between 69 and 60, then grade = D
if score is below 60, then grade = F.

1.24 Construct an algorithm and a flowchart to determine if a number is positive, negative or zero. Use a select case structure to make the decisions.

1.25 Construct an algorithm and a flowchart to read in two whole numbers and find the sum of all *odd* numbers between these two. Include in the sum both numbers if they are odd.

1.26 Construct an algorithm and a flowchart to compute the terms in the following series:

$$1 \quad 1 \quad 2 \quad 3 \quad 5 \quad 8 \quad 13 \quad 21 \quad 34 \quad 55 \quad 89 \quad 144 \quad 233 \quad ...$$

The first two numbers are 1 and 1. All the other terms are determined by adding the previous two terms. Calculate n terms of this series, where n is read into the program.

1.27 Construct an algorithm and a flowchart to read in a number x and repeatedly divide it by 2 until the result is smaller than 0.001. Print out how many divisions it took.

1.28 Construct an algorithm and a flowchart to calculate the terms in this series:

$$a = 2\left[1 - \frac{1}{2} + \frac{1}{3} - \frac{1}{4} + \frac{1}{5} - \cdots \right]$$

Calculate the series until any one term is less than 0.1% of the value of the sum of the previous terms. Note that the sign of each term alternates.

1.29 Construct an algorithm and a flowchart to calculate the value of a, where

$$a = \frac{x - y}{x^y} - \frac{y - x}{y^x}$$

for values of $x = 1, 2, 3, \ldots, 10$ and for values of $y = 0.1, 0.2, 0.3, \ldots, 1.0$.

1.30 Construct an algorithm and a flowchart for a main program and a module to receive two numbers and determine which one is greater.

1.31 Construct an algorithm and a flowchart for a module to approximate the sine of an angle:

$$\sin(x) = x - \frac{x^3}{3!} + \frac{x^5}{5!} - \frac{x^7}{7!} + \cdots$$

Then use this module to test the identity $(\sin(3a) = 3\sin(a) - 4\sin^3(a))$ for $a = 1, 2, \ldots, 5$.

Answers to Selected Supplementary Problems

1.18 Print out X, Y, Z

1.19 Read A, B
RTSIDE=(tan(A)+tan(B))/(1−tan(A)tan(B))
LEFTSIDE=tan(A+B)
Print RTSIDE, LEFTSIDE

1.20 Read RATIO, TS
$TM=TS[1-(RATIO)^2]^{1/2}$
DIFFERENCE=TS−TM
Print DIFFERENCE

(Comment: The variable RATIO is the fraction of the speed of light that the rocket is traveling. In this case, RATIO=0.96.)

1.21 Read K, V, I0, VR
Is V ≥ VR?
If yes, then $I=I0(e^{KV} - 1)$
If no, then $I=-I0(e^{-KV} - 1)$
End Branch

1.22 Read I, J, K, L
NUM = 0
Is I = J? – if yes, NUM = NUM + 1
Is I = K? – if yes, NUM = NUM + 1
Is I = L? – if yes, NUM = NUM + 1
Is J = K? – if yes, NUM = NUM + 1
Is J = L? – if yes, NUM = NUM + 1
Is K = L? – if yes, NUM = NUM + 1
Print NUM "numbers are equal"

1.23 Read SCORE
Is SCORE ≥ 90 and SCORE ≤ 100?
If yes, GRADE = A
Is SCORE ≥ 80 and SCORE ≤ 89?
If yes, GRADE = B
Is SCORE ≥ 70 and SCORE ≤ 79?
If yes, GRADE = C
Is SCORE ≥ 60 and SCORE ≤ 69?
If yes, GRADE = D
Is SCORE < 60? – if yes, GRADE = F

1.24 Read X
Select Case (based on X)
X < 0:   Print "X is negative"
X = 0:   Print "X is zero"
X > 0:   Print "X is positive"
End Select Case

1.25 Read I, J
SUM = 0
Loop (LCV start = I, stop = J, step = 1)
Is (LCV/2)*2 = LCV?
If yes, then skip
If no, then SUM = SUM + LCV
End Branch
End Loop

*(Comment: The statement LCV*2/2 = LCV checks to see if LCV is even. If it is, then we skip that value of LCV, and go on to the next one.)*

1.26 Read N
F1 = 1

1.27 Read X
NUM = 0

```
        F2 = 1
        Print F1, F2
        Loop (start = 3, stop = N, step = 1)
            F3 = F1 + F2
            F2 = F3
            F1 = F2
            Print F3
        End Loop
```

```
Conditional Loop: (While X ≥ 0.001)
    X = X/2
    NUM = NUM + 1
End Loop
Print NUM
```

1.28
```
    I = 2
    SIGN = +1
    TERM = 2
    SUM = 2
    Loop: (While |TERM|/|SUM| ≥ 0.001)
        SIGN = − SIGN
        TERM = SIGN/I
        SUM + SUM + TERM
        I = I + 1
    End Loop
    Print SUM
```

(Comment: We need to independently calculate the sign (+ or -) and the magnitude for each term in the series. We then estimate the importance of the term by its   ratio |TERM|/|SUM|.   If   the contribution is negligible, then we stop calculating other terms.)

1.29
```
Loop (LCV1 start=1 to 10, step=1)
    Loop (LCV2 start=0.1 to 1.0, step=0.1)
```

$$A = \frac{X - Y}{X^Y} - \frac{Y - X}{Y^X}$$

```
        Print A
    End Loop
End Loop
```

1.30   <u>Main Program:</u>

```
    Read A, B
    C = MAX( A, B)
    Print C
```

<u>Module for MAX:</u>

```
    Is A > B?
        If yes, MAX = A
        If no, MAX = B
    End Branch
```

1.31   <u>Main Program:</u>

```
    Loop (LCV start = 1 to 5, step = 1)
    Print A
    U = sin(A)
    V = [sin(A)]³
    RTSIDE = 3U − 4V
    LFTSIDE = sin(3A)
    Is (|LFTSIDE−RTSIDE| < 0.01)?
        If yes, then print "identity valid"
        If no, then print "identity invalid"
    End Branch
    End Loop
```

Module for SIN(X) Approximation:

```
SUM = X
TERM = X
SIGN = +1
I = 3
Loop: (While |TERM|/|SUM| ≥ 0.0001)
    SIGN = - SIGN
    TERM = SIGN*X^I/I!
    SUM = SUM + TERM
    I = I + 2
End Loop
```

Module for Factorial of I:

```
FACT = 1
Loop (LCV start = 2, stop = I, step =1)
    FACT = FACT * LCV
End Loop
```

Chapter 2

Getting Started

2.1 INTRODUCTION

In the last chapter, we presented the basic building blocks required for programming. So now it is time to introduce the specific details needed to construct simple Fortran programs using some of these basic ideas. To allow you to write your first program, we need to discuss four items:

- How a program is organized
- The different types of data, constants, and variables
- The assignment statement as a means of calculating and storing data
- Simple input and output

We will also review selected library functions for performing common mathematical operations and debugging tips. When you complete this chapter, you should be able to write a simple program consisting of input, sequential calculations and output to a terminal screen.

2.2 PROGRAM ORGANIZATION

A program is constructed with a *text editor*, which is nothing more than a simple word processor. The organization of each program line must follow very specific rules and you must be very careful to follow them. For instance, the various columns have significance as summarized in the table below. Columns 1 through 5 are reserved for statement labels and column 6 is reserved for a continuation character that indicates that the current line is a continuation of the previous line. Columns 7 through 72 store the Fortran commands. Finally, columns 73 and higher are ignored and can be used for comments. Sometimes, you may wish to document various parts of your program. This can be done by using *Comments*, which are created by placing the letter C or an asterisk (*) in column 1. Any text that follows on that line will be ignored.

Column	Purpose
1	C or * in column indicates a comment line
1—5	Statement labels that are used to identify specific lines
6	Continuation character (any character is allowed)
7—72	Fortran program statements
73—	Everything that follows is ignored; can be used for short comments

EXAMPLE 2.1

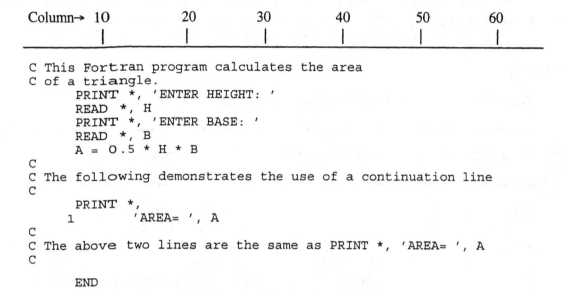

```
Column→  10        20        30        40        50        60
         |         |         |         |         |         |

C This Fortran program calculates the area
C of a triangle.
      PRINT *, 'ENTER HEIGHT: '
      READ *, H
      PRINT *, 'ENTER BASE: '
      READ *, B
      A = 0.5 * H * B
C
C The following demonstrates the use of a continuation line
C
      PRINT *,
     1         'AREA= ', A
C
C The above two lines are the same as PRINT *, 'AREA= ', A
C
      END
```

The END statement indicates the end of the *main* program. Later on, we will introduce the concept of *subprograms*, which can be considered as separate programs. Therefore, the END statement is needed to divide the different parts, or *modules*. Without the END statement, we would have no way of knowing where one module ends and next one begins.

Optionally, a program may start with the PROGRAM *name* statement, where you can substitute a convenient label for *name* that indicates the program function. The sole purpose of this name is to make it easier for you to recognize each program at a later date.

EXAMPLE 2.2

```
C The program name (AREAOFCIRCLE) suggests its use
C
      PROGRAM AREAOFCIRCLE
C
C This example calculates the area of a circle.
C
      PRINT *, 'Enter Circle Radius'
      READ *, R
      A = 3.1416 * R * R
      PRINT *, 'Area of circle is ', A
      END
```

2.3 DATA TYPES AND INTEGER CONSTANTS

Fortran 77 contains six *intrinsic* data types that are built automatically into the language. These are divided into two categories: *numerical* and *nonnumerical*. Numerical types are *integer, real, double precision,* and *complex*. Nonnumerical types are *character* and *logical*. In this chapter, we are mostly concerned with the numerical types.

Integer Constants

Integer values are those that represent whole numbers. The range of values that can be represented on a computer depends specifically on the computer. However, a typical range is from -2^{32-1} to $+2^{32-1} - 1$ (approximately $\pm 2 \times 10^9$) for a 32-bit computer.

EXAMPLE 2.3

The following illustrate correct and incorrect examples of integer constants:

Valid Examples	Invalid Examples	Comment
-999		*Negative sign required*
+10		*Plus sign optional*
111 111 111		*Spaces ignored – useful for large numbers*
	111,111,111	*No commas*
	174.00	*No decimal points in integer numbers*
	-7 1/2	*No fractions*

Real and Double Precision Constants

The second type of numerical constant is called *real*. Real numbers are stored in the computer as two components: a mantissa ranging between 0.1 and 1.0 and an exponent that indicates the appropriate power of 10. Real constants are those that we think of as fractional numbers which may be positive or negative and *always* have a decimal point.

EXAMPLE 2.4

The following examples illustrate valid and invalid uses of real constants:

Valid Examples	Invalid Examples	Comment
-21.4		*Negative required*
+132.7		*Plus sign optional*
0.0000034		*Small numbers permitted*
123 456.0		*Spaces ignored*
	$ 1.23	*Only numbers permitted (no $)*
	0	*Requires a decimal point, otherwise this is an integer*
	123,456.00	*No commas*

Real constants can also be used with *scientific notation*. Recall that this is a useful method for noting very large or very small numbers. It relies on the use of a mantissa between 0.1 and 1.0 and an exponent that is a power of 10 and given by <mantissa> × 10 <exponent>. The limit of accuracy of real constants is approximately seven digits with a magnitude from 10^{-39} to 10^{+38}.

EXAMPLE 2.5

The following examples show the use of real constants using scientific notation:

Valid Examples	Invalid Examples	Comment
0.6023E24		*Avogadro's number 6.023×10^{23}*
−0.123E24		*Negative mantissa permitted*
0.123E-24		*Negative exponent permitted*
0.0E0		*Zero!*
1E2		*Decimal point not required*
	0.1E−12.5	*Exponent must be integer*
	0.1E−123	*Value too small on most computers*
	0.1E+123	*Value too large on most computers*

If more than 7 digits of accuracy are required, you can use a *double precision* constant, which is accurate to 14 to 16 decimal places, depending on the machine. Double precision is simple to use. Instead of using E for the exponent, double precision simply substitutes the letter D.

EXAMPLE 2.6

The following examples illustrate double precision constants using scientific notation:

Valid Examples	Invalid Examples	Comment
0.0D0		*Double precision form of zero*
0.23D-94		*Double precision will give greater range*
	0.123456789E23	*Not double precision! Extra digits ignored*

A word of caution: double precision numbers require two to ten times the computational time compared to single precision real numbers. Therefore, you should be careful to use double precision only when absolutely required.

Complex Constants

We often need to use complex numbers such as $4+3i$, which contain real and imaginary parts. Since computers cannot work with imaginary numbers programmers have developed a convention where a complex constant is represented by two real components.

Fortran representation: $(REAL_1 , REAL_2)$

Algebraic representation: $real_1 + i (real_2)$

The first number $(REAL_1)$ represents the real part of the complex number, and the second number $(REAL_2)$ represents the imaginary part $(i^2 = -1)$. The rules for complex constants are not standard for Fortran 77, yet most commercial versions of the Fortran 77 language use a similar set of rules in defining complex data. The following example summarizes these rules.

EXAMPLE 2.7

Here are some examples of commonly encountered complex constants:

Valid Examples	Invalid Examples	Comment
(1.23, -3.45)		*Either component may be negative*
(+1.23, 0.0)		*Positive sign is optional*
(1.23E-2, 3.45)		*Exponential format is permitted*
	(1.23D-128, 3.45)	*Both components must match in precision*
	(1, 2)	*Integers not allowed*

Complex numbers are not officially part of the Fortran 77 standard. However, almost all compilers support them as extensions, so that there are few problems in using them.

Character Constants

There are occasions when we need to work with nonnumerical data, which cannot be handled with the data types just discussed. Examples would be data such as names and addresses. Accordingly, we will use a different type of constant, the *character* constant. A character constant is any set of the allowed symbols defined below and enclosed in single quote marks (').

Letters of the alphabet (upper- or lower-case)
Numbers 0 through 9
Special characters $+ - ( ) . , * / = ' \$$
Blank space

Even though you can create symbols such as ☺ on your computer, Fortran will not accept them.

EXAMPLE 2.8

Here are some commonly encountered examples of character constants:

Valid Examples	Invalid Examples	Comment
'Helen'		*Mixing upper/lower case OK*
'12345'		*All numbers OK*
'I''M OK'		*If you want an apostrophe inside the single quotes, you must use two apostrophes. Result is I'M OK.*
	"Helen"	*Must use single quotes (apostrophe)*
	Helen	*Missing quote marks*
	'I ♥ NY'	*Illegal character (♥)*

Be sure not to confuse the character constant '1234' with its numerical counterpart 1234. While it is possible to perform mathematical operations with numerical constants, you cannot do the same thing with numbers stored as character constants. For example, you can add 123 to 456 (both numerical constants), but you cannot write '123' + '456', since these are character constants.

Logical Constants

The final intrinsic data type is the *logical* constant, which can take on only two values. Thus, the rules are very simple since the only allowed values of logical constants are .TRUE. and .FALSE. (note the use of the periods). The role of the logical constant will be made more apparent in the following chapters when we discuss control structures.

EXAMPLE 2.9

Here are some examples of common uses of logical constants:

Valid Examples	Invalid Examples	Comment
.True.		*Mixed case is acceptable*
	FALSE	*Requires periods (.FALSE.)*
	.T.	*Must spell out complete word*

2.4 VARIABLES AND SIMPLE INPUT/OUTPUT

Variables provide a means by which you can manipulate data. By using input and output statements, variables become another way by which you can introduce data into your program. When you studied algebra, you learned that variables could be used to represent a quantity in a formula. In programming, variables have this function also. However, we also use variables to represent memory in the computer. The following example is a program that requests the radius of a circle and returns its circumference and area.

EXAMPLE 2.10

Below is a simple program to compute the area and circumference of a circle of radius r. In the program, the variables used are PI, AREA, CIRCUM, and R. Note that we try to choose variable names that indicate their function in the program.

```
      PROGRAM AREAOFCIRCLE
C The following statements request the user to type in
C a value of the radius
      PRINT * , 'Enter circle radius'
      READ * , R
C Once the radius is fed in, the area is calculated
      PI = 3.1416
      AREA = PI * R * R
      CIRCUM = 2 * PI * R
C The value of the area is now printed out
      PRINT * , 'Area of circle is ', AREA
      PRINT * , 'Circumference of circle is ', CIRCUM
      END
```

When we execute this program, the following sequence of events will occur:

Enter circle radius	*(Printed by computer — line #4)*
5	*(Value typed in by user —line #5)*
Area of circle is 78.54	*(Printed by computer — line #11)*
Circumference of circle is 31.416	*(Printed by computer — line #12)*

The value of R was entered into the program with a READ Statement and PI was given a value by using a real constant. AREA and CIRCUM were calculated by using simple mathematical expressions. Finally, the calculated values of AREA and CIRCUM were displayed at the terminal screen by using the two PRINT statements in lines 11 and 12.

When you give variables their names, try to choose names that describe their function within the program. The rules for defining Fortran 77 variable names are as follows:

- Names are 1 to 6 characters long
- Only letters (A — Z) and numbers (0 — 9) are allowed
- First character must be a letter
- Upper/lower case are equivalent
- Blank spaces are ignored

EXAMPLE 2.11

Here are some common forms of variable names:

Valid Examples	Invalid Examples	Comment
X		*OK, but not very illustrative*
TAXDUE		*Better, since it describes its function*
TEMP1		*OK to mix letters and numbers*
AMT DUE		*OK, spaces are ignored*
Amt Due		*Same as previous example, since lower case is treated the same as upper case in Fortran*
	AMOUNTDUE	*Too many characters (max of 6)*
	$OWED	*Illegal character ($)*
	2BEES	*Must start with a letter*

Implicit Data Typing

In the previous sections, we discussed the six basic data types, but we did not discuss how to tell the computer how to define the variables. With constants, it was obvious what data type each constant was. For example, if a number had a decimal point it was real, and if it had no decimal point, it was treated as an integer, and so forth. But with variables we must develop another way. With Fortran, we have two options, *implicit* or *explicit* typing.

The variables in Example 2.10 were *implicitly* defined, which means that each was assigned to a data type based on the first letter of the variable name and the following rules:

Variable names that begin with the letters A—H or 0—Z are real.
Variables names that begin with the letters I—N are integer.

EXAMPLE 2.12

Here are some examples of implicit typing:

Variable	Type		Variable	Type
R	Real		CIRCUM	Real
PI	Real		LENGTH	Integer
AREA	Real		ICOUNT	Integer

Explicit Data Typing

Implicit typing rules make it easy to define whether variables will be real or integer. But these rules do not apply to complex, character or logical variables. To use these types, you must use *explicit* typing rules. Explicit typing is simply the procedure of specifying how to treat each variable. These rules are also used if you want to override the implicit typing for integers and reals.

To declare a variable to be a specific type, enter the type followed by a list of the variables to be so treated, with each variable separated by a comma. This so-called *declaration statement* <u>must</u> come before any executable statement where some sort of processing takes place. There may be several declaration statements at the beginning of the program, and their form will always be:

$$TYPE \ \ variable1 \ , \ variable2 \ , \ . \ . \ .$$

EXAMPLE 2.13

Here are some examples of explicit typing:

Declaration Statement	Result
REAL X , Y , Z	Declares X, Y, and Z as a real variables
REAL LENGTH	Defines LENGTH as a real variable
INTEGER COUNT	Defines COUNT as an integer variable
CHARACTER GRADE	Defines GRADE as a character variable of length 1
CHARACTER*20 NAME	Defines NAME as a character variable of length 20
COMPLEX PHASE	Defines PHASE as a complex variable
LOGICAL YESNO	Defines YESNO as a logical variable
DOUBLE PRECISION X	Defines X as a double precision variable
CHARACTER A*10, B*20	Defines A as a character variable of length 10 and B as a character variable also, but of length 20

The following example shows a full program with <u>explicit</u> variable typing to define the several variables.

EXAMPLE 2.14

The following program is similar to Example 2.10, except that the types of the variables are now explicitly stated:

```
      PROGRAM AREAOFCIRCLE
C The following statements requests the user to type in
C a value of the radius
      REAL R, PI, AREA, CIRCUM
      PRINT * , 'Enter circle radius'
```

(Program continues on next page)

```
      READ * , R
C Once the radius is fed in, the area is calculated
      PI = 3.1416
      AREA = PI * R * R
      CIRCUM = 2 * PI * R
C The value of the area is now printed out
      PRINT * , 'Area of circle is ', AREA
      PRINT * , 'Circumference of circle is ', CIRCUM
      END
```

Simple Input and Output

Most programs require the user to enter data into the program. And once calculations have been performed, the results must be sent to some sort of display device such as a CRT screen. These two functions are known as *input* and *output*, or collectively as I/O. We have already seen examples of I/O in Example 2.10. For the purpose of this section, only free formatted output (also called list directed) will be presented, and we will assume that all I/O will be at the terminal screen.

To input a value to a variable, we use the READ * statement with the general form:

READ *, *variable1, variable2, . . .*

To display the value of a variable or variables on the terminal screen, we use the PRINT * statement, whose general form is:

PRINT *, *variable1, variable2, . . .*

Character constants can be included in the output list of the PRINT * command, by placing the string to be printed inside single quotation marks.

EXAMPLE 2.15

The following example reads in a person's name and age in years. It then converts the age from years into months:

```
      PROGRAM AGEINMONTHS
C The declaration statement must come first
      CHARACTER*10 NAME
      REAL AGEYRS, AGEMTH
C Here is where we input the person's name and age
      PRINT *, 'Enter your name and your age in years'
      READ *, NAME, AGEYRS
C Now we convert the age from years into months
      AGEMTH = AGEYRS * 12
C Print out the results
      PRINT *, NAME, ' is approximately ', AGEMTH, ' months old'
      END
```

This is how the input and output would appear on the CRT screen:

Enter your name and your age in years   *(Prompt from line #6)*
'Martin C.', 32   *(Entered by user; note apostrophes)*
Martin C.   is approximately 384.000 months old   *(Printed by computer from line #11)*

Note that in the output produced by the computer, any unused characters in NAME are given blank spaces. For example, when the name was entered, it contained only 9 characters. So, when the computer goes to print out the name, there is an extra space that has not been filled. In such cases, the computer will pad the variable with blank spaces.

2.5 ASSIGNMENT STATEMENTS, EXPRESSIONS, AND HIERARCHY

The *assignment statement* is the primary means of storing data in variables. We have seen a number of simple examples of assignment statements in the "AREAOFCIRCLE" program (Example 2.10) and the "AGEINMONTHS" program (Example 2.15). As the name assignment statement implies, we are telling the computer to assign a value to a given variable. The general form of the assignment statement is:

$$\text{Target} \leftarrow \text{Value from an expression}$$

The interpretation of this statement is "The target receives a value obtained from the expression." The way this is implemented in Fortran is:

$$\text{Variable} = \text{Value from an expression}$$

The expression on the right-hand side (RHS) of the equal sign can be one of several types as discussed below.

EXAMPLE 2.16

In the table below are several examples of assignment statements involving constants, variables, and mathematical operators:

Expression	Type of Expression
PAY = 5.12	Constant assigned to the variable *pay*
TAXES = CALC	The value of the variable *calc* assigned to *taxes*
PAY = GROSS - NET + 5.00	Value of the numerical expression assigned to *pay*
X = SQRT(Y)	Function used to evaluate the square root of y ($\sqrt{y}$)

In each of these examples, something happens on the right-hand side to determine what value goes into the left-hand side. This is an important difference between an algebraic equation and an assignment statement. You must keep in mind that these assignment statements are not equations to be solved. Instead, the right hand-side is evaluated first, and the answer is then assigned to the variable on the left-hand side.

EXAMPLE 2.17

In a conventional algebraic equation such as:

$$x = 1 - x$$

we could solve for x very easily and obtain:

$$x = 1/2$$

But, the same line (X = 1 − X) in a program has a very different meaning. It is not an equation to be solved. Rather, it is an expression to be evaluated followed by an assignment of the result to a specific variable. For example, consider the following lines of code (program) and try to predict the final value of X:

```
X = 1.0
X = 1.0 - X
PRINT *, X
```

When the first command (X=1.0) is executed, the real variable X is given a value 1.0. When the second line (X=1.0 − X) executes, the expression is evaluated as 1.0 − (1.0), since the old value of X is retrieved and substituted into the expression. The result, which is 0, is placed into the variable X. X now has the value 0. This process of following the logic of a program is known as *tracing*. It is a very useful device, especially when you are attempting to debug a program. To aid in tracing a program, you should create a table of all the variables in the program, where each row represents one of the variables. Whenever a variable is assigned a value, it is entered into the table and whenever a value is required, the last value entered is used.

EXAMPLE 2.18

Trace through the following program segment and predict its output:

```
X = 1.0
Y = 2.0
Z = 3.0
X = -X
PRINT *, 'Value of X is: ', X
Y = Y - 1.0
PRINT *, 'Value of Y is: ', Y
Z = Z + X
Z = Z + X - Y
PRINT *, 'Value of Z is: ', Z
```

The variable table would look like this after performing the trace:

X	1.0	− 1.0	
Y	2.0	1.0	
Z	3.0	2.0	0.0

Note that the values of X and Y were changed once during the program after the initial assignment, but that Z changed value two times. So, after execution, here is the final output:

```
Value of X is:   -1.000000
Value of Y is:    1.000000
Value of Z is:    0.000000
```

Lines 1, 2, and 3 are constant assignment statements. They initialize the variables X, Y, and Z to the values 1.0, 2.0, and 3.0, respectively. Line 4 tells the computer to take the current value of X (which is 1.0) and change its sign. The value is placed back into X. X is now −1. Line 6 states to take Y and subtract 1 from it, or 2 − 1 is 1. That value is placed back into Y. Y is now 1. Line 8 states to take Z + X and place that value back into Z, or 3 + (−1) is 2. Z is now 2. Line 9 states to calculate Z + X − Y and place the result back into Z, or 2 + (−1) − 1 is 0. Finally, Z is assigned the value 0. Note that during these evaluations the right-hand side is processed first, and then the answer is placed into the variable on the left-hand side.

Expressions and Hierarchy of Operations

All of the examples of expressions have been simple ones. They've consisted simply of multiplication, or addition and subtraction. There are only five basic arithmetic operations possible with Fortran. They are addition, subtraction, multiplication, division, and exponentiation, as presented in the following table:

Priority	Algebraic Symbol	Fortran Symbol	Meaning
1	(.....)	(.....)	Parentheses
2	A^b	**	Exponentiation
3	×	*	Multiplication
3	÷	/	Division
4	+	+	Addition
4	−	−	Subtraction

In order to create mathematical expressions, you must use the symbols listed in the table on a single text line entered into your program. While algebra permits the use of multiple line expressions, Fortran requires you to place the expression on a single line.

For all of the operators with equivalent position within the hierarchy (except **), evaluation is from left to right. For exponentiation, the direction is from right to left. For example 8.0/2.0*4.0 gives 16.0, since the division is done first and then the multiplication.

EXAMPLE 2.19

Here is how you might write a mathematical expression in algebra:

$$y = \frac{a + 2b + c}{d}$$

but in Fortran, this is how we would write the same expression:

$$Y = (A+2*B+C)/D$$

There are several key points that you should notice in this simple example:

- *Implied* operations are not allowed in Fortran. In algebra, we know that 2B means 2 multiplied by B. But, in Fortran, you must explicitly write out the implied multiplication as 2*B.
- Everything is written on one line. In the algebraic expression, the numerator is written above the denominator, like a fraction. But, in Fortran, we place the numerator and the denominator on the same line and separate them with a slash (/) to indicate division.

In algebra it is understood that you should perform the multiplication (2B) before any addition. Thus, in the expression A + 2B + C, 2B is evaluated first and then added to A and C. Therefore, all mathematical operations have a well-defined hierarchy. This is true also for Fortran as summarized in the preceding table.

EXAMPLE 2.20

Based on the hierarchy of mathematical operations, evaluate the following expression:

$$9.2 - (2.0**3 - 14.0 / 7.0) + 14.0 * 0.1$$

1. First priority is ( ), so the expression inside the parentheses (2.0**3 − 14.0 / 7.0) is evaluated first.
2. Next in the hierarchy is exponentiation. Thus, the expression inside the ( ) is evaluated by performing the exponentiation first, which gives (8.0 − 14.0 / 7.0).
3. The next priority is the division, resulting in (8.0 − 2.0).
4. Finally, perform the subtraction (6.0).
5. Return to the original expression with this result, so the expression becomes 9.2 − 6.0 + 14.0 * 0.1.
6. Next is multiplication and the expression becomes 9.2 − 6.0 + 1.4.
7. Finally, addition and subtraction have the same priority. Therefore, they are evaluated left to right, which gives 3.2 + 1.4 = 4.6.

EXAMPLE 2.21

When two exponentiation operations appear together, they are evaluated right to left:

$$2 ** 3 ** 2 \quad \rightarrow \quad 2 ** 9 \quad \rightarrow \quad 512$$

Here are some more examples to see if you fully understand the rules for evaluating an expression.

EXAMPLE 2.22

For the examples below, we supply the answer. Trace through each and make sure you get the same result:

Expression	Value	Comments
16.0 − 4.0 − 2.0	10.0	*Left to right*
16.0 − (4.0 − 2.0)	14.0	*Evaluate expression within ( ) first*
16.0 + 4.0 * 2.0	24.0	*Multiplication first*
16.0 / 4.0 / 2.0	2.0	*Left to right*
16.0 ** 4.0 * 2.0	131072.0	*Exponentiation first*
16.0 ** (4.0 * 2.0)	4294967296.0	*Expression within ( ) first*

In the preceding examples, we have been careful to make all the constants and variables real. This was done because there are special rules that govern integer arithmetic. Also, when you try to mix real and integer data types, complications arise as illustrated in the following section.

2.6 INTEGER AND MIXED-MODE ARITHMETIC

When performing arithmetic with real numbers, the results show what you would algebraically expect. However, when performing calculations with integers or a mixture of integers and real numbers, different results may be obtained.

The two operations that are affected by data type are division and exponentiation. Division of two integers results in an integer value. This value is equal to the real number result with the decimal portion deleted.

EXAMPLE 2.23

The result can be very different if we do mathematics with real numbers and integers. Note in the following example that the integer division produces an unexpected result:

Using reals: 3.0 / 2.0 = 1.5   (note that 3.0 and 2.0 are real as is 1.5)

Using integers: $3 / 2 = 1$ (not 1.5! Note that 3 and 2 are integers as is 1)

In the second example above, both 3 and 2 were integers because we did not use decimal points. Therefore, when the computer does the division, it will give an integer result. This is obtained by *truncating* any noninteger remainder.

You must be careful when using integer arithmetic, since unintended results can creep into your program. So be careful! But sometimes this effect is desired, as shown in the next example.

EXAMPLE 2.24

The following program makes change in terms of dollars, quarters, dimes, nickels, and pennies by making use of integer division:

```
        INTEGER CENTS, DOLLAR, QUARTR, NICKEL, DIME, PENNY
        PRINT *, ' Enter value in cents '
        READ *, CENTS
C
C Whole dollar part is the integer division of CENTS by 100
C
        DOLLAR = CENTS / 100
C
C What is left is the remaining change in CENTS
C
        CENTS = CENTS - DOLLAR * 100
C
C Repeat this process for QUARTR, DIME, NICKEL and PENNY
C
        QUARTR = CENTS / 25
        CENTS = CENTS - QUARTR * 25
        DIME = CENTS / 10
        CENTS = CENTS - DIME * 10
        NICKEL = CENTS / 5
        PENNY = CENTS - NICKEL * 5
C
C   Print out the results
C
        PRINT *, 'Dollars: ', DOLLAR
        PRINT *, 'Quarters: ', QUARTR
        PRINT *, 'Dimes: ', DIME
        PRINT *, 'Nickels: ', NICKEL
        PRINT *, 'Pennies: ',PENNY
        END
```

We took advantage of integer arithmetic in this example to give us the desired results. For example, if the change were 78 cents, division by 25 would produce exactly 3 (not 3 plus a remainder). Thus, the program would say to return 3 quarters.

The second area where the results will depend on whether you use reals or integers is exponentiation. Under certain circumstances, an error will occur depending on the choice of variable type. This is because the method of performing the calculation is different depending on whether the exponent is integer or real.

In the case where the exponent is an integer, the value is determined by successive multiplications. But when the exponent is a real number, Fortran will take the log of the base, multiply the result by the exponent, and then take the inverse log of that result. This may cause the computer to take the logarithm of a negative number, which produces an error.

EXAMPLE 2.25

Try to use integer values for exponents. Otherwise, Fortran will use logarithmic functions to calculate the result.

$$2**6 \text{ is calculated as } 2*2*2*2*2*2 = 64$$

but

$$2**6.0 \text{ is calculated as } Log^{-1}(6*Log(2)) = 64.0$$

The result is the same, but there *may* be a problem, as shown below:

$$(-2)**3 \text{ is calculated as } -2*-2*-2 = -8$$

but

$(-2)**0.3$ is calculated as $Log^{-1}(0.3*Log(-2)) = $ ERROR since log of a negative number is not defined.

In situations where integer and real numbers are mixed during division, the integer value is converted to a real number. The result is the expected value. What must be realized is that these rules for integer and mixed-type division are applied on an operator by operator basis.

EXAMPLE 2.26

Evaluate the following mixed-mode arithmetic expression:

$$J = 2.3 * (3 / 2) - 5$$

First evaluate 3 / 2:

$3 / 2 = 1$ *(Fraction is truncated because both numbers are integers)*

Next perform multiplication. An integer times a real yields a real number.

$$J = 2.3 - 5$$

Finally perform the subtraction. A real minus an integer yields a real.

$J = -2.7 = 2$ *(Fraction is truncated because J is an integer)*

2.7 SELECTED LIBRARY FUNCTIONS

Fortran functions behave much like the definitions for mathematical functions such as square root, sine, and so forth. You use a function by placing its name (followed by its arguments) in an expression. You must take great care to match the type, number and order of arguments required for the function. We summarize the most common functions below.

Name	Description	Argument	Result	Example	
ABS(X)	absolute value	integer real double	integer real double	J X Z	= ABS(-51) = ABS(-17.3) = ABS($-0.1D04$)
ACOS(X)	arccosine	real double	real (rad) double (rad)	X X	= ACOS(0.5) = ACOS(0.5D0)
ALOG(X)	natural logarithm	real double	real double	X X	= ALOG(2.71828) = ALOG(0.2718D01)
ALOG10(X)	logarithm base 10	real double	real double	X X	= ALOG10(10.0) = ALOG10(0.1D0)
AMAX(...)	returns largest value	integer real double	integer real double	I X X	= AMAX(5,1,6,2) = AMAX(0.2,5.6) = AMAX(1D0,3D3)
AMIN(...)	returns smallest value	integer real double	integer real double	I X X	= AMIN(4,3,-4) = AMIN(0.2,5.6) = AMIN(1D0,3D3)
ASIN(X)	arcsine	real double	real (rad) double (rad)	X X	= ASIN(0.5) = ASIN(0.5D0)
ATAN(X)	arctangent	real double	real (rad) double (rad)	X X	= ATAN(1.0) = ATAN(1.0D0)
COS(X)	cosine	real (rad) double	real double	X X	= COS(1.04712) = COS(1.04712D0)
DBLE(X)	converts to double	integer real	double double	X X	= DBLE(3) = DBLE(3.0)

(table continues on next page)

Name	Description	Argument	Result	Example
EXP(X)	exponential, e^x	real double	real double	X = EXP(1.0) X = EXP(1.0D0)
INT(X)	converts to integer	real double	integer integer	J = INT(3.9999) J = INT(0.3999D01)
FLOAT(I)	converts to real	integer double	real real	X = FLOAT(4) X = FLOAT(0.4D01)
MOD(I,J)	integer remainder of I/J	integer	integer	J = MOD(29,4)
NINT(X)	round to nearest integer	real double	integer integer	J = NINT(3.99) J = NINT(0.6D01)
REAL(I)	convert to real	integer double	real real	X = REAL(3) X = REAL(0.23D02)
SIN(X)	sine	real (rad) double (rad)	real double	X = SIN(0.5202) X = SIN(0.52D0)
SORT(X)	square root	real double	real double	X = SQRT(17.6) X = SQRT(0.17D2)
TAN(X)	tangent	real (rad) double	real double	X = TAN(0.785) X = TAN(0.785D0)

Be careful when using the trigonometric functions, since they require angles in radians (rad), not degrees. Similarly, the inverse trigonometric functions will report the results in radians.

EXAMPLE 2.27

The following program reads in two points and calculates the distance between them:

```
C Distance Between Two Points (X1,Y1) and (X2,Y2)
C
      PRINT *, 'Enter X,Y location for first point'
      READ *, X1, Y1
      PRINT *, 'Enter X,Y location for second point'
      READ *, X2, Y2
      DIST = SQRT ( ( X2 - X1 ) ** 2 + ( Y2 - Y1 ) ** 2 )
      PRINT *, 'Distance between the points is ', DIST
      END
```

Once the values of (X_1, Y_1) and (X_2, Y_2) have been entered, they are used in the equation to determine the distance d by the formula $d = \sqrt{(x_1 - x_2)^2 + (y_1 - y_2)^2}$. Note that we have used the Fortran function SQRT to perform this calculation.

It is permissible to place one function within another. In fact, many times common sense and defensive programming practices will require it. For example, if you are going to take the square root of a number, you may have to make sure that the number is positive before you can attempt the square root. Otherwise, you may be asking the computer to perform an illegal operation.

EXAMPLE 2.28

Here is the program of Example 2.27 that has been modified to take the absolute value of a number before attempting to take the square root of a number:

```
C Distance Between Two Points (X1,Y1) and (X2,Y2)
C
      PRINT *, 'Enter X,Y location for first point'
      READ *, X1, Y1
      PRINT *, 'Enter X,Y location for second point'
      READ *, X2, Y2
      DIST=SQRT(ABS((X2-X1)**2 + (Y2-Y1)**2))
      PRINT *, 'Distance between the points is ', DIST
      END
```

In this situation, it made no difference that we added the ABS function, since the argument $(x_1 - x_2)^2 + (y_1 - y_2)^2$ is always positive (or zero). So taking the absolute value makes no difference. But there will be many occasions when this might be needed.

2.8 DEBUGGING TIPS

Debugging is the process of removing errors from your program. For the types of programs presented in this chapter, two error types are most likely to occur; improper use of integer/mixed-mode arithmetic and simple typographical errors.

You may also have programs that contain *run-time* and *logic* errors. Run-time errors are those that occur while the program is running, and can usually be traced to illegal mathematical operations such as the logarithm of a negative number. Logic errors are those where the program executes to completion, but gives you the wrong answer. You simply gave the computer a wrong series of instructions to execute. Both of these types of errors are most easily solved by tracing.

Typographical errors (typos) occur when you accidentally mistype the name of a variable or command. Since Fortran utilizes implicit typing, new variables can be created when you make a simple typo error. You can detect such mistakes by:

- Including the statement IMPLICIT NONE at the beginning of your program.
- Declaring all the variables that you intend to use in the program by explicit typing.

By disabling the implicit typing feature, variables that are not declared will result in a compiler error. This is one way of locating variables created by "typos."

EXAMPLE 2.29

Here is an example of how to use the IMPLICIT NONE statement to help locate typographical errors. Note that if we turn off the implicit typing feature by using the IMPLICIT NONE statement, we will then have to declare every variable with the explicit typing.

```
C The IMPLICIT NONE statement is placed first in the program
C We must then explicitly name all the variables in a type
C declaration statement(s)
      IMPLICIT NONE
      REAL X1, Y1, X2, Y2, LENGTH
      READ *, X1, Y1, X2, Y2
      LENGHT=SQRT((X2-X1)**2 + (Y2-Y1)**2)
      PRINT *, 'Length is ', LENGTH
      END
```

On line 7 LENGTH is misspelt as LENGHT. Because implicit typing is turned off, the compiler will generate an error due to an undeclared variable. If the IMPLICIT NONE statement is omitted, the computer would accept both spellings as different variables and will report no error.

Errors due to mixed-mode arithmetic can often be located by adding PRINT statements before and after each expression. Before an expression, print out the variables being used in the calculation. After an expression, PRINT the result. Trace the program and see if the values being printed out at each step of the program agree with what you expect.

EXAMPLE 2.30

This program always returns the result "Length is 1.000000," no matter what values are entered. Find the error.

```
      IMPLICIT NONE
      REAL X1, Y1, X2, Y2, LENGTH
      READ *, X1, Y1, X2, Y2
      PRINT *, X2, X1, Y2, Y1
      LENGTH=((X2-X1)**2 + (Y2-Y1)**2)**(1/2)
      PRINT *, 'Length is ', LENGTH
      END
```

We have added PRINT statements *before* and *after* the calculation of LENGTH. The computer will always report "LENGTH=1.000000," but when you trace through by hand you should get a different result. By adding the PRINT statements, we find that the program line that calculates LENGTH is in error. The problem is the improper use of integer arithmetic in the exponentiation (** (1/2)). Because 1/2 involves integer division, the result is 0. This problem can be fixed by simply adding decimal points, producing (**(1./2.)).

Solved Problems

2.1   The following examples illustrate various types of literal constants. Some examples are valid, while other are invalid. Where appropriate, we indicate the default data type (Real, Integer, etc). Explanations for the invalid examples are provided.

a)	1.00	*(Real)*
b)	123	*(Integer)*
c)	+8	*(Integer)*
d)	13 7/8	*(Invalid: Fraction is not allowed)*
e)	$ 78.24	*(Invalid: $ is not allowed)*
f)	−0.123E7.1	*(Invalid: Exponent must be an integer)*
g)	'She''s happy'	*(Character)*
h)	(1.2, 3.4)	*(Complex)*
i)	(1E0, 3E0)	*(Complex)*
j)	1,234	*(Invalid: commas are not allowed.)*
k)	.False	*(Invalid: must have trailing "." to be logical)*

2.2   The following are examples of valid and invalid variables. Reasons for invalid examples are provided.

a)	X	*(Valid)*
b)	Height	*(Valid)*
c)	R P M	*(Valid; Spaces ignored)*
d)	1station	*(Invalid: 1st character must be letter)*
e)	.TEST	*(Invalid: "." not allowed)*

2.3   The following examples demonstrate implicit data typing based on the first letter of the variable name.

a)	X	*(Real)*
b)	Volume	*(Real — note that lower case letters are OK)*
c)	KOUNT	*(Integer)*
d)	InDia	*(Integer — mixing lower/upper case letters OK)*

2.4   The following examples demonstrate explicit data typing.

a)	REAL X, Y, Z	*(Valid, defines three real variables)*
b)	INTEGER COUNT	*(Valid, defines one integer variable)*
c)	CHARACTER NAME*20	*(Valid, defines one variable 20 characters long)*
d)	LOGICAL OK	*(Valid, defines one logical variable)*
e)	DOUBLE PRECISION VOL	*(Valid, defines one double precision variable)*

2.5 The following examples illustrate valid and invalid assignment statements.

a)   X = 3.1416*R^2   *(Invalid — "^" is not a valid operator)*
b)   X 1 = 3*Area   *(Valid — blanks in variable name are permitted)*
c)   X = SQRT((X1−X2)**2)   *(Valid)*
d)   SQRT((X1−X2)**2) = X   *(Invalid — target of assignment must be on left side)*

2.6 The following examples illustrate the hierarchy of operations. The results of each operation are assigned 1st, 2nd, 3rd, etc. Those results are then used in following operations:

a)   ROOT = (A + 2 * B + C) / D
   → 1st   = 2 * B
   → 2nd = A + 1st
   → 3rd   = 2nd + C
   → 4th   = 3rd / D

b)   X1 = (−B + (B * B − 4 * A * C) ** 0.5) / (2 * A)
   → 1st   = B * B
   → 2nd = 4 * A
   → 3rd   = 2nd * C
   → 4th   = 1st - 3rd
   → 5th   = 4th ** 0.5
   → 6th   = −B + 5th
   → 7th   = 2 * A
   → 8th   = 6th / 7th

c)   A = 0.5 * B * H + H ** 2
   → 1st   = H ** 2
   → 2nd = 0.5 * B
   → 3rd   = 2nd * H
   → 4th   = 3rd + 1st

d)   R = SQRT (3 * T ** 2 + (M * G) ** 2)
   → 1st   = M * G
   → 2nd = T ** 2
   → 3rd   = 1st ** 2
   → 4th   = 3 * 2nd
   → 5th   = 4th + 3rd
   → 6th   = SQRT (5th)

2.7 The following examples illustrate how to evaluate expressions with mixed-mode arithmetic.

a)   10 * 3.0 + 10 / 3
   → 1st   = 10 * 3.0   = 30.0000   *(Integer times a real yields a real)*
   → 2nd = 10 / 3   = 3   *(Since both numbers are integers, the result must be integer or 3 by truncation)*
   → 3rd   = 30.0 + 3   = 33.0000   *(Real plus an integer yields a real)*

b)   4 ** (1 / 2.)
        → 1st = 1 / 2.   = 0.50000   *(Result remains real)*
        → 2nd = 4 ** 0.5   = 2.00000   *(Result is real since types are mixed)*

c)   (−5) ** 3.
        → ERROR   *(Raising to a real power is the same as $\log^{-1}(3*\log(-5))$. It is not possible to take the log of a negative number, so an error occurs.)*

d)   10 − 10 / 3 * 3
        → 1st = 10 / 3   = 3   *(Simple division of two integers)*
        → 2nd = 1st * 3   = 9   *(No mixed mode)*
        → 3rd = 10 - 2nd   = 1   *(No mixed mode)*

2.8   The following examples illustrate the process of tracing a program.

a)   Assume an input of 100, 45

```
PI = 3.1416
PRINT *, 'Enter Velocity (ft/sec) and Elevation (deg)'
READ *, V, THETA
THETA = THETA * PI / 180.0
VX = V * COS ( THETA )
VY = V * SIN ( THETA )
PRINT *, 'X-component of velocity is ', VX ,' ft/sec'
PRINT *, 'Y-component of velocity is ', VY ,' ft/sec'
END
```

TRACE TABLE: OUTPUT:

V	100.0	X-component of velocity is 70.711 ft/sec
THETA	45.0, 0.7854	Y-component of velocity is 70.711 ft/sec
VX	70.711	
VY	70.711	

b)   Assume an input of 10, 20, 30

```
REAL N1, N2, N3, X
READ *, N1, N2, N3
X = 0.0
X = X + N1
X = X + N2
X = X + N3
PRINT *, 'Value of X is: ', X
END
```

TRACE TABLE: OUTPUT:

X	0.0, 10.0, 30.0, 60.0	Value of X is 60.00
N1	10.0	
N2	20.0	
N3	30.0	

c)   Assume an input of 12.5

```
INTEGER FEET, INCHES
PRINT *, 'Enter distance in feet'
READ *, DIST
FEET = DIST
INCHES = ( DIST - FEET ) * 12 + 0.5
PRINT *, 'Distance is ', FEET, 'feet and ', INCHES, ' inches'
END
```

TRACE TABLE: OUTPUT:

DIST	12.5	Distance is 12 feet and 6 inches
FEET	12	
INCHES	6	

2.9   Convert the following mathematical expressions into valid Fortran code:

a) $2\,a\,b$ $\rightarrow 2.0 * A * B$

b) $(a + 3\,b)\,c$ $\rightarrow (A + 3.0 * B) * C$

c) $(a + 3\,b)(c + d)$ $\rightarrow (A + 3.0 * B) * (C + D)$

d) $a^2 - 3\,a\,b + 4\,b^2$ $\rightarrow A ** 2 - 3.0 * A * B + 4.0 * B ** 2$

e) $\dfrac{a - b}{c + 4\,d}$ $\rightarrow (A - B) / (C + 4.0 * D)$

f) $\dfrac{(a - b)^2}{(c + 4\,d)^3}$ $\rightarrow (A - B) ** 2 / (C + 4.0 * D) ** 3$

2.10 Convert the following mathematical expressions into valid Fortran code:

a) $|\,a\,b\,|$ $\rightarrow ABS (A * B)$

b) $\sin^{-1}(3\,\pi\,x)$ $\rightarrow ASIN (3.0 * 3.14159 * X)$

c) $\sqrt{|\,a\,b\,|}$ $\rightarrow SQRT (ABS (A * B))$

d) $e^{|\,2a\,|} \tan(b)$ $\rightarrow EXP (ABS (2.0 * A)) * TAN (B)$

e) $(e^{|\,2a\,|})^3$ $\rightarrow EXP (ABS (2.0 * A)) ** 3$

Supplementary Problems

2.11 Which of the following are valid and invalid examples of literal constants? For the invalid examples provide the reasons why they are invalid. For the valid example indicate the constant type.

a) 3.1415927   b) −987   c) +9.   d) 123 456 789
e) 1E10   f) 0D0   g) 'This is a test'   h) 'he said, "hi"'

2.12 For each variable name indicate whether the variable is valid or invalid.

a) Amt Due   b) Amt_Due   c) TotalVolume   d) TIME
e) Circumference

2.13 Indicate the implicit data type based on the variable name.

a) LENGTH   b) COUNT   c) JOINT   d) VOLUME
e) Imax

2.14 Indicate whether the following declaration statements are valid. For invalid declaration statements describe why they are invalid.

a) REAL X Y Z   b) CHARACTER NAME
c) CHARACTER*20 FIRST, LAST   d) CHARACTER(10) A, B

2.15 Indicate which of the following are valid assignment statements. For those statements that are invalid, provide the reason.

a) Y + 2 = X   b) Dist := Y2 − Y1   c) NUM = NUM + 1

2.16 Illustrate the operator hierarchy by listing the results of each operation. The results of each operation are to be indicated as 1st, 2nd, 3rd, etc.

a) Dist = SQRT((X1 − X2) ** 2 + (Y1 − Y2) ** 2)
b) A = X ** Y ** Z + 10
c) D = 1 / (4 * N) * (M * G + T * (D + H) / B)
d) P = 2 * F * E / (C * (1 − A / B))

2.17 Evaluate the following mixed mode arithmetic expressions. Use the same format as in the previous problem.

a) $4 ** (1 / 2)$ b) $-5 ** 3$ c) $10 / (1.0 * 3) - 10 / 3$
d) AREA $= 1 / 2 * B * H$

2.18 Trace the following programs and predict their output:

a)   Assume an input of 1,2,3 for the 1st input request and 4,5,6 for the second request.

```
READ *, X1, Y1, Z1
READ *, X2, Y2, Z2
X3 = X1 + X2
Y3 = Y1 + Y2
Z3 = Z1 + Z2
PRINT *, 'Sum of two vectors is ', X3, Y3, Z3
END
```

b) Assume an input of 1, 1, 1, 2, 3, 4

```
PRINT *, 'Enter two 3 component vectors'
READ *, X1, Y1, Z1, X2, Y2, Z2
ANS = 0
ANS = X1 * X2 + ANS
ANS = Y1 * Y2 + ANS
ANS = Z1 * Z2 + ANS
PRINT *, 'The answer is ', ANS
END
```

c) Assume an input of 1, 1, 1, 2, 3, 4

```
READ *, X1, Y1, Z1, X2, Y2, Z2
X3 = Y1 * Z2 - Y2 * Z1
Y3 = Z1 * X2 - Z2 * X1
Z3 = X1 * Y2 - X2 * Y1
PRINT *, 'The Answer is ', X3, Y3, Z3
END
```

d) Assume an input of 0, 0, 0, 100, 50, 25

```
PRINT *, 'Enter Position 1 (x,y,z) and Position 2 (x,y,z):'
READ *, X1, Y1, Z1, X2, Y2, Z2
DIST = SQRT((X1-X2)**2 + (Y1-Y2)**2 + (Z1-Z2)**2)
XM = ( X1 + X2 ) / 2.0
YM = ( Y1 + Y2 ) / 2.0
ZM = ( Z1 + Z2 ) / 2.0
PRINT *, 'Distance between points ', DIST
PRINT *, 'Midpoint location ', XM, YM, ZM
END
```

2.19 Create a program to solve each of the following problems.

a)   There are 5280 feet in a mile. Write a program to read in a distance in miles and return the equivalent number of feet.

b)   There are 25.4 millimeters/inch. Write a program that reads in feet and inches and converts the distance to millimeters.

c)   The equation to convert degrees F to degrees C is C=5/9*(F−32). Write a program to request temperature in degrees C and return the temperature in degrees F.

d)   There are 4 quarts to a gallon, 2 pints to a quart, and 16 fluid ounces to a pint. Write a program which will read in a decimal value for gallons and return gallons, quarts, pints and oz. For example 5.5 gallons is 5 gallons 2 quarts, 0 pints and 0 ounces. HINT: refer to the make change example (Example 2.24) in this chapter.

2.20 Convert the following mathematical expressions into valid Fortran code. Do not use any of the library functions.

a) $\dfrac{a}{b} - \dfrac{c}{d}$

b) $\dfrac{a}{b-c}$

c) $\dfrac{m_0}{[1-(v/c)^2]^{1/2}}$

d) $\dfrac{a}{b\,c}$

e) $\sqrt{\sqrt{\dfrac{a-b}{c+4d}}}$

2.21 Convert the following mathematical expressions into valid Fortran code:

a) $e^{b}\tan^3(a)$

b) $\dfrac{a^{c-1}}{\ln(b)}$

c) $\tan^{-1}\sqrt{\sin^2|a|}$

Answers to Selected Supplementary Problems

2.11 a) Real   b) Integer
       c) Real   d) Integer
       e) Real   f) Double Precision
       g) Character   h) Character

2.12 a) Valid – Space ignored   b) Invalid – "_" not allowed
       c) Invalid: 6 characters maximum   d) Valid
       e) Invalid: 6 characters maximum

2.13 a) Integer   b) Real
       c) Integer   d) Real
       e) Integer

2.14 a) Valid (declares one variable)   b) Valid
       c) Valid   d) Invalid (use *10 to indicate length)

2.15 a) Invalid: target must be a variable   b) Invalid: Assignment operator is "="
     c) Valid

2.16 a) 1st=X1 − X2; 2nd=Y1 − Y2; 3rd=1st ** 2; 4th=2nd ** 2; 5th=3rd + 4th;
       6th=SQRT(5th).
     b) 1st=Y ** Z; 2nd=X ** 1st; 3rd=2nd + 10.
     c) 1st=D + H; 2nd=4 * N; 3rd=M * G; 4th=T * 1st; 5th=4th / B; 6th=3rd + 5th;
       7th=1 / 2nd; 8th=7th * 6th.
     d) 1st=A / B; 2nd=1 − 1st; 3rd=C * 2nd; 4th=2 * F; 5th=4th * E; 6th=5th / 3rd.

2.17 a) 1st=1 / 2 = 0 since both are integers.
       2nd=4 ** 0 = 1 since integer raised to integer is an integer.
     b) 1st=− 5 ** 3 = − 125 integer exponentiation evaluated by repeated multiplication
       (−5)*(−5)*(−5).
     c) 1st=1.0 * 3 = 3.0 mixed multiplication converted to real numbers.
       2nd=10 / 1st = 3.3333... integer value of 10 converted to real 10.0.
       3rd=10 / 3 = 3 integer result due to both numbers being integers.
       4th=2nd - 3rd = 3.3333 − 3 = 0.3333.
     d) 1st=1 / 2 = 0 integer division will result in any remainder being dropped.
       All remaining operations will result in a zero result.

2.18 a) X1: 1   Y1: 2   Z1: 3   X2: 4   Y2: 5   Z2: 6
       X3: 5   Y3: 7   Z3: 9
       Output: Sum of two vectors is 5.00000   7.00000   9.00000
     b) X1: 1   Y1: 1   Z1: 1   X2: 2   Y2: 3   Z2: 4
       Output: The answer is 9.00000
     c) X1: 1   Y1: 1   Z1: 1   X2: 2   Y2: 3   Z2: 4
       X3: (1*4−3*1)=1   Y3: (1*2−4*1)=-2   Z3: (1*3−2*1)=1
       Output: The Answer is 1.00000   −2.00000   1.00000
     d) X1: 0   Y1: 0   Z1: 0   X2: 100   Y2: 50   Z2: 25
       XM: 50   YM: 25   ZM: 12.5   DIST: 114.564
       Output: Distance between points 114.564; Midpoint location 50.0000 25.0000 12.5000

2.20 a) A/B−C/D   b) A/(B−C)
     c) M0/(1.0−(V/C)**2)**0.5   d) A/(B*C) *or* A/B/C
     e) ((A−B)/(C+4.0*D))**0.25

2.21 a) EXP(B)*TAN(A)**3   b) (A**(C−1)/ALOG(B))
     c) ATAN(SQRT(SIN(ABS(A))**2))

Chapter 3

Input and Output

3.1 LIST-DIRECTED INPUT AND OUTPUT

The easiest way to input and output data from a program is via the so-called *list-directed* statements. In these types of statements we are not concerned about the appearance of the data, but rather about *what* we input or output. The general form of the list-directed input statement is:

READ *, *variable1, variable2, . . .*

and for output, the corresponding statement is:

PRINT *, *variable1, variable2, . . .*

The star (*) which appears in each of these statements indicates that we are using *free format*. Free format means that the computer will use a set of predetermined instructions to read or print data. For example, the machine will figure out how many decimal places to print, how many blank spaces to leave between each number, and so forth. Your only concern is to provide the proper information about what to print out or read in. In the next sections, we will replace the star with a series of specific instructions that will give us some control over the appearance of the data.

The list that appears after the READ or PRINT statements is called the *I/O list* and indicates the variables for either input or output. It also contains other information that we will discuss shortly. In the case of such *list-directed I/O*, the computer will control all aspects of the appearance of the output.

EXAMPLE 3.1

To illustrate how list-directed I/O works, consider the following statement:

```
READ *, X, Y, Z
```

This will cause the first three numbers that you type in to be assigned to the corresponding variables. A typical input by you might look like this:

```
14.3, -27.943, 0.0034567  <carriage return>
^^^^^^^^^^^^^^^^^^^^^^^^^^^^^^^^^^^^^^^^^^^^^^^^^^^^
        |       |        |        |        |
       10      20       30       40       50
```

67

Reading the three data values is equivalent to the three assignment statements:

```
X  =  14.3
Y  =  -27.943
Z  =  0.0034567
```

In the example input just described, we have shown what an input line might look like. For convenience, we have numbered all the columns, since spacing will be of great concern to us shortly. In practice, this column spacing is usually not present, but we have shown it for convenience. Note that each number is separated by a comma (technically known as a delimiter). Also note that the line is completed with the <carriage return> (or <CR> for short). No data are entered until you press the carriage return key.

One advantage of the READ statement over the equivalent assignment statements is that you do not need to rewrite and recompile the program if you enter a different set of data. All you need to do to run the program with different data is merely enter the new data in response to the READ statement.

EXAMPLE 3.2

The PRINT command shown below will send the value of each variable to the CRT screen. For example, if we enter the data given above, we can print them out using the following program segment:

```
READ *, X, Y, Z
PRINT *, X, Y, Z
```

the computer will print out the same values that you typed in:

```
14.3,  -27.943,  0.0034567   <CR>                    (what you type in)
14.30000   -27.94300   0.003456700   (printout on CRT screen)
^^^^^^^^^^^^^^^^^^^^^^^^^^^^^^^^^^^^^^^^^^^^^^^^^^^^^^^^^^^^^
        |           |           |           |           |
        10          20          30          40          50
```

There are a few things to note in this example. First, the computer will use its own rules about printing out the results. These will vary from one compiler to another. The real numbers, for example, were printed here in decimal notation, but on another computer they might be printed in scientific (exponential) notation. The second point to note is that the numbers were printed out with seven significant digits, even though none of the numbers that we typed in had this many digits of accuracy. This occurs because the computer internally stores real numbers with approximately seven digits of accuracy. Thus, the output will contain all seven digits even if the numbers were not entered this way.

The PRINT statement can also contain character strings in the output list. If you enclose a string inside apostrophes, the string will be printed out intact. Finally, you may include mathematical operations in the list of items to be printed.

EXAMPLE 3.3

Here is an example of enhancing the PRINT statement with strings that describe the data being printed:

```
X = 2.4
PRINT *,'X = ', X,'X ** 2 = ', X*X
```

This will produce the following output on the screen:

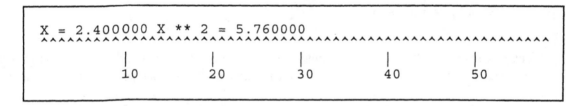

Once again seven digits of accuracy appear in the output. Note that the only time spaces appear in any formatted output is when we have included them <u>inside</u> the apostrophes.

With these simple tools, you can produce a readable printout of your data. However, since you are restricted by the internal rules of the computer, you have little flexibility in the output appearance. Yet, free formatting and list-directed I/O are useful for getting quick answers. To improve the appearance of the output, you will need formatted I/O.

3.2 THE FORMAT STATEMENT

Formatting provides a degree of control over the I/O functions that the simple list-directed commands do not. Using formatting you can make the output more attractive and more readable. Formatting instructions must be used only with either an input or output command, which we often call an *I/O FORMAT pair*. Without the matching input or output commands, the FORMAT statement is useless. In general, the input pair will have the following structure:

> READ *sl* , *variable1* , *variable2* , . . .
> *sl*   FORMAT (*list of instructions*)

In a similar way, the output pair will look like this:

> PRINT *sl* , *variable1* , *variable2* , . . .
> *sl*   FORMAT (*list of instructions*)

The difference between the simple list-directed I/O and the formatted I/O is that the "*" has been replaced with a label number, which points to a FORMAT statement. The statement label (*sl*) in front of the FORMAT statement must go in columns one to six, and the statement itself begins in column seven.

The list of instructions that follows the FORMAT statement is composed of a carriage control character (output only) and a list of *edit descriptors*. The carriage control character resets a printer (if used), and the edit descriptor specifies the output instructions for each output item. Among the things that we can specify are

- Type of variable and number of significant digits
- Column in which to start printing
- Floating point or exponential form (real numbers only)
- Number of blank spaces and blank lines
- Any text to be included

There are specific rules for controlling each of these functions. Note that when you give up the free formatting and take control, there are a number of things that you will have to control yourself.

The general form of a FORMAT statement is

$$sl \qquad FORMAT \; (CCC \;, specifier1 \;, specifier2 \;, \ldots, specifierN)$$

where   sl   = statement label (integer up to five digits).
         CCC   = carriage control character.
         specifier   = instruction for individual variable.

The carriage control character CCC is always the first item inside the parentheses and is only present when formatting output. Its purpose is to reset a printer by moving the printing head to column 1. Sometimes you will not need the CCC (for example, when you are printing to a CRT screen), and it can be omitted.

There are four different CCC characters to handle the printer reset:

Character	Description of Function
' '	Single vertical spacing
'0'	Double vertical spacing
'1'	New page
'+'	No advance; reset to beginning of current line

The most common carriage control character is the one for single spacing (' '), while the last CCC ('+') is used rarely for printing special characters by overstriking (e.g., create the $\neq$ character by printing '/' over '='). Do not forget to include the carriage control character in your output FORMAT statements when sending output to a printer. Failure to do so may cause a "runaway printer." Ask your instructor for local rules for any required CCC characters.

3.3 EDIT DESCRIPTORS

Edit descriptors provide detailed information on how data are to be printed or read. For now, we will deal only with output, since formatted input is rarely used. Input can be handled in a similar way, and we will delay any discussion of formatted input until the exercise section. Format specifiers fall into two main categories. The first contains the rules for controlling numerical and character data, while the second controls spacing functions.

Category	Descriptor	Function	Form	Example
Numerical data	I	Integer	Iw	I5
	F	Real	Fw.d	F6.2
	E	Real (exponential)	Ew.d	E12.4
	D	Double precision	Dw.d	D20.8
	G	Real (general): switches between F and E format	Gw.d	G8.2
Character data	A	Character variable	Aw	A20
	' '	Character strings	'xxx'	'Example'

When we wish to print out data, whether real, integer or double precision, we usually have two primary concerns. These are the total number of spaces and the total number of significant digits to be displayed. The general form of the data edit descriptor is

$$\text{TYPE } width \ (.decimals)$$

where TYPE   = a letter (I, F, E, G, or D) indicating the type of the data to be printed.
     width   = total width of space desired.
     decimals   = total number of decimal places (not needed for integers or characters).

The second set of format specifiers are those which control the physical layout, such as spacing (both vertical and horizontal), tab stops, and alignment in column format. These are summarized in the following table:

Category	Descriptor	Function	Form	Example
Spacing	X	Individual space	rX	5X
	T	Tab to column c	Tc	T20
	TR	Tab right s spaces	TRs	TR3
	TL	Tab left s spaces	TLs	TL5
	/	New line	/	/
Repeat	r( )	Reuse specifiers in ( )	r( )	2(F6.2,I3)

In these tables, the symbols have the following meanings:

c = column number.
s = number of spaces to move (left or right).
r = repeat factor, which is optional.

One of the key things to note when using formatted output is that the edit descriptor must match the type of data that you are printing. For example, if you are printing a real number, you can use only the Fw.d, Ew.d, or Gw.d descriptors.

EXAMPLE 3.4

When we print out integers, our only concern is that we leave enough space in the printed line for all the digits of the number. We do not need to worry about the number of decimal places since integers can only be whole numbers. Therefore, the form of the specifier becomes:

$$I\,w$$

where I indicates an integer number and w indicates the total amount of reserved space. To illustrate, consider the following example:

```
        ICOUNT = 237
        JCOUNT = -14
        PRINT 33, ICOUNT, JCOUNT
33      FORMAT(' ', I6, I9)
```

In this example, the first descriptor inside the FORMAT statement is the CCC giving the command to start a new line. In the I/O list, the variable ICOUNT is the first variable and therefore will be printed with the first edit descriptor inside the FORMAT statement, which is I6. The second variable in the list, JCOUNT, will be printed with the second descriptor, I9. Thus, the output page will look like this:

```
  ← I6 →← I9 →                              (how the line is divided)
     237        -14                         (the actual output)
  ^^^^^^^^^^^^^^^^^^^^^^^^^^^^^^^^^^^^^^^^^^^^^^^^^^^^^^^^^^^^^^^^^^^^^
        |           |           |           |           |
       10          20          30          40          50
```

The descriptor I6 tells the computer to reserve six spaces for the numerical value of ICOUNT. Similarly, the descriptor I9 reserves 9 spaces for JCOUNT. When the computer fills in these reserved spaces with the numerical values, the values are *right-justified*. This means that the printer places them as far to the right as possible within the field reserved for the number. If the number is smaller than the space reserved for it, the printer will leave extra blank spaces. If, however, the number is too large for the reserved space, the printer fills the field with asterisks (*) as in the next example.

EXAMPLE 3.5

Consider the following program segment where the program does not allow sufficient space to print out the data:

```
        ICOUNT = 12345
        JCOUNT = -98765
        PRINT 98, ICOUNT, JCOUNT
98      FORMAT(' ', I5, I5)
```

→ SHOULD BE AN I6 descriptor w/ AN I5 descriptor an overflow condition is the result.

This will result in the following output:

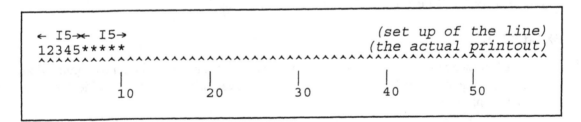

```
  ← I5 →← I5 →                              (set up of the line)
  12345*****                                (the actual printout)
  ^^^^^^^^^^^^^^^^^^^^^^^^^^^^^^^^^^^^^^^^^^^^^^^^^^^^^^^^^^^^^^^^^^^^^
        |           |           |           |           |
       10          20          30          40          50
```

This may appear to be a strange result until you realize that even a minus sign takes up one column in the output line. Thus, the variable JCOUNT, which is equal to -98765, requires 6 columns for printing. However, the FORMAT descriptor I5 allots only 5 columns. Therefore, an overflow condition will occur. If this problem occurs, you must go back to the program and open up the field width. In this example, we would increase the edit descriptor to at least I6.

When we wish to print out real data, we need to worry about both the total number of spaces (w) and the number of decimal places (d). So when we use the form Fw.d, w must be at least three larger than d to allow for the decimal point, the leading negative sign (for negative numbers), and a leading zero (for numbers less than 1.0).

EXAMPLE 3.6

Here is an example of how to use the F edit descriptor:

```
        DIST  = 12.345
        TIME  = 0.00345
        VELOC = DIST/TIME
        PRINT 5, DIST, TIME, VELOC
5       FORMAT(' ',F7.2, F9.6, F10.1)
```

will produce the following output:

```
 ← F7.2→ ←  F9.6  →  ← F10.1 →              (set up of the line)
   12.35 0.003450     3578.3                (the actual printout)
 ^^^^^^^^^^^^^^^^^^^^^^^^^^^^^^^^^^^^^^^^^^^^^^^^^^^^^^^^^^^^^^^^^
          |           |          |           |           |
          10          20         30          40          50
```

If you study the output for a moment, you will see that the computer has rounded off the value for DIST to fit into the allotted space. The same thing has happened to VELOC (3578.2608), which retains only 1 decimal place. The variable TIME, on the other hand, has had a zero added to it before printing to fill out the allotted space.

In addition to the edit descriptors to control the appearance of the data, you may also include *spacing control* and *strings*. The spacing control allows you to spread out the data on a line by leaving the desired number of spaces between the numbers. Strings are lines of text that you can add to improve the readability of the output.

EXAMPLE 3.7

The following example demonstrates how to control the number of decimal digits printed and the spacing between two numbers. Also, we have included strings inside the FORMAT statement.

```
        X = 1.234567
        Y = 9.876543
        PRINT 10, X, Y
10      FORMAT(' ','Value of X= ',F8.3,3X,'Value of Y= ',F9.1)
```

To better understand the format specifiers, we should interpret each one separately:

' '	The carriage control character – start a new line in column 1;
'Value...'	Character string – just print out what is inside the apostrophes;
F8.3	Descriptor for controlling the printout of the first variable, X. F8.3 specifies a total of eight columns with three decimal places;
3X	Skip three spaces;

'Value...'   Another string – do as above;

F9.1   Descriptor for printing the value of the second variable Y in nine columns
                     and one decimal place.

When the above program segment is executed, this is what would appear on the screen:

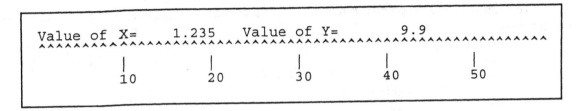

We can also express real numbers in scientific notation as we discussed in Chapter 2. The general form for printing a real number in this exponential format is:

$$E\ w.d$$

where   E = indicates exponential format (mantissa $\times 10^n$).

w = total width of field reserved for number.

d = desired number of decimal places for mantissa.

As with the F format, the E format has a special rule about how many additional spaces must be reserved. Besides the number of significant digits of the mantissa, the E format requires a total of 7 additional spaces. Thus, the rule for the E$w.d$ format is:

$$w \geq d + 7$$

EXAMPLE 3.8

To demonstrate the exponential format, let's reexamine Example 3.6, but now with the E format:

```
        DIST  = 12.345
        TIME  = 0.00345
        VELOC = DIST/TIME
        PRINT 5, DIST, TIME, VELOC
5       FORMAT(' ', E12.4, E14.6, F10.1)
```

This will produce the following output:

```
 ←    E12.4   →←     E14.6    →←   F10.1 →      (set up of line)
    0.1235E+02  0.345000E-02      3578.3   (the actual output)
^^^^^^^^^^^^^^^^^^^^^^^^^^^^^^^^^^^^^^^^^^^^^^^^^^^^^^^^^^^^
       |           |            |          |          |
      10          20           30         40         50
```

Numbers will be rounded or zeros will be added if required to fit into a field. Also, the two different formats for real numbers can be mixed as this example shows. Finally, note that the + sign indicating the sign of the mantissa and the sign of the exponent are optional. If either the mantissa or exponent is negative, however, the printout will include the appropriate minus sign. Check with your instructor to find out what local variations exist.

We print out double precision numbers with a format very similar to that for exponential notation:

$$D\ w.d$$

where D = indicates double precision format (e.g. 0.123D+003).

         w = total width of field reserved for number.

         d = desired number of decimal places for mantissa.

The principal difference between E and D formats is that the exponent for double precision can be significantly larger than that for single precision. Therefore, you must allow for a three-digit exponent with the D format compared to two digits for E format. The following rule summarizes these requirements:

$$w \geq d + 8$$

Otherwise, the D format is identical to the E format.

EXAMPLE 3.9

To demonstrate the double precision format, let's reexamine Example 3.8, but now with the D format:

```
      DOUBLE PRECISION DIST, TIME, VELOC
      DIST  = 12.345
      TIME  = 0.00345
      VELOC = DIST/TIME
      PRINT 5, DIST, TIME, VELOC
    5 FORMAT(' ', D12.4, D11.3, D10.1)
```

will produce the following output:

```
←    D12.4   →←    D11.3   →←   D10.1 →          (set up of line)
   0.1235D+002 0.345D-002   0.4D+004          (the actual output)
  ^^^^^^^^^^^^^^^^^^^^^^^^^^^^^^^^^^^^^^^^^^^^^^^^^^^^^^^^^^^^^^^^
        |           |           |           |           |
       10          20          30          40          50
```

The final format that we will use with real numbers is the *general purpose* format G indicated by

$$G \ w.d$$

where G = indicates general purpose format.
      w = total width of field reserved for number.
      d = desired number of significant digits.

The G format combines both the floating point and exponential formats into a single code. With the G format, the computer selects the format automatically by using either a modified (F$(w-4).d$ + 4X) descriptor or an E$w.d$ descriptor. The computer has a specific rule to decide which format to choose based on the value of the exponent of the number. It compares the exponent to d in the G$w.d$ specification. If the exponent is between approximately 0 and d, the computer uses the modified F format. Otherwise, the E format will be used. The modified format (F$(w-4).d$ + 4X) consists of the floating point format, where d represents the number of significant digits followed by four blank spaces.

EXAMPLE 3.10

To see how the G$w.d$ format works, examine the following examples:

Value	G Format	Equivalent E/F Format	Output
0.010000	G11.3	E11.3	0.100E−01 ~ ~
0.100000	G11.3	F7.3+4X	0.100 ~ ~ ~ ~ ~ ~
1.000000	G11.3	F7.3+4X	1.00 ~ ~ ~ ~ ~ ~ ~
10.00000	G11.3	F7.3+4X	10.0 ~ ~ ~ ~ ~ ~ ~
100.0000	G11.3	F7.3+4X	100. ~ ~ ~ ~ ~ ~ ~
1000.000	G11.3	E11.3	0.100E+04 ~ ~

(Note: ~ = blank space)

In the first example above, the number 0.01 is equivalent to 0.1×10^{-1}, which has an exponent of -1. Since this does not fall in the range of $0 \leq$ exponent ≤ 3, the computer selects the E format. The next four examples all have exponents between 0 and 3. Thus, the computer prints them with the modified F format. Finally, the last number (1000.0 or 0.1 x 10^{+4}) places the exponent outside the range of 0 to 3. Thus, it reverts to the E format. Note that when we specify the G$w.3$ format, any number less than 0.1 or greater than 100.0 will be printed in scientific notation. Only if the number is within these tight limits will the machine choose the floating point (F$w.d$) format.

In the previous examples, we saw that you can print out a character string by placing it inside quotation marks inside the PRINT statement:

```
PRINT *, 'PLEASE ENTER X , Y , Z :'
```

All you need to do to get the same effect with a FORMAT statement is to move the character string inside the parentheses as a descriptor.

EXAMPLE 3.11

Strings which are placed inside single apostrophes in the FORMAT statement are printed intact:

```
        PRINT 21
21      FORMAT(' ', 'PLEASE ENTER X, Y, Z:')
```

This will result in the following output:

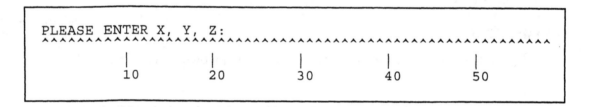

For this trivial example, moving the string inside the FORMAT statement is no improvement over the list directed example. However, if we combine numerical data output with strings, we can combine descriptive text with numerical data to improve comprehension.

```
        X = 12.34
        Y = -0.025
        PRINT 34, X, Y, X*Y
34      FORMAT(' ','X = ',F6.2,' Y = ',F6.3, ' PROD = ',F10.5)
```

will produce the following output:

```
X = ←F6.2→ Y = ←F6.3→ PROD = ←   F10.5 →
X =   12.34 Y = -0.025 PROD =   -0.30850
^^^^^^^^^^^^^^^^^^^^^^^^^^^^^^^^^^^^^^^^^^^^^^^^^^^^^^^^^^^^
      |        |        |        |        |
     10       20       30       40       50
```

Let's examine the descriptors within the FORMAT statement a little more carefully. We reproduce each below with a brief explanation of its meaning:

' '   Carriage Control Character – begin new line

'X = '	Character string – Print X =
F6.2	Floating point format – print out first number as XXX.XX
' Y = '	Character string – Print Y =
F6.3	Floating point format – Print out second number as XX.XXX
' PROD = '	Character string – Print PROD =
F10.5	Floating point format – Print out third number as XXXX.XXXXX

You should carefully match these descriptions with the printer output. Note that a blank space inside the apostrophes produces a blank space in the output. Thus, ' Y = ' produces [blank]Y [blank]=[blank] on the output line.

We do formatting of character variables in a way similar to that for integers, where the only thing we need to worry about is the total number of reserved spaces. The general form of the FORMAT specifier is:

$$A\ w$$

where   A = indicates character format.
      w = total width of field reserved for character output.

Recall that characters can be of any length. This distinguishes them from numerical data, which have a constant length (7 significant digits for reals for instance). Thus, when we declared character variables in the previous chapter, we had to specify the anticipated length. In a similar way, we must tell the computer how many spaces to reserve for character data.

EXAMPLE 3.12

Consider the following simple example:

```
        CHARACTER NAME*20
        PRINT 19, NAME
19      FORMAT(' ', A20)
```

This produces an output similar to (assuming arbitrarily that NAME = 'martin cwiakala'):

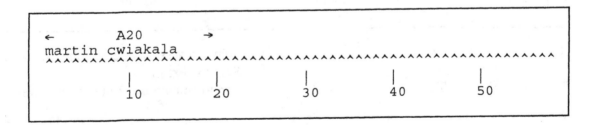

The only thing unusual about this printed line is that the character is *left-justified* , which means that the printer begins printing at the far left. Any extra spaces will appear on the right-hand side of the field. By contrast, numerical data are *right-justified*.

Character data is also different from numerical data in that it is not possible to overflow a field with characters. If the field is too small for numerical data, recall that a string of asterisks will appear. But if the field is too small for character data, it simply truncates the extra characters.

EXAMPLE 3.13

Here is what happens when the character data and the edit descriptor are mismatched:

Character Variable	Format	Output
BOSTON RED SOX	A1	B
BOSTON RED SOX	A10	BOSTON RED
BOSTON RED SOX	A15	BOSTON RED SOX ~
BOSTON RED SOX	A20	BOSTON RED SOX ~ ~ ~ ~ ~ ~
BOSTON RED SOX	A	BOSTON RED SOX

In the last example, we have used an *option* that is available in many versions of Fortran. The simple specifier A without any indication of the field width, will automatically allocate just the right number of spaces for that variable. Note that there are no extra leading or trailing blank spaces in the example given.

Character output varies from system to system. So be sure to check your local manuals to see how the computer reads and prints characters. Among the things to check are whether the *default* format specifier A is allowed and if your compiler distinguishes between upper and lower case. Also, check to see that character data is left justified.

There are several additional format specifiers that are useful for spacing data output, aligning it into tables and improving the general appearance. These specifiers do not work with any data or variable in an I/O list. Rather, when the computer encounters them in a FORMAT statement, the descriptors will produce the spacing requested. There are three specifiers in this group:

Descriptor	General Form	Example	Function
X	nX	3X	Skip n spaces (3 spaces in the example)
/	/	/	Skip to next line
T	Tn	T32	Tab to column n (32 in this example)

EXAMPLE 3.14

The spacing edit descriptors are easy to use and are very effective in improving the appearance of your output. Below is an example combining all three. Assume that BASE =

12.4, HEIGHT $= 9.6$ and VOL $= 119.04$.

```
       PRINT 9, BASE, HEIGHT, VOL
9      FORMAT(' ',5X,F9.3,/,3X,' X',T7,F9.3,/,
  1          T6,'_____',/,T7,F9.3)
```

will produce the following output:

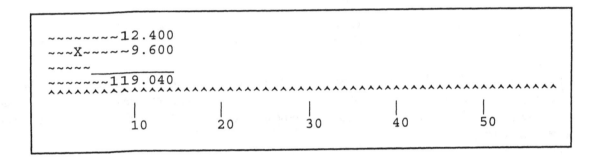

This may appear to be a complex example, but if you take the time to break down the descriptors one by one, you should be able to follow the process leading to the above printout. So follow the descriptions given below for each specifier:

' '	Carriage control character – begin new line (line 1)
5X	Spacing command – skip 5 spaces (line 1)
F9.3	Floating point format – print out first number as XXXXX.XXX
/	Spacing command – begin new line (line 2)
3X	Spacing command – skip 3 spaces (line 2)
' X'	Character string – print X preceded by a blank space (line 2)
T7	Spacing command – tab to column 7 (line 2)
F9.3	Floating point format – print out 2nd number as XXXXX.XXX
/	Spacing command – begin new line (line 3)
T6	Spacing command – tab to column 6 (line 3)
'_____'	Character string – print _____ (line 3)
/	Spacing command – begin new line (line 4)
T7	Spacing command – tab to column 7 (line 4)
F9.3	Floating point format – print out 3rd number as XXXXX.XXX

There is one additional form of the T specifier that you may see occasionally. This form tells the computer to move left or right a certain number of spaces from its current position. These instructions are

TR*n*   (*move right n spaces from current position*)
TL*n*   (*move left n spaces from current position*)

Note that these two commands depend on the current position within a line, while the T*n* command is independent of the line position. Be careful when using these commands since they can "overwrite" what has been printed before. Therefore, if you try to tab left on the CRT screen, anything which was previously written will be erased, and the new text will be written over the old text. Thus, on a CRT screen, the text seems to disappear. But on a hard-copy printer, the text will be printed as intended. For this reason, you may wish to avoid the TR and TL edit descriptors.

There are many times when you need to reuse the same descriptor. A common situation is where all the data are of the same type and are to be printed out with the same format.

```
         PRINT 47, A, B, C, D, E, F, G, H
47       FORMAT(' ',F9.5,F9.5,F9.5,F9.5,F9.5,F9.5,F9.5,F9.5)
```

As you can see, all eight variables are to be printed with the same F9.5 format. Fortunately, Fortran offers a shortcut to avoid repetitious use of a descriptor. All you need to do is to place the *Repeat Descriptor* in front of the format to be repeated. Thus, the above FORMAT statement can be rewritten as:

```
         PRINT 47, A, B, C, D, E, F, G, H
47       FORMAT(' ', 8F9.5)
```

This form of the Repeat Descriptor can be used with the I, F, E, D, G, and A formats. It cannot be used in this form with the / descriptor.

There is another form of the repeat descriptor where more complex combinations can be repeated. The Repeat Descriptor for complex instructions consists of an integer value representing the number of times something is to be repeated and a set of parenthesis containing the repeat unit. Consider this example:

```
         PRINT 47, A, B, C, D, E
47       FORMAT(' ',F9.5,3x,F9.5,3x,F9.5,3x,F9.5,3x,F9.5)
```

Note that there is a unit consisting of (F9.5, 3x) which repeats 5 times. The idea introduced above to place a repeat descriptor in front of the repeat unit can also be used here. However, you must place the unit inside a set of inner parentheses:

```
         PRINT 47, A, B, C, D, E
47       FORMAT(' ', 5(F9.5, 3x))
```

There is a slight difference between these two format statements that you probably did not catch. Note that if you write out the unit (F9.5,3x) five times, the sequence will end in 3x. By comparison, the original format statement ended in F9.5. If you think about this though, you will realize that the shortened form, 5(F9.5,3x), will leave 3 extra blank spaces at the end of the line. In many cases, this is not a problem and can be ignored. But if other things follow on the same line, then you must take these extra three spaces into account.

The only exception to the above rules is the '/' descriptor. The '/' mark indicates that you are finished with the current line and you want the next bit of output on the following line. If you wish to skip three lines however (the first terminates the current line), the following are equivalent:

$$/ , / , / , / \quad or \quad //// \quad or \quad 4(/)$$

EXAMPLE 3.15

Here are a few additional examples to show how the repeat descriptor works:

Original Format	Equivalent Format
F7.3, F7.3, F7.3	3F7.3
/ , / , / (*skip two lines*)	3(/) or ///
F7.3, I6, /, F7.3, I6, /	2(F7.3, I6, /)
F7.3, I6, 2X, I6, 2x, F7.3, I6, 2X, I6	2(F7.3, 2(I6, 2X))
F7.3, 2X, I6, F7.3, 2X, I6, F9.4, I4, F9.4, I4	2(F7.3, 2X, I6), 2(F9.4, I4)

Although FORMAT statements can be used with either READ or PRINT statements, they are usually used for controlling output. The reason is that if you use FORMATs with a READ statement, the data must be entered exactly as spelled out in the FORMAT statement. If you type in too many or too few zeros or spaces, the data will be read incorrectly. Therefore, we recommend that you <u>avoid formatted READ statements</u>. The exception is when you want to read data from a data file, which we will discuss in a later chapter. In some situations like this, you usually have no choice but to use formatted READs. Remember though, that when a FORMAT statement is used with a READ statement, there is no Carriage Control Character. These are limited to output on a printer.

EXAMPLE 3.16

Examine the following program segment to see if you understand the appearance of the output (assume TEMP1 = 5.0, TEMP2 = 10.0, TEMP3 = 15.0, TEMP4 = 20.0, TEMP5 = 25.0, X1 = 12.400, X2 = 12.736, X3 = 13.055, X4 = 13.343, X5 = 13.587, EXPAN1 = 0.00, EXPAN2 = 2.710, EXPAN3 = 2.505, EXPAN4 = 2.206, EXPAN5 = 1.829):

```
        PRINT 23
        PRINT 19, TEMP1, X1 , EXPAN1
        PRINT 19, TEMP2, X2 , EXPAN2
        PRINT 19, TEMP3, X3 , EXPAN3
        PRINT 19, TEMP4, X4 , EXPAN4
        PRINT 19, TEMP5, X5 , EXPAN5
23      FORMAT(' ',T5,'TEMP (C)',T16,'LENGTH OF BAR (CM)',
     1        T36,'EXPANSION (%)',TL44,9('_'),TR2,18('_'),
     1        TR2,13('_'))
19      FORMAT(' ', T5, F7.1, T15, F11.3, T35, F9.3)
```

Here's how each of these descriptors works:

' '	Carriage control character — begin new line (line 1)
T5	Spacing control — tab to column 5 (line 1)
'TEMP (C)'	Character string — print TEMP (oC) (line 1)
T16	Spacing control — tab to column 16 (line 1)
'LENGTH ... '	Character string — print LENGTH OF BAR (CM) (line 1)
T36	Spacing command — tab to column 36 (line 1)
'EXPAN ...'	Character string — print EXPANSION (%) (line 1)
TL44	Spacing control — tab left 44 spaces (line 1)
9('_')	Repeat specifier — print character string "_" 9 times (line 1)
TR2	Spacing command — tab right 2 spaces (line 1)
18('_')	Repeat specifier — print character string "_" 18 times (line 1)
TR2	Spacing control — tab right 2 spaces (line 1)
13('_')	Repeat specifier — print character string "_" 13 times (line 1)

We will not discuss details of each of the specifiers for the data since you should be able to do that for yourself by now. Here is what the printout looks like:

```
      TEMP (C)    LENGTH OF BAR (CM)     EXPANSION (%)
          5.0          12.400              0.000
         10.0          12.736              2.710
         15.0          13.055              2.505
         20.0          13.343              2.206
         25.0          13.587              1.829
    ^^^^^^^^^^^^^^^^^^^^^^^^^^^^^^^^^^^^^^^^^^^^^^^^^^^^^^^^^^^^^^^^^
         |              |              |              |              |
         10             20             30             40             50
```

There are two things to note in this example. First, you may have a PRINT statement without an I/O list, such as PRINT 23. Second, you may refer to the same FORMAT statement as often as you need without having to repeat the instructions. Each time a PRINT statement references the FORMAT statement, the computer will simply reuse the edit descriptors from the beginning.

3.4 DEBUGGING TIPS

There are several types of problems that you are likely to encounter when you begin to use formatting. Some of these can be avoided by using good programming technique. Others can be solved by good debugging skills. For convenience, we will break this discussion into these two broad categories: good programming style and good debugging skills.

Programming style is often thought of as "defensive" programming. If you develop good basic skills, and pay attention to what is thought of as good style, then you will avoid many of the common programming errors and you will find your programs easier to debug. We present four guidelines at this point that will help you to improve your programming style:

- Use prompts to assure that you enter data in the correct sequence.
- Echo the entered data onto the screen to verify correct input.
- Do not insert any formatting statements until you have perfected the logic of your programs.
- Avoid the use of the F format for real numbers in early versions of the program.

Prompts are short messages that your program prints on the CRT screen to remind you of the order in which to enter data. Without prompts, it is very easy to forget the sequence of the input data. Also, it is a very good idea to have your program print out the input data as soon as it reads it. This is called an *echo* and is an excellent way to detect errors early.

The third and fourth guidelines above suggest that you should be slow to introduce FORMAT statements. First, make sure your program logic is correct before you add any FORMAT statements. Then, use only E-type edit descriptors for real data until you have a good idea of the approximate range of the output data. Only then should you add the F edit descriptors.

EXAMPLE 3.17

Here is an example in which we use prompts and echoes to assist in entering data.

```
C Here is an example of a prompt to remind the user of
C the sequence of the input data.
      PRINT *, 'ENTER X, Y AND Z:'
      READ * , X, Y, Z
C Here is an echo, where the values of X, Y, and Z will be
C sent to the CRT screen so that you can check correct entry.
      PRINT *, 'VALUE OF X ENTERED = ', X
      PRINT *, 'VALUE OF Y ENTERED = ', Y
      PRINT *, 'VALUE OF Z ENTERED = ', Z
```

will produce the following output (assuming X = 123.45, Y = 345.67, Z = 567.89):

```
ENTER X, Y AND Z:                       (Prompt from the program)
123.45, 345.67, 567.89    <CR>      (Values that you type in)
VALUE OF X ENTERED = 0.1234500E+03       (Echo from program)
VALUE OF Y ENTERED = 0.3456700E+03       (Echo from program)
VALUE OF Z ENTERED = 0.5678900E+03       (Echo from program)
^^^^^^^^^^^^^^^^^^^^^^^^^^^^^^^^^^^^^^^^^^^^^^^^^^^^^^^^^^^^^^^^
      |            |            |            |            |
      10           20           30           40           50
```

Note in this example that we do not use any FORMAT statements. We will add them only when we really need them. The first PRINT statement is the prompt. Its only purpose is to remind us in what order we are to enter the data. Once we enter the data (on a single line, separated by commas), the program prints out the string "VALUE OF X ENTERED = ," followed by the value of X that we entered. This is the echo portion of the input section. The only undesirable thing about this program segment is that the real data is printed in exponential format, which is somewhat difficult to read. But now that we know that it works, we can modify the program segment to give a somewhat nicer output appearance:

```
C Here is an example of a prompt to remind the user of
C the sequence of the input data.
      PRINT *, 'ENTER X, Y AND Z:'
      READ * , X, Y, Z
C Here is an echo, where the values of X, Y, and Z will be
C sent to the CRT screen so that you can check correct entry.
      PRINT 5, X, Y, Z
5     FORMAT('VALUE OF X ENTERED = ', F10.5, /,
1             'VALUE OF Y ENTERED = ', F10.5, /,
1             'VALUE OF Z ENTERED = ', F10.5)
```

will produce the following output (assuming $X = 123.45$, $Y = 345.67$, $Z = 567.89$):

```
ENTER X, Y AND Z:              (Prompt from the program)
123.45, 345.67, 567.89  <CR>   (Values that you type in)
VALUE OF X ENTERED =  123.45000 (Echo from program)
VALUE OF Y ENTERED =  345.67000 (Echo from program)
VALUE OF Z ENTERED =  567.89000 (Echo from program)
^^^^^^^^^^^^^^^^^^^^^^^^^^^^^^^^^^^^^^^^^^^^^^^^^^^^^^^^^^^
        |         |         |         |         |
        10        20        30        40        50
```

The bugs that you are mostly likely to encounter when using formatted I/O are the following:

- Overflow (data do not fit into the space allotted).
- Parentheses unbalanced.
- Data type of the output variable and the edit descriptor do not match.

The first problem occurs during execution when you do not allow enough space to print the output data. For example, if you use an I5 edit descriptor to print out the value of $J = 1234567$, the computer will print ***** as the output line. Obviously, J is a seven-digit number and cannot fit into five columns. The solution is obvious – add additional digits to the edit descriptor, or in the case of real numbers, switch to the E edit descriptor.

The second error (unbalanced parenthesis) occurs during compilation because FORMAT statements tend to contain several sets of parentheses, and it is very easy to have too few or too many. Remember, that there must be an equal number of left and right parentheses. When this error occurs, simply count the number of left and right parentheses, and make sure they balance.

The third error (incompatible variable and edit descriptor) is the most frequent formatting bug. Recall that a real variable can only use the F, E, or G edit descriptor. If you accidently forget, and use another descriptor (I, for example), an error occurs during compilation. Make sure that the type of the variables and the edit descriptors match.

EXAMPLE 3.18

The following example contains several common formatting errors.

```
        X = 12.345
        Y = 98.765
        I = 123
        J = 987
        PRINT 5, X, Y, X*Y, I, J, I*J
5       FORMAT(' ', 3(F7.3, 3X), /, 1x, 3(I3, 3X))
```

will not compile, since there is an extra right parenthesis in the FORMAT statement. Your compiler will detect this error and send you an appropriate error message. Once the extra parenthesis is removed, and the program is recompiled and executed, you should get the following output:

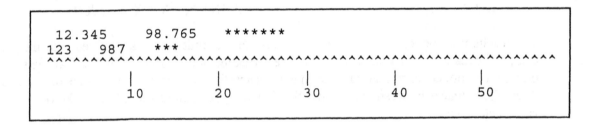

Notice that the product of X times Y (1219.2539) will not fit into the space allotted (F7.3), nor will the product of I times J (121401) fit into I3. So, the result is an overflow. To correct these problems, we should enlarge each of the output fields. In the corrected program below, we will use the E format for the product of the real numbers and expand I3 to something larger for the integer data.

```
        X = 12.345
        Y = 98.765
        I = 1234
        J = 9876
        PRINT 5, X, Y, X*Y, I, J, I*J
5       FORMAT(' ', 2(F7.3, 3X), E15.5, /, 1x, 3(I10, 3X))
```

The output will now look like this:

```
    12.345     98.765        0.12193E+04
        1234         9876        12186984
^^^^^^^^^^^^^^^^^^^^^^^^^^^^^^^^^^^^^^^^^^^^^^^^^^^^^^
        |           |           |           |           |
        10          20          30          40          50
```

Solved Problems

Note: We assume that all output statements require a carriage control character. This is always true when you are printing to a hard copy printer, but may not be required if printing to a CRT terminal. Therefore, you may have to modify the FORMAT statements accordingly.

3.1 Predict the output for the following program segments:

(a) I = 1234
    X = 12.34
    PRINT *, I, X

(b) I = 1234
    X = 12.34
    PRINT *, ' I = ', I, ' X = ', X

(c) I = 1234
    X = 12.34
    PRINT *, I
    PRINT *, X

(d) I = 1234
    X = 12.34
    PRINT *, ' I * I = ', I**2
    PRINT *, ' X * X = ', X**2

The results may be machine dependent because of the limit on storage of real and integer data, and because of the default rules on free formatted output. But, assuming that reals are printed in exponential format with seven significant digits and integers with nine digits, and three blank spaces between data items, this is what your output should look like (note: ~ is a blank space):

(a) ~ ~ ~ ~ ~ 1234 ~ ~ ~ 0.1234000E+02
(b) ~I ~ = ~ ~ ~ ~ ~ ~ 1234 ~ ~ ~ ~ X ~ = ~ 0.1234000E+02
(c) ~ ~ ~ ~ ~ 1234
    0.1234000E+02
(d) ~I ~ * ~I ~ = ~ ~ ~ 1522756
    ~X ~ * ~X ~ = ~ 0.1522756E+03

3.2 What would be the value of each variable after executing the following program segments?

(a) READ *, A, B, C   *(Input on one line: 12.34, 56.78, 98.76)*
(b) READ *, A, B, C   *(Input on three lines: 12.34, 56.78, 98.76)*
(c) READ *, I   *(Input: 1.5)*
(d) READ *, A   *(Input on line #1: 12.34, 56.78)*
    READ *, B, C   *(Input on line #2: 98.76, 54.32)*

(a) A = 12.3400, B = 56.7800, C = 98.7600
(b) Same as (a). It doesn't matter whether the data values are entered on the same or on different lines.
(c) I = 1, since I is an integer by default, so the decimal part is dropped.
(d) A = 12.3400, B = 98.7600, C = 54.3200. The first READ statement needs only one value to complete its job, so the second number on the first line is never read. The second READ statement starts reading a new line.

3.3   Assume that the real variable X has the value of 1234.567 and that it is printed out with PRINT 12, X. How would the output appear for each of the following FORMAT statements?

(a) 12   FORMAT(F12.4)   (b) 12   FORMAT(F8.4)
(c) 12   FORMAT(' ', F12.4)   (d) 12   FORMAT('+', F12.4)
(e) 12   FORMAT(' ','X= ', F12.4)   (f) 12   FORMAT(' ','X= ', /, F12.4)

(a) ~1234.5670   (Since there was no carriage control character, the computer interpreted the first character of the value to be printed (~) as the CCC. This is why there is only one blank space in front of the number.)

(b) ********   (If we insist on four decimal places, the number cannot fit into eight columns. Remember that the decimal point also takes up one column.)

(c) ~ ~1234.5670   (Compare this to example (a), where we left out the carriage control character.)

(d) ~ ~1234.5670   (Same as (c) except that this would be on current line, not on the next line.)

(e) X= ~ ~ ~ ~1234.5670   (The blank space after the = sign in the string is also printed.)

(f) X= ~
    ~ ~1234.5670   (The CCC is needed for the second line.)

3.4   Assume that the real variable X has the value of −1234.567 and that it is printed out with PRINT 12, X. How would the output appear for each of the following FORMAT statements?

(a) 12   FORMAT(E11.4)   (b) 12   FORMAT(E8.4)
(c) 12   FORMAT(' ', E11.4)   (d) 12   FORMAT('+', E11.4)
(e) 12   FORMAT(' ','X= ', E11.4)   (f) 12   FORMAT(' ','X= ', /, E11.4)

(a) 0.1235E+04   (Since there was no carriage control character, the computer interpreted the first character (minus sign) as the CCC.)

(b) no output   (Would not compile since w is too small. Must be at least 7 greater than d.)

(c) −0.1234E+04   (Compare this to example (a), where we left out the carriage control character.)

(d) −0.1234E+04   (The only difference between (c) and (d) is the line on which they appear. Example (c) appears on the next line, while (d) appears on the current line.)

(e) X= ~ −0.1235E+04   (The blank space after the = sign in the string is also printed.)

(f) X= ~
    0.1235E+04   (The CCC is needed for the second line.)

3.5   Assume that the real variable X has the value of -123.4567 and that it is printed with PRINT 12, X. How would the output appear for each of the following FORMAT statements?

(a) 12   FORMAT(G11.2)   (b) 12   FORMAT(G8.5)
(c) 12   FORMAT(' ', G14.5)   (d) 12   FORMAT(' ', G11.3)
(e) 12   FORMAT(' ','X= ', G8.3)   (f) 12   FORMAT(' ','X= ', /, G11.2)

(a) ~ ~0.12E+03   (Since the exponent value (3) is greater than the d value (2) in Gw.d, the E format is used. Also, since there was no CCC, the computer interprets the first character (blank space) as the CCC.)

(b) *******   (The exponent value of 3 is now *less* than d in Gw.d, so the computer switches to the F format. But, this does not leave enough room to print the answer, so we get an overflow.)

(c) ~ ~ ~ ~ -123.46~ ~ ~ ~   (Since the exponent value of 3 is smaller than the d value of 5, the F format is used. But, the computer alters the size of the field to roughly center it. To do this, it creates a new combination of $F(w-4).d + 4X$, where w = initial width and d = number of significant digits in the G format. For this example, w = 14 and d = 5 from G14.5 and the revised format becomes $F(14-4).5 + 4X$, or $F10.5 + 4X$, where 4X indicates 4 blank spaces.)

(d) ~ ~ -123. ~ ~ ~ ~   (The exponent (3) is equal to d in Gw.d, so we use the F format. But we must resize it using the rules in the previous example. $F(w-4).d + 4X$ becomes $F(11-4).3 + 4X$, or $F7.3 + 4X$.)

(e) X=********   (The minus sign occupies one column. Thus, the number cannot fit into the allotted 3 columns)

(f) X=~
     ~ ~0.12E+03   (The CCC is needed for the second line.)

3.6   Assume that the real double precision variable X has the value of -12345.6789 and that it is printed out with PRINT 12, X. How would the output appear for each of the following FORMAT statements?

(a) 12   FORMAT(D15.5)   (b) 12   FORMAT(' ', D15.5)
(c) 12   FORMAT(' ', D12.5)   (d) 12   FORMAT(' ', F11.3)
(e) 12   FORMAT(' ', G13.5)   (f) 12   FORMAT(' ', G15.3)

(a) ~ -0.12346D+005   (Since there is no carriage control character, the computer interprets the first character (~) as the CCC.)

(b) ~ ~ -0.12346D+005   (The first blank space was interpreted in (a) as the carriage control character. But this has now been corrected.)

(c) ***********   (Not enough space reserved, so an overflow results.)

(d) No output   (Compilation error, since the number is double precision and can only use D or G formats.)

(e) $\sim\sim-12346.\sim\sim\sim$ (The exponent (5) is equal to d in Gw.d, so we use the F format. But we must resize it using the rules previously discussed. F(w−4).d + 4X becomes F(13−4).5 + 4X, or F9.5 + 4X.)

(f) $\sim\sim\sim\sim-0.123D+005$ (The exponent (5) is smaller than d in Gw.d, so we use the D format.)

3.7 Assume that the integer variable I has the value of -123 and that it is printed out with PRINT 12, I. How would the output appear for each of the following FORMAT statements?

(a) 12   FORMAT(I3)   (b) 12   FORMAT(' ', I3)
(c) 12   FORMAT(' ', I5)   (d) 12   FORMAT(' ', 3X, F5.0)
(e) 12   FORMAT(' ','I= ', I5)   (f) 12   FORMAT(' ','I= ',/, I5)

(a) **   (The minus sign takes up one column, so you need to allow for it. Also, the CCC was left out).

(b) ***   (Even after the CCC is included, we still need to enlarge the field to make room for the negative sign.)

(c) ~-123 (Everything is OK now.)

(d) no output   (Compiler error since I is an integer, but F is the edit descriptor for a real number, not an integer.)

(e) I=$\sim\sim-123$ (The blank space after the = sign in the string is also printed.)

(f) I=$\sim$
   -123 (The CCC is needed for the second line.)

3.8 Assume that the character variable NAME has the value of "Joe Montana" and that it is printed out with PRINT 12, NAME. How would the output appear for each of the following FORMAT statements?

(a) 12   FORMAT(A1)   (b) 12   FORMAT(' ', A1)
(c) 12   FORMAT(' ', A12)   (d) 12   FORMAT(' ', A)

(a)   (The line would be blank! Since we only allowed one column for the output, only the first letter (J) should be printed. But we also left out the Carriage control character, so this would be used for the CCC instead.)

(b) J   (The problem from the previous example has been solved.)
(c) Joe Montana$\sim$ (Characters are left justified, so the blank space comes at the end.)

(d) Joe Montana   (No extra blank space.)

3.9 Assume that the real variables X and Y have the values of 1.2345 and 9.8765, respectively, and that the integer variables I and J have the values 12345 and 98765, respectively. How would the output appear for each of the following PRINT/FORMAT pairs?

(a)   PRINT 12, X, Y, I, J
     12 FORMAT(F10.3, T15, F10.3, T29, I10, T43, I10)

(b)   PRINT 12, X, Y, I, J
     12 FORMAT(' ', F10.3, T15, F10.3, T29, I10, T43, I10)

(c)   PRINT 12, X, Y, I, J
     12 FORMAT(' ', 2(F10.3, 4X), 2(I10, 4X))

(d)   PRINT 12, X, Y, I, J
     12 FORMAT(' ',2(F10.3, 4X), //, 1x, 2(I10, 4X))

(a) ~ ~ ~ ~ 1.235 ~ ~ ~ ~ ~ ~ ~ ~ ~ ~ 9.877 ~ ~ ~ ~ ~ ~ ~ ~ ~ 12345 ~ ~ ~ ~ ~
~ ~ ~ ~ 98765   (Note missing first blank space because CCC was left out.)

(b) ~ ~ ~ ~ ~ 1.235 ~ ~ ~ ~ ~ ~ ~ ~ ~ ~ 9.877 ~ ~ ~ ~ ~ ~ ~ ~ ~ 12345 ~ ~ ~ ~
~ ~ ~ ~ ~ 98765   (Slightly different from previous example since CCC now present.)

(c) ~ ~ ~ ~ ~ 1.235 ~ ~ ~ ~ ~ ~ ~ ~ ~ 9.877 ~ ~ ~ ~ ~ ~ ~ ~ ~ ~ 12345 ~ ~ ~ ~ ~ ~
~ ~ ~ 98765   (Last four blank spaces not shown.)

(d) ~ ~ ~ ~ ~ 1.235 ~ ~ ~ ~ ~ ~ ~ ~ ~ 9.877
               (Blank line – the // command double spaces.)
~ ~ ~ ~ ~ 12345 ~ ~ ~ ~ ~ ~ ~ ~ ~ 98765

3.10 Find the syntax errors, if any, in each of the following program segments. Assume implicit typing rules in effect for all variables.

(a)   PRINT I , J , K   (b)   READ *, 'ENTER THE VALUE OF X:',X

(c)   PRINT *, X , Y   (d)   PRINT *, "THE ANSWER IS:", X

(e)   PRINT 10, X   (f)   PRINT 20, X
    10 FORMAT(I3)   20 FORMAT(' ','X= ')

(a) Comma and * missing   (b) No printouts permitted with a READ statement

(c) Correct   (d) Should use apostrophes, not quote marks

(e) Integer descriptor for real variable (f) No edit descriptor for X

3.11 Trace through the following program segments and predict their output. For problems with formatted I/O, pay close attention to spacing.

(a)   X = 1.5   (b)   X = 123.4567
        Y = 2.56   PRINT 10, X, X, X, X, X, X
        Z = 100.01   10 FORMAT(1X,2(F8.1,2(F8.2,2(F8.3))))
        PRINT 10, X, Y, Z, Y   END
        PRINT 10, Z * Y
    10 FORMAT(1X, 2(F6.1), 2F6.2)
        END

(c)   X1 = 1.0   (d)   X1 = 1.0
         X2 = 2.0   X2 = 2.0
         X3 = 3.0   X3 = 3.0
         PRINT 100,X1,X2,X3,X3,X2,X1   PRINT 90, X1,X2,X3,X3,X2,X1,X2,X3,X1
    100 FORMAT(' ',10(1X,F6.2))   90 FORMAT(' ',3(1X,F6.2))
         END   END

(a) ~ ~ ~ 1.5 ~ ~ ~ 2.6100.01 ~ ~ ~ 2.56
    ~ 256.0
(b) ~ ~ ~ 123.5 ~ ~ 123.46 ~ 123.457 ~ 123.457 ~ ~ 123.46 ~ 123.457
(c) ~ ~ ~ 1.00 ~ ~ ~ 2.00 ~ ~ ~ 3.00 ~ ~ ~ 3.00 ~ ~ ~ 2.00 ~ ~ ~ 1.00
(d) ~ ~ ~ ~ 1.00 ~ ~ ~ 2.00 ~ ~ ~ 3.00
    ~ ~ ~ 3.00 ~ ~ ~ 2.00 ~ ~ ~ 1.00
    ~ ~ ~ 2.00 ~ ~ ~ 3.00 ~ ~ ~ 1.00

3.12 Write a program which reads in a REAL number and prints out the whole number portion
without using any of the intrinsic functions.

```
         PRINT *, 'Enter a Real Number:'
         READ *, X
         I = X
         PRINT 10, I
    10   FORMAT(' '. 'Whole Portion of Number is:'. I7)
         END
```

3.13 Suppose there is a program which calculates the month, day and year (stored in MONTH,
DAY, and YEAR) and also the time in hours, minutes, and seconds (stored in HOURS,
MINUTE and SECOND). Write the Fortran code to output this information in military time
(24-hour basis) following this example: *The date is 10/23/90, and the time is now 15:45:37
hours*. Assume that all variable types are integer.

```
         INTEGER DAY, YEAR, HOURS, SECOND
         PRINT 10, MONTH, DAY, YEAR, HOURS, MINUTE, SECOND
    10   FORMAT(' ', 'The Date is', I2,'/',I2,'/',I2,'and the time is now ',I2,':',I2,':',
    1                I2,' hours')
         END
```

3.14 Write a program assigning I1 = 1, I2 = 2, I3 = 3, I4 = 4, I5 = 5, and I6 = 6. Have your program
print these integers in the following ways:

(a) In a single row
(b) In two rows containing (I1, I2, I3) and (I4, I5, I6), using two PRINT statements but
     only one FORMAT statement
(c) In two rows, as above, but with only one PRINT statement

(a) 12 FORMAT(A18)   (b) 12 FORMAT(' ', A18)
(c) 12 FORMAT(' ','Course=',A15) (d) 12 FORMAT(' ','Course=', 5x, A)

3.23 Assume the real variables X and Y have the values of -0.12345 and -0.98765, respectively, and the integer variables, I and J, have the values 4567 and 890, respectively. How would the output appear for each of the following PRINT/FORMAT pairs?

(a)   PRINT 12, X, Y, I, J
        12 FORMAT(' ',F8.3, T13, F8.3, T25, I5, T34, I5)
(b)   PRINT 12, X, Y, I, J
        12 FORMAT(' ', 2(F8.3, 4X), 2(I5, 4X))
(c)   PRINT 10
        10 FORMAT(' ', T4, 'X', T16, 'Y', T27, 'I', T36,'J',//)
        PRINT 12, X, Y, I, J
        12 FORMAT(' ',2(F8.3, 4X), 2(I5, 4X))

3.24 Find the syntax errors, if any, in each of the following program segments. Assume implicit typing rules in effect for all variables.

(a)   PRINT 30, I , J , K , X   (b)   PRINT 40
        30 FORMAT(4(I5,2X))   40 FORMAT('AMTDUE: ', AMTDUE)
(c)   PRINT 27, X , Y , Z ,   (d)   READ 41, U , V , W , I , J , K
        27 FORMAT('+',3(F12.4),I4)   41 FORMAT(3(F12.4, I6))
(e)   PRINT 200, A , I , B , K   (f)   PRINT 19, X , Y , I , U , V
        200 FORMAT(F10.4, 3X, I4)   19 FORMAT(' ',2E12.7,2(I7,1X,2D12.4))
(g)   READ 12, I , X , Z*Y
        12 FORMAT(' ',I4,4X,2F12.5)

3.25 Trace through the following program segments and predict their output.

(a)   X1=1.0   (b)   X=1.2
        X2=2.0   Y=1.3
        X3=3.0   Z=1.4
        PRINT 102,X1,X2,X3,X3,X2,X1   PRINT 10, X, Y, Z
        102 FORMAT(' ',3(3(1X,F6.2),/,1X)) 10 FORMAT(T10,F6.2,/,T10,F6.2,/,T10,F6.2)
        END   END

(c)   PRINT 2   (d)   X=100.2
        PRINT 3   PRINT 10, X
        2   FORMAT(' ','O')   10 FORMAT(F6.2)
        3   FORMAT('+','/')   END
        END

3.26 Write a program which reads in a REAL number and prints out the fractional portion without using any of the intrinsic functions.

3.27 Write a program which will read in an angle reported as DEGREES, MINUTES, and SECONDS and print it out in a decimal format as in the following example: *An angle of 22 degrees, 13 minutes, 47 seconds is equal to 22.3472 degrees.*

3.28 Write a program that will print out a table heading with "Student ID" starting in column 5, "Midterm Exam" in column 25, "Final Exam" in column 45, and "Grade" in column 65. On the next line, underline all of the headings.

3.29 Write a program that reads in a real number and rounds it off to two decimal places. Use a prompt statement to assist the user.

Answers to Selected Supplementary Problems

3.15 (a) ~ ~ ~ ~ -4567 ~ ~ ~ ~ ~ ~ 123 ~ ~ ~ $-0.1234567E-02$
   (b) ~I~ = ~ ~ ~ ~ ~ -4567 ~ ~ ~ ~J~ = ~ ~ ~ ~ ~ ~ ~ 123 ~ ~ ~ ~
        X~ = ~ $-0.1234567E-02$
   (c) ~ ~ ~ ~4567 ~ ~ ~ ~ ~ ~ 123
        $-0.1234567E-02$
   (d) ~I~ * ~J~ = ~ ~ ~ ~ -561741
        ~X~ * ~J~ = ~ $0.1518517E+00$

3.16 (a) A = -0.1234, I = 12, J = 11 (computer does not round off in this case).
   (b) Same as (a). It doesn't matter whether the data values are entered on the same or different lines.
   (c) X = 1.0 (computer adds decimal point).
   (d) A = -0.1234, B & C are undefined. The first READ statement needs only one value to complete its function, so the second and third numbers on the first line are never read. Subsequent READ statements are still waiting for data.

3.17 (a) ~ ~ ~ ~ ~ -0.001 (Since there was no carriage control character, the computer interpreted the first character ($\sim$) as the CCC.)
   (b) 0.0012   (The leading negative sign was used for the carriage control since the CCC was left out.)
   (c) ~ ~ ~ ~ ~ ~ -0.001 (Compare this to example (a), where we left out the CCC.)
   (d) ~ ~ $-0.001234567x$ (Real numbers can store only 7 significant digits. So, if we

request more in the printout, you can never be sure what the machine will print out. We highlight this by showing the last digit as x.)

(e) X= ~ ~ −0.00123

(The last digit is rounded. In this case, it is rounded down.)

(f) X= ~
    ~ ~ −0.001235

(In this case, the last digit is rounded up.)

3.18 (a) 0.1235E −02

(Since there was no carriage control character, the computer interpreted the first character (minus sign) as the CCC.)

(b) ~ −0.12E−02

(Similar to (a), except that a blank space was used for carriage control.)

(c) −0.1235E−02

(Compare this to example (a), where we left out the carriage control character.)

(d) ~ ~ −0.123457E−02   (Note that the mantissa is rounded up.)

(e) X= ~ −0.1235E−02

(The blank space after the = sign in the string is also printed.)

(f) X= ~
    0.1235E −02

(The CCC is needed for the second line.)

3.19 (a) ~ ~ −1.2~ ~ ~ ~

(Since the exponent in E format is one and is less than d(2) in Gw.d, the F format is used. The revised F format is F(11−4).2 + 4x, or F7.2 + 4x. Also, since there was no carriage control character, the computer interpreted the first character (blank space) as the CCC.)

(b) *******

(Since the exponent is less than d (2), the F format is used with F(8−4).5 + 4X, or F4.5 + 4X. Notice that the number cannot fit in this space, so an overflow condition results. Also, one of the blank spaces is used for carriage control, so only 7 stars are printed, not 8.)

(c) ~ ~ −1.2346~ ~ ~ ~   (Convert to F(14−4).4 + 4X, or F10.4 + 4X.)

(d) ~ −1.23~ ~ ~ ~ ~   (Convert to F(11−4).2 + 4X, or F7.2 + 4X.)

(e) X= ~ ~ −1.23~ ~ ~ ~   (Don't forget the blank space after =.)

(f) X= ~
    ~ ~ −1.2~ ~ ~ ~

(Format becomes F7.1 + 4X.)

3.20 (a) 0.12346D+001

(Since there was no carriage control character, the first character (minus sign) is used as the CCC.)

(b) −0.12346D+001   (Carriage control problem now solved.)

(c) ***********   (Not enough space reserved, so an overflow results.)

(d) No output

(Compilation error, since the number is double precision and can only use D or G formats.)

(e) ~ ~ −1.2346~ ~ ~ ~   (Convert to F(14−4).4 + 4X, or F10.4 + 4X.)

(f) ~ ~ ~ −1.~ ~ ~ ~   (Convert to F(11−4).0 + 4X, or F7.0 + 4X. Notice that F7.0 is permitted and will print no decimal places.)

3.21 (a) 87654   (Since the CCC was left out, the computer used the first digit for carriage control.)

(b) 987654   (CCC problems now solved.)
(c) ~ ~ ~987654   (Integers are right justified within output field.)
(d) no output   (Compiler error since I is an integer and cannot use G format.)

(e) I = ~987654   (The blank space after the = sign in the string is also printed.)

(f) I = ~
   87654   (The CCC is needed for the second line.)

3.22 (a) ocket Science 101   (No CCC, so the first character is used.)
(b) Rocket Science 101   (Problem from the previous example has been solved.)
(c) Course = Rocket ~ Science ~ (No overflow condition with character data.)
(d) Course = ~ ~ ~ ~ ~Rocket ~ Science ~ 101
               (The A format allows just enough spaces.)

3.23 (a) ~ ~ −0.123 ~ ~ ~ ~ ~ ~ −0.988 ~ ~ ~ ~ ~4567 ~ ~ ~ ~ ~ ~890
(b) ~ ~ −0.123 ~ ~ ~ ~ ~ ~ −0.988 ~ ~ ~ ~ ~4567 ~ ~ ~ ~ ~ ~890
(c) ~ ~ ~X ~ ~ ~ ~ ~ ~ ~ ~ ~ ~ ~Y ~ ~ ~ ~ ~ ~ ~ ~ ~ ~ ~I ~ ~ ~ ~ ~ ~ ~ ~ ~J
             (this line is blank)
   ~ ~ −0.123 ~ ~ ~ ~ ~ ~ −0.988 ~ ~ ~ ~ ~4567 ~ ~ ~ ~ ~ ~890

3.24 (a) X is real and cannot use I5 descriptor
(b) Variable to printout must be in PRINT statement
(c) Extra comma at end of I/O list
(d) Should be 3F12.4,3I6
(e) Correct, since the FORMAT is reused
(f) E edit descriptors do not allow enough space. Use the edit descriptors as many times as needed (twice). U and V are not double precision.
(g) Cannot do math in READ statement

3.25 (a) ~ ~ ~1.00 ~ ~ ~2.00 ~ ~ ~3.00
     ~ ~ ~3.00 ~ ~ ~2.00 ~ ~ ~1.00
(b) ~ ~ ~ ~ ~ ~ ~ ~ ~ ~ ~1.20
     ~ ~ ~ ~ ~ ~ ~ ~ ~ ~ ~1.30
     ~ ~ ~ ~ ~ ~ ~ ~ ~ ~ ~1.40
(c) Ø   (a slash (/) superimposed over a zero (0))
(d) 00.20

3.26   PRINT*, 'Enter a Real Number:'
      READ *, X
      I = X
      FRAC = X − I
      PRINT 10, FRAC
   10 FORMAT(' ', 'Fractional Part of Number is:', F7.4)
      END

3.27   INTEGER DEGREE, SECOND
      PRINT *, 'Enter degrees, minutes, and seconds:'
      READ *, DEGREE, MINUTE, SECOND
      DECIMAL=DEGREE+MINUTE/60.0+SECOND/360.0
      PRINT 10, DEGREE, MINUTE, SECOND, DECIMAL
   10 FORMAT(' ','An angle of ',I3,' Degrees, ',I2,' Minutes, ',I2,
    1   ' Seconds is equal to ', F8.4,' degrees')
      END

3.28   PRINT 10
   10 FORMAT(' ', T5, 'Student ID', T25, 'Midterm Exam',
    1   T45, 'Final Exam', T65, 'Grade',
    1   /,T5, 10('_'), T25, 12('_'), T45, 10('_'), T65, 5('_'))

3.29   PRINT 10
   10 FORMAT(' ', 'Enter any real number with more than two decimal places')
      READ *, X
      PRINT 20, X, X
   20 FORMAT(' ', 'The original number:', F15.5, /, 'rounded to 2 decimal places:', F10.2)
      END

Chapter 4

Decision-Based Control Structures

4.1 OVERVIEW

So far you have learned to construct simple sequential Fortran programs with formatted input and output. While such programs are useful for straightforward tasks, there are a great many problems that require decision making. In this chapter we will discuss various kinds of *control* structures. These structures will allow you to select one set of instructions for execution from two or more groups of instructions.

The topics to be covered in this chapter include:

- Unconditional transfer;
- Conditional statements and constructs;
- Special forms of the IF construct;
- The SELECT CASE structure; and
- Debugging tips for branching operations.

Conditional and unconditional transfer statements provide fundamental functions from which more complex control structures can be created. For example, suppose we would like to sum a list of 100 numbers. With what we know so far, we would have to write a program that reads in 100 numbers, adds them together, and then finally prints the result. This would be a tedious and long program to write. However, by using the statements provided in this chapter, such a problem can be solved with just a few lines. What's more, the program can be written to read in any arbitrary number of numbers. This is just one example of the power of control structures.

4.2 UNCONDITIONAL TRANSFER

The unconditional transfer statement, or GO TO statement, is the simplest transfer operation. It provides a means by which control transfers to another line in the program. The line to receive the control must be labeled using a statement label. The general form of the GO TO statement is:

GO TO *statement label*

where the statement label is a positive integer value placed in columns one through five and indicates a specific line to which we can transfer.

The unconditional transfer is usually used for two purposes:

- Skip over a set of instructions; and
- Repeat a set of instructions.

At first glance, it may appear that the GO TO statement is all that we need to set up the two remaining building blocks of programming that we described in Chapter 1. But as we will see shortly, using the GO TO often gets programmers into trouble and can result in nearly unreadable code (sometimes jokingly called *spaghetti code*). There are better ways to implement the branching and looping operations without the use of the GO TO, but there are a <u>few</u> times when the GO TO is the simplest way to solve a logic problem. So we will review this simplest control structure first.

EXAMPLE 4.1

Here is a program that produces a list of the squares of positive integers

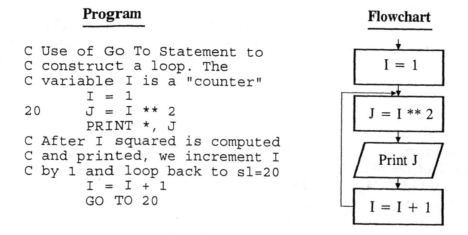

```
C Use of Go To Statement to
C construct a loop. The
C variable I is a "counter"
        I = 1
20      J = I ** 2
        PRINT *, J
C After I squared is computed
C and printed, we increment I
C by 1 and loop back to sl=20
        I = I + 1
        GO TO 20
```

When we first start this program, I has the value of 1. Its square is computed and printed, after which I increases by 1 and the whole process repeats. While this program works and produces the desired result, it is a very poor way to accomplish this. Note for example, that the process presented is an *infinite loop*, and there is no way to get out.

The second way that we use the GO TO statement is to produce a branch, where we can jump over one set of instructions to perform another set.

EXAMPLE 4.2

In the simple example program below, we use the GO TO statement to skip over another line within the program.

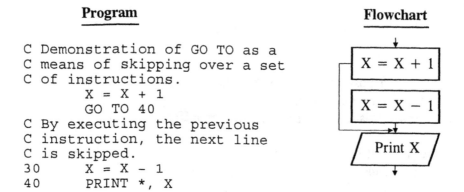

```
C Demonstration of GO TO as a
C means of skipping over a set
C of instructions.
        X = X + 1
        GO TO 40
C By executing the previous
C instruction, the next line
C is skipped.
30      X = X - 1
40      PRINT *, X
```

In this example, after executing the statement "X = X + 1," the program transfers control to the line labeled 40 where the computer executes the PRINT statement. The only way of executing the statement labeled 30 would be for some other part of the program to issue a GO TO 30 command.

GO TO statements, FORMAT statements and other structures yet to be presented utilize statement labels. While there are few rules for statement labels, here are a few suggestions that will help you make your program more understandable and easier to debug.

- Arrange statement labels in ascending order throughout your program. In other words, the lowest numbered statement label appears first in your program and the highest numbered statement label appears last. This will help you to locate the statement quickly when you are reading or tracing your program.
- Because programs are rarely correct the first time you write them, it is a good idea to increment your statement label by 10's, or even 100's. By initially assigning statement labels this way, you will be able to insert additional labels while maintaining the ascending order rule.

GO TO statements should be used sparingly and only when absolutely necessary since their excessive use can lead to programs which are more likely to contain logic errors and are hard to debug. We will show you alternate constructs that make any use of the GO TO rare.

4.3 CONDITIONAL STATEMENTS AND CONSTRUCTS

In this section we will present the IF statement and the IF construct. By using these commands it will be possible for you to construct conditional tests. Based on that test you will be able to branch to other lines of code for other operations.

The IF statement provides a way to test a condition and execute a single command if the test condition is true. The general form is:

IF *(test condition)* *statement-to-execute-if-true*

The *test condition* is a comparison between two quantities (a variable with a constant for example). If the test condition is true, then the *statement-to-execute-if-true* is executed before control passes to the next line. If the test condition is false, however, control is immediately passed to the next line. Graphically, this is how the logic flows:

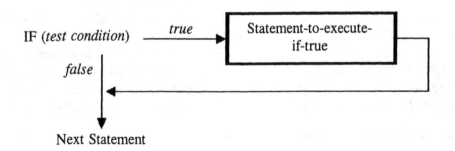

The test condition can be any expression or statement that returns a logical value of *true* or *false*. For most applications, the test condition will be constructed of *relational operators* and *logical operators*. Relational operators are used to compare two numerical values and can return only one of two possible answers — *true* or *false*. The logical operators, on the other hand, are the mathematical operations to compare two truth values, such as those returned by the relational operators.

Relational Operators

Relational operators compare two quantities and return an answer of true or false. There are only six relational operators available in Fortran 77, and they are listed in the table below:

Operator	Description	Example	Result
.LT.	Less than ($<$)	1 .LT. 2	True
.LE.	Less than or equals ($\leq$)	3.14 .LE. 10.0	True
.EQ.	Equals ($=$)	0 .EQ. 10	False
.NE.	Not equals ($\neq$)	0 .NE. 10	True
.GT.	Greater than ($>$)	1 .GT. 2	False
.GE.	Greater than or equals ($\geq$)	4 .GE. 3	True

When you use relational operators, you can compare a variable with a constant, a variable with another variable, a variable with an expression, and so forth. This comparison is done inside the parentheses following the IF statement.

EXAMPLE 4.3

Here are several examples of the use of the relational operators:

Example Relational Operator	Description
IF (DENO .EQ. 0) STOP	Halt the program if the value of DENO $= 0$
IF (TEMP .LT. 0) PRINT *, TEMP	If TEMP < 0 then print value of TEMP
IF (X .LE. XMIN) XMIN = X	If X $\leq$ XMIN, set value of XMIN to X
IF (S .GT. 1E6) S = 1E6	Set S to 1×10^6 if S $> 1 \times 10^6$
IF (A .GE. 0) GO TO 10	Permissible to transfer to a statement label
IF (SQRT(X*Y) .NE. 4) X = Y	You can use expressions for comparison
IF (ABS(X) .EQ. Y*Z) A=SQRT(X)	You can compare an expression to an expression
IF (I/2*2 .EQ. I) PRINT *,'even'	How to determine if an integer I is even or odd

Logical Operators

In some instances you may wish to check more than one condition before carrying out an instruction. You can think of this as a compound test. For example, two things may need to be true simultaneously before a calculation can proceed. You were already familiar with this when you had a test like "Is x between 3.0 and 10.0?," expressed by:

$$3.0 \leq x \leq 10.0$$

This is equivalent to two individual relational comparisons:

$$3.0 \leq x \text{ and at the same time is } x \leq 10.0$$

We treat this as two separate comparisons and connect them with a *logical operator*. Logical operators perform operations on truth values and return a truth value as their result. The following table lists the logical operators available in Fortran:

Operator	Description	Number of arguments
.NOT.	Negation	1 argument
.AND.	Both simultaneously	2 arguments
.OR.	Either/or	2 arguments

These logical operators can only operate on logical expressions. The first (.NOT.) changes the logical value of its argument. Thus, if A is *true*, then (.NOT. A) is *false*. The other operators compare two logical values and return a single value based upon the two input values and the operator being used. The easiest way to summarize these is with the *truth tables* shown below:

.AND. Truth Table		
A	B	A .AND. B
T	T	T
T	F	F
F	T	F
F	F	F

.OR. Truth Table		
A	B	A .OR. B
T	T	T
T	F	T
F	T	T
F	F	F

.NOT. Truth Table	
A	.NOT. A
T	F
F	T

The .AND. operator is *true* only when <u>both</u> inputs are *true* while the .OR. operator is *true* when <u>either</u> input is *true*. Note carefully that these logical operators require two inputs. The .NOT. operator simply changes the input value and requires only a single input value.

EXAMPLE 4.4

Construct a logical operator to see if a number x is within the range $1.0 < x < 10.0$. This test actually consists of two separate tests, both of which must be true simultaneously:

$$1.0 < x \quad and \quad x < 10.0$$

We construct the two tests and connect them with the .AND. logical operator:

```
READ *, X
IF(1.0.LT.X.AND.X.LT.10.0)PRINT *,X,'is between 1 and 10'
```

When you first look at this, you might have been tempted to write, as we do in mathematics:

$$1.0 \ .LT. \ X \ .LT. \ 10.0$$

But this statement is incorrect. The reason is that the operators can only compare data of the same type. They cannot compare *true* or *false* values with numerical data for example. Let's assume $X = 5.0$ and trace through our hypothetical solution:

$$1.0 \ .LT. \ X \ .LT. \ 10.0 \quad \rightarrow \quad 1.0 \ .LT. \ 5.0 \ .LT. \ 10.0 \quad \rightarrow \quad true \ .LT. \ .10.0$$

An error occurs at this point since the .LT. operator attempts to compare two things that are incompatible (logical data with a real number in this instance).

In this last example, we combined relational operators (.LT.) with logical operators (.AND.). It is likely also that you will write complex test conditions that include mathematical operators. This may lead you to ask which operator would be performed first in such a complex test. Do we do the logical operators, the relational operators, or the mathematical operations first? The answers lie in the table below, which updates the hierarchial rules to include the two new operators:

Priority	Math Symbol	Fortran Symbol	Meaning
1	(...)	(...)	Parentheses
2	A^b	**	Exponentiation
3	$x \div$	*, /	Multiplication & division
4	$+ \ -$	+, −	Addition & subtraction
5	$= \neq <$	.EQ., .NE., .LT.	Relational operators
	$\leq \ > \ \geq$	.LE., .GT., .GE.	
6	$\bar{x}$	.NOT.	Logical negation
7	$\odot$	.AND.	Logical AND
8	$\oplus$	.OR.	Logical OR

There are three new mathematical symbols in this table that you may not be familiar with. These are $\bar{x}$ (read as *bar x*) for logical negation, $\odot$ (read as *and*) for the logical AND function, and $\oplus$ (read as *or*) for the logical OR function. In this hierarchial list, the mathematical operators are performed first, the relational comparisons second, and the logical comparisons last. Thus, in a complex test, there is now an established order that you can use to decide which operations to perform first.

EXAMPLE 4.5

Evaluate the following expressions, assuming that X = 10.0, Y = −2.0, and Z = 5.0:

(X*Y .LT. Z/X .OR. X/Y .GT. Z*X .AND. Z*Y .LT. X)

First, substitute the values for X, Y, and Z, and perform the mathematical operations:

(10.0*−2.0 .LT. 5.0/10.0 .OR. 10.0/−2.0 .GT. 5.0*10.0 .AND. 5.0*−2.0 .LT. 10.0)

Next, perform the relational comparisons (.LT., .GT., .LT. left to right):

(*true* .OR. *false* .AND. *true*)

From the hierarchy table, we see that .AND. takes precedence over .OR.. Thus, this reduces to

(*true* .OR. *false*)　　→　　(*true*)

4.4 THE BLOCK IF STRUCTURE

The IF statement that we discussed in the previous section is useful when you have only a single instruction to execute after the test condition is evaluated. But if you have more than a single instruction, you need a different structure. In Fortran, this is the *block IF* structure. As its name implies, it consists of blocks of instructions to execute. One block executes when the test condition is *true*, while a second block of instruction will execute when the test condition is *false*. The general form of the block IF construct is as follows:

```
IF (Test-Condition) THEN
        Block of statements if test-condition is true
ELSE
        Block of statements if test-condition is false
END IF
```

Nothing appears on the same line as the THEN, ELSE, or END IF key words. For convenience, we have indented the individual blocks to make it easier to visualize breaks in the control. But the indentation is not required. The individual blocks of statements can be as complex as you wish. They may be a single line or they may be hundreds of lines with complex structures.

EXAMPLE 4.6

The following segment checks to see if the number x you have entered is greater than or equal to zero. If it is not, the user is sent an error message and requested to reenter the data.

Program   **Flowchart**

```
C Use a prompt to request
C input for X
10     PRINT *,'Enter Value:'
       READ *, X
C If X is negative, then
C print a message and go
C back to the input section.
C Otherwise, accept the
C value.
       IF(X .LT. 0) THEN
          PRINT *,'Invalid'
          GO TO 10
       ELSE
          PRINT *,'Valid'
       END IF
```

In this example, the IF statement checks to see if the entered number is less than zero. If it is, then the test condition is *true* and the series of instructions between THEN and ELSE will be executed. In this case, the computer prints out the error message and returns to the input section. But if the number is greater than or equal to zero, the test condition is *false*, and control transfers to the block between the ELSE and the END IF statements. The only result here is to produce the message "Valid." A key point is that no matter what the outcome of the test condition, only *one* block of instructions or the other is performed, not both!

When you write an IF-THEN-ELSE-ENDIF block, it is good programming practice to indent the block of instructions. All the key words (IF, ELSE, ENDIF) begin in the same column, while the instructions in each of the blocks are indented by an amount of your choosing. You will find this to be useful when you need to trace through your program while debugging. The indentations help you to visualize groups of instructions as blocks, and will become a valuable aid later on. We will also offer this same advice when we get to the other block structures.

There are times, some of which will be discussed shortly, when it is advantageous to reverse the logic of the test condition. For example, if we set up the test to ask "Is x is equal to y?," it may be better to rephrase the question as "Is x not equal to y?" Of course, if we do this, we must reverse the block of instructions that accompany each of the answers (true or false).

EXAMPLE 4.7

The following program segment modifies Example 4.6 to reverse the logic.

Program	**Flowchart**

```
C Use a prompt to request
C input for X
10      PRINT *,'Enter Value:'
        READ *, X
C The logic is reversed from the
C previous problem. The opposite
C of .LT. is .GE. We also need
C to switch the instructions to
C be executed for a true or
C false answer.
        IF(X .GE. 0) THEN
            PRINT *,'Valid'
        ELSE
            PRINT *,'Invalid'
            GO TO 10
        END IF
```

The program produces the same result as the segment in Example 4.6, but the route is somewhat different. When we reversed the logic, we also had to exchange the instructions to be executed when the decision is made. How you choose to write programs is a matter of personal style. Select the method that is most understandable to you.

Along with the introduction of the block IF construct came the introduction of *program blocks*. Aside from the IF statement, many other Fortran commands also utilize program blocks. We will see them again when we discuss the Select Case structure and loops. Therefore, it is worthwhile to stop here and discuss briefly the rules for program blocks that will help you later. These rules are:

- From inside the block, control can be transferred to a statement *outside* of the block.
- It is valid to transfer control from one statement of a block to another statement *within* the same block.
- You cannot transfer control from outside of a block to *inside* of a block except by way of the controlling structure.
- It is possible to nest constructs as long as the inner construct is completely within the outer block (no crossing of block boundaries is permitted).
- It is valid for a GO TO to send control to the closing statement of a construct.

We will demonstrate more fully what these rules mean in the next few examples.

EXAMPLE 4.8

The following example demonstrates that it is permissible to transfer *out* of a block IF construct. We will see shortly that the reverse operation (transferring *into* the body of a block) is never permitted.

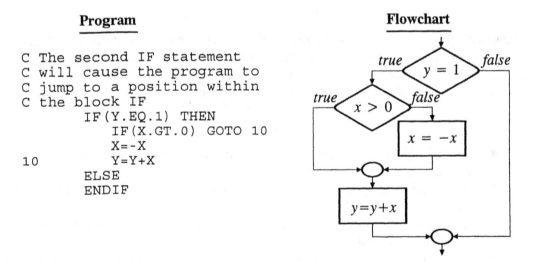

Program

```
C The GO TO statement in
C this example transfers
C out of the block IF
        IF(D.EQ.0) THEN
            PRINT *,'D = 0'
            GO TO 10
        ELSE
        END IF
        ANS = 1 / D
        PRINT *,ANS
10      STOP
        END
```

If the value of d is zero, the block IF prints out a statement that $d=0$ and transfers outside the block (to the STOP statement). But for any other value of d, the program proceeds to calculate the reciprocal of d and print it.

EXAMPLE 4.9

It is permissible to transfer control from one statement of a block to another statement *within* the same block.

Program

```
C The second IF statement
C will cause the program to
C jump to a position within
C the block IF
        IF(Y.EQ.1) THEN
            IF(X.GT.0) GOTO 10
            X=-X
10          Y=Y+X
        ELSE
        ENDIF
```

In this example, control jumps over the line $x=-x$ when x is greater than zero. This is permitted since the jump is entirely within the IF-ENDIF block. As long as the transfer begins and ends within the block IF construct, it is permitted. Thus, if we wished, we could have transferred to a line before the IF (X .GT. 0) statement and created a loop. The only restriction is that the line to which we are transferring must be situated within the block.

One final note about this and the previous examples is that there are no instructions to be executed between the ELSE and the ENDIF statements. This is allowed, and in such cases the ELSE statement can be omitted without loss of clarity.

If jumping out of a block structure is allowed, how about jumping into the middle of a block? This <u>cannot</u> be allowed, since it would bypass the mechanism that controls a block of instructions.

EXAMPLE 4.10

In the following example, we show how you might attempt to transfer into the middle of a block. The Fortran compiler however, will not allow you to do this.

```
      IF (X .EQ. 0) GO TO 20
      IF (Y .EQ. 0) THEN
20       X=X+1                    (This statement is inside the block IF construct)
      ELSE
      END IF
```

When the program attempts to jump to statement label 20, the statement that controls the branching operation (IF (Y .EQ. 0)) is completely bypassed.

It is possible to place one block IF within another block IF, provided that they do not violate any of the previous rules. Not only is this structure acceptable, but it is often desirable, since it allows you to construct branching operations with more than two outcomes. In general, if you desire a structure with n outcomes, you will need $n-1$ nested block IF structures.

EXAMPLE 4.11

Here is a sample program to determine if a is positive, negative, or zero. Notice that this requires two nested block IFs, since there are three possible outcomes:

Program   **Flowchart**

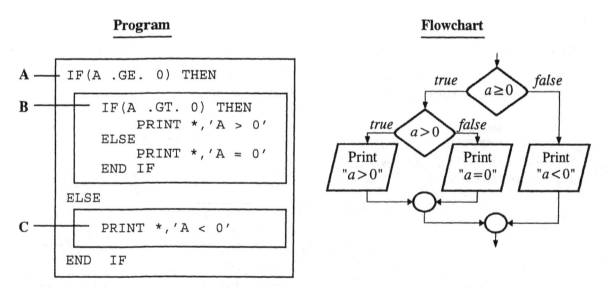

Note that block B is completely within the *true* section of the block IF represented by A. Similarly, block C is completely within the *false* block. As a result, the blocks are *properly nested*. If, however, the blocks are not properly nested, the program will not compile.

Here is an example of invalid nesting:

EXAMPLE 4.12

Here is the same program as in Example 4.11, except that the blocks are improperly nested:

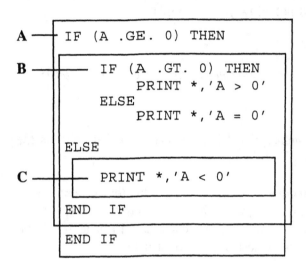

```
A ──┬─ IF (A .GE. 0) THEN

B ──┬───── IF (A .GT. 0) THEN
    │           PRINT *,'A > 0'
    │      ELSE
    │           PRINT *,'A = 0'
    │
    │      ELSE
    │
C ──┴────── PRINT *,'A < 0'

       END  IF

    END IF
```

In this example, the *true* block, labeled B, overlaps the boundaries of block A. Thus, one of the components of the block-IF actually extends outside the block that is supposed to contain it. Thus, this is not a legal structure, and the compiler will report a nesting error.

Block C is correctly nested, so there is no error for this part of the nested structure. One way to tell that the two structures are improperly nested is to look at one of the *key words* — ELSE. Notice that this structure has two consecutive ELSE statements. If the structures are properly nested, you will not have the situation where the same key word is repeated consecutively.

The final rule about block structures is that it is permissible to transfer to the end of the structure.

EXAMPLE 4.13

In this example, a GO TO statement inside a block IF structure is used to transfer to the end of the structure, which in this case is the END IF statement.

Program   **Flowchart**

```
C The GO TO 10 statement
C transfers control to the
C end of the block IF.
      IF(A .GT. 10) THEN
          A = A + B
          Y = Y + 1
          IF(Y .GT. 10)GOTO 10
          X = X - 1
      ELSE
          PRINT *, A, B
10        END IF
```

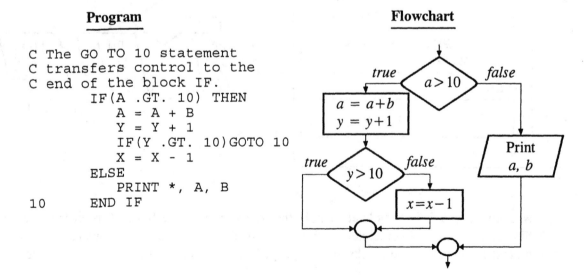

4.5 THE ELSE IF CONSTRUCT

The previous section introduced the IF construct and some of the rules appropriate for using it. In this section we will discuss a special form of the IF construct called the ELSE IF form. The ELSE IF construct is a nested block IF structure in which a block IF is placed inside the false block of an outer block. By using the ELSE IF form, a *list* of conditions can be tested more concisely than with the full blown block IF. The general form of the IF-THEN-ELSE-IF is:

```
IF (Test-Condition-1) THEN
            Block-1
ELSE IF (Test-Condition-2) THEN
            Block-2
               ⋮
ELSE IF (Test-Condition-N) THEN
            Block-N
ELSE
            Block-N+1
END IF
```

This is the only time that an instruction is allowed to be on the same line with the ELSE key word. If the first test condition is true, Block-1 executes. After completing the execution of Block-1, control then passes to the single END IF. If test condition 1 is false, however, control passes to the next ELSE IF. If that test condition is true, then its block is executed and so on. This structure can have any number of ELSE IF blocks and offers the possibility of setting up a structure that has N+1 alternatives. Recall that the block IF structure can have only two alternatives. But, by nesting these within each other, we can construct more complex structures, such as this multiple alternative form.

There are two ways of achieving the desired result. The first is to embed full-blown block IFs within each other. In this case, there will be an equal number of ELSE and ENDIF statements. The second way is to use the ELSE IF construct, where there will be only one ENDIF statement, and the construct will contain fewer lines. As you will see in the following example, the ELSE IF construct is easier to read than the equivalent nested IF-THEN-ELSE-ENDIF structures.

EXAMPLE 4.14

The following program reads in a temperature in degrees C and prints out an appropriate message using the following criteria:

Temperature $\leq 0°C$	Print "It's below freezing"
$0°C <$ Temperature $\leq 10°C$	Print "It's cold out"
$10°C <$ Temperature $\leq 20°C$	Print "It's cool out"
$20°C <$ Temperature $\leq 30°C$	Print "It's warm"
Temperature $> 30°C$	Print "It's hot!"

First, we show the logic of the program with the nested block IF structures. To help you identify the various blocks, we have enclosed all the blocks. Note that the structure is properly nested since none of the lines from any of the blocks crosses any other block.

```
PRINT *,'Enter the temperature in degrees C'
READ *,C
```

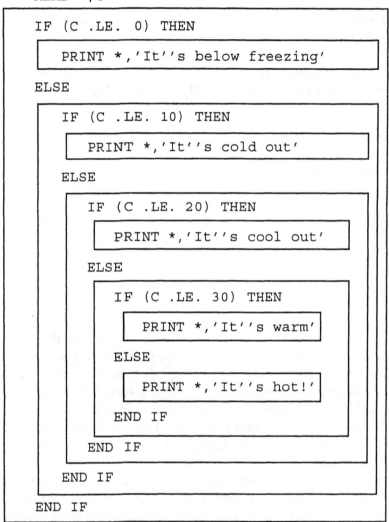

```
IF (C .LE.  0) THEN

    PRINT *,'It''s below freezing'

ELSE

    IF (C .LE. 10) THEN

        PRINT *,'It''s cold out'

    ELSE

        IF (C .LE. 20) THEN

            PRINT *,'It''s cool out'

        ELSE

            IF (C .LE. 30) THEN

                PRINT *,'It''s warm'

            ELSE

                PRINT *,'It''s hot!'

            END IF

        END IF

    END IF

END IF
```

This program can also be written more concisely with the ELSE IF form of the IF construct.

```
PRINT *, 'Enter the temperature in degrees C'
READ *, C
IF (C .LE.  0) THEN
   PRINT *, 'It''s below freezing'
ELSE IF (C .LE. 10) THEN
   PRINT *, 'It''s cold out'
ELSE IF (C .LE. 20) THEN
   PRINT *, 'It''s cool out'
ELSE IF (C .LE. 30) THEN
   PRINT *,'It''s warm'
ELSE
   PRINT *,'It''s hot!'
END IF
```

This is a more compact structure that the equivalent nested block IF structure shown in the first part of the example. Note that the ELSE-IF option works by passing control to the END IF only when a *true* test condition is found.

The choice of which structure to use — the nested block IFs or the ELSE IF structure is up to you since they perform equivalent functions. Most programmers, however, tend to prefer the ELSE IF construct because generally it is easier to follow.

4.6 THE SELECT CASE STRUCTURE

Many Fortran compilers offer the *select case* structure as an extension of the Fortran 77 standard. However, not all compilers offer this control structure. So check your compiler manual to see if the select case is available before reading any further. If it is not, then you will have to use the nested block IFs and/or ELSE IF structure to choose from among multiple alternatives.

The select case provides a means of selecting an action (which can be a block of statements) by comparing the value of an expression against a list of values. The general form of the select case construct is:

```
SELECT CASE (expression)
        CASE (selector list 1)
            block-1
        CASE (selector list 2)
            block-2
                ⋮

                ⋮

        CASE DEFAULT
            block-n
END SELECT
```

As with the previous block structures, there are key words to mark the beginning and end of the structure — the SELECT CASE and END SELECT statements respectively. In between are a series of CASES, only one of which is executed based on the value of the expression in the SELECT CASE statement. The expression is a scalar (single-valued) expression which can have integer, character, or logical data type. Once this expression is evaluated, its value is compared with the values contained in the *selector lists* until a match is found. The list of instructions that follow this CASE is then executed. If the expression in the CASE SELECT expression has no match among the various selector lists, then the instructions in the CASE DEFAULT are executed. The CASE DEFAULT statement is optional.

The selector list for each of the CASES can be a single value, a list, or a range of values specified by low-value:high-value, or a list of values which include ranges. This will become more obvious in the following examples. Also, the selector lists must not overlap in values.

The type of the expression and selectors must match. Thus, if the expression is a character string, then the selectors must also be character strings. Lengths of strings do not necessarily have to match. If the expression is of type integer or logical, then the selectors also be of the same type.

The SELECT CASE construct determines which block is to be executed by checking if the expression equals any of the values defined by the selectors. If the equality is true, then that block is executed and control passes to the END SELECT command.

EXAMPLE 4.15

Here is a simple SELECT CASE example that will type out a message about which set of instructions have been selected by the user:

Program

```
C Demonstration of Select Case Structure. An integer
C is read into N. If the value read in is 1, 2, or 3
C a message such as "#2 Entered" is printed. But if any
C other number is read in, the message "Error" is printed.
      PRINT *,'Select value 1-3'
      READ *, N
      SELECT CASE (N)
         CASE (1)
            PRINT *,'#1 Entered'
         CASE (2)
            PRINT *,'#2 Entered'
         CASE (3)
            PRINT *,'#3 Entered'
         CASE DEFAULT
            PRINT *,'Error'
      END SELECT
```

Flowchart

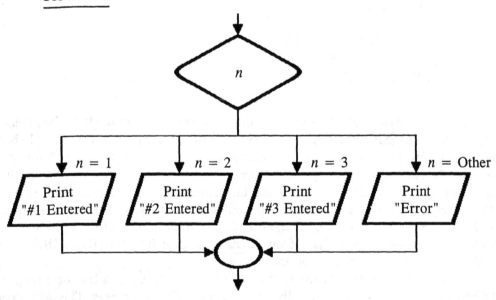

After the value of n is read in, the SELECT CASE structure examines its value, and decides which section to execute. If $n=1$, 2 or 3 for example, control transfers to the instructions inside the first, second or third CASE, respectively. But if n is any other value, control transfers to the section labeled CASE DEFAULT where the computer will print out an error message. Note that the CASE DEFAULT statement is optional in the SELECT CASE structure.

The switching within this structure depends upon the value of the expression following the SELECT CASE command and the list of selectors that define each of the CASEs. Therefore, it is important that the expression and the corresponding selector list be as flexible as possible. In the example below, we illustrate the many ways that you can set up the selector lists.

EXAMPLE 4.16

Shown below are several examples of allowed selector lists along with an interpretation of their meanings.

Selector	Description
CASE(1)	Single value (1)
CASE(1, 3, 5)	List of values (1, 3 or 5)
CASE(1:5)	The range of integer values 1,2,3,4 and 5
CASE(:0)	The range of integer values less than or equal to 0
CASE(1:)	The range of integer values greater than or equal to 1
CASE(1,10,100:)	List of integer values 1, 10, plus all values more than 100
CASE('A')	String with value 'A'
CASE('A':'H')	Range of characters A through H
CASE(1,'a')	Invalid: selector must be of one type only
CASE(2.25)	Invalid: real values are not allowed

The value inside the parentheses of the above examples will be used by the computer to decide which block of instructions to execute. If, for example, we set up CASE(1, 3, 5), and the CASE SELECT expression evaluates to 1, 3, or 5, then the set of instructions that follow this CASE would be executed.

In addition to the rule about matching the expression and selector types, it is also necessary that selectors do not overlap in values.

EXAMPLE 4.17

Shown below are two examples of valid select case structures and one invalid example:

```
a)      SELECT CASE (N)              (Choice of CASE depends on value of n)
           CASE (:-1)
              NSIGN=-1               (Sets NSIGN to -1 for values of n less than 0)
           CASE (0)
              NSIGN=0                (Sets NSIGN to 0 for value of n equal to 0)
           CASE(1:)
              NSIGN=1                (Sets NSIGN to 1 for values of n greater than 0)
        END SELECT
```

```
(b)        SELECT CASE (N)              (Value of n used to select CASE)
              CASE (1,3,5)
                 X = -X                 (If n=1, 3, or 5, change sign of x)
              CASE (2,4,6)
                 X = ABS(X)             (If n=2,4, or 6, replace x by its absolute value)
              CASE(:0)                  (If n is zero or negative, do nothing)
              CASE DEFAULT
                 X = X**2               (For any other value of n, replace x by its square)
           END SELECT


(c)        SELECT CASE(I)               (Invalid example because value of 7 used twice)
              CASE(1,3,5,7)             (One of the allowed values is 7)
                 RANGE=1
              CASE (7,9)                (Value of 7 used again, which is not allowed)
                 RANGE=2
           END SELECT                   (Error detected at compilation time)
```

EXAMPLE 4.18

If we are want to know the temperature to the nearest degree, we can rewrite Example 4.14 using the select case construct.

```
C We can use the select case structure to give a rough
C weather report. First, we convert the temperature to
C an integer value with the NINT function. Then this value
C is used to select a range. For example, if IC=23, it
C would fall into the range for CASE(21:30), and the
C program would print the message "It's warm"
      PRINT *,'Enter the temperature in degrees C'
      READ *, C
      IC = NINT( C )
      SELECT CASE (IC)
         CASE( :0)
            PRINT *,'It''s below freezing'
         CASE(1:10)
            PRINT *,'It''s cold out'
         CASE (11:20)
            PRINT *,'It''s cool out'
         CASE (21:30)
            PRINT *,'It''s warm'
         CASE DEFAULT
            PRINT *,'It''s hot!'
      END SELECT
```

Note that in order to use the CASE construct, we had to convert the temperature entered from a real to an integer value. The reason for this is that the CASE structure can operate only with integer, character, or logical data. Real, double precision, and complex data cannot be used.

4.7 DEBUGGING TIPS

Debugging is something that no programmer can escape. Most inexperienced programmers start with the assumption that debugging is a *post mortem* event and begins only after the program crashes. An experienced programmer, however, knows that debugging starts when you are writing the program at the earliest stages. Good programming style pays handsome dividends when it comes time to debug. Thus, many of our debugging tips focus on style, so that we try to make our programs bug proof from the beginning.

Here are some things you can do to develop good programming style:

- *Assign Statement Labels in Ascending Order*
  By arranging statement labels in ascending order, the location of statement labels can be more easily seen. By initially incrementing statement labels by 10's or 100's you will leave room for future modifications. Remember, programs rarely work correctly the first time. Be sure to prepare for future changes.

- *Indent Block Structures*

- *Use Comment Statements Liberally*
  One of the most useful capabilities of any programming language is the ability to include comment statements. Use comment statements to describe the functionality of a program block. Think of your comment statements as a road map. When you return to your program, you will understand more easily the logic you were trying to implement when you worked on the program. Comments might include the objectives of the program, descriptions of all the variables used, and the logic you are implementing.

- *Enter the Key Words of a Construct First*
  By completely writing the key words of the construct and then entering the blocks, you guarantee that all of the components will be in the correct location. By using this technique you can eliminate misplaced END IF's, ELSE's, and other construct pieces that are always so bothersome.

EXAMPLE 4.19

Here is an example of the process that we recommend when entering constructs. First, here is the final program that we will be producing:

```
C Demonstration of construction of nested block IF structures.
C Focus on the key words (IF, ELSE, ENDIF) which establish
C the boundaries of the blocks for execution.
      IF (A .GT. 0) THEN
          IF (B .LE. 10) THEN
              PRINT *, 'A > 0 and B <=10'
          ELSE
              PRINT *, 'A > 0 and B > 10'
          END IF
      ELSE
          PRINT *, 'A <= 0'
      END IF
```

We start with only one block based on the IF (A.GT.0) construct, and put down only the skeleton consisting of the key words (IF-THEN-ELSE-ENDIF).

Step 1:
```
IF (A .GT. 0) THEN
ELSE
END IF
```

Next, fill in blocks, being sure to indent for clarity. In this case however, one of the blocks contains another block IF construct. So we will follow our own advice and fill in only the skeleton of this inner construct:

Step 2:
```
IF (A .GT. 0) THEN
    IF (B .LE. 10) THEN
    ELSE
    END IF
ELSE
    PRINT *, 'A <= 0'
END IF
```

Finally, fill in the blocks for the second, innermost IF construct. Once again, remember to indent the blocks that you are adding:

Step 3:
```
IF (A .GT. 0) THEN
    IF (B .LE. 10) THEN
        PRINT *, 'A > 0 and B <=10'
    ELSE
        PRINT *, 'A > 0 and B > 10'
    END IF
ELSE
    PRINT *, 'A <= 0'
END IF
```

A convenient way to think of this process is to think of the constructs as the general logic of the program and the blocks as the specific actions. By entering the constructs first, you are laying out the logic and then filling in the details of the action at a later time. Notice that by writing the program in this fashion, it is impossible for you to misplace an END IF or ELSE statement.

Even if you faithfully carry out all of the suggestions we have given you, you will still have bugs in your programs. Hopefully, they will be far fewer in number, and easier to find. So how do you locate them? The first way is to trace through your program as we discussed in Chapter 2. To review, tracing is the process of manually predicting the output of a program. We will be doing the same thing here, but it is somewhat more involved because of the transfer operations introduced so far (GO TO, Block IF, ELSE IF, and SELECT CASE constructs).

When tracing programs that contain constructs, you will have to determine which IF-THEN statements matches which END IF. The same is true for the SELECT CASE and END SELECT statements. If you had used indentations when you wrote the program, this would be a simple task. But if you did not use indentations when you wrote the program, the method presented in the following example can be used.

EXAMPLE 4.20

The following example illustrates how to match the initiating and terminating statements for block constructs:

```
IF (A .GT. 0) THEN
IF (B .LE. 10) THEN
PRINT *, 'A > 0 and B <=10'
ELSE
PRINT *,'A > 0 and B > 10'
END IF
SELECT CASE (N)
CASE (:-1)
NSIGN=-1
CASE (0)
NSIGN=0
CASE(1:)
NSIGN=1
END SELECT
IF (A+B.LT.10) STOP
ELSE
PRINT *,'A <= 0'
END  IF
```

The first step is to connect terminating statements to initiating statements as we did in the example. This is accomplished by starting at the top of the program and reading down until a terminating statement is encountered (END IF, or END SELECT). Draw a line from the terminating statement back to the first initiating statement that is appropriate (IF-THEN or SELECT-CASE). Repeat until all terminating statements are matched.

At this point, indent any line that is inside any of the connecting lines. Then locate the connecting intermediate and optional statements. This is accomplished by drawing lines (shown here as dashed lines) from the intermediate statement out to the connecting lines. The first line encountered indicates the ownership of the intermediate statement.

```
IF (A.GT.0) THEN
    IF (B.LE.10) THEN
        PRINT *,'A > 0 and B <=10'
    ELSE
        PRINT *,'A > 0 and B > 10'
    END IF
    SELECT CASE (N)
        CASE (:-1)
        NSIGN=-1
        CASE (0)
        NSIGN=0
        CASE(1:)
        NSIGN=1
    END SELECT
    IF (A+B.LT.10) STOP
ELSE
    PRINT *,'A <= 0'
END IF
```

The final step is to see if any of the block structures are improperly nested. You can easily see this by checking to see if any of the lines cross each other. Since no lines cross each other in the example above, the blocks are properly nested.

Tracing as a Debugging Tool

The process of manually tracing a program can be time consuming. However, by providing yourself with tools such as indentations of block structures and variable tables, you can trace even the most complex programs to find logic errors. To help guide you, we offer two more guidelines:

- *Document your trace.*
  Document your trace by writing out what key components of the manual trace. If you are unable to complete the trace, a documented trace will help the next person who looks at it.

- *Use variable tables as outlined in Chapter 2.*

EXAMPLE 4.21

To aid in documenting a trace, it is recommended that you assign a number to each line of the program. This way, as you trace through the program, you can write down the lines of code your are evaluating. Also, identify each of the key words in block structures, and identify the nesting level if appropriate. For the following trace, assume A=5, B=1, and N=15:

Program Line		Identify Key Word and Level
001	IF (A .GT. 0) THEN	*IFTHEN (level 1)*
002	IF (B .LE. 10) THEN	*IFTHEN (level 2)*
003	PRINT *, 'A > 0 and B < = 10'	
004	ELSE	*IFTHEN (level 2)*
005	PRINT *, 'A > 0 and B > 10'	
006	END IF	*IFTHEN (level 2)*
007	SELECT CASE (N)	*SELECT CASE (level 1)*
008	CASE (:-1)	*CASE (level 1)*
009	NSIGN=-1	
010	CASE (0)	*CASE (level 1)*
011	NSIGN=0	
012	CASE(1:)	*CASE (level 1)*
013	NSIGN=1	
014	END SELECT	*CASE (level 1)*
015	IF (A+B.LT.10) STOP	
016	ELSE	*IFTHEN (level 1)*
017	PRINT *,'A < = 0'	
018	END IF	*IFTHEN (level 1)*

For the input data given, this is how the program would be executed:

Line 01 Is (15 .GT. 0)? True, go to line 02 (the true-block of IFTHEN1.)
Line 02 Is (1 .LE. 10)? True, go to line 03 (the true-block of IFTHEN2.)
Line 03 Prints: A > 0 and B < =10.
Line 04 Else of IFTHEN2, go to ENDIF of IFTHEN2.
Line 06 END IF of IFTHEN2.
Line 07 SELECT CASE (15), go to next line.
Line 08 CASE(:-1) 15 in range of negative integers? False, go to next CASE line 10.
Line 10 CASE(0) is 15 equal to 0? False, go to next CASE line 12.
Line 12 CASE(1:) 15 in the range of positive integers? True, go to next line (CASE block).
Line 13 NSIGN is set to 1, go to next line.
Line 14 END SELECT: end of structure, go to next line.
Line 15 Is (5+1.LT.10)? True, so execute STOP statement. End of program.

And here is the output:

A > 0 and B < =10

Variable Table:

A	5.0
B	1.0
N	15
NSIGN	1

Tracing is a tedious task. So, if you can get the computer to do some of the work for you, your job will be much easier. Most compilers have options, one of which is known as "list," which creates a file of your program with line numbers, tables of variables used, and any errors encountered by the compiler. When performing a trace, this is a convenient place to start.

In addition to line numbers and error listing, a table of all your variables is usually also presented. This table can be used for the variable table during tracing. Another use for the variable table is to check for variable typing. Along with the list of variables will be a column indicating the type of variable. This is a way to check that all variables are declared as you would like them.

If the results of the program are incorrect, use PRINT statements to display the value of variables and the results of expressions. If your manual calculations of an expression do not agree with the computer-generated result, then check for mixed mode arithmetic and proper hierarchy of operations. The following list summarizes these newest guidelines:

- *Use PRINT statements liberally to display values of variables and expressions.*
  Include PRINT statements in your program and have the computer do the tracing for you.

- *Validate your results using known solutions.*
  This is sometimes called the "magic bullet" approach. Look for data that will test as many of the branches of your program as possible. Leave no block untested.

Solved Problems

4.1   Locate errors in the following IF-THEN Constructs:

(a) `IF(A > B) Print *,'A>B'`   (b) `IF(A .GT. 10)`
    `ENDIF`   `X = 1`
                                      `END IF`
(c) `IF(A .EQ. B) THEN X = 1`   (d) `IF (A .LT. 10 .AND. B) THEN`
    `ELSE X = 2`   `PRINT *,'A is less than 10 and',B`
                                      `END IF`

(a) Relational comparison (>) not valid. No ENDIF needed for one-line IF statement.
(b) THEN is missing.
(c) No statement can appear after the THEN or ELSE statements. Any desired statement must go on the next line. Also, the entire structure must be terminated by an ENDIF.
(d) Expression is incorrect. Rewrite as A .LT. 10 .AND. A .LT. B

4.2   Indicate which of the following logical expressions are valid. If the expression is invalid, explain why. For each of the following examples, assume *LOG1* is a logical variable. Assume default typing (Implicit) for all other variables.

(a) (A = B)   Invalid. Should be .EQ. instead of =
(b) (1 .LT. X & X .LT. 10)   Invalid. "&" is not a valid operator. Use .AND.
(c) (.NOT.(A.GT.10.AND.A.LT.2))   Valid
(d) (SQRT(A) .EQ. LOG1)   Invalid. Cannot compare real and logical data.

4.3   Trace through the following logical expressions step by step illustrating the hierarchy of operations. For each problem assume $X = 10.0$, $Y = -2.0$, and $Z = 5.0$. For clarity, underline the next operation to be performed.

(a) (X .EQ. Y .OR. X / Y + Z .EQ. 0.0 .OR. Y .GE. Z)
(b) (.NOT. (X .EQ. Y .OR. X * Y + Z .EQ. 0.0))
(c) (.NOT. (X .GT. 10 .AND. Z .LT. 2))
(d) (Y .LT. Z .AND. X .LT. Z)
(e) (.NOT. (Y .LT. Z .AND. .NOT. X .GT. Z))

(a) (10.0 .EQ. −2.0 .OR. <u>10.0/−2.0</u> +5.0 .EQ. 0.0 .OR. −2.0 .GE. 5.0)
    (10.0 .EQ. −2.0 .OR. <u>−5.0 + 5.0</u> .EQ. 0.0 .OR. −2.0 .GE. 5.0)
    (<u>10.0 .EQ. −2.0</u> .OR. <u>0.0 .EQ. 0.0</u> .OR. <u>−2.0 .GE. 5.0</u>)
    (*false* .OR. *true* .OR. *false*)
    (<u>*true* .OR. *false*</u>) → *true*
(b) (.NOT. (10.0 .EQ. −2.0 .OR. <u>10.0 * −2.0</u> + 5.0 .EQ. 0.0))
    (.NOT. (10.0 .EQ. −2.0 .OR. <u>−20.0 +5.0</u> .EQ. 0.0))
    (.NOT. (<u>10.0 .EQ. −2.0</u> .OR. −15.0 .EQ. 0.0))
    (.NOT. (*false* .OR. <u>−15.0 .EQ. 0.0</u>))

(.NOT. (*false .OR. false*))

(.NOT. (*false*)) → *true*

(c) (.NOT. (10.0 .GT. 10 .AND. 5.0 .LT. 2)))

(.NOT. (*false* .AND. 5.0 .LT. 2)))

(.NOT. (*false .AND. false*))

(.NOT. *false*) → *true*

(d) (−2.0 .LT. 5.0 .AND. 10.0 .LT. 5.0)

(*true* .AND. 10.0 .LT. 5.0)

(*true .AND. false*) → *false*

(e) (.NOT. (−2.0 .LT. 5.0 .AND. .NOT. 10.0 .GT. 5.0))

(.NOT. (*true* .AND. .NOT. 10.0 .GT. 5.0))

(.NOT. (*true* .AND. *.NOT. true*))

(.NOT. (*true .AND. false*))

(.NOT. *false*) → *true*

4.4　Which program segments have incorrect transfer instructions?

```
(a) IF (X .GT. 10) THEN          (b)    SELECT CASE (N)
        A = X**2 + 1                    CASE (:-1)
        B = 10 + X                         A=SQRT(X**2 + Y**2)
        GO TO 10                           GO TO 30
    ELSE                               CASE (0)
        A = X + 1                          IF(X.LT.10) GOTO 20
10      C = 10                      20     Z=Z+1
    END IF                             CASE DEFAULT
                                30         Q = Q + Q**2
                                       END SELECT
```

(a) GO TO 10 is incorrect. Transfers control to a line inside the ELSE block.

(b) GO TO 30 is incorrect since the line with this statement label appears inside another block.

4.5　Which program segments are incorrect due to overlapping blocks?

```
(a) IF ... THEN               (b)    SELECT CASE...
    IF ...THEN                       CASE...
    SELECT CASE ...                  SELECT CASE ...
    CASE...                          CASE...
    IF...                            CASE DEFAULT
    IF...THEN                        CASE...
    ELSE                             CASE...
    CASE                             END SELECT
    END SELECT                       END SELECT
    ELSE
    END IF
    END IF
```

(a) CASE and third IF-THEN structures cross.

(b) CASE DEFAULT appears as an intermediate case to the second SELECT CASE. One END SELECT should come after the CASE DEFAULT block.

4.6   Determine which SELECT CASE constructs are valid or invalid. For invalid constructs indicate why. Assume default typing of the variables.

```
(a) SELECT CASE (N)                (b)    SELECT CASE (X)
        CASE (:-1)                             CASE (1.0,3.0,5.0)
            NSIGN = -1                             PRINT *,'N was 1,3 or 5'
        CASE (-1)                              CASE DEFAULT
            NSIGN=0                                PRINT *,'N was NOT 1,3,5'
        CASE (1:)                          END SELECT
            NSIGN=1
    END SELECT
```

(a) Invalid. Overlapping of CASE values in first and second cases.
(b) Invalid: Case selector must be an integer, character, or logical value. X is real.

4.7   Predict the output for the program presented in Example 4.21 based on the input values given below. Be sure to use a trace table and to document your trace.

(a) $A = 2$, $N = -1$, and $B = 5$ (b) $A = 0$, $N = 0$, and $B = 15$

(a) Program Trace:
    Line 01 (2 .GT. 0):true, go to line 2
    Line 02 (5 .LE.10):true, go to line 3
    Line 03 PRINT "A>0 and B < = 10", go to next line
    Line 04 ELSE of IFTHEN2. Go to ENDIF for IFTHEN2
    Line 06 ENDIF for IFTHEN2. Go to next line
    Line 07 SELECT CASE (−1) go to first case
    Line 08 CASE (:−1): true. Execute block for case
    Line 09 NSIGN=−1. Last statement in block. Go to END SELECT
    Line 14 END SELECT, go to next line
    Line 15 is (2+5 .LT. 10)? true. Execute STOP
Output:
    A > 0 and B < = 10
Trace Table:
    A: 2
    N: −1
    B: 5
    NSIGN: −1

(b) Program Trace:
    Line 01 Is (0 .GT. 0)? False. Go to ELSE block for IFTHEN1
    Line 17 Print 'A < = 0' Last line of ELSE block. Go to ENDIF
    Line 18 ENDIF

Output:
   A < = 0
Trace Table:
   A: 0
   N: 0
   B: 15
   NSIGN: never assigned a value

4.8   Write a program to read in values for *a*, *b*, and *c*, and print their sum. Repeat this procedure until all values of *a*, *b*, and *c* are negative.

```
10   READ *, A, B, C
     IF( A. LT. 0 .AND. B .LT. 0 .AND. C.LT. 0) STOP
     SUM =A + B + C
     PRINT *, 'SUM = ', SUM
     GO TO 10
     END
```

4.9   Read in three integer values *i*, *j*, *k* and determine if *all* are odd or *all* are even.

```
C An integer I is even if I/2*2 = I. Recall that if we use
C the rules of integer division that any remainder is dropped.
C Thus, if I is odd, division by two will produce a remainder.
     READ *, I, J, K
     IF(MOD(I,2).EQ.0.AND.MOD(J,2).EQ.0.AND.MOD(K,2).EQ.0) THEN
        PRINT *, 'ALL EVEN'
     ELSE
          IF(MOD(I,2).EQ.1.AND.MOD(J,2).EQ.1.AND.MOD(K,2).EQ.1)THEN
             PRINT *, 'ALL ODD'
        ELSE
             PRINT *, 'MIXED'
        ENDIF
     ENDIF
```

4.10   Write a program to read in the radius *r* of a circle centered at the origin. Then read in coordinate pair (*x*, *y*) of a point and determine if that point lies within the circle.

```
     PRINT *, 'Enter R'
     READ *, R
10   PRINT *, 'Enter X, Y'
     READ *, X, Y
     RXY = SQRT(X**2+Y**2)
     IF(RXY.LT.R) THEN
        PRINT*, 'Inside Circle'
     ELSE
        PRINT*, 'Outside Circle'
     ENDIF
     END
```

4.11 When we write a program, we often have the program ask questions which are answered yes or no. People have a tendency however, to answer with things like yes, YES, y, Y, true, TRUE and so forth. A good program should consider how people are likely to answer such a question. Write a program that will convert yes, YES, y, Y, true, TRUE, t, and T into TRUE. Similarly, your program should report FALSE for n, NO, N, no, false, f, FALSE or false. Can you think of any other possible responses that someone might use?

```
CHARACTER *5, ANS
PRINT *, 'Enter Answer'
READ *, ANS
SELECT CASE (ANS)
   CASE('t', 'T', 'y', 'Y', 'true', 'TRUE', 'yes', 'YES')
      PRINT *, 'TRUE'
   CASE('f', 'F', 'n', 'N', 'false', 'FALSE', 'no', 'NO')
      PRINT *, 'FALSE'
   CASE DEFAULT
      PRINT *, 'Answer not recognized'
END SELECT
```

(Also consider mixed capitalization such as Yes, True, No, etc.)

Supplementary Problems

4.12 Locate errors in the following IF-THEN constructs.:

(a) ```
IF (A.GE.B) THEN Z=Y
   ENDIF
```

(b) ```
REAL A,B,C
IF(A.LT.B.LT.C) THEN
PRINT *,' A < B < C'
END IF
```

(c) ```
IF (C.LE.0) THEN
    PRINT *,'freezing'
ELSE (C.LE.10)
    PRINT *,'cold'
ELSE (C.LE.20)
    PRINT *,'cool'
ELSE (C.LE.30)
    PRINT *,'nice'
ELSE
    PRINT *,'hot'
ENDIF
```

(d) ```
IF A.GT.10 GO TO 100
```

(e) ```
IF (B.NOT.10) PRINT *,'B is not equal to 10'
```

**4.13** Indicate which of the following logical expressions are valid. Assume *LOG1* and *LOG2* are logical variables. Assume default typing for all other variables.

(a) (A EQ B)

(b) (.NOT. LOG1)

(c) (LOG1 .AND. X + 1 .GT. 10)

(d) ((.NOT. (X+B)) .EQ. 0.0)

(e) (.NOT. LOG2 .OR. .NOT. LOG1)
```

4.14 Trace through the following logical expressions step by step, illustrating the hierarchy of operations. For each problem assume that $x = 10.0$, $y = -2.0$, and $z = 5.0$:

(a) (X .NE. Y .AND. Y .NE. Z .AND. X .NE. Z)

(b) (X.GE.Z.AND..NOT.((Z*Y.LE.X).OR..NOT.(X.EQ.Y)))

(c) (X*Y .LT. Z / X .OR. X / Y .GT. Z * X)

(d) (.NOT. Y .LT. Z .AND. X .GT. Z)

(e) (–INT(X / Y) .EQ. X / Y)

4.15 Which of these program segments has incorrect transfer operations?

(a)
```
    IF(A+B.GE.2.34)GOTO 15
    IF(X.EQ.10) THEN
        Z=A+B+X
15  DIST=10+Z
    END IF
```

(b)
```
    IF(X+Y.GT.0) THEN
    IF(X.GT.0)GOTO 10
        Y=X+Y
10  ENDIF
```

4.16 Which of these program segments is incorrect due to overlapping blocks?

(a)
```
IF...THEN
ELSE
IF...THEN
ELSE
ENDIF
IF...THEN
ELSE IF...THEN
ELSE
SELECT CASE...
CASE...
ENDIF
CASE...
CASE DEFAULT
END SELECT
ENDIF
```

(b)
```
IF...THEN
ELSE IF...THEN
IF...THEN
ELSE IF...THEN
ELSE
SELECT CASE
CASE...
IF...
END SELECT
CASE...
END SELECT
ELSE IF...THEN
ELSE
ENDIF
```

4.17 Determine which constructs are valid. Assume that STRING is a character variable.

(a)
```
SELECT CASE(STRING)
    CASE("A":"H")
        TEST=1
    CASE ("Y","Z")
        TEST=2
END SELECT
```

(b)
```
SELECT CASE(N/2)
    CASE (1)
        PRINT *,'RANGE 1'
    CASE DEFAULT
        PRINT *,'RANGE 2'
    CASE (2)
        PRINT *,'RANGE 3'
END SELECT
```

4.18 Predict the output for the program presented in Example 4.21 based on the input values given below. Be sure to use a trace table and to document your trace.

(a) $A = 0$, $N = -1$, and $B = 15$ (b) $A = 2$, $N = 0$, and $B = 5$
(c) $A = 0$, $N = 1$, and $B = 15$.

Answers to Selected Supplementary Problems

4.12 (a) Assignment statement Z=Y must go on the following line
(b) Expression is invalid. Replace with A.LT.B.AND.B.LT.C
(c) Missing IF and THEN statements on the ELSE (test) lines
(d) The ( ) is missing around the logical expression
(e) NOT is a logical operator. A relational operator is needed to check a numerical value. The line should be IF (B .NE. 10)....

4.13 (a) Invalid: " EQ " should be ".EQ."
(b) Valid
(c) Valid
(d) Invalid: cannot use .NOT. operator on real numbers
(e) Valid

4.14 (a) (<u>10.0 .NE. −2.0</u> .AND. <u>−2.0 .NE. 5.0</u> .AND. <u>10.0 .NE. 5.0</u>)
(<u>*true* .AND. *true*</u> .AND. *true*)
(<u>*true* .AND. *true*</u>) → *true*
(b) (10.0 .GE. 5.0 .AND. .NOT. ((<u>5.0 * −2.0</u> .LE. 10.0) .OR. .NOT. (10.0 .EQ. −2.0)))
(10.0 .GE. 5.0 .AND. .NOT. ((<u>−10.0 .LE. 10.0</u>) .OR. .NOT. (10.0 .EQ. −2.0)))
(10.0 .GE. 5.0 .AND. .NOT. (*true* .OR. .NOT. (<u>10.0 .EQ. −2.0</u>)))
(10.0 .GE. 5.0 .AND. .NOT. (*true* .OR. <u>.NOT. *false*</u>))
(10.0 .GE. 5.0 .AND. .NOT. (<u>*true* .OR. *true*</u>))
(<u>10.0 .GE. 5.0</u> .AND. .NOT. *true*)
(*false* .AND. <u>.NOT. *true*</u>)
(<u>*false* .AND. *false*</u>) → *false*
(c) (<u>10.0*−2.0</u> .LT. 5.0/10.0 .OR. 10.0/−2.0 .GT. 5.0*10.0)
(−20.0 .LT. <u>5.0/10.0</u> .OR. 10.0/−2.0 .GT. 5.0*10.0)
(−20.0 .LT. 0.5 .OR. <u>10.0/−2.0</u> .GT. 5.0*10.0)
(−20.0 .LT. 0.5 .OR. −5.0 .GT. <u>5.0*10.0</u>)
(<u>−20.0 .LT. 0.5</u> .OR. −5.0 .GT. 50.0)
(*true* .OR. <u>−5.0 .GT. 50.0</u>)
(<u>*true* .OR. *false*</u>) → *true*
(d) (.NOT. <u>−2.0 .LT. 5.0</u> .AND. 10.0 .GT. 5.0)
(.NOT. *true* .AND. <u>10.0 .GT. 5.0</u>)

$$(.NOT. \ \underline{true} \ .AND. \ true)$$
$$(\underline{false \ .AND. \ true}) \rightarrow false$$

(e) $(-INT(\underline{10.0/-2.0}) \ .EQ. \ 10.0/-2.0)$
$(\underline{-INT(-5.0)} \ .EQ. \ 10.0/-2.0)$
$(5 \ .EQ. \ \underline{10.0/-2.0})$
$(\underline{5 \ .EQ. \ -5.0}) \rightarrow false$ *(May not work since the real number (5.0) may not be exactly equal to the integer (5) because of roundoff errors)*

4.15 (a) Invalid transfer from IF Statement
(b) Branching to the ENDIF is acceptable

4.16 (a) ENDIF of third IF-THEN crosses the SELECT CASE 1st block
(b) Invalid structure; one too many END SELECTs and too few END IFs

4.17 (a) Program is valid
(b) CASE DEFAULT must be at the end of the construct

4.18 (a) Program Trace:
Line 01 0.GT.0: False. Go to ELSE block for IFTHEN1
Line 17 Print 'A < = 0' Last line of Else block. Go to ENDIF
Line 18 ENDIF
Output:
A < = 0
Trace Table:
A: 0
N: 0
B: 15
NSIGN: never assigned a value

(b) Program Trace:
Line 01 Is (2 .GT. 0)? true, go to line 2
Line 02 Is (5 .LE. 10)? true, go to line 3
Line 03 PRINT "A > 0 and B < = 10", go to next line
Line 04 ELSE of IFTHEN2. Go to ENDIF for IFTHEN2
Line 06 ENDIF for IFTHEN2. Go to next line
Line 07 SELECT CASE (0) go to first CASE
Line 08 Is 0 in the range of all negative integers? False. Go to next CASE
Line 10 Is 0 equal to 0? True. Execute next line
Line 11 NSIGN=0. Last statement of block. Go to END SELECT
Line 14 END SELECT, go to next line
Line 15 Is (2+5.LT. 10)? True. Execute STOP
Output:
A > 0 and B < = 10

Trace Table:
    A: 2
    N: −1
    B: 5
    NSIGN: 0

(c) Program Trace:
    Line 01 Is (0 .GT. 0)? False. Go to ELSE block for IFTHEN1
    Line 17 Print 'A < = 0' Last line of ELSE block. Go to ENDIF
    Line 18 ENDIF
Output:
    A < = 0
Trace Table:
    A: 0
    N: 0
    B: 15
    NSIGN: never assigned a value

Chapter 5

Loops

5.1 OVERVIEW

The third type of control structure is the *loop*. As we discussed in Chapter 1, there are two types of loops in common usage:

- The counted loop
- The conditional loop

The counted loop executes a predetermined number of times and the variables controlling the loop *cannot* be altered during the loop execution. The conditional loop, on the other hand, lacks a predetermined stopping point, and the loop *must* alter the variables controlling it.

We will review these loop structures in this chapter. Fortran 77 officially supports only the counted loop, but most commercial compilers also support the conditional loop. So we will devote some effort to discuss this important type of loop. However, in case your compiler does not support the conditional loop as an extension, we will show you alternate ways of doing the same thing.

5.2 THE COUNTED LOOP

The counted loop is the most widely used loop among the high level languages (such as Fortran, C, Basic, and Pascal) used by engineers and scientists. As we discussed in Chapter 1, these loops have a very rigid structure. They execute for a predetermined number of iterations, and the variables controlling the loop *cannot* be altered once the loop begins. In Fortran, we call these *DO loops*, which have the following general structure (anything in brackets is optional):

> DO *statement label*　　*Loop Control Variable = start, stop [, step]*
> ⋮
> *[series of instructions]*
> ⋮
>
> *statement label*　CONTINUE

The DO statement marks the beginning of the loop and contains all the information necessary to control the loop. The statement shows where to find the end of the loop by specifying a *statement label*. Of course, the statement label marking the end of the loop must correspond to the one used in the DO statement. Also, each statement label must be an integer <u>less</u> than five digits and <u>must not</u> be duplicated within the program.

The DO statement also contains the information on the *loop control variable* (LCV). The program assigns the starting value to this variable, and, after each cycle through the loop, the computer increases the LCV by the *step* size. Before the loop can recycle, however, the computer checks to see if the new value of the LCV exceeds the *stop* value. If it does, then the loop stops and control passes to the next line after the CONTINUE.

The (*statement label* CONTINUE) statement marks the end of the loop. By itself though it does nothing, since it is a contrived statement to avoid confusion. Any executable statement, such as PRINT, can be used in its place. But if you use such a statement, it is not always clear whether the program should execute it every time. So to avoid this confusion, we use the CONTINUE statement.

The computer has complete control of the loop and handles all the tasks associated with it. These include:

- *Initialize* the LCV to the start value;
- *Increment* the LCV by the step value each time through the loop;
- *Test* the LCV to see if it exceeds the stop value;
- *Decide* when to terminate the loop.

After starting the loop, you don't need to do any of these things yourself. The computer does all this automatically. The only pitfall that you might encounter is if you attempt to modify the LCV inside the loop. The LCV belongs to the computer. You may use it for calculations, but you may not change it.

EXAMPLE 5.1

Here is an example of a DO loop in action.

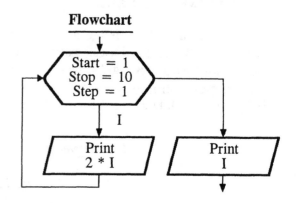

| **Program** | **Flowchart** |

```
C The following loop will
C execute 10 times and use
C I as the loop control
C variable. Note that we
C can look at the value of I
C inside or outside the loop.
      DO 5 I=1,10,1
          PRINT *, 2*I
5         CONTINUE
      PRINT *, I
```

This is a simple loop, which will print out the even numbers from 2 to 20. An interesting point is that the LCV increments inside the loop until it *exceeds* the final value (10 in this example.) Of course, the first integer number that exceeds 10 is the number 11. Therefore, the PRINT statement outside the DO loop will print the final value of I as 11.

Notice in the example above that we can *use* the LCV inside the loop, but we cannot *modify* it. Thus, we were allowed to use the LCV to perform the calculation 2*LCV and then print it. But notice that we did not change the value of the LCV; we merely used it in a computation.

EXAMPLE 5.2

In the following program segment, we attempt to change the value of the LCV inside the loop. But since this is not allowed, we would receive an error message from the compiler.

```
      DO 5 I=1, 10, 1
         I = I + 1
5     CONTINUE
```

Inside the loop body of this example, the program attempts to reset the value of the variable I, which is the loop control variable. So there is a conflict. The LCV is under the control of the computer, but the program is attempting to override this control. This kind of error is sometimes not so obvious, especially when you begin to use subroutines (see Chapter 7). The results can be disastrous. So be careful when using the LCV inside a loop.

The *start*, *stop*, and *step* values need not always be constants as in the previous examples. In fact, it is common practice to use variables instead. This will allow you to set up your loops so that they are general purpose and do not need to be modified every time you run the program with a different set of input data.

EXAMPLE 5.3

The loop control variables themselves can be either variables that are read in at execution time or the results of a computation. In this example, we will read in the variables i and j, and use these as the start and stop variables in the DO loop to compute all the even integers between and including $2i$ and $2j$.

Program

```
C We will read in I and J
C for use as the loop
C control variables.
      PRINT *, 'ENTER I, J'
      READ *, I, J
      DO 10 L = I, J, 1
         PRINT *, 2*L
10    CONTINUE
```

Flowchart

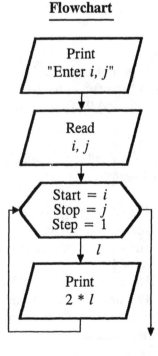

With this structure, we can enter values for i and j at execution time. For example, if we type in 1 and 10, we will simply obtain the results of Example 5.1. If we run the segment a second time and type in new values of 5 and 9, we will obtain a different set of output data: 10, 12, 14, 16, 18. These values correspond to 2×5, 2×6, 2×7, 2×8, and 2×9. In this example, we indicated a step size of 1. But this is redundant, since the computer assumes a step size of 1 if no step size is specified. Although it was not used in this example, you may also use a variable for the step size.

EXAMPLE 5.4

The step size of a DO loop may be a variable that is read in at execution time.

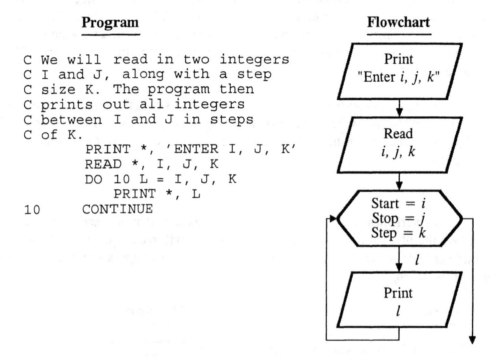

| **Program** | **Flowchart** |

```
C We will read in two integers
C I and J, along with a step
C size K. The program then
C prints out all integers
C between I and J in steps
C of K.
      PRINT *, 'ENTER I, J, K'
      READ *, I, J, K
      DO 10 L = I, J, K
         PRINT *, L
10    CONTINUE
```

To illustrate how this works, let's enter 3, 10, and 3 for i, j, and k, respectively, to produce the numbers between 3 and 10 in increments of 3. The loop control variable l will take on values of 3, 6, and 9. These will be the values printed on the CRT screen.

There are several rules and guidelines for setting up the loop and the loop control variables that you will find useful. These are:

- The LCV <u>should</u> be an integer. While a real variable can be used, it may produce unexpected results.
- The start, stop, and step size values used to establish the LCV can themselves be variables.
- The LCV cannot be changed inside the body of the loop.
- The step size can be omitted. If it is, the computer assumes a step size of 1.
- It is permissible to leave the body of a loop. But you may not enter a loop body from outside.

EXAMPLE 5.5

Here are some examples of correct and incorrect usage of the DO statements:

Correct	Incorrect	Comments
DO 10 I = 1, 10		*(Step is optional (assumed=1))*
DO 20 I = J, 10		*(Mixing variables, constants OK)*
DO 30 I = 10, 1, −1		*(Decreasing index OK)*
	DO 40 I = 1.0, 5.0, 0.1	*(Mixed mode)*
	DO 50 I = 1, 10, I	*(Subtle attempt to modify LCV)*
	DO 60 I = 10, 1	*(Loop does not converge)*
	DO 70 I = 1, 10, 0	*(Zero step size is not allowed)*

The compiler will probably report all seven examples above as correct. But when you go to run them, the last four will perform in unexpected ways:

- In example four (DO 40) there is mixed mode. The LCV is an integer (I), while the start, stop, and step size are real. Therefore the computer will convert the real numbers to integer values, resulting in an equivalent statement of DO 40 I=1,5,0. Notice that the step size is reduced to zero as a result of this conversion. This creates an infinite loop because of the zero step size.
- In example five (DO 50 I=1,10,I) there is a subtle attempt to change the LCV. Note that if the machine did as we directed the step size (I) would be the same as the LCV (I). Therefore, it is not clear what will happen when this runs. On some compilers, a divide by zero error is reported.
- In example six (DO 60, I=10,1), the loop will never execute, but it will compile. If we had included a negative step size, the loop would execute. But because we left it out, the compiler assumes a step size of 1. Consequently, the LCV would start out with a value of 10, and increase by 1 every time through the loop. Consequently, it could never converge on the final value (1). In these situations the compiler recognizes the difficulty and simply skips over the loop without ever executing a single iteration. In some older Fortran compilers (Fortran IV and earlier), a loop must always execute at least once. But in Fortran 77, loops can be skipped without ever executing.
- In the final example (DO 70, I=1, 10, 0) the zero step size causes an infinite loop. The compiler will usually not recognize this problem in advance.

Alternate Form of the DO Loop

All Fortran compilers will recognize the DO loop structure just discussed. In addition, many Fortran compilers also recognize another form of the DO loop structure. This alternate form may simplify your loops by eliminating the statement label, and substituting an END DO statement to mark the end of the loop.

$$\text{DO} \quad \textit{Loop Control Variable = start, stop [, step]}$$

$$\vdots$$

$$\textit{[series of instructions]}$$

$$\vdots$$

END DO

Other than the elimination of the statement label and the substitution of the END DO statement, the function of the loop is identical to what we have just discussed.

EXAMPLE 5.6

Here is Example 5.1 written with the DO–END DO structure:

```
DO  I = 1, 10, 1
   PRINT *, 2 * I
END DO
PRINT *, I
```

This program segment will produce exactly the same results as that shown in Example 5.1. There are two reasons for eliminating the *sl* CONTINUE as the end of the DO loop. First, the END DO does not require you to worry about which statement labels have been used or the sequence of labels. Thus, it eliminates the overhead of worrying about whether you have used the same statement label more than once. The second reason for eliminating the *sl* CONTINUE statement is the desirable goal of eliminating as many statement labels as possible to improve the readability of your program.

Nesting and the DO Loop

So far, the loops that we have shown you contain only simple instructions within the body of the loop. But the body can have any desired complexity. For example, you can put other branching and looping instructions in the body. In fact, one of the most common structures in Fortran is to *nest* one loop inside another. You will see this frequently with arrays and complex I/O. The only problem that you may have when nesting a control structure inside a loop is the possibility that the boundaries of the two structures cross.

EXAMPLE 5.7

The Fibonacci series is a famous sequence that dates back to the thirteenth century:

$$1, 1, 2, 3, 5, 8, 13, 21, 34, \ldots$$

The first two terms in the series are 1 and 1, but every term after that is the sum of the two previous terms. In this problem, we are going to calculate the series up to the *n*th term, where *n* is a number entered at execution time. In cases like this we have to be careful that the value of *n* is a valid number. Thus, in the program below, we will first see if *n* is a number less than 3 (with a block IF). If it is, then we will go ahead and compute *n* terms in the series (with a loop). Note that we will nest the DO loop within the block IF structure.

| **Program** | **Flowchart** |

```
C First we read in N
      INTEGER FIB1, FIB2
      PRINT *, 'Enter N:'
      READ *, N
C Now check to see if N is
C less than 3. If it is, then
C use the DO loop to compute
C N terms of the series.
      IF(N.LT.3) THEN
         PRINT *,'ERROR'
      ELSE
         FIB1=1
         FIB2=1
         PRINT *, FIB1, FIB2
         DO 10 I=3,N
            NEW=FIB1+FIB2
            FIB1 = FIB2
            FIB2 = NEW
            PRINT *, NEW
10       CONTINUE
      ENDIF
      END
```

Note carefully that the DO loop is completely inside the false branch of the IF-THEN-ELSE-ENDIF structure. If the DO loop had extended over the two branches or outside the block IF structure, the compiler would have reported an error.

In this example we use the two variables *fib1* and *fib2* as the first two terms in the series and assign initial values of 1 and 1. We then enter a loop to calculate the next term *new* by equating it to *fib1* + *fib2*. The next step is to update *fib1* and *fib2* by assigning *fib2* to *fib1* and *new* to *fib2*. As we generate each new number in the series, we will retain only the last two terms in the series. Here is a trace of the program for *n*=4 to show you how the DO loop works:

Step	Instruction	FIB1	FIB2	NEW	Output
1	Print prompt				Enter N:
2	Read in value of 4				
3	Is N < 3? No, so transfer to false branch of block IF				
4	FIB1 = 1	1			
5	FIB2 = 1		1		
6	Print values of FIB1 and FIB2				1, 1
7	Enter DO loop for I=3 to 4				
8	Calculate NEW (I=3)			2	
9	Reassign FIB1	1			
10	Reassign FIB2		2		
11	Print value of NEW				2
12	Calculate NEW (I=4)			3	
13	Reassign FIB1	2			
14	Reassign FIB2		3		
15	Print value of NEW				3
16	Terminate loop				
17	Terminate program				

When nesting loops, the inner loop must lie completely within the outer loop. Also, the two loops must use different LCVs. The general form is as follows:

$$DO\ label1\ LCV1 = start1,\ stop1\ [,\ step1]$$
$$DO\ label2\ LCV2 = start2,\ stop2\ [,\ step2]$$
$$\vdots$$

label2   CONTINUE
label1   CONTINUE

Notice that the DO *label2* loop begins and ends completely within the DO *label1* loop, and that each loop has its own loop control variable. A common error that programmers make is to give the two LCVs the same name. For example, if the LCV in the outer loop is named I, the inner loop must have a different name, such as J. Otherwise the inner loop will be attempting to change the LCV of the outer loop. Finally, you may use the value of LCV1 as the start, stop, or step value in the inner loop.

When the nested loops execute, the innermost loop will increment to completion before the LCV in the outer loop changes to its next value.

EXAMPLE 5.8

Here are examples of properly and improperly nested DO loops:

Properly Nested	Improperly Nested

```
      DO 10 I =                    DO 10 I =
           ⋮                            ⋮
      DO 20 J =                    DO 20 J =
           ⋮                            ⋮
20    CONTINUE              20     CONTINUE
           ⋮                            ⋮
      DO 30 K =                    DO 30 K =
           ⋮                            ⋮
30    CONTINUE              10     CONTINUE
           ⋮                            ⋮
10    CONTINUE              30     CONTINUE
```

Improper nesting of loops is an easy error to catch since compilers can recognize this error. Also, since the beginning and end of DO loops are clearly marked, it is easy to spot nesting errors.

EXAMPLE 5.9

Here is an example of how to use nested loops to generate a simple multiplication table. At this point, we don't yet have the means to produce a nice square table. But at least this program will generate the values.

Program   **Flowchart**

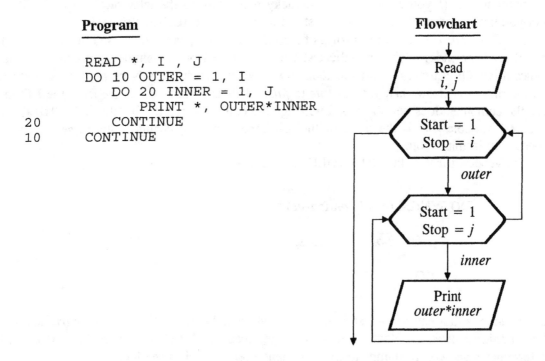

```
      READ *, I , J
      DO 10 OUTER = 1, I
          DO 20 INNER = 1, J
              PRINT *, OUTER*INNER
20        CONTINUE
10    CONTINUE
```

Suppose that we enter 2 for I and 3 for J. The nested loops tell us that the innermost loop will execute more rapidly than the outer loop. Thus, for example, OUTER will be fixed at a value of 1 while INNER will cycle through the values 1, 2, and 3. Only then will OUTER move to the next value of 2. Here is a trace table for the variables:

OUTER	INNER	Output
1	1	1
1	2	2
1	3	3
2	1	2
2	2	4
2	3	6

Once the trace starts, the variable OUTER remains fixed while the variable INNER goes through its range. After the inner loop finishes, OUTER increases by one and then the inner loop begins all over again. Be sure that you understand how these nested loops execute, since you will see them repeatedly when we get to arrays.

5.3 THE CONDITIONAL LOOP

The conditional loop is available on most Fortran compilers, but there are still a few that may not support it. So, if you are one of the unlucky ones, skip to the later section (page 144) that shows you how to generate an equivalent structure using IF-THEN-ELSEs and GOTOs.

The *DO WHILE* structure is a form of a conditional loop, as we discussed in Chapter 1. The loop will execute indefinitely until the test condition based on the single loop control variable becomes *false*. Of course, to start the loop, the condition must initially be *true*. Obviously, the condition must somehow change from *true* to *false*. This is a stark difference from the DO loop, where the computer does not allow us to change the control variable. For the DO WHILE loop, the control variable that is the basis of the test condition <u>must</u> change. Otherwise, we will be trapped in an infinite loop.

The general form of the DO WHILE construct is

DO WHILE (*condition is true*)
⋮
[block of instructions]
⋮

END DO

When the loop is first entered, a test is performed whose only allowed outcomes are *true* and *false*. If the condition is *true*, the block of instructions is executed. But if the test condition is *false*, the loop terminates and control jumps to the statement after the end of the loop.

The test condition that controls the operation of the while loop is set up just like the test in the IF constructs, and is based on a control variable. One of the keys to the while construct is that this control variable must change within the body of the loop. Sometimes this is done with a READ statement. More often, it is done through reassignment of a variable, through either an assignment statement or equivalent statement.

EXAMPLE 5.10

The DO WHILE loop should be used where we do not know in advance how often to execute the loop. A good example is where we wish to read in some data from an experiment. Generally, we do not know how many data items there will be. A common solution to this problem is to set up the loop to read in one data item at a time. But we set up the loop so that if the data value has a specific value (a negative value for example), then the loop will stop.

To demonstrate how this works, let's assume that we are calculating the average weight of rabbits in a laboratory. Since rabbits multiply so fast, we never know in advance how many there will be. So we set up the loop to read in the weights, one at a time, until one of the weights is greater than 500 pounds. When this occurs, the loop will stop. We sometimes call this special value a *sentinel* value. The loop is set up so that we watch for this key value, which we have chosen so that it is unlikely to be found in the data set. So when you enter this value, the program will recognize it as the signal to stop.

Program	**Flowchart**

```
TOT = 0.0
NUM = 0
WGT = 0.0
DO WHILE(WGT .LE. 500.0)
   PRINT *,'Enter Weight'
   READ *, WGT
   TOT = TOT + WGT
   NUM = NUM + 1
END DO
AVG = (TOT-WGT)/(NUM-1)
PRINT *,'Avg Wgt=', AVG
```

The variables TOT, NUM, and WGT represent the total weight of all the rabbits, the total number of rabbits, and their individual weights, respectively. When the loop begins, the computer checks to see if WGT is less than or equal to 500. The first time through, of course, WGT equals zero, so the loop proceeds. Inside the loop, we read in a weight, add it to the total, and increase the counter (NUM) by one. The loop then repeats. Notice if the weight that we enter is greater than 500 the loop will stop, but not until after this very large value is added to the total. That is why we subtract this artificially high value after we leave the loop. Also, we need to subtract 1 from NUM to calculate the average weight (AVG).

Why did we set the sentinel value to 500? Actually, we could have chosen any value as long as it was unlikely that any genuine value would be as large as this. Since no rabbit weighs 500 pounds, this condition will always be *true* while we are entering realistic values. When we have entered all the data, we purposely type in a weight of something like 99999, and the loop will end. Since a weight of 99999 exceeds 500, the condition is now *false* and the loop will stop. There are other ways to do the same thing (one of which is known as a structured read loop), and we will explore some of these in future exercises and examples.

Some compilers have slightly different statements for the conditional loop, such as WHILE DO, END WHILE, and so forth. So check your manual to find out the precise form. Hopefully, you will find this construct in your compiler.

Alternate Way to Construct the DO WHILE Loop

If your system does not support the DO WHILE construct, you must set up your programs with other structures that we have already discussed, namely, the IF-THEN-ELSE and the GOTO statements.

EXAMPLE 5.11

Here is the previous rabbit weighing program written with the Block IF and GOTO commands:

```
         TOT = 0.0
         NUM = 0
         WGT = 0.0
10       IF (WGT .LE. 500) THEN
             PRINT *, 'Enter Weight'
             READ *, WGT
             TOT = TOT + WGT
             NUM = NUM + 1
             GO TO 10
         ELSE
             AVG = (TOT-WGT)/(NUM-1)
         END IF
         PRINT *,'Avg Weight=', AVG
```

In this program segment, the computer first tests to see if WGT is within range. If it is, then the program will read the next value and process it. The GO TO statement at the end of the true block of the IF-THEN-ELSE-ENDIF then transfers control back to the beginning of the IF statement for a recheck. Thus we have converted a conditional statement into a loop.

This structure should be avoided if possible, however, because of the GO TO, which may eventually cause serious debugging problems. So if at all possible, use the DO WHILE structure.

The EXIT and CYCLE Statements

Many Fortran compilers offer several different forms of the DO loop that consolidate the counted loop and the conditional loop into a single DO structure. These structures are not part of the Fortran 77 standard, but they are commonly found in commercial compilers.

The available extension sets up only a single type of DO loop, with the general structure shown below. Anything included inside brackets is optional.

DO *[label]* *[loop control structure]*

           ⋮

[IF (condition is true) EXIT]

           ⋮

[IF (condition is true) CYCLE]

           ⋮

[label] END DO

The same DO–END DO construct is used to perform either a counted loop or a conditional loop. If the loop control variable is included, the loop becomes a counted loop. But if the loop control variables are left out, the loop becomes a conditional one. In this case, however, there must be a means of stopping the loop. This is done with the two new commands: EXIT and CYCLE. As their names imply, the EXIT command inside the loop causes the loop to terminate, while the CYCLE command causes the loop to go back to the beginning of the loop. In effect, both commands are substitutes for the GO TO command. The EXIT command is equivalent to GO TO a point outside of loop. Similarly, the CYCLE command is equivalent to GO TO the end of the loop.

EXAMPLE 5.12

Below is the rabbit weighing program rewritten to use the EXIT command as the means to terminate the loop.

```
TOT = 0.0
NUM = 0
DO
    PRINT *, 'Enter Weight'
    READ *, WGT
    IF (WGT .GT. 500) EXIT
    TOT = TOT + WGT
    NUM = NUM + 1
END DO
AVG = TOT/NUM
PRINT *,'Avg Weight=', AVG
```

Compare this structure carefully with that shown in Example 5.10. In this version, the execution is much more natural. As soon as we read in a weight, we check to see if it exceeds the sentinel value. If it does, then we exit the loop and compute the average weight. Note that we don't have to make corrections (TOT−WGT) and (NUM−1) that we had to make in the previous example.

The key point to note here is that we can conduct our check whenever we wish. It's most natural to do this just after we read in the value as in this example. But with the DO WHILE structure, we had to wait until the next iteration of the loop to perform this check.

EXAMPLE 5.13

The program below shows how to use the CYCLE command. Once again, we will use the rabbit weighing problem. But here we will allow for a typographical error during the data entry. Experienced programmers will often think defensively when writing programs. They often ask themselves "What can possibly go wrong?" In the rabbit weighing problem, one of the potential problems is that someone may accidentally type in a negative or zero weight. In the previous versions of this program, this value would be accepted. In this version however, we will print out an appropriate message and ignore the input.

```
TOT = 0.0
NUM = 0
DO
   PRINT *, 'Enter Weight'
   READ *, WGT
   IF (WGT .GT. 500.) EXIT
   IF (WGT .LE. 0.) THEN
      PRINT *, 'Invalid Weight, Please Reenter'
      CYCLE
   ELSE
      TOT = TOT + WGT
      NUM = NUM + 1
   ENDIF
END DO
AVG = TOT/NUM
PRINT *,'Avg Weight=', AVG
```

We have retained the EXIT command introduced in the last example, but added the additional IF-THEN-ELSE construct. If the weight is zero or negative, the program prints out an error message and asks the user to reenter the data. Otherwise, we proceed with the calculations as before.

5.4 DEBUGGING TIPS

Previously, we gave you several suggestions to help locate syntax errors related to assignment statements and branching operations. These suggestions are equally valid for finding syntax errors for loops. So we won't repeat them here. Instead, we want to focus on locating logic and run time errors. These errors are typically more difficult to remove.

Before you try to trace through a loop, you may want to do a few preliminary things. One of the first things to do is to print out the program and *highlight* the loop bodies and the other control structures. A convenient method of doing this is by drawing boxes or lines around the body of each loop. (Of course, if you had indented while writing the program, this would have already been done.) By blocking out the control structures you will be able to locate errors such as missing key words and improper nesting. Also, it will be easier to spot errors in the program logic. Finally, by blocking out the loops, it will be easier to trace through the program.

EXAMPLE 5.14

The following program is an example of nested loops without any highlighting. Its purpose is to print out a table of lengths in feet and inches (up to 12 feet, 0 inches) together with the corresponding measure in total inches. As an example, it will print out messages such as "10 Feet and 4 Inches = 124 Inches".

In the following program, the outer loop will increment the number of feet to be converted, while the inner loop will increment the number of inches. Thus, the value of feet will be fixed, while the inches loop through the possible values of 1 to 11.

Program   **Flowchart**

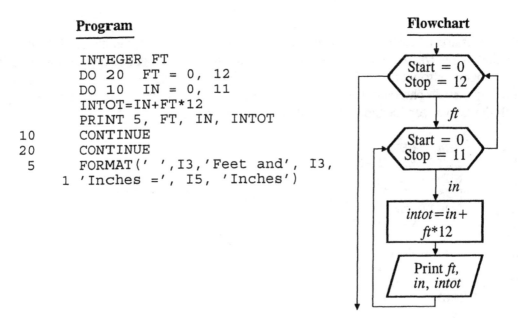

```
         INTEGER FT
         DO 20  FT = 0,  12
         DO 10  IN = 0,  11
         INTOT=IN+FT*12
         PRINT 5, FT, IN, INTOT
10       CONTINUE
20       CONTINUE
 5       FORMAT(' ',I3,'Feet and', I3,
     1   'Inches =', I5, 'Inches')
```

We show the same programs below with the loop structures highlighted using both methods.

Blocked Out   **Indented**

```
         INTEGER FT                        INTEGER FT
         DO 20 FT = 0,  12                 DO 20 FT = 0,  11
         DO 10 IN = 0,  11                   DO 10  IN = 0,  11
         INTOT = IN + FT * 12                 INTOT = IN + FT * 12
         PRINT 5, FT, IN, INTOT               PRINT 5, FT, IN, INTOT
10       CONTINUE                    10       CONTINUE
20       CONTINUE                    20       CONTINUE
```

The indentation method is strongly recommended even if you prefer the line method, because you can do it while entering the program. By using the indentations, you prepare for the likelihood of tracing.

The most important step in locating logic errors is to trace through the structures, since tracing will allow you to find where the program logic goes wrong. Tracing a DO loop takes a bit of patience since some of the variables change frequently. Because of the large number of changes within loops, trace tables are even more important than with other structures. Therefore, we recommend that the first step in performing a trace to detect faulty logic is to set up a complete trace table.

EXAMPLE 5.15

Let us now use some of these ideas to help debug a program containing a logic error. We designed this program to produce the following sequence of fractions:

$$\frac{2}{1} \quad \frac{3}{2} \quad \frac{5}{3} \quad \frac{8}{5} \quad \cdots$$

The numerator of each fraction is the sum of the numerator and denominator of the previous fraction, while the denominator of the new fraction is the numerator of the previous fraction. The program shown below is supposed to print out the first 40 terms of this sequence using real arithmetic. The output contains the term number (2/1 is term number 1 for example), with the numerator, denominator, and value of the fraction.

```
        REAL NUM
        INTEGER TERM
        NUM = 2.0
        DEN = 1.0
        DO 10 TERM = 1, 40
            VAL = NUM / DEN
            PRINT *,TERM,'# ',NUM,'/',DEN,' = ',VAL
            NUM = NUM + DEN
            DEN = NUM
10      CONTINUE
        END
```

When we go to execute the above program, the computer prints the following output on the CRT screen:

```
    1#   2.00000/ 1.00000  =   2.00000
    2#   3.00000/ 3.00000  =   1.00000
    3#   6.00000/ 6.00000  =   1.00000
                    ⋮
```

As you can see from the output, the program is incorrect since the numerators and denominators are equal, except for the first term. The first debugging step is to perform a trace on the program. Below is a listing of the variable table and the trace for the first few terms:

Variable Trace Table:

NUM	2.0, 3.0
DEN	1.0, 3.0
VAL	2.0
TERM	1, 2

Program Execution:

```
        NUM = 2.0
        DEN = 1.0
        Enter DO Loop, assign TERM=1
        Is TERM > 40? No, then execute loop
        VAL = NUM/DEN = 2.0
        PRINT TERM, NUM, DEN, VAL
        NUM=NUM+DEN=3.0
        DEN=NUM=3.0
```

We can carry out this trace further, but it is not necessary since the error has already occurred. After the first iteration through the loop, the expected values of each variable and the actual values already differ as summarized below:

Variable	Expected Value	Actual Value
NUM	3.0	3.0
DEN	2.0	3.0
VAL	1.5	1.0

We copied the expected values from the problem statement. For the term 3/2 we expect the denominator to be 2.0 and the numerator to be 3.0. The program however, returns the values of 3.0 and 3.0. Clearly then, the problem lies with the variable DEN. The problem is that the statement that updated the numerator destroys the value of the previous numerator (which we need to define the new denominator). One method of solving this is to use additional variables to store the previous numerator and denominator. Using those values, we can then calculate the new numerator and denominator. The corrected program now includes the two new variables, PRENUM and PREDEN:

```
      REAL NUM
      INTEGER TERM
      NUM = 2.0
      DEN = 1.0
      DO 10 TERM = 1, 40
            VAL = NUM / DEN
            PRINT *,TERM,'# ',NUM,'/',DEN,' = ',VAL
            PRENUM = NUM
            PREDEN = DEN
            NUM = PRENUM + PREDEN
            DEN = PRENUM
10          CONTINUE
      END
```

Once we correct the logic error, the output is now correct:

```
1#  2.00000/ 1.00000 =  2.00000
2#  3.00000/ 2.00000 =  1.50000
3#  5.00000/ 3.00000 =  1.66667
            ⋮
40#  2.679143E+08/ 1.655801E+08 =  1.61803
```

As you can see from this output, the program is now working correctly. You will find that there is no substitute for tracing in removing logic errors. You must be willing to trace through the program by hand to confirm that the logic is correct.

Solved Problems

5.1   Locate syntax errors in each of the following loops:

```
(a)      DO 10 I = 1, 5, I          (b)      DO 20, J = I, K, L
(c)      DO 10 I = K, L, M          (d)      DO 10 J = 1, 9, 2
            DO 10 I = L, M, K                    J = J**2
            PRINT *, I, K, L, M                  PRINT *, J
    10   CONTINUE                       10   CONTINUE
(e)      DO 10 J = 1, 3             (f)      DO 10 J = 1, 3
            PRINT *, J                          DO 20 K = 1, 4
            DO 10 K = 1, 3                       L = K ** 2
               PRINT *, K                        PRINT *, L
    10   CONTINUE                       20   CONTINUE
    10   CONTINUE                                J = L
                                                DO 30 L = 1, 3
                                                   PRINT *, L
                                        30   CONTINUE
```

(a) You cannot use I both as the step size and loop control variable.

(b) No error. The comma after DO 20 is permitted.

(c) You cannot use I as the LCV for the inner loop since it is already being use as the loop control variable in the outer loop.

(d) Attempt to change LCV inside the loop.

(e) There are two 10 CONTINUE statements. Eliminate one of them.

(f) Missing 10 CONTINUE. Also, the statement J = L may change the LCV depending on position of the missing statement (10 CONTINUE).

5.2   Locate errors in the following nonstandard structures:

```
(a)      DO   J = 1, 10, 0.5         (b)      DO , J = 1, 10
(c)      DO   I = 1, J               (d)      DO J = 2, 95
            DO J = I, 2*I                         IF(MOD(J,25).EQ.0) CYCLE
               PRINT *, I, J                   END DO
            END DO
         END DO
```

(a) The step size of 0.5 will be converted to zero, which is not allowed. A step size of zero would result in an infinite loop and produce a run-time error.

(b) Correct since comma is allowed.

(c) The inner loop will change the upper limit in the outer loop. Some compilers may not allow this.

(d) Correct.

5.3   Convert the following structures into loops:

(a)
```
      X = 1.0
   10 IF (X .LE. 10) THEN
      Z = Z/C
      P = C ** 2
      X = X + 1
      GOTO 10
      ELSE
      PRINT *, P
      END IF
```

(b)
```
      I = 1
    5 IF ( I .LE. 10) THEN
      J = 1
   10 IF (J .LE. 10) THEN
      PRINT *, I, J
      J = J + 1
      GO TO 10
      END IF
      I = I + 1
      GO TO 5
      END IF
```

(a)
```
      DO 10 I = 1, 10, 1
         Z = Z/C
         P = C ** 2
   10 CONTINUE
      PRINT *, P
```

(b)
```
      DO 10 I = 1, 10
         DO 10 J = 1, 10
            PRINT *, I, J
   10 CONTINUE
```

5.4　　Trace through the following program segments and predict the output:

(a)
```
      DO 10 J = 1, 9, 2
         K = J ** 2
   10 CONTINUE
      PRINT *, J
```

(b)
```
      DO 10 J = 1, 3
         IF (J .LE. 2) K = J**2
         IF (J .GT. 2) K = J
         A = J**2 + K**2
         PRINT *, A
   10 CONTINUE
```

(c)
```
      INTEGER A, B, C
      DO 10 A = 2, 8, 2
         DO 10 B = A, 2
            DO 10 C = 1, B, 2
               PRINT *, A, B, C
   10       CONTINUE
```

(d)
```
      L = 0
      DO 10 J = 1, 100, 50
         PRINT *, J
   10 CONTINUE
      DO 20 K = J, 100-J, -50
         L = L + J
   20 CONTINUE
      PRINT *, L
```

(a) Trace Table:

J:	1, 3, 5, 7, 9, 11
K:	1, 9, 25, 49, 81

Output:
11

(b) Trace Table:

J:	1, 2, 3
K:	1, 4, 3
A:	2, 20, 18

Output:
2
20
18

(c) Trace Table:

A:	2, 4
B:	2, 3, 4
C:	1, 3

Output:
2 2 1

(d) Trace Table:

L:	0, 101, 202, 303
J:	1, 51, 101
K:	101, 51, 1, −49

Output:
1
51
303

5.5 Determine if the structures below are properly nested:

(a)
```
      DO 10
        ⋮
      DO 20
        ⋮
      DO 30
        ⋮
   20 CONTINUE
        ⋮
   30 CONTINUE
   10 CONTINUE
```

(b)
```
   DO 10
     ⋮
   IF(   ) THEN
     ⋮
   ELSE
     ⋮
10 CONTINUE
     ⋮
   ENDIF
```

(a) DO 30 and DO 20 loops overlap.

(b) The end of the Block IF structure must be inside the loop.

5.6 Locate syntax errors in each of the following loops:

(a)
```
DO WHILE (X .NGT. 0)
```

(b)
```
DO WHILE (I .LE. 5)
   PRINT *, I
END WHILE
```

(c)
```
DO WHILE (X .EQ. 0)
   DO WHILE (Y .NE. X)
      PRINT *, X, Y
END DO
```

(d)
```
DO WHILE (X .GE. Y)
   IF(X .GT. 0) THEN
      PRINT *, X
END DO
```

(a) NGT is not a valid relational operator.

(b) Terminating statement on most compilers is END DO, not END WHILE.

(c) Must have two terminating statements, one for each DO WHILE.

(d) Missing terminating statement for Block-IF construct.

5.7 Trace through the following program segments and predict the output:

(a)
```
J = 1
DO WHILE (J .LE. 100)
   PRINT *, J
   J = J + 1
END DO
```

(b)
```
X = 1.0
DO WHILE (X .GE. 0.01)
   SUM = SUM + X
   X = X/10.0
END DO
PRINT *, SUM
```

(c)
```
X = 1.0
Y = 1.0
DO
   IF(X .LE. 0.01) EXIT
   X = X /10.0
   Y = 2.0 * Y
   IF(Y . GE. 4.0) CYCLE
   SUM = SUM + X * Y
   PRINT *, X, Y, SUM
END DO
```

(d)
```
TERM = 1.0
ISIGN = +1
X = 1.0
DO
   ISIGN = -ISIGN
   X = X + 1.0
   TERM = ISIGN / X**2
   IF(ABS(TERM).LT.0.05)EXIT
   SUM = SUM + TERM
   PRINT *, SUM
END DO
```

(a) Trace Table:
     J: 1, 2, 3, 4, ..., 100
   Output:
     1
     ⋮
     100

(b) Trace Table:
     X: 1.0, 0.1, 0.01
     SUM: 1.0, 1.1, 1.11
   Output:
     1.11000

(c) Trace Table:
     X: 1.0, 0.1, 0.01
     Y: 1.0, 2.0, 4.0
     SUM: 0.2
   Output:
     0.10000 2.00000 0.20000

(d) Trace Table:
     TERM: 1.0, −0.25, 0.111,
             −0.0625, 0.04
     ISIGN: +1, −1, +1, −1, +1
     X: 1.0, 2.0, 3.0, 4.0, 5.0
     SUM: −0.25, −0.1389, −0.20139
   Output:
     −0.250000
     −0.138889
     −0.201389

5.8   The following suggestions are designed so that you can find out the limitations or extensions of your Fortran compiler. Run small programs to find out if the following suggestions work. You may need also to consult the documentation for your system.

(a) Some compilers will always execute a loop at least once, even if the structure of your loop tells it otherwise. Try the following:

```
      DO 10 I = 1, 0
          PRINT*, I
   10 CONTINUE
```

(b) See if your compiler supports the DO WHILE extension. Some compilers use the DO WHILE structure. Others may use the WHILE(..)DO structure. Try both:

```
DO WHILE (X .LE. 1.0)           WHILE(X .LE. 1.0) DO
    PRINT *, X                      PRINT *,X
    X = X + 1                       X = X + 1
END DO                          END WHILE
```

5.9   Write a program that prints out all even numbers including the end points between two positive values (*i* and *j*) that are read in at execution time.

```
      READ *, I, J
      LIMIT1 = I/2*2 + 2
      DO 10 LCV = LIMIT1, J, 2           DO
          PRINT *, LCV                     ⋮
   10     CONTINUE                       END DO   (if available)
```

5.10   Write a program to read in a real value x and repeatedly divide it by 2 until $x < 0.001$. Print out the result after every five divisions, along with the total number of divisions.

```
READ *, X
DO WHILE (X .GE. 0.001)                    DO
    X = X/2.0                                ⋮
    NOSDIV = NOSDIV + 1                       ⋮
    IF(MOD(NOSDIV,5) .EQ. 0) THEN         IF(X .LE. 0.001) EXIT
        PRINT *, X, NOSDIV                   ⋮
    END IF                                    ⋮
END DO                                    END DO   (if available)
```

(Note: If NOSDIV is a multiple of 5, MOD(NOSDIV,5) will be zero.)

5.11 Write a program to read in a series of numbers and find the largest and smallest. Stop reading data when a negative value is entered.

```
READ *, X
XMIN = X
XMAX = X
DO WHILE (X .GE. 0)                       DO
    XMIN = MIN(XMIN, X)                      READ *, X
    XMAX = MAX(XMAX, X)                      IF(X .LT. 0) EXIT
    READ *, X                               XMIN=MIN(XMIN,X)
END DO                                      XMAX=MAX(XMAX,X)
PRINT *, 'Min Value: ', XMIN             END DO   (if available)
PRINT *, 'Max value: ', XMAX
```

5.12 Write a program that prints the powers of 2 between 1 and 256.

```
DO 10 I = 0, 8                            DO  I=0, 8
    PRINT *, 2.0**I                          ⋮
10 CONTINUE                               END DO   (if available)
```

5.13 Write a program segment to find all integers that are divisible by three and lie between two integers that you enter at execution time.

```
PRINT *, 'Enter Limits'
READ *, I, J
DO 10 NUM = I, J                          DO   NUM = I, J
    IF(MOD(NUM, 3) .EQ. 0) THEN              ⋮
        PRINT*, NUM, 'is divisible'          ⋮
    ELSE                                     ⋮
        PRINT*, NUM, 'not divisible'         ⋮
    ENDIF                                    ⋮
10 CONTINUE                               END DO   (if available)
```

5.14 Write a program to compute the value of a given by the first ten terms of the following series:

$$a = 1 + \frac{1}{2} + \frac{1}{3} + \frac{1}{4} + \ldots$$

```
      A = 0.0
      DO 10 I = 1, 10                   DO    I=1,10
         A = A + 1.0/I                     ⋮
   10 CONTINUE                          END DO    (if available)
      PRINT *, 'A = ', A
```

5.15 Write a program to compute the value of *b* given by the series shown below. Continue computing the sum of the terms until the absolute value of any individual term falls below 0.01. By doing this, we evaluate the series for all terms that are significant. We will ignore any term whose value is so small that it has little effect on the series total.

Note in this series that the terms have an alternating sign. This is best handled by defining a variable SIGN whose initial value is set at 1.0. For each successive term in the series, we will multiply SIGN by -1.0, in effect, alternating the sign.

$$b = 1 - \frac{1}{2} + \frac{1}{3} - \frac{1}{4} + \dots$$

```
      TERM = 1.0
      SUM = 1.0
      SIGN = -1.0
      I = 2
      DO WHILE (ABS(TERM) .GE. 0.01)     DO
         TERM = 1.0/I*SIGN                  ⋮
         SIGN = -SIGN                    IF(TERM.LT.0.01) EXIT
         SUM = SUM + TERM                   ⋮
         I = I + 1
      END DO                            END DO    (if available)
      PRINT *, 'B = ', SUM
```

5.16 The factorial of a number (*n*!) is the product of all integers between 1 and *n*. Write a program to compute the factorial of an integer value entered at execution time.

```
      PRINT *, 'Enter N:'
      READ *, N
      FACT = 1.0
      DO 10 I = 2, N                     DO    I = 2, N
         FACT = FACT * I                    ⋮
   10 CONTINUE                          END DO    (if available)
      PRINT *, N,'! =', FACT
```

5.17 Write a program to read in the radius *r* of a circle centered at the origin. Then read in the coordinate pairs (x, y) of a point and determine if that point lies within the circle. Use the condition that if

$$(x^2 + y^2)^{0.5} < r$$

then the point is inside the circle. Terminate the program the first time that $(x^2 + y^2)^{0.5} > 2r$.

```
READ *, R
PRINT *, 'Enter X, Y: '
READ *, X, Y
DO WHILE(X**2+Y**2.LT.4*R**2)          DO
   IF(X**2+Y**2.LT.R*R) THEN              PRINT *, 'Enter X, Y:'
      PRINT *, 'Inside'                   READ *, X, Y
   ELSE                                   Z=X**2+Y**2
      PRINT *, 'Outside'                  IF(Z.GT.4*R**2) EXIT
   ENDIF                                     :
   PRINT *, 'ENTER X, Y'                     :
   READ *, X, Y                              :
END DO                                 END DO    (if available)
```

5.18 The value of $e = 2.718282$ can be approximated by the infinite series:

$$e = \sum_{n=0}^{n=\infty} \left(\frac{1}{n!} \right) \approx \left(\frac{1}{0!} \right) + \left(\frac{1}{1!} \right) + \left(\frac{1}{2!} \right) + \left(\frac{1}{3!} \right) + \dots$$

The factorial function $n!$ is the product of integers from 2 to n and $0! = 1$ by definition. Write a program to approximate the value of e for five terms in the series. Then modify it to compute the approximation for n terms in the series, where n is read in at execution time.

```
PRINT *, 'Enter Number of Terms:'
READ *, N
SUM = 0.0
DO 10 I = 0, N-1                    DO  I=0, N-1
   FACT = 1.0                          :
   DO 5 II = 2, I                      DO  II=2, I
      FACT=FACT * II                      :
5  CONTINUE                           END DO
   SUM = SUM + 1.0/FACT                 :
10 CONTINUE                          END DO    (if available)
   PRINT *, 'Approx = ', SUM
```

5.19 Write a program to determine if a number is *prime*. A prime number is one which is divisible only by itself and 1. Use the following algorithm:
(a) Successively divide n by all integers lying between 2 and $n/2$;
(b) With each division, check for a remainder;
(c) If there is no remainder for a given division, then the number is not a prime, so stop.
(d) Print out a message in either case (prime or nonprime).

```
PRINT *, 'Enter Number: '
READ *, N
DO 10 I = 2, N/2                    DO  I=2, N/2
   IF(MOD(N,I) .EQ. 0) THEN            :
      PRINT *, 'not prime'            :
      STOP                           :
   ENDIF                             :
10 CONTINUE                          END DO    (if available)
   PRINT *, 'prime'
```

5.20 Write a program to simulate a population explosion. Start out with a single bacteria cell that can produce an offspring by division every 4 hours. The new cell must incubate for 24 hours before it can divide. The parent cell meanwhile will continue to divide every 4 hours. Assume that any new cells will follow this pattern. How many cells will you have in 1 day, 1 week, and 1 month, if none of the new cells die?

```
C H24 is the number of cells that are 24 hours old or older.
c Similarly, H20 is the number of cells that are 20 hours old,
c H16 is the number of cells 16 hours old and so forth. Every
c four hours, we move the number stored in each variable to the
c next higher level. Thus, H16 receives the value from H12. The
c number of new cells created (NEWCEL) is the value stored in
c H24.
      H24=1
      PRINT *, 'Enter Number of hours'
      READ *, HOURS
      DO 10 I = 1, HOURS/4
         NEWCEL=H24
         H24=H24+H20
         H20=H16
         H16=H12
         H12=H8
         H8 =H4
         H4 =H0
         H0 =NEWCEL
10    CONTINUE
      TOT=H0+H4+H8+H12+H16+H20+H24
      PRINT *, 'Number of Cells=', TOT
```

Supplementary Problems

5.21 Locate syntax and run-time errors in each of the following loops:

```
(a)     DO 30 L = 1, M,           (b)     DO 40 M = 1, I**2, -1
(c)     DO 10 J = 1, 9, 2         (d)     DO 10 J = 1, 10.5, 1.5
           K = J**2                          PRINT *, J
           PRINT *, K                10 CONTINUE
           J = J + 1
      10 CONTINUE
(e)     DO 10 J = 1, 10           (f)     DO 10 J = 1, 2
           PRINT *, J                        DO 20 K = 2, 5
           DO 20 J = 1, 5                        DO 30 K = 1,3
              PRINT *, J**2                          PRINT *, J, K
      20    CONTINUE              30             CONTINUE
      10 CONTINUE                 10          CONTINUE
                                  20    CONTINUE
```

5.22 Locate errors in the following nonstandard structures:

```
(a)      DO 10 I = 1, 10        (b)      DO
            DO K = 1, 10                    J = J + 2
               PRINT *, I, K                PRINT *, J
      10      CONTINUE               END DO
         END DO
(c)      DO   I = 1, 10, K       (d)      DO I = 1, 10
            K = 2 * K                      PRINT *, I**2, I
            PRINT *, I, K                  K = I + 1
         END DO                         CONTINUE
```

5.23 Convert the following structures into loops:

```
(a)      I = 10                 (b)      I = 1
      5  IF (I .LE. 1) THEN          5  IF (I .LE. 10) THEN
            PRINT *, I                   J = I
            I = I - 2              10  IF (J .LE. 2*I) THEN
            GO TO 5                      PRINT *, J
         ENDIF                           J = J + 2
                                         GO TO 10
                                      END IF
                                      PRINT *, I
                                      I = I + 2
                                      GO TO 5
                                      END IF
```

5.24 Trace through the following program segments and predict the output:

```
(a)      DO 10 J = 1, 1         (b)      DO 10 J = 1, 2
            DO 20 K = 1, 2                  DO 20 K = J, 3
               L = J + K                       L = J + K
               PRINT*,'L=', L                  PRINT*, 'L=', L
      20      CONTINUE                20      CONTINUE
      10 CONTINUE                        M = J - K
                                         PRINT *, 'M=', M
                                 10 CONTINUE
                                    PRINT*, J + K
(c)      DO 10 J = 1, 2         (d)      DO 90 I = 5, 17, 3
            DO 10 K = 1, 2                 II = I / 5
               DO 30 L = 1, 2              DO 99 III = 7, II, 4
                  Z = J+K+L                   IF(I.EQ.I/III*III)CYCLE
      30         CONTINUE            99      CONTINUE
               L = J + K                     PRINT*, I, II, III
               M = L**2             90 CONTINUE
               PRINT *, Z, M
      10      CONTINUE
```

5.25 Determine if the structures below are properly nested:

(a)   DO 10
              ⋮
         DO 20
              ⋮
    20   CONTINUE
              ⋮
    10   CONTINUE
              ⋮
         DO 30
              ⋮
         DO 40
              ⋮
    30   CONTINUE
              ⋮
    40   CONTINUE

(b)   DO 10
              ⋮
    10   CONTINUE
              ⋮
         DO 20
              ⋮
    20   CONTINUE
              ⋮
         DO 30
              ⋮
    30   DO 40
              ⋮
    40   CONTINUE

5.26 Locate syntax and run time errors in each of the following loops:

```
(a)   DO WHILE(X.GT.Y.OR..LT.Z)
          PRINT *, Y
      END DO

(b)   DO WHILE (A * B .LT. 0)
          DO 10 I = 1, 10
              PRINT *, I/A*B
   10     CONTINUE
      END DO

(c)   DO WHILE(X * X .GE. 0.0)
          READ *, X
          PRINT*, X, X*X
      END DO

(d)   IF (X.LT.A.AND.B.GT.X)
          DO 10 I = 1, 6
              DO WHILE (I.GT.0)
                  READ *, I
                  X = I * X
              END DO
   10     CONTINUE
      END IF
```

5.27 Trace through the following program segments and predict the output:

```
(a)   X = 1.5
      DO WHILE (X .LE. 5.0)
          PRINT *, X
          X = X * 1.5
      END DO

(b)   X = 1.0
      DO WHILE (X .LE. 100.0)
          PRINT *, X
          X = (X-1)**2 + 2.0
      END DO

(c)   X = 2.0
      Y = 1.0
      SUM = 0.0
      DO
          X = X * Y
          Y = X * Y
          IF(X .GT. 5.0) EXIT
          IF(Y .GE. 4.0) CYCLE
          SUM = SUM + X*Y
          PRINT *, X, Y, SUM
      END DO

(d)   TERM = 0.0
      ISIGN = +1
      X = 1.0
      DO
          ISIGN = -ISIGN
          X = X + 1.0
          SUM = 2.0 * X**ISIGN
          TERM = 2**X*ISIGN
          IF (X .GE. 5) EXIT
          SUM = SUM + TERM
          PRINT *, TERM, SUM
      END DO
```

5.28 The following suggestions are designed so that you can find out the limitations or extensions of your Fortran compiler. Run small programs to find out if the following suggestions work. You may need also to consult the documentation for your system.

(a) Most FORTRAN compilers will not allow you to transfer into the middle of a DO loop. Try the following code to see if your compiler catches this problem.

```
      READ *, N
      IF (N .NE. 0) GO TO 10
      DO 20 I = 1, 10
   10    PRINT *, 'I = ', I
   20 CONTINUE
```

(b) Using real values to control a DO loop is generally not a good idea because reals are stored imprecisely. Run both segments on your system and compare results.

```
      SUM = 0.0                    ISUM = 0
      DO 1 X=0.0, 1.0, 0.0001      DO 1 I = 1, 10000
         SUM = SUM + X                ISUM = ISUM + I
    1 CONTINUE                   1 CONTINUE
      PRINT *, SUM                 PRINT *, ISUM / 10000.0
```

5.29 Write a program segment that reads in two integer values (i and j) and prints out all integer values between them in reverse order. Do not include i and j in the output.

5.30 Write a program to read in a series of numbers and keep track of the running total and the number of data items. Stop collecting data when a negative sentinel value is entered. Then calculate the average and report it.

5.31 Write a program to read in a dollar amount and a monthly interest rate. Calculate the interest earned each month and the total amount on deposit. Terminate the program when the initial deposit has doubled.

5.32 Write a program to calculate the values of y, where y is given by:

$$y = 1/x - 4.3 \log(x) + x^4$$

for values of x between 0.01 and $+10.0$ in increments of 0.01. Since this will produce almost 1,000 values of y, provide output statements to print out the values of x and y for every nth x value (for example, every hundredth value for $n=100$). The value of n is to be read in at execution time.

5.33 One difficulty with the approach of problem 5.18 (approximating the value of an infinite series like e=2.718282) is that you never know how many terms to use for the approximation. One way that has proven to be very successful is to have the summation terminate when each new term adds little to the approximation. For example, the thirteenth term is 1/13! or 1.6059×10^{-10}, which is insignificant compared to the sum of the previous terms. Therefore, you should modify the program for problem 5.18 to allow for termination of the series when any term is less than ϵ, which is a variable that you read in.

5.34   One of the most famous series is that due to Fibonacci

$$1\ 1\ 2\ 3\ 5\ 8\ 13\ 21\ 34\ \ldots$$

This series is known to describe many naturally occurring phenomena. For example, successive rows of sunflower seeds duplicate the series. It also describes a population explosion among rabbits. The first two numbers in the series are 1 and 1. All the additional terms of the series are the sum of the two previous terms. Thus, the ninth term (34) is the sum of the seventh and the eighth terms, or 13 + 21. Write a program to calculate the first *n* terms of the series.

5.35   A lot of people place much faith in the study of numbers. They believe that they can predict your future if they know one of your vital statistics such as your social security number. They base their method on reducing your number to a single digit number by adding all the digits together. For example, if your SS# is 123-45-6789, the sum of the digits is 45. Since this is still a two-digit number, the process needs to be repeated. The result (4 + 5) is 9. Write a program to carry out this unusual addition process for any general number such as a phone number or body weight.

Answers to Selected Supplementary Problems

5.21   (a) Extra comma at end of loop control variable.
(b) Loop does not converge. I**2 will always be a positive value.
(c) Attempt to change LCV inside the loop.
(d) Cannot mix real and integer values inside the loop control statement.
(e) Cannot use J as the LCV for the inner loop.
(f) Improper nesting, and K as the LCV in the innermost loop is prohibited.

5.22   (a) Improper nesting.
(b) Infinite loop since there is no way for the loop to stop.
(c) Correct. The loop control is set up only when the loop is first entered. Thus, the *initial* value of K is used to create the loop. Subsequent changes to K do not create an error. The only variable that cannot be changed is I.
(d) CONTINUE is not a legal termination for this loop.

5.23 (a)
```
      DO 10 I = 10, 1, -2
         PRINT *, I
   10 CONTINUE
```
(b)
```
      DO 10  I = 1, 10, 2
         DO 20 J = I, 2*I, 2
            PRINT *, J
   20       CONTINUE
         PRINT *, I
   10 CONTINUE
```

5.24 (a) Trace Table:

J:	1
K:	1, 2
L:	2, 3

Output:
L = 2
L = 3

(b) Trace Table:

J:	1, 2
K:	1, 2, 3, 2, 3
L:	2, 3, 4, 4, 5
M:	−2, −1

Output:
L = 2
L = 3
L = 4
M = −3
L = 4
L = 5
M = −2

(c) Trace Table:

J:	1,2
K:	1,2,1,2
L:	1,2,2,1,2,3,1,2,3,1,2,4
Z:	3,4,4,5,4,5,5,6
M:	4,9,9,16

Output:

4.00000	4
5.00000	9
5.00000	9
6.00000	16

(d) Trace Table:

I:	5, 8, 11, 14, 17
II:	1, 1, 2, 2, 3
III:	7, 7, 7, 7, 7

Output:

5	1	7
8	1	7
11	2	7
14	2	7
17	3	7

5.25 (a) Do 30 and DO 40 loops overlap.
(b) DO 40 cannot be the terminating statement of the DO 30 loop.

5.26 (a) Improper compound conditional. Should be (X .GT. Y .OR. X .LT. Z).
(b) Infinite loop — no way for DO WHILE construct to stop.
(c) Infinite loop — X*X will always be positive. Therefore, the loop cannot stop.
(d) READ statement inside the DO WHILE loop attempts to change value of I. This is forbidden since I is the LCV for the DO 10 loop. Also, THEN key word is missing.

5.27 (a) Trace Table:
X: 1.5, 2.25, 3.375, 5.0625

(b) Trace Table:
X: 1.0, 2.0, 3.0, 6.0, 27.0, 678.0

Output: Output:
  1.500000   1.00000
  2.250000   2.00000
  3.375000   3.00000
                            6.00000
                          27.0000

(c) Trace Table: (d) Trace Table:
  X: 2.0, 2.0, 4.0, 32.0   TERM: 0.0, -4.0, 8.0, -16.0, 32.0
  Y: 1.0, 2.0, 8.0, 256.0   ISIGN: $+1$, -1, $+1$, -1, $+1$
  SUM: 0.0, 4.0, 36.0   X: 1.0, 2.0, 3.0, 4.0, 5.0
Output: SUM: 1.,-3.,6.,14.,0.5,-15.5,10.
  2.00000 2.00000 4.00000   Output:
                         -4.00000 -3.00000
                          8.00000   14.0000
                       -16.0000 -15.5000

5.29
```
        READ *, I, J
        DO 10 LCV = J-1, I+1, -1      DO LCV=J-1, I+1, -1
           PRINT *, LCV                  ⋮
     10 CONTINUE                      END DO        (if available)
```

5.30
```
        NOS = 1
        SUM = 0.0
        DO WHILE(X .GE. 0)           DO
           READ *, X                    READ *, X
           NOS = NOS + 1                IF(X .LT. 0) EXIT
           SUM = SUM + X                NOS = NOS + 1
        END DO                          SUM = SUM + X
        AVG = (SUM - X)/(NOS - 1)    END DO
        PRINT *, AVG                 AVG = SUM/NOS (if available)
```

5.31
```
        READ *, AMT, PERCENT
        START = AMT
        DO WHILE(AMT .LT. 2*START)   DO
           ADD = AMT * PERCENT          ⋮
           PRINT *,'Interest:',ADD      ⋮
           AMT = AMT + ADD              ⋮
           PRINT *, 'Total: ', AMT      IF(AMT .GT. 2*START) EXIT
        END DO                       END DO       (if available)
```

5.32
```
        PRINT *, 'How many times?'
        READ *, N
        DO 10  I = 1, 1000           DO  I= 1, 1000
           X = I/100.0                  ⋮
           Y = 1/X-4.3*ALOG10(X)+X**4   ⋮
           IF(MOD(I,N) .EQ. 0) THEN     ⋮
              PRINT *, X, Y             ⋮
           ENDIF                        ⋮
     10 CONTINUE                     END DO        (if available)
```

(Note: the LCV <u>should</u> be an integer. So we created I to control the loop and then we calculated X inside the loop to match the problem statement.)

5.33
```
        PRINT *, 'Enter EPS:'
        READ *, EPS
        SUM = 0.0
        TERM = 1
        I = 2
        DO WHILE (TERM .GT. EPS)         DO
            FACT = 1.0                        :
            DO 5 II = 1, I                DO II = 1, I
                FACT=FACT*II                  :
    5       CONTINUE                      END DO
            TERM = 1/FACT                     :
            SUM = SUM + TERM              IF(TERM .LE. EPS) EXIT
            I = I + 1                         :
        END DO                           END DO          (if available)
        PRINT *, 'Approx = ', SUM
```

5.34
```
        PRINT *, 'Number of terms?'
        READ *, N
        TERM1=1
        TERM2=1
        PRINT *, 'Term1:', TERM1
        PRINT *, 'Term2:', TERM2
        DO 10 I = 3, N                   DO   I=3, N
            TERM = TERM1 + TERM2              :
            PRINT *,'Term',I,':',TERM         :
            TERM2 = TERM1                     :
            TERM1 = TERM                      :
    10  CONTINUE                         END DO
```

5.35
```
        PRINT *,'Enter number(max 9 digits)'
        READ *, NUM
        DO WHILE (NUM .GE. 10)           DO
            SUM = 0                           :
            DO WHILE (NUM .GE. 10)        DO
                SUM=SUM+MOD(NUM,10)           :
                NUM=NUM/10                    :
            END DO                        IF(NUM .LT. 10) EXIT
            SUM=SUM+NUM                   END DO
            NUM=SUM                           :
        END DO                                :
        PRINT *,'Sum of Digits:',NUM     IF(NUM .LT. 10) EXIT
                                         END DO
```

Chapter 6

Subscripted Variables and Arrays

6.1 OVERVIEW

Arrays are a convenient way to work with large quantities of data. For example, by using arrays you can easily control 100 numbers with only a single variable. Without arrays, you would need 100 conventional single-valued variables to do the same thing.

Each array has an *index* that allows you to locate and manipulate the quantities stored in the array. We sometimes also call the subscript the *subscript*. The idea of the subscripted variable is a common one in mathematics. For example, if you have a series of numbers, $x_1, x_2, \ldots, x_n$, you can represent the average $\bar{x}$ by a mathematical shorthand.

$$\bar{x} = \frac{1}{n} \sum_{i=1}^{i=n} x_i = \frac{1}{n} (x_1 + x_2 + \cdots + x_n)$$

Here we represent the individual numbers as x_i, where i is the subscript that locates the desired number in the list. Thus, x_1 represents the first number in the list, x_2 is the second number, and so on. The summation sign Σ indicates that we are to add together the specified numbers in the list. All we need do to manipulate these numbers is to specify the position (1, 2, 3, etc.) within that list. Thus, if we wanted to add together the third and fourth numbers in the list, we would write:

$$total = x_3 + x_4$$

As we will soon see, this method will increase our ability to manipulate large quantities of data.

The topics to be covered in this chapter include:

- The need for arrays
- Declarations and one-dimensional arrays
- Manipulation of arrays
- Two-dimensional and higher order arrays
- Input/output of arrays
- Debugging tips

6.2 THE NEED FOR ARRAYS

Scientists and engineers often work with large amounts of data. For example, we may run an experiment in which there are several thousand data points to process. Using only the techniques that we have presented so far, this would be a difficult task. To demonstrate this, let's focus on a

165

simple task to write a program that reads in ten numbers and prints them out in reverse order. One possible solution is:

```
READ *, X1, X2, X3, X4, X5, X6, X7, X8, X9, X10
PRINT *, X10, X9, X8, X7, X6, X5, X4, X3, X2, X1
```

This program segment will work of course, but it's neither elegant nor very practical. If we want to do the same thing for 11 numbers, we would have to modify our program. So if we wanted to perform this task on 100 numbers, we would have a lot of work ahead of us.

Before we show you the structure of an array, you must understand the difference between the *single-value variable* and the *subscripted variable*. The variables that you have studied so far are all *single-valued*. This means that they can take on only a single value:

```
X = 1.23456
```

In this simple assignment statement, the variable X has only a single value. When we wish to create a *subscripted variable*, we must add one additional piece of information —the *subscript*:

```
X(1) = 1.23456
X(2) = 9.87654
```

The number that appears within the parentheses is the *index* and indicates the position within the array X that contains the list of data. Thus, the first number in the list is X(1) or 1.23456. In mathematics, we indicate this type of variable by using a subscript. In Fortran however, the rule is that we must write the subscript inside the parentheses. The quantity that goes inside the parenthesis can be a constant, a variable, or an expression. Thus, we could have:

```
X(1) = ......
X(J) = ......
X(2*K-1) = ......
```

The advantage is that the subscript can be a variable that can be controlled by the program.

EXAMPLE 6.1

The array subscript can be controlled by a DO loop. The most common way is to use the loop control variable (LCV) as the subscript of the array. In the following example, we will use I as the LCV, and then use it to store values in $x_1, x_2, \ldots, x_{10}$. The values will be i^2. When this program segment is finished, x_1 will contain 1^2, x_2 will contain 2^2 and so forth, up to x_{10} storing 10^2.

```
        DO 10 I = 1, 10
           X(I) = I**2
10      CONTINUE
```

The variable I will change each time through the loop. Thus, when $I=1$, a value will be assigned to $X(1)$. When $I=2$, a value will be assigned to $X(2)$, and so forth.

The primary restriction on the subscript is that it must be an *integer* constant, variable, or expression. Also, there may be restrictions on the complexity of the allowed integer expressions.

EXAMPLE 6.2

The subscript of an array may be an <u>integer</u> constant, a variable, or an expression. The integer expression, however, is limited to the following on some older Fortran compilers:

Rule for Subscript	Correct Example	Incorrect Example
Constant	X (1)	X (1.2)
Variable	X (J)	X (Z)
Variable + constant	X (J+1)	X (1+J)
Constant × variable	X (2*J)	X (J*2)
Constant × variable ± constant	X (2*J−1)	X (J*2−K)

Almost all compilers will allow you to use other forms for subscripts. The above rules are only guidelines which will help to insure that your program is portable and will work on all machines. Even if your compiler allows other subscript forms, you should try to avoid using them if you expect to run your program at a later date under other compilers.

6.3 THE DECLARATION STATEMENT

Before you can use arrays, you must first *declare* them. Declaration statements go at the beginning of the program before any executable statements and provide important information that allows the compiler to reserve enough memory space for the arrays. The declaration is usually done with the *type declaration* statement, which also indicates the *size* or number of elements in the array. The general form is:

> *type arrayname (Lower limit : Upper limit)*

where, *type* indicates the type of the array (REAL, INTEGER, LOGICAL, etc.)
  arrayname is any valid Fortran variable name (X, TIME, etc.)
  Lower limit indicates the lowest value for the subscript
  Upper limit indicates the maximum value for the subscript.

The "Lower limit : Upper limit" of numbers can be any integers (even negative) as long as the upper limit is larger than the lower limit. Usually, though, arrays will begin with a lower limit of 1. In most applications it makes a lot of sense to start your arrays this way, since the conventional way of thinking of a list is that it begins with the "first" item. If you set up your arrays this way, you may omit the lower limit and specify only the upper limit without the colon. In some instances, however, it may make sense to start the array at some value other than a lower limit of 1.

An important point about declaring arrays is that you promise the compiler what the maximum size of the array will be. You are not required to use all this space. All that you are doing is telling the compiler to reserve sufficient space for the data. For example, if you create an array with 100 elements and use only 10 of those, there is no problem. The reverse situation (using more than you reserve) is not allowed.

Keep in mind the difference between the array name and the subscript. The array represents a group of data as a list, while the subscript represents the position within that list.

EXAMPLE 6.3

The following illustrate some correct and incorrect usage of array declaration statements:

Valid	Invalid	Comments
REAL X(5)		*(X is a real array with 5 elements.)*
INTEGER A(10), B(3)		*(A are both integer arrays with 10 elements and 3 elements, respectively)*
REAL X(1:10)		*(OK, but 1 is unnecessary.)*
REAL X(10)		*(Same result as previous example.)*
REAL X(−5:10), Y(20)		*(Declares X and Y to be real with 15 and 20 elements, respectively.)*
INTEGER AMT, M(10)		*(OK to declare scalar variables and arrays in the same declaration statement.)*
	REAL X(N)	*(Variable-size arrays not allowed.)*
	REAL X(10.0)	*(Limits must be integer, not real.)*
	REAL X(5:−5)	*(Wrong order of limits.)*

6.4 MANIPULATING ARRAYS

Now that we have gone though the formality of setting up our arrays with the declaration statement, we can begin to focus on the main topic — how to manipulate arrays. One thing to keep in mind is that one-dimensional arrays are an efficient way to store and manipulate lists (and later, tables) of data. Quite often, these data will be systematically stored, retrieved, and manipulated. For example, when we enter data, we usually intend to store the items in ascending order (1st, 2nd, and so forth). Similarly, if we add all the data we usually add them in a systematic way (1st + 2nd+ 3rd and so forth). Because of the organized way in which we handle the data, the process is an ideal candidate for control by loops. Therefore, you will find that arrays and loops are almost inseparable. Chances are that if you are using an array, you will be using loops.

EXAMPLE 6.4

Sigma notation (Σ) is used very frequently in engineering, science, and mathematics as a shorthand notation. So we will explore this subject in considerable detail in this and subsequent examples. Recall that sigma notation indicates the sum of the individual elements of the subscripted expression is to be computed. Here is a simple example:

$$a = \sum_{i=1}^{i=100} y_i$$

This expression represents the sum of all the elements stored in the subscripted variable y and the statement stores the result in a. We add one element of the array at a time, and systematically change the subscript from $i=1$ to $i=100$. We implement this in Fortran with a DO loop (we leave out the input statements since we haven't discussed I/O of arrays yet):

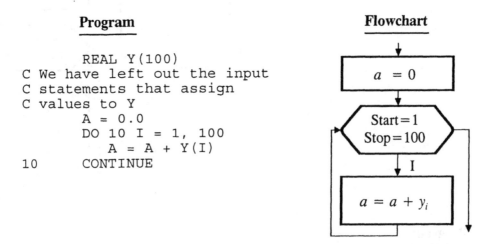

```
        Program

        REAL Y(100)
C We have left out the input
C statements that assign
C values to Y
        A = 0.0
        DO 10 I = 1, 100
          A = A + Y(I)
10      CONTINUE
```

The DO 10 loop takes each element of the array and adds it to the running total. For example, when I=1, Y(I) or Y(1) is added, and when I=2, Y(2) is added, and so forth. An important thing to note is that the subscript of the array is also the loop control variable.

EXAMPLE 6.5

Create a program that reads in a list of numbers from the terminal, calculates the average, and finally prints a list of the individual deviations of each number from the average. The deviation is the difference between the number and the average. Assume a maximum of 100 numbers will be entered.

To solve this problem, we will use two arrays: X and DEV. The X array will store the numbers as we enter them. Once all the numbers are entered, we will be able to compute the average. Finally, we can then compute the deviations by subtracting the average value from each of the input numbers. Note that we have to save the entered numbers so that we can use them a second time for the computation of the deviations. A simple algorithm and flowchart to do this are:

Algorithm

1. Read in number of data points, N
2. SUM = 0.0
3. Loop (1 to N)
   Read in a value and assign to X(I)
   Add X(I) to SUM
4. Compute average (AVG = SUM/N)
5. Loop (1 to N)
   DEV(I) = X(I) − AVG
   Print X(I) and DEV(I)

Flowchart

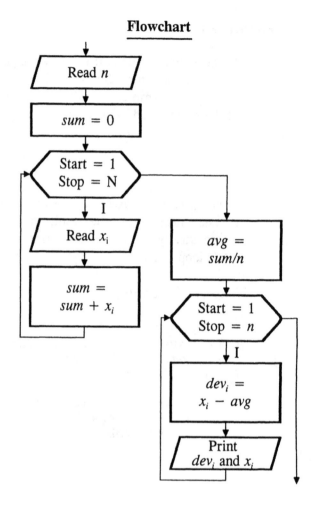

Program

```
      REAL X(100), DEV(100)
C Enter the number of data items for the computation
      PRINT *, 'Number of values (less than 100)?'
      READ *, N
C We will read in one data value at a time and store it in X(I)
      SUM = 0.0
      DO 10 I = 1, N
            READ *, X(I)
            SUM = SUM + X(I)
  10     CONTINUE
      AVG = SUM/N
C Once the average has been computed, we can use it to
C calculate the deviations defined by X(I)-AVG:
      PRINT *, 'Average = ', AVG
      DO 20 I = 1, N
            DEV(I) = X(I) - AVG
            PRINT *, 'NUMBER=', X(I)
            PRINT *, 'DEVIATION=', DEV(I)
  20     CONTINUE
      END
```

Another area where one dimensional arrays are useful is the processing of vectors. Vectors, as you may recall, are quantities that have components. Force, for example, is a vector that has components in three directions.

EXAMPLE 6.6

The *dot product z* of two vectors *a* and *b* is defined by:

$$z = \vec{a} \odot \vec{b} = \sum_{i=1}^{i=3} a_i b_i$$

We start by noting that the summation process can be implemented with a single DO loop as shown in the previous example. Inside the loop, we will add the product of the appropriate components of each vector. For example, for the two vectors $a = (1.2, 3.5, 4.1)$ and $b = (2.0, 5.1, -1.1)$, the dot product is given by $1.2 \times 2.0 + 3.5 \times 5.1 + 4.1 \times (-1.1) = 2.4 + 17.85 - 4.51 = 15.74$. The algorithm for doing this is:

Algorithm

1. Z = 0.0
2. Loop (1 to 3)
   Read A_I and B_I
   Add $A_I \times B_I$ to Z
3. Print Z

Flowchart

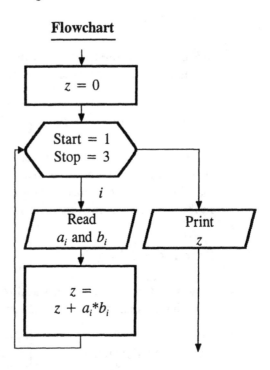

Program

```
C The two vectors A and B each contain 3 components. So
C we declare each to be a one-dimensional array with 3 elements.
      REAL A(3), B(3)
      Z = 0.0
C Inside the following loop, we read in the components of each
C vector and perform the required summation of the products.
      DO 10 I = 1, 3
          READ *, A(I), B(I)
          Z = Z + A(I) * B(I)
   10     CONTINUE
      PRINT*, 'Dot Product = ', Z
      END
```

Another common application of the one-dimensional array is to process a list of numbers, such as sorting in ascending order. We give here one example of such a sorting process.

EXAMPLE 6.7

A common application is to take a list of numbers and put them into ascending or descending order. For example, if you had a list such as 7, 3, 2, 6, 9, 0 and put it into ascending order, the list becomes 0, 2, 3, 6, 7, 9. One of the simplest methods to do this is the *min–max* sort. It works by searching all of the elements in a list for the minimum value. The values at the minimum value location and the first location are then swapped. Now the first element has the minimum value; the program next searches element 2 through the end of the list for the smallest value and then swaps them. This process is repeated until the entire list has been sorted.

To demonstrate how this works, consider the following list and watch how the numbers swap after each search:

Starting Values	7	3	2	6	9	0

We assume that the minimum value is in the first position. But, as we search through the list, we find the smallest value is in the sixth position. So, we switch the first and sixth values:

Swap 1st and 6th values	0	3	2	6	9	7

Now we start the search at the second position (since we know that the first position has the smallest value). We assume that the minimum value is in the second position. But, we find that the value in the third position is smallest (in the shortened list), so we swap the values in the second and third positions:

Swap 2nd and 3rd values	0	2	3	6	9	7

Now we start the search at the third position, assuming that its value is the smallest. This time the assumption is correct, so we do nothing:

Leave 3rd value alone	0	2	3	6	9	7

Now we start the search at the fourth position, assuming that its value is the smallest. Once again, the assumption is correct, so we do nothing:

Leave 4th value alone	0	2	3	6	9	7

Next, we start at the fifth position, and we find that we must swap the fifth and sixth values:

Swap 5th and 6th values	0	2	3	6	7	9

Flowchart

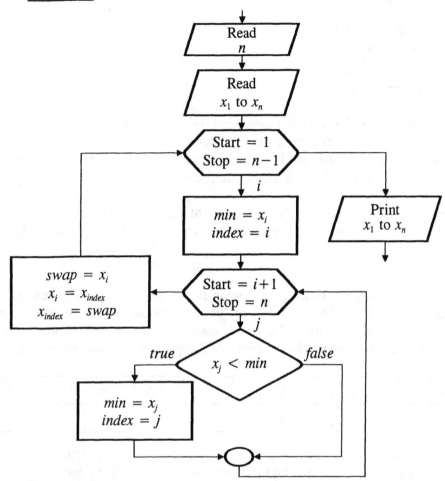

Program

```
      REAL X(100)
      PRINT *, 'How many numbers?'
C Input N values into X(1) to X(N)
      READ *, N
      DO 10 I = 1, N
        READ *, X(I)
 10     CONTINUE
C The DO 30 loop continues until all the values are sorted
      DO 30 I = 1, N-1
        XMIN = X(I)
        INDEX = I
C The Do 20 loop locates the position of the smallest value
        DO 20 J = I+1, N
          IF (X(J) .LT. XMIN) THEN
            XMIN = X(J)
            INDEX = J
          END IF
 20       CONTINUE
C The following section swaps the value in X(I) and the
```

(Program continues on next page)

```
C smallest value located in X(INDEX)
      SWAP = X(I)
      X(I) = X(INDEX)
      X(INDEX) = SWAP
  30  CONTINUE
      DO 40 I = 1, N
      PRINT *, X(I)
  40  CONTINUE
```

For convenience, we have used a shorthand notation in the flowchart when we entered or printed the data. Instead of using a loop to enter all the values, we have condensed this block of instructions into a single read instruction, such as Read X_1 to X_N. As we will see shortly, Fortran has an instruction corresponding to this shorthand notation.

Another common application is the compiling of statistics from a list of data. For example, we may want to know how many students achieved scores of 90 to 100 on an examination.

EXAMPLE 6.8

A data set contains a list of integers ranging from 0 to 10 where the same number may be entered multiple times. The following program counts the number of occurrences for each value. We will create an array C(I) that contains a count of each number as it is entered. Thus, C(0) represents the number of zeros, C(1) represents the number of ones, and so forth:

C(0)	C(1)	C(2)	C(3)	C(4)	C(5)	C(6)	C(7)	C(8)	C(9)	C(10)

When we read in a value, we will put that number into the appropriate bin. For example, if we read in the number 5, we would increase the count in C(5) by one:

C(0)	C(1)	C(2)	C(3)	C(4)	C(5)	C(6)	C(7)	C(8)	C(9)	C(10)
					1					

Flowchart

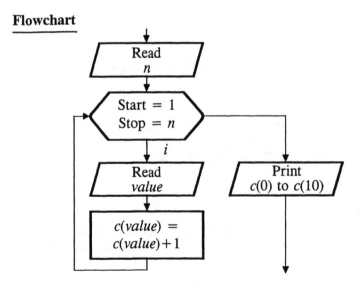

Program

```
C When we declare the array C, it makes sense to declare it to
C start at C(0). Note also that VALUE must be declared as an
C integer since we will be using it later as a subscript to store
C a value in C(VALUE)
        INTEGER C(0:10), VALUE
        PRINT *, 'Number of values?'
        READ *, N
C First, we initialize all elements of C to zero.
        DO 10 I = 0, 10
          C(I) = 0
  10    CONTINUE
C Read in a value and increment the appropriate list position.
        DO 20 I = 1, N
          READ *, VALUE
          C(VALUE) = C(VALUE) + 1
  20    CONTINUE
C Print out the results
        DO 40 I = 0, 10
          PRINT *, 'Number of', I, '''s were', C(I)
  40    CONTINUE
        END
```

This example utilizes an array as a group of counters. Because the values read in were integers, it was possible to use these values to select the counter. COUNT(0) was used to keep track of the zeros, for example. By selecting the counter based on the value, the process was straightforward. Because this example included values starting at 0, this was a good opportunity to take advantage of the special index range feature of Fortran for arrays. That is why the declaration statement (INTEGER C(0:10)) had the array start at element 0.

The previous examples were concerned with manipulation of lists. But, we can also use lists to look up data. For example, we may wish to find a certain number within a long list of data.

EXAMPLE 6.9

The following example illustrates a search algorithm for locating a value in a list. The program requires that the entered list be sorted in ascending order. The process to locate a given number will be to read down the list until the value being sought is located. Once found, the index value (or position within the list) will be reported. As an example, assume that we have the following list of numbers and we are searching for a specific value of 19

Search value = 19	−4	5	11	13	19	20	41	52

When the search is completed, we find that the search value (19) is in the fifth position.

The reason that the list must be in ascending order (such as that shown in Example 6.7) is that we will stop the search once any value exceeds the search value. If the list were not in ascending order, then we would have to test every number before we say that the number is not in the list. By requiring the list to be in ascending order, the search is more rapid.

Program   **Flowchart**

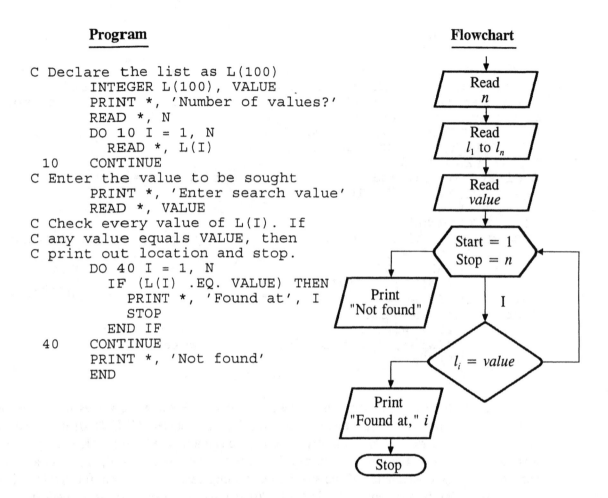

```
C Declare the list as L(100)
      INTEGER L(100), VALUE
      PRINT *, 'Number of values?'
      READ *, N
      DO 10 I = 1, N
         READ *, L(I)
   10    CONTINUE
C Enter the value to be sought
      PRINT *, 'Enter search value'
      READ *, VALUE
C Check every value of L(I). If
C any value equals VALUE, then
C print out location and stop.
      DO 40 I = 1, N
         IF (L(I) .EQ. VALUE) THEN
            PRINT *, 'Found at', I
            STOP
         END IF
   40    CONTINUE
      PRINT *, 'Not found'
      END
```

This process is inefficient since we repeatedly search through the same list of numbers. A much more efficient method known as the *binary* search is outlined in the following example.

EXAMPLE 6.10

The *binary search* method works by bracketing a group of values within a list that is in ascending order. By comparing the search value with the value in the middle of the list, it is possible to determine which half of the list contains the value. This process is then repeated on the narrowed portion of the list until the value is found or the range goes to 0.

To demonstrate how this works, consider the following list already in ascending order:

Starting values

2	9	11	23	49

We start by comparing the search value (*e.g.*, 23), with the value at the center of the list:

Compare search value (23) with midpoint value

2	9	11	23	49

If the search value (23) is less than the value in this position, then the number is in the lower half of the list; otherwise, it is in the upper half. In this case, the search value (23) is larger than the value in the middle (11), so the search will focus on the second half. We then repeat the process by dividing the remaining numbers into two halves:

Cut search area in half and repeat previous step

		11	23	49

The value in the center of the reduced search area is now equal to the search value (23), so our search stops. The program will then print out that it found the value in the fourth position. If the search area ever goes to zero, then the search number is not in the list.

Flowchart

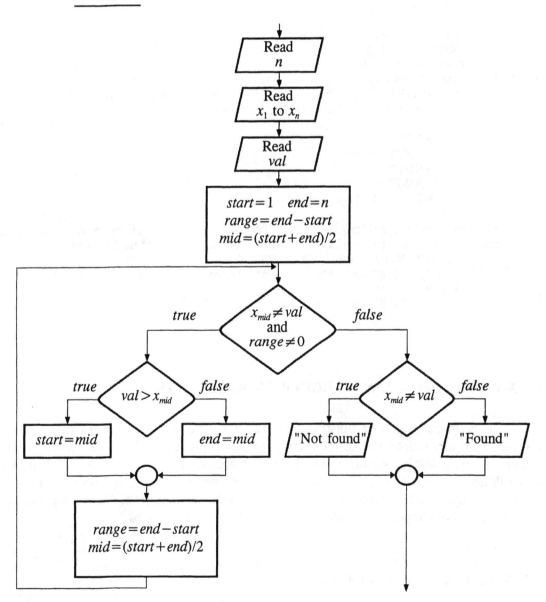

Program

```
        INTEGER X(100)
        INTEGER RANGE
        INTEGER START, END
C The input section
        PRINT *, 'Number of values?'
        READ *, N
        DO 10 I = 1, N
          READ *, X(I)
  10    CONTINUE
C Enter the value to be sought
        PRINT *, 'Enter value'
        READ *, VAL
C Define the range and midpoint
        START = 1
        END = N
        RANGE = END - START
        MID = (START + END)/2
C As long as the value is not found, cut the range in half
C and check which half the value might be in.
        DO WHILE (X(MID) .NE. VAL .AND. RANGE .NE. 0)
          IF (VAL .GT. X(MID)) THEN
            START = MID
          ELSE
            END = MID
          ENDIF
          RANGE = END - START
          MID = (START + END)/2
        END DO
C If the value being sought is not in the middle of the last
C range, then the value is not in the original list.
        IF (X(MID) .NE. VAL) THEN
            PRINT *, VAL, 'not found'
        ELSE
            PRINT *, 'Value at', MID
        ENDIF
        END
```

6.5 TWO-DIMENSIONAL AND HIGHER-ORDER ARRAYS

In the previous section we illustrated several applications of one- dimensional arrays. You can think of the array dimension as the number of subscripts required to locate a value stored in the array. As an example, one-dimensional arrays represent lists of values. All we had to do to locate a desired value was to specify a single index or subscript. Two-dimensional arrays can be thought of as representing a table of information. To select a value from a table, we will need to specify the row and column. Consequently, two subscripts are required.

EXAMPLE 6.11

Consider the following list A and table B:

A
4
7
18

B		
3	–2	30
47	15	0
70	–8	39

Since a list requires only one subscript to locate a value, we can see immediately that A(2) has the value 7. A table, however, requires two subscripts to locate a value. The only question is which subscript (row or column) comes first? Fortran adopts the convention that the <u>row</u> will come first. Thus, B(2,3) has the value 0. Similarly, B(3,2) has the value –8. Note very carefully that B(3,2) is <u>not</u> equal to B(2,3). If we wanted to add the values in the second column, we could do this with B(1,2) + B(2,2) + B(3,2) = 5. As we did when processing one-dimensional arrays, we will use subscripts to process the data contained within an array. But this time, we will need two subscripts.

Processing of two dimensional arrays is very similar to processing of one-dimensional arrays except that there is a second index to worry about. Therefore, you will very often use nested loops. One loop usually controls the row index, while the other loop controls the column index.

EXAMPLE 6.12

The table below shows the result of a survey of the computing experience levels of engineering students. The columns represent the different classes (freshman, sophomore, junior, and senior). The rows represent the experience levels (none, < 1 year, 1–2 years, 2–3 years, and more than 3 years).

	Freshman	Sophomore	Junior	Senior
None	13	5	2	1
Less than 1 year	27	30	20	18
Between 1–2 years	30	32	36	38
Between 2–3 years	16	19	22	25
More than 3 years	7	11	13	14

When the survey questionnaires are passed out, the student is requested to indicate his/her class and indicate his/her class and level of experience using these categories:

Class: 1) freshman   2) sophomore 3) junior   4) senior

Experience: 1) none   2) < 1 yr   3) 1–2 yrs   4) 2–3 yrs   5) >3 yrs

The data are entered as a pair of numbers such as 2, 3 (sophomore, 1–2 years experience). When these numbers are read in, our program will increment the appropriate cell by 1.

Flowchart

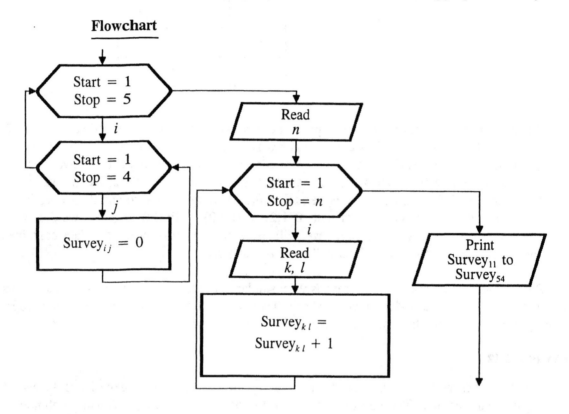

At the beginning of the flowchart is the initialization section that consists of nested loops setting all elements of the array to zero. It is a good idea to do this even if your compiler automatically initializes variables, including arrays, to zero.

In the next section of the flowchart is an input statement to read in the number of survey results. This value (n) is then used to control a counted loop, where a single pair of numbers (k, l) is read in indicating the year and experience level. This pair is then used to increment the appropriate counter by 1.

The final section of the program is the output section, where the two-dimensional array (SURVEY(1, 1) to SURVEY(5, 4)) is sent to the CRT screen. This will actually be implemented with a loop, although we show it here as only a simple I/O instruction.

Program

```
C Declare SURVEY to be a two-dimensional 5 row, 4 column array
      INTEGER SURVEY(5,4), TOTAL
C Initialize the entire array to zero.
      DO 10 I = 1, 5
         DO 10 J = 1, 4
            SURVEY(I,J) = 0
10    CONTINUE
      PRINT *, 'Number of Responses?'
      READ *, N
```

(Program continues on next page)

```
C As each response is read in, increment the appropriate
C position in the table.
      DO 20 I = 1, N
         PRINT *, 'Enter year and experience level'
         READ *, K, L
         SURVEY(K,L) = SURVEY(K,L) + 1
20       CONTINUE
C Print out the survey results
      PRINT *, 'Results'
      DO 30 I = 1, 5
         PRINT *, SURVEY(I,1), SURVEY(I,2), SURVEY(I,3),
     1               SURVEY(I,4)
30       CONTINUE
              ⋮
```

(More program to follow)

⋮

Once the above table has been generated with this program, we can begin to manipulate the data to answer such questions as "How many freshmen are nonprogrammers?" or "What percentage of the students are expert programmers (> 3 years experience)?" The following example illustrates how to manipulate values in the array to get such answers.

EXAMPLE 6.13

After a table of data has been created, we can compile statistics about the data by using some of the operations already discussed. This time, however, we need to worry about two indices. So very often we will need to have nested loops. To demonstrate this, we will construct program segments to answer the following questions based on the program in Example 6.12.

a) How many freshmen are nonprogrammers? Freshmen nonprogrammers have year equal to 1 and experience level equal to 1. Thus, all we need do is look at SURVEY(1,1). You could do this with a simple PRINT statement such as:

```
PRINT *,'Number of freshmen nonprogrammers=',SURVEY(1,1)
```

b) How many sophomores are experienced programmers with 1 year or more of programming experience? Sophomores with 1–2 years of experience, 2–3 years of experience, and more than 3 years of experience would fall into this category. Thus, year is equal to 2, and experience levels of 3, 4, and 5 are needed. One way to compute this total is:

```
TOTAL = SURVEY(3,2) + SURVEY(4,2) + SURVEY(5,2)
```

Notice that one of the indices remains fixed, while the other index cycles through a range of values in a systematic manner (3, 4, 5 in this example). Thus, this problem is a candidate for a DO loop, where we will replace the second index (indicating the column) with a loop control variable:

```
TOTAL = 0
DO 10 I = 3, 5
```

```
                    TOTAL = TOTAL + SURVEY(I,2)
    10          CONTINUE
```

In this example, the DO loop actually results in a lengthier program segment. Yet, it may be more desirable. What if the table had contained more than three entries? The DO loop approach would have been much easier to construct and debug than the simple assignment statement.

c)   How many total nonprogrammers were in the survey? This would be the sum of nonprogramming freshmen, sophomores, juniors, and seniors:

```
SUM=SURVEY(1,1) + SURVEY(1,2) + SURVEY(1,3) + SURVEY(1,4)
```

We can also write this with a loop:

```
        SUM = 0
        DO 10 J = 1, 4
            SUM = SUM + SURVEY(1,J)
    10      CONTINUE
```

d)   How many students participated in the survey? To determine this, we would add up all the values in the array. The most direct way to do this is with:

```
TOT = SURVEY(1,1)+SURVEY(1,2)+SURVEY(1,3)+SURVEY(1,4)+
      SURVEY(2,1)+SURVEY(2,2)+SURVEY(2,3)+SURVEY(2,4)+
      SURVEY(3,1)+SURVEY(3,2)+SURVEY(3,3)+SURVEY(3,4)+
      SURVEY(4,1)+SURVEY(4,2)+SURVEY(4,3)+SURVEY(4,4)+
      SURVEY(5,1)+SURVEY(5,2)+SURVEY(5,3)+SURVEY(5,4)
```

Clearly, this approach has gotten out of hand. So nested loops are better:

```
        TOT = 0.0
        DO 10 I = 1, 5
            DO 10 J = 1, 4
                TOT = TOT + SURVEY(I,J)
    10      CONTINUE
```

Another common area where arrays are useful is the processing of matrices, such as multiplication of a matrix by a scalar, or addition or multiplication of two matrices. We will think of a matrix as a table in which we can locate a data item by referring to its row and column in the matrix, just as we did with tables of data.

EXAMPLE 6.14

The process of multiplying two arrays together can be expressed using sigma notation.

$$c_{ij} = \sum_k a_{ik} b_{kj}$$

This expression indicates how to calculate each entry in the product array c. Note that the number of columns in the a array must match the number of rows in the b array. The resulting array will have the same number of rows as a and the same number of columns as b. To illustrate how this summation works, let's compute the term c_{12}. This will require the summation of the individual products of $a_{1k}b_{k2}$. Assume for example, that we have the a matrix of size 3×2 and the b matrix of size 2×3, which when multiplied produce a c matrix with 3 columns and 3 rows:

$$a = \begin{bmatrix} 1 & 2 \\ 4 & 6 \\ 1 & 0 \end{bmatrix} \qquad b = \begin{bmatrix} 2 & 1 & 4 \\ 3 & 0 & 7 \end{bmatrix}$$

The desired term c_{12} would be $a_{11}b_{12} + a_{12}b_{22}$ or $(1)(1) + (2)(0) = 1$. In a similar way, we can generate all other elements in c, which will have three rows and three columns:

$$c = \begin{bmatrix} (1)(2) + (2)(3) & (1)(1) + (2)(0) & (1)(4) + (2)(7) \\ (4)(2) + (6)(3) & (4)(1) + (6)(0) & (4)(4) + (6)(7) \\ (1)(2) + (0)(3) & (1)(1) + (0)(0) & (1)(4) + (0)(7) \end{bmatrix}$$

Before you look at the flowchart and program, be sure you can follow how each of the elements of C is generated. See if you can duplicate the results given above.

Program	**Flowchart**

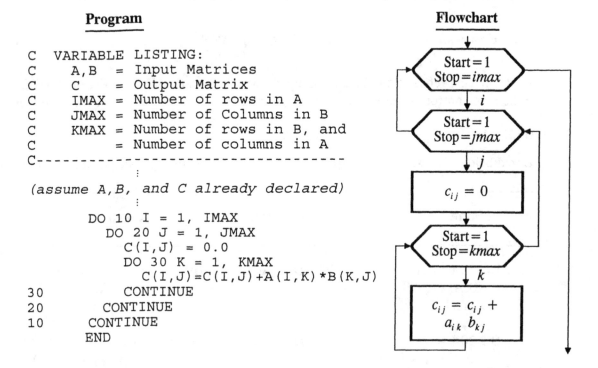

```
C   VARIABLE LISTING:
C     A,B  = Input Matrices
C     C    = Output Matrix
C     IMAX = Number of rows in A
C     JMAX = Number of Columns in B
C     KMAX = Number of rows in B, and
C          = Number of columns in A
C---------------------------------
          ⋮
    (assume A,B, and C already declared)
          ⋮
          DO 10 I = 1, IMAX
            DO 20 J = 1, JMAX
              C(I,J) = 0.0
              DO 30 K = 1, KMAX
                C(I,J)=C(I,J)+A(I,K)*B(K,J)
30            CONTINUE
20          CONTINUE
10        CONTINUE
          END
```

The innermost loop of this example multiplies the ith row of a by the jth column of b. After summation of the products, the result is placed into C(I,J). Note that we first initialized each element of C to zero.

6.6 INPUT AND OUTPUT OF ARRAYS

The simplest way to print arrays is to refer to each element individually, just as you would with a single valued variable (scalar). For example, if we wished to print out the first two elements of the array X, we could do it with this command:

```
PRINT *,X(1),X(2)
```

While this is the simplest way, it is impractical if we wish to print out a long list of array elements. Instead, we more often use a loop with the input or output statement to simplify the process:

```
        DO 10 I = 1, 100
            PRINT *, A(I)
  10     CONTINUE
```

While this approach is more versatile, it does pose a problem. Whenever the computer encounters a PRINT statement, a new line is created. The preceding example would generate 100 lines of output, for example! To solve this problem, we use a special form of the DO loop known as the *implied DO loop*, whose use is limited to input/output statements and the DATA statement presented in the next section. We cannot use this special form of the DO loop for arithmetic processing. The general form of an implied DO loop to print out arrays is as follows:

I/O Command (array(LCV), LCV = Start, Stop, Step)

I/O Command refers to any input/output statement such as READ, PRINT, or WRITE. The LCV is the loop control variable, and start, stop, and step set up the values for the loop control.

EXAMPLE 6.15

Listed below are examples of explicit forms of I/O and their equivalent implied DO loops:

Explicit Form	Implied Form	Comments
DO 10 I=1, 10 READ *, A(I) 10 CONTINUE	READ *,(A(I),I=1, 10)	Reads 10 values into array A.
DO 20 I=1, 10 READ *, X(I), Y(I) 20 CONTINUE	READ *,(X(I),Y(I),I=1, 10)	Reads in 10 sets of data as (x_1, y_1), (x_2, y_2), through (x_{10}, y_{10}).

(Table continues on next page)

Explicit Form	Implied Form	Comments
DO 30 I = 1,20 DO 30 J = 1,10 READ*, Z(I,J) 30 CONTINUE	READ *,((Z(I,J),J=1,10),I=1,20)	An implied DO loop within another implied DO loop is permitted.

You must understand that the implied DO loop prints out all of the array variables to a single line unless formatting is used to control the output appearance. But with the READ statement, the computer will attempt to read in the values from the <u>current</u> line. If all of the required data are not present on a single line, then the next line of input is used. Thus, if an input statement for an array uses an implied DO loop to read in 100 values, those 100 values can appear on a single line or 100 lines with a single value per line.

When printing output, however, you must be more careful since you typically want the data to have a style that is easily readable. So you must take care in using implied DO loops with output of arrays. Among the things you must consider are the number of data items per line and vertical alignment, in addition to conventional formatting instructions.

EXAMPLE 6.16

For the following example, A is a one-dimensional integer array of 10 elements and B is a 3×3 two-dimensional integer array. The value assigned to each element is:

A	1	2	3	4	5	6	7	8	9	10

B

1	2	3
4	5	6
7	8	9

Below are examples of how the output would appear for a variety of implied DO loops:

Program Segment	Output
a) PRINT *, A(1), A(2), A(3)	1 2 3
b) PRINT *, (A(I), I = 1, 3)	1 2 3
c) PRINT *, (A(I), I = 2, 8, 2)	2 4 6 8

(Table continues on next page)

Program Segment		Output
d)	PRINT *, ((B(I,J), I=1,3), J=1,3)	1 4 7 2 5 8 3 6 9
e)	PRINT *,B	1 4 7 2 5 8 3 6 9
f)	PRINT *, ((B(I,J), J=1,3), I=1,3)	1 2 3 4 5 6 7 8 9
g)	DO 10 I=1, 3	1 2 3
	PRINT *, (B(I,J), J=1,3)	4 5 6
10	CONTINUE	7 8 9
h)	PRINT *, ('+', I=1,10)	+ + + + + + + + + +

Example "a" illustrates the method that we have been using up to this point to output array elements, whereas example "b" performs the same task using an implied DO loop. Note that even in this simple example of printing out only 3 array elements, the implied DO loop requires less typing. The savings are more significant when printing larger numbers of elements.

Example "c" illustrates how to use the loop control variable to print the even-numbered elements from element 2 to element 8. Example "d" illustrates how to print a two-dimensional array using nested implied DO loops. In this example the first subscript represents the most rapidly changing one. Thus, the first elements printed are B(1,1), B(2,1), and B(3,1). Only when I runs through all its values does the value of J change. Example "e" illustrates Fortran's default output of an array. In this case, the computer will print the array elements by columns, starting with column 1. These two examples ("d" and "e") are equivalent, if the two dimensional array is declared to be a 3 × 3 array. Example "f" illustrates the effect of making the second subscript change more rapidly than the first. The result is that the computer prints the array by rows. The only problem with examples "d," "e," and "f" is that the computer prints all of the array elements on a single line. We solve this problem in example "g" where we combine an explicit DO loop with an implied one. Each time the computer encounters a PRINT statement, it starts a new output line.

The final example, "h," illustrates that implied DO loops do not have to be used only with arrays. By placing a character constant (+) within the implied DO loop, ten "+" characters were produced. This can be used as a way of creating special effects such as an underlined table heading.

EXAMPLE 6.17

The following program will print out a crude graph of a sine wave over a range of 0 to 2π.

```
DO 10 I = 0, 20
    X = I*2*3.1416/20.
    Y = SIN(X)
    N = NINT(30+Y*30+1)
    PRINT *, ('*', J = 1, N)
10    CONTINUE
    END
```

The loop calculates the position of the curve at 21 different positions. Inside the loop, x will vary between 0 and 2π, and y represents the value of sin(x) for each value. The purpose of n is to scale the sine wave so that it will fit conveniently on your screen. Note that the minimum and maximum values of y are -1 and 1 respectively. Thus, n will be between 1 and 61. So in the next program line, when we use n to print out a string of stars on the screen, the stars will be between columns 1 and 61, which should easily fit on your screen. Run this program on your computer to see the effect.

6.7 FORMATTING OF ARRAY OUTPUT

Because of the large quantities of data that arrays can output, formatting requires careful planning and relies very heavily on the use of the repeat specifier. Recall that repeat specifiers (see example 3.15) allow you to repeat a section of formatting instructions without having to explicitly retype it.

EXAMPLE 6.18

In the following example, A is a one-dimensional real array of 10 elements and B is a 3×3 two dimensional real array. The value assigned to each element is:

A	1	2	3	4	5	6	7	8	9	10

B	1	2	3
	4	5	6
	7	8	9

Below are several examples of how the output would appear for a variety of formatted implied DO loops:

Program Segment	Output
a) PRINT 10, (A(I), I = 1, 5) 10 FORMAT (' ', 5(F4.1, 1X))	1.0 2.0 3.0 4.0 5.0
b) PRINT 10, (A(I), I = 1, 5) 10 FORMAT (' ', 20(F4.1, 1X))	1.0 2.0 3.0 4.0 5.0
c) PRINT 10, (A(I), I = 1, 10) 10 FORMAT (' ', 5(F4.1, 1X))	1.0 2.0 3.0 4.0 5.0 6.0 7.0 8.0 9.0 10.0

(Table continues on next page)

Program Segment	Output
d) PRINT 10, ((B(I,J), J=1, 3), I=1, 3) 10 FORMAT (' B:', 3(/, 1X, 3(F4.1, 1X)))	B: 1.0 2.0 3.0 4.0 5.0 6.0 7.0 8.0 9.0
e) PRINT 10, ((B(I,J), J=1, 3), I=1, 3) 10 FORMAT (' ', 3(F4.1, 1X))	1.0 2.0 3.0 4.0 5.0 6.0 7.0 8.0 9.0

f)   N = 3
      DO 20 I = 1, N
        PRINT 10, (B(I,J), J = 1, N)
     10   FORMAT (' ', 100(F4.1, 1X))
     20   CONTINUE
	1.0 2.0 3.0
	 4.0 5.0 6.0
	 7.0 8.0 9.0

The first example is a straightforward use of the repeat specifier. In the FORMAT statement, 5(F4.1, 1X) repeats the descriptors "F4.1, 1X" five times. In effect, the FORMAT statement in example "a" is the same as FORMAT(' ', F4.1, 1X, F4.1, 1X, F4.1, 1X, F4.1, 1X, F4.1, 1X). Example "b" illustrates what happens if there are more formatting instructions than actually needed. The result is that the unused formatting is simply ignored. Example "c" illustrates the reverse problem — an insufficient number of edit descriptors. In this case, the output is printed until all the formatting instructions are used. Then the output continues on a new line and the format instructions are reused. For example "c" this results in printing two rows of five columns each, even though the array is one-dimensional.

Example "d" demonstrates the use of the repeat specifiers and the end-of-line descriptor (/). When using the end-of-line descriptor to generate output on a new line, remember to include a carriage-control character. Most often, this is most conveniently done with the 1X edit descriptor. Example "e" illustrates how to take advantage of the fact that when formatting runs out, the computer repeats the edit descriptors on a new line. This allows for a simple format statement to print out a two-dimensional array. The only drawback of this approach is that you must know the size in advance, and you cannot change it without changing your FORMAT statement. Example "f" illustrates a means around this by combining explicit and implicit DO loops.

6.8 THE PARAMETER AND DATA STATEMENTS

The PARAMETER statement is an easy way of creating *named constants*. Named constants have elements of both constants and variables. On the one hand they are constants whose value cannot change under any circumstances, and on the other hand they are given names like a variable. A good example would be PI. Once we assign a value to the named constant PI with the PARAMETER statement, its value cannot change. Any attempt to change a named constant results in an error during compilation.

One of the most common uses of the named constant is to declare arrays whose size is likely to change. The advantage of this approach is that you can make many changes throughout the program by making a single change in the named constant. The general form of the PARAMETER statement is:

PARAMETER (*variable1* = *value, variable2* = *value,* . . .)

Each named constant is given its value inside the parentheses following the PARAMETER key word. Once a name is specified here, it cannot be used as a conventional variable within the program, and its value <u>cannot</u> be reassigned by an assignment statement, function, or READ statement.

EXAMPLE 6.19

Here is an example of a PARAMETER statement that allows you to declare several arrays simultaneously. First, suppose you write a program to process 100 data points with the following array declarations (without the PARAMETER):

```
REAL VOLTS(100), I(100), IMPED(100), RESIST(100)
INTEGER TIME(100), COUNTS(100), SIZE(100)
```

If you use this approach and now wish to change the program to allow for 1000 data points, you must use your editor to change each array dimension from 100 to 1000. An easier way is to use the PARAMETER statement when you first set up your program to define a named constant such as N below:

```
PARAMETER (N = 100)
REAL VOLTS(N), I(N), IMPED(N), RESIST(N)
INTEGER TIME(N), COUNTS(N), SIZE(N)
```

Now, when you want to increase the size of the arrays, you need only change a single PARAMETER statement. This method is especially useful for changing values scattered throughout your program. For example, you might have declaration statements for arrays and DO loop variables to process the data, and I/O statements with implied DO loops.

```
PARAMETER (N = 100)
REAL VOLTS(N), I(N), IMPED(N), RESIST(N)
INTEGER TIME(N), COUNTS(N), SIZE(N)
      ⋮
READ *, (VOLTS(K), K = 1, N)
      ⋮
DO 10 L = 1, N
      ⋮
```

```
10     CONTINUE
       ⋮
       PRINT *, (IMPED(M), M = 1, N)
       END
```

Another useful structure is the DATA statement. It is used to assign <u>initial</u> values to a variable. Whereas the PARAMETER statement assigns <u>permanent</u> values, the DATA statement assigns <u>temporary</u> values. DATA statements are most useful to replace READ statements at the beginning of a program; they save you the trouble of having to type in repetitive data every time you run a program. The general form of the DATA statement is:

DATA *variable1, variable2, . . . / value1, value2, . . . /*

The list of variables after the DATA statement can include either single-valued variables or arrays. Values to be assigned to these variables are contained within the slash (/) marks and will be assigned to the corresponding variable by virtue of its *position* within the list. The third value, for example, will be assigned to the third variable, and so forth.

If arrays are specified within the DATA variable list, we may use an implied DO loop, just as we did with the input statements:

DATA *(array(subscript), subscript = start, stop, step) /value1, value2, . . ./*

The implied DO loop will specify the array elements to receive the values listed inside the slashes.

EXAMPLE 6.20

a)   One common area where we use DATA statements is to assign initial values to a list of single-valued variables:

<u>Without DATA Statements:</u>

```
VOLTS = 5.3
RESIST = 1000.0
CAPICT = 0.000035
```

<u>With DATA Statements:</u>

```
DATA VOLTS, RESIST, CAPICT /5.3, 1000.0, 0.000035/
```

b)   Quite often when we use DATA statements, several of the variables may receive the same value. In this case, we have a shorthand notation

<u>Long Way:</u>

```
DATA A, B, C, D, E, F /1.0, 1.0, 1.0, 1.0, 1.0, 1.0/
```

Short Way:

```
DATA A, B, C, D, E, F /6*1.0/
```

The star (*) here does not imply multiplication. Instead, it indicates that the number which follows is to be repeated the indicated number of times.

c)   DATA statements are particularly useful when initializing arrays:

```
REAL A(100)
DATA (A(I), I = 1, 100) /50*0.0, 50*1.0/
```

These statements assign 0.0 to the first 50 elements of A, and 1.0 to the last 50 elements.

d)   The implied DO loop may not be necessary if all elements are to be assigned. Here is a shorter way of writing example c):

```
REAL A(100)
DATA A /50*0.0,50*1.0/
```

If the array is a two-dimensional array, the data values will be assigned by columns if you use this simple form:

```
REAL B(3, 3)
DATA B /1.0, 2.0, 3.0, 4.0, 5.0, 6.0, 7.0, 8.0, 9.0/
```

This will result in the following assignments:

B:		
1.0	4.0	7.0
2.0	5.0	8.0
3.0	6.0	9.0

e)   If you wish to assign the data by rows instead of by columns, you must use the full implied DO loop:

```
REAL A(10, 10)
DATA ((A(I,J), J=1,10), I=1,10)/50*10.0, 50*100.0/
```

The first five rows are filled with 10.0's and the remaining five are filled with 100.0's. If the implied DO loops were not present, then this array would have been filled differently (the first five columns would have 10.0's and the remaining columns would have 100.0's). When in doubt about how the data will be assigned, use an implied DO loop.

6.9 DEBUGGING TIPS

One of the topics presented in this section was the use of the PARAMETER statement when declaring an array. This statement is an ideal tool for debugging purposes where we would like to have the ability to rescale the program to something more manageable. After all, debugging a program with a 5 × 5 array is a much easier task than debugging a program with a 100 × 100 array. Here are a few suggestions about how to debug arrays containing arrays:

SUGGESTION #1:   Whenever you declare an array, use a PARAMETER statement.

SUGGESTION #2:   When you are initially testing your program, use small arrays.

Tracing arrays can be very time consuming. With a single declaration statement it is easy to create thousands of storage locations with a single variable. By reducing the size of the problem to something manageable (suggestion #2), it is possible to perform a manual trace as described in earlier chapters.

Finally, learn how your compiler deals with array errors. For example, what happens if you go beyond the limit of a subscript? Does your program stop, or do you get erroneous data? This type of error can be very difficult to find, particularly if you are not looking for it. So write a small program (five lines or less), and deliberately make errors to go outside the bounds of the arrays that you have declared in order to find out what happens.

SUGGESTION #3:   Test the limits of your compiler to learn how your compiler deals
                   with array errors such as "subscript out of bounds" or a real value
                   for a subscript.

Proper declaration of arrays is very important. If the array is improperly declared, errors will propagate through your program, producing dozens of error messages.

SUGGESTION #4:   If you encounter a large number of errors on every line where you
                   use a particular array, then check your declaration statements.

Solved Problems

6.1   Locate the syntax errors in the following program segments:

(a)   `INTEGER I`
        `REAL ARRAY(I)`

(b)   `REAL A(1,10)`
        `DO 10 I=1, 10`
        `    A(I)=I**2`
`10   CONTINUE`

(c)   `INTEGER I(10)`
        `DO 10 I=0, 9`
        `    I(I+1)=I**2`
`10   CONTINUE`

(d)   `REAL A[10]`
        `DO 10 I=0, 9`
        `    A(I+1)=I**2`
`10   CONTINUE`

(a) ARRAY(I) does not indicate the SIZE.

(b) A is a two-dimensional array, but inside the loop is used as a one-dimensional array.

(c) I is being referred to both as an array and as a scalar (DO loop).

(d) Declaration statement uses square brackets instead of the required parentheses.

6.2 Write program segments to accomplish the following:

(a) Add the third and fourth elements of the array X.

(b) Determine the average of the ten elements of an array Y.

(c) If the 10 elements of the x, y, and z subscripted variables are defined by:

$$y_i = i + 3$$
$$x_i = i$$
$$z_i = x_i + y_i$$

determine the following:

$$a_i = [\sum_{j=1}^{3} (x_j)(y_j)(z_j)]^{0.5}$$

(d) If the elements of the one-dimensional arrays X and Y are defined as $X(I) = 3*I-15$ and $Y(I) = 2*I+5$, write a program segment to print the results of $X(I) + Y(I)$ for all values of I up to IMAX.

(a)   `SUM=X(3)+X(4)`

(b)   ```
SUM=0.0
DO 10 I=1, 10
  SUM=SUM+Y(I)
10 CONTINUE
AVG=SUM/10.0
```

(c)         ```
DO 10 I=1, 10
  X(I)=I
  Y(I)=I+3
  Z(I)=X(I)+Y(I)
10 CONTINUE
DO 20 I=1, 10
  PROD=0.0
  DO 30 J=1, 3
    PROD=PROD+X(J)*Y(J)*Z(J)
30   CONTINUE
  A(I)=PROD
20 CONTINUE
```

(d)   ```
DO 10 I=1, IMAX
  X(I)=3*I-15
  Y(I)=2*I+5
10 CONTINUE
DO 20 I=1, IMAX
  PRINT *, X(I)+Y(I)
20 CONTINUE
```

**6.3**  Write program segments to accomplish the following. Assume all arrays are 10 × 10 unless specified otherwise.

(a) Set the corresponding elements of B(I, J) equal to C(I, J) if A(I, J) > 0. Otherwise, set B(I, J) equal to 0.
```

(b) Create a 4 × 5 array whose elements are created by copying elements from every third row and every second column from a larger 10 × 10 array.

(c) Declare an integer two-dimensional array with three rows and three columns, and set all the values in the first column to 1, all the values in the second column to 2, and all the values in the third column to 3.

(d) Declare a real one-dimensional array with five elements and initialize the array to the values (1, 0, 1, 0, 1).

```
(a)     REAL A(10, 10), B(10, 10), C(10, 10)
        READ *, ((A(I,J), I=1,10), J=1,10)
        READ *, ((C(I,J), I=1,10), J=1,10)
        DO 10 I = 1, 10
          DO 10 J = 1, 10
            IF(A(I,J) .GT. 0.0) THEN
              B(I,J) = C(I,J)
            ELSE
              B(I,J) = 0.0
            ENDIF
   10   CONTINUE
(b)     REAL A(10,10), B(4,5)
        READ *, ((A(I,J), I=1,10), J=1,10))
        DO 10 I = 1, 4
          DO 10 J = 1, 5
            B(I,J) = A(3*(I-1)+1, 2*(J-1+1)
   10   CONTINUE
(c)     INTEGER NUM(3,3)
        DO 10 I = 1, 3
          DO 10 J = 1, 3
            NUM(I,J) = J
   10   CONTINUE
(d)     REAL A(5)
        DATA A/1.0, 0.0, 1.0, 0.0, 1.0/
```

6.4   The standard deviation σ of a series of numbers is determined by the following:

$$\sigma = [\frac{1}{n-1} \sum_{i=1}^{i=n} (x_i - \bar{x})^2]^{0.5}$$

where n = number of samples
        x_i = list of data values
        $\bar{x}$ = average of data items.

Write a program to read in a list of numbers (up to 100) and calculate σ.

```
        REAL X(100)
        PRINT *, 'Number of Points?'
        READ *, N
        READ *, (X(I), I = 1, N)
```

```
              SUM = 0.0
              DO 10 I = 1, N
                 SUM = SUM + X(I)
        10    CONTINUE
              XBAR = SUM/N
              SUM = 0.0
              DO 20 I = 1, N
                 SUM = SUM + (X(I)-XBAR)**2
        20    CONTINUE
              STD = SQRT(SUM/(N-1))
              PRINT *, 'Std Deviation is', STD
              END
```

6.5   Write separate programs to perform the following tasks on the arrays A(100, 100) and B(100, 100):

(a) Sum any column.
(b) Sum the entire two-dimensional array.
(c) Find the minimum in a two-dimensional array.
(d) Subtract a scalar value (S) from all elements in a two-dimensional array.

```
(a)           REAL A(100,100)
              PRINT *, 'Column Number?'
              READ *, JCOL
              SUM = 0.0
              DO 10 I = 1, 100
                 SUM = SUM + A(I,JCOL)
        10    CONTINUE
              PRINT *, 'Sum =', SUM
              END
(b)           REAL A(100,100)
              SUM = 0.0
              DO 10 I = 1, 100
                DO 10 J = 1, 100
                  SUM = SUM + A(I,J)
        10    CONTINUE
              PRINT *, 'Sum =', SUM
              END
(c)           REAL A(100,100)
              AMIN = A(1,1)
              DO 10 I = 1,100
                DO 10 J = 1,100
                  IF (A(I,J) .LT. AMIN) THEN
                     AMIN = A(I,J)
                  ENDIF
        10    CONTINUE
              PRINT *, 'Minimum:', AMIN
              END
(d)           REAL A(100,100)
              PRINT *, 'Enter scalar:'
              READ *, S
              DO 10 I = 1, 100
                DO 10 J = 1, 100
```

```
          A(I,J) = A(I,J)-S
     10   CONTINUE
          END
```

6.6   Trace the following program segments and predict the output of each one. Line numbers are
provided for your convenience and are not part of the program.

```
(a) 01      REAL II(100)          (b) 01      REAL X(2), Y(2), NUM
    02      DO 10 I=1, 100            02      DATA X,Y/1, 2, 3, 4/
    03        II(I)=I*2               03      DATA NDIM,Z,P/2,2.0,0.0/
    04  10  CONTINUE                  04      DO 10 I = 1, NDIM
    05      PRINT*,II(II(II(1)))      05        TERM = 1
    06      END                       06        DO 20 J=1, NDIM
                                      07          IF(I.NE.J) THEN
                                      08            DEN=X(I)-X(J)
                                      09            NUM=Z-X(J)
                                      10            TERM=TERM*NUM/DEN
                                      11          ENDIF
                                      12  20    CONTINUE
                                      13        TERM=TERM*Y(I)
                                      14        P=P+TERM
                                      15  10  CONTINUE
                                      16      PRINT *, P
                                      17      END
```

(a) Each element in the II array has a value equal to its index times 2. So, let's use this
shortcut to examine the PRINT statement:

    PRINT *, II(II(II(1)))

    PRINT *, II(II(2))

    PRINT *, II(4)

    PRINT *, 8.00000   OUTPUT → 8.00000

(b) Trace Table:

X(1):	1.0	Z:	2.0
X(2):	2.0	P:	0.0, 0.0, 0.0, 4.0
Y(1):	3.0	I:	1, 2, 3
Y(2):	4.0	TERM:	1.0, 0.0, 0.0, 1.0, 1.0, 4.0
NDIM:	2	J:	1, 2, 3, 1, 2, 3
NUM:	0.0, 1.0	DEN:	−1.0, 1.0

Trace Steps:

01: Declare X and Y arrays.

02: DATA statement assigns X(1)=1.0, X(2)=2.0, Y(1)=3.0, and Y(2)=4.0.

03: DATA statement assigns NDIM=2, X=2.0, and P=0.0.

04: Enter DO 10: initialize I to 1, check if it exceeds 2 — false, execute loop.

05: TERM=1.0

06: Enter DO 20: initialize J to 1, check if it exceeds 2 — false, execute loop.

07: IF (I.NE.J) — (1.NE.1) is false, do not execute statement.

08: Increment J by 1 (J=2) and go to line 06.

06: Check if J exceeds 2 — false, execute loop.

07: IF (I.NE.J) — (1.NE.2) is true, execute TERM=TERM*(Z-X(J))/(X(I)-X(J))

TERM$=1.0*(2.0-2.0)/(1.0-2.0)$, TERM$=0.0$
08: Increment J by 1 (J$=3$) and go to line 06.
06: Check if J exceeds 2 — true, skip loop.
09: TERM$=$TERM$*$Y(1), TERM$=0.0$
10: P$=$P$+$TERM, P$=0.0+0.0$, P$=0.0$
11: Increment I by 1 (I$=2$) and go to line 04.
04: Check if I exceeds 2 — false, execute loop.
05: TERM$=1.0$
06: Enter DO 20: initialize J to 1, check if it exceeds 2 — false, execute loop.
　07: IF (I.NE.J) — (2.NE.1) is true, execute TERM$=$TERM$*$(Z$-$X(J))/(X(I)$-$X(J))
　　TERM$=1.0*(2.0-1.0)/(2.0-1.0)$, TERM$=1.0$
08: Increment J by 1 (J$=2$) and go to line 06.
06: Check if J exceeds 2 — false, execute loop.
07: IF (I.NE.J) — (2.NE.2) is false, do not execute THEN block.
08: Increment J by 1 (J$=3$) and go to line 06.
06: Check if J exceeds 2 — true, skip loop.
09: TERM$=$TERM$*$Y(2), TERM$=1.0*4.0$, TERM$=4.0$
10: P$=$P$+$TERM, P$=0.0+4.0$, P$=4.0$
11: Increment I by 1 (I$=3$) and go to line 04.
04: Check if I exceeds 2 — true, skip loop.
12: PRINT *, P
13: STOP
Output:
4.00000

6.7　Two vectors are said to be *orthogonal* if they are perpendicular to each other. One way of checking orthogonality of two vectors is to take their dot product and see if it is zero (or very close to it taking into account roundoff errors). The dot product between vectors x and y is defined by:

$$dot\ product\,(x,y) = x \odot y = \sum_{i=1}^{i=3} x_i y_i$$

Write a program which reads in two vectors and determines if they are orthogonal.

```
      REAL A(3), B(3)
      PRINT *, 'Components of A and B and allowed error?'
      READ *, A, B, EPS
      DOT = 0.0
      DO 10 I = 1, 3
        DOT = DOT + A(I)*B(I)
   10 CONTINUE
      IF(ABS(DOT) .LE. EPS) THEN
          PRINT*, 'The vectors are orthogonal'
      ELSE
          PRINT *, 'The vectors are not orthogonal'
      ENDIF
      END
```

6.8   Write a program that reads in a list of values, stores them in an array, and returns the minimum value and its position in the array.

```
      REAL X(1000)
      PRINT *, 'Number of items?'
      READ *, N
      PRINT *, 'Enter data'
      READ *, (X(I), I=1, N)
      AMIN=X(1)
      IMIN=1
      DO 10 I=1, N
         IF(X(I).LT.AMIN)THEN
            AMIN=X(I)
            IMIN=I
         END IF
  10  CONTINUE
      PRINT *, 'Min value = ', AMIN
      PRINT *, 'Found at ', IMIN
      END
```

6.9   A list of real numbers whose values range from 0 to 100 is read in from the keyboard. Write a program that creates a list showing how many numbers from the list are in each of the following ranges. (HINT: Consider integer conversion of the real values.)

Range 1: $00 \leq$ Number ≤ 10

Range 2: $10 <$ Number ≤ 20

$\vdots$

Range 10: $90 <$ Number ≤ 100

```
      INTEGER N(10)
      REAL X(1000)
      DATA N/10*0/
      PRINT *, 'Enter number of items and data:'
      READ *, M, (X(I), I=1, M)
      DO 10 I = 1, M
         J = INT((X(I)+1))/10
         N(J) = N(J)+1
  10  CONTINUE
      PRINT 20, (I, N(I), I=1, 10)
  20  FORMAT(' ', 'Range', I2, ':', I3)
      END
```

6.10   We've seen two-dimensional arrays used as tables. Another use of two-dimensional arrays is to create graphical images where the rows and columns of the array can be considered as the (x,y) coordinates. Write a program to plot a curve according to the following steps:

- Initialize all elements of a two dimensional array to 0.0.
- Set up a variable J that represents the 41 columns in an array of size $(-20:20, -20:20)$. For each row, calculate the position from -20 to 20 where we wish to print a symbol (1 for example). The position will represent the value of the sine function from -2π to 2π.

```
      INTEGER PLOT(-20:20, -20:20)
      DATA PLOT, PI/1681*0, 3.14159/
      DO 10 J = -20, 20
         Y = SIN(PI*J/10.0)
         I = NINT(-Y*20.0)
         PLOT(I, J) = 1
   10 CONTINUE
      DO 20 I = -20, 20
         PRINT 15, (PLOT(I, J), J = -20, 20)
   20 CONTINUE
   15 FORMAT(' ', 41I1)
      END
```

To show you how this program works, let's select a single column (the fourth column for example) in the graph. This will correspond to a J value of -17 in PLOT(I, J), since we started with $J = -20$. Inside the DO 10 loop, when $J = -17$, Y will be $\sin(-17\pi/10.0)$ or approximately -0.81. I then becomes 16. Thus, the number 1 will be placed into PLOT(16, -17). All the other elements in that column will be zero.

6.11 Based on Examples 6.12 and 6.13, write program segments to accomplish the following:
(a) Percentage of freshmen in the survey.
(b) Total number of most experienced programmers (> 3 years experience).
(c) Percentage of nonprogrammers.
(You may use the variables defined in Examples 6.12 and 6.13.)

```
(a)       INTEGER SURVEY(5,4), TOT, TOTEXP, TOTNON
              ⋮
          NOS = 0
          DO 10 I = 1, 5
            NOS = NOS + SURVEY (I,1)
       10 CONTINUE
          PERFRE = NOS/TOT
(b)       TOTEXP = 0
          DO 10 J = 1, 4
              TOTEXP = TOTEXP + SURVEY(5,J)
       10 CONTINUE
          PRINT *,'Number of most experienced programmers =', TOTEXP
(c)       TOTNON = 0
          DO 10 J = 1, 4
              TOTNON = TOTNON + SURVEY (1,J)
       10 CONTINUE
          PERNON = TOTNON/TOT
          PRINT *, 'Percentage of nonprogrammers = ', PERNON
```

6.12 Based on the search method illustrated in Example 6.9 for a one-dimensional array, modify the program to search for a value in a two-dimensional array. Have the program return the row and column subscripts when it locates the desired value. Assume that the maximum limits for rows and columns are 200 and 100, respectively.

```
      INTEGER X(200,100), VALUE
      PRINT *, 'Nos of rows?'
      READ *, N
      PRINT *, 'Nos of columns?'
      READ *, M
      PRINT *, 'Enter data by columns:'
      READ *, ((X(I, J), I=1, N), J=1, M)
      PRINT *, 'Search Value?'
      READ *, VALUE
C  Start the search operation
      DO 40 I=1, N
        DO 40 J=1, M
          IF(X(I, J).EQ.VALUE)THEN
             PRINT *, 'Value at', I, J
             STOP
          END IF
40      CONTINUE
      END
```

6.13 For each of the following DATA statements, determine the values that will be assigned to each array element.

(a) INTEGER A(10)
    DATA (A(I), I=10, 1, -1)/1, 2, 3, 4, 5, 6, 7, 8, 9, 10/
(b) INTEGER A(3, 3)
    DATA ((A(I, J), I=1, 3), J=1, 3)/1, 2, 3, 4, 5, 6, 7, 8, 9/
(c) INTEGER A(2, 2, 2)
    DATA A/1, 2, 3, 4, 5, 6, 7, 8/

(a) A(1)=10, A(2)=9, A(3)=8, A(4)=7, A(5)=6, A(6)=5, A(7)=4, A(8)=3, A(9)=2, A(10)=1
(b) A(1,1)=1, A(1,2)=4, A(1,3)=7
    A(2,1)=2, A(2,2)=5, A(2,3)=8
    A(3,1)=3, A(3,2)=6, A(3,3)=9
(c) A(1,1,1)=1, A(2,1,1)=2, A(1,2,1)=3, A(2,2,1)=4, A(1,1,2)=5, A(2,1,2)=6, A(1,2,2)=7, A(2,2,2)=8
    (This is the first demonstration of a three-dimensional array).

6.14 Write program segments to perform the following tasks:
(a) Change all negative values in a two-dimensional array A to the positive reciprocal value.
(b) A real array A(40, 40) has values ranging from 0 to 100. Write a program segment to create a new integer array B according to the following rules:
    – if the element of A is < 50.0, then the corresponding value of B is 0
    – if the element of A is ≥ 50.0, then the corresponding value of B is 1

```
(a)    DO 10 I = 1, IMAX
        DO 10 J = 1, JMAX
          IF(A(I,J) .LT. 0.0) A(I,J) = 1.0/ABS(A(I,J))
10     CONTINUE
```

```
(b)        REAL A(40,40)
           INTEGER B(40,40)
           DO 10 I = 1, 40
              DO 10 J = 1, 40
                 IF(A(I,J) .LT. 50.0) THEN
                    B(I,J) = 0
                 ELSE
                    B(I,J) = 1
                 ENDIF
     10    CONTINUE
```

6.15 Trace through the following program and predict its output. Line numbers are provided for your convenience and are not part of the program.

```
01              REAL A(3,3), B(3), C(3)
02              DATA A/1, 2, 3, 4, 5, 6, 7, 8, 9/
03              DATA B/1, 2, 3/
04              DO 20 I = 1, 3
05                 C(I) = 0.0
06                 DO 10 J = 1, 3
07                    C(I) = C(I) + A(I, J)*B(J)
08    10        CONTINUE
09    20     CONTINUE
10           PRINT 30, C
11    30     FORMAT(' ', 3(F6.1, 1X))
12           STOP
13           END
```

Trace Table:

A:

1.0	4.0	7.0
2.0	5.0	8.0
3.0	6.0	9.0

B:

1.0	2.0	3.0

I: 1, 2, 3, 4
J: 1, 2, 3, 4, 1, 2, 3, 4, 1, 2, 3, 4
C(1):0.0, 1.0, 9.0, 30.0
C(2):0.0, 2.0, 12.0, 36.0
C(3):0.0, 3.0, 15.0, 42.0

OUTPUT
    30.0 36.0 42.0

Supplementary Problems

6.16 Locate the syntax errors in the following program segments:

(a)   `REAL A(1,100)`   (b)   `REAL SIN(10)`
       `DO 10 I = 1, 10`   `PI=3.14159`
         `A(I-5) = I**2`   `DO 10 I = 1, 10`
  `10  CONTINUE`   `SIN(I) = SIN(I*PI)`
                        `10  CONTINUE`

(c)   `REAL X(100)`   (d)   `PARAMETER (N=5, M=10)`
       `DATA X/100*2.0/`   `REAL X(N, M)`
       `DO 10 I = 1, INT(X(I))`   `READ *,N, M`
        `I=INT(X(I))`
  `10  CONTINUE`

6.17 Write program segments to accomplish the following:

(a) Read in a series of numbers and then determine their sum.
(b) The recurrence series is 1, 3, 5, 11, 21, 43, ... The first two numbers in the series are 1 and 2. All other numbers in the series s_i ($i \geq 3$) are generated by $s_i = s_{i-1} + 2s_{i-2}$. Write a program to determine the first 50 terms of this series.
(c) For a given array X determine the repeated fraction:

$$X(10) + \cfrac{1}{X(9) + \cfrac{1}{X(8) + \cfrac{1}{\ldots + X(2) + \cfrac{1}{X(1)}}}}$$

(d) Merge two one-dimensional arrays A and B into a new one-dimensional array C, such that the even subscripts of C are generated from consecutive elements of A and the odd subscripts are generated by successive elements of B. For example, if A=(7, 3, 9, 13) and B=(5, 8, 10, 2), then C=(5, 7, 8, 3, 10, 9, 2, 13).

6.18 Write program segments to accomplish the following:

(a) Assign the values of a real 10×10 array so that each element has a value equal to the sum of its indices (e.g., A(4, 6) = 10).
(b) Set all the elements of a real 10×10 array to 0 if they were originally less than 0.

6.19 Write program segments to perform the following tasks on the arrays A(100, 100) and B(100, 100):

(a) Sum a row.

(b) Determine the maximum value within each array.

(c) Transpose an array. The transposed array (B) is the original array (A) with rows and columns switched.

(d) Subtract each element in the array B from the corresponding element of the A array. Have the results returned in the A array. In general, this can be represented as $A(I,J) = A(I,J) - B(I,J)$.

6.20 Trace through the following program segments and predict their outputs. Line numbers are provided for your convenience and are not part of the program.

```
(a) 01      REAL A(10)             (b) 01      INTEGER A(10)
    02      DO 10 I=1, 10              02      DO 10 I=1, 9, 2
    03        A(I)=I**2                03        A(I)=I**2
    04 10 CONTINUE                     04 10 CONTINUE
    05      DO 20 I=2, 10, 2           05      DO 20 I=2, 8, 2
    06        PRINT *, A(I/2+1)        06        A(I)=A(I-1)-A(I+1)
    07 20 CONTINUE                     07 20 CONTINUE
    08      STOP                       08      PRINT 30,(A(I),I=1,10)
    09      END                        09 30 FORMAT(' ',2(I7,3x),/)
                                       10      STOP
                                       11      END
```

6.21 Write a program that reads in a list of values from the terminal, stores them in an array, and returns the maximum absolute value.

6.22 Modify the min/max sort program (Example 6.7) so that a second array will be sorted based on the sorting sequence for the first array. For example, if the first and third values in the first array are swapped, then the first and third values in the second array will also be swapped:

A	B	After Sorting on A:	A	B
5	5000		5	5000
4	2347		4	2347
1	45		2	247
2	247		1	45

Your program should read in a maximum of 100 pairs of numbers. Have the first number in the pair stored in the A array and the second in the B array. Sort the numbers as described and print the results.

6.23   A list of real numbers ranges in value from 0.0 to 100.0. Write a program that reads in the upper limits for five possible ranges into which the data can be sorted as illustrated below. Have the program create a list showing how many numbers exist in each of the ranges. Stop reading in numbers when any value is less than 0.

Range 1:	0	$\leq$ number $<$ upper limit 1
Range 2:	lower limit 2	$\leq$ number $<$ upper limit 2
Range 3:	lower limit 3	$\leq$ number $<$ upper limit 3
Range 4:	lower limit 4	$\leq$ number $<$ upper limit 4
Range 5:	lower limit 5	$\leq$ number $\leq$ upper limit 5

6.24   We've seen two-dimensional arrays used as tables. Another common usage concerns the creation of graphical images where the rows and columns of a two-dimensional array can be thought of as (x, y) coordinates on a graph. Write a program to generate curves by taking the value of a two-dimensional function $z(x, y)$ and converting its range of real values to a range of integers. Begin with an array of size $(-20:20, -20:20)$. Then calculate values of the function $z(x,y) = \cos(\sqrt{x^2 + y^2})$ for 41 values of x and y. Then fill in the array for plotting by converting the z values to integers ranging from 0 to 9, with 0 representing values of $z(x, y) = -1$ and 9 representing values of $z(x, y) = 1$. Values of z between -1 and 1 should be scaled to integer values between 0 and 9.

6.25   A national survey of smoking habits as a function of age was taken. Age values range from 10-years-old to 100. Smoking levels ranged from nonsmoker, to intermediate smoker (1–2 packs per day), to heavy smoker (3 or more packs per day). Smoking habits were then rated as 1 for nonsmoker, 2 for intermediate level smoker, and 3 for heavy smoker. Additional questions of gender and state residence were also added. Responses were given a list of code numbers. For gender, the data were coded 1 for male and 2 for female. The states were given code numbers ranging from 1 to 50. If we store this information in an array,

(a) How many dimensions must this array have?
(b) Write a program to read the survey results and examine the data to generate a statistics table (number of 25-year-old women who live in state #5 and are nonsmokers, etc.).
(c) Write a program segment to calculate total number of respondents.
(d) Write a program segment to report total number of nonsmokers.
(e) Write a program segment to report percentage of male and female smokers. For example, assuming there were 100 smokers in the survey, the output would look like this: Of the 100 smokers, 46% were women and 54% were men.

6.26   The operation of scalar multiplication of an array is the process of multiplying each element in the array by the desired scalar value. For example, if we multiply an array by the constant 2, we would multiply each element of the array by this constant. Write a program that reads in an array of size M $\times$ N, requests a scalar value, and returns the result of the scalar multiplication. The maximum number of rows and columns should be 100.

6.27 Given the following data statements, determine what values will be assigned to each array element:

(a) `INTEGER A(3,3)`
     `DATA A/3*1,3*2,3*3/`
(b) `INTEGER A(2,2)`
     `DATA ((A(I,J),J=1,3),I=1,3)/1,2,3,4,5,6,7,8,9/`
(c) `INTEGER A(2,2,2)`
     `DATA (((A(I,J,K),I=2,1,-1),J=1,2),K=2,1,-1)/1,2,3,4,5,6,7,8/`

6.28 Modify the program presented in Example 6.17 (printing a sine wave) so that it prints using a width of 100 characters and a length of 60 lines.

6.29 Write program segments to perform the following tasks.

(a) Change all positive values of a two-dimensional array to the $\log_e$ of their value and all negative values to 0.
(b) An integer array has elements that have both even and odd values. Change all even values to 0 and all odd values to the value $+ 1$.

6.30 Trace through the following program and predict its output. Line numbers are provided for your convenience and are not part of the program.

```
01          REAL MAT(10, 10)
02          DATA ((MAT(I, J), I=1, 3), J=1, 4)
03       1     /1, 2, 3, 4, 5, 6, 7, 8, 9, 10, 11, 12/
04          DO 15 I=1, 2
05            DO 10 J=1, 4
06              MAT(I+1, J)=MAT(I+1, J)+MAT(I, J)
07   10       CONTINUE
08   15     CONTINUE
09          PRINT *, ((MAT(I, J), I=1, 3), J=1, 3)
10          END
```

Answers to Selected Supplementary Problems

6.16 (a) The array element $(I-5)$ is out of bounds when I is less than or equal to 5.

(b) By declaring SIN to be an array, the intrinsic function is no longer available. Consequently, $SIN(i*\pi)$ will be in error due to a real subscript in what the compiler thinks is a one-dimensional array.

(c) The control variable of the loop cannot change while the loop is operating.

(d) Once the variables N and M are named in a PARAMETER statement, they cannot be changed by any other statement, including the READ statement.

6.17 (a)
```
        REAL X(1000)
        READ *, N, (X(I), I=1, N)
        SUM = 0.0
        DO 10 I = 1, N
          SUM = SUM + X(I)
     10 CONTINUE
        PRINT *, SUM
```
(b)
```
        INTEGER S(50)
        DATA S(1), S(2)/1, 3/
        DO 10 I=3, 50
          S(I)=S(I-1)+2*S(I-2)
     10 CONTINUE
        PRINT *, (S(I), I=1, 50)
```
(c)
```
        REAL X(10)
        READ *, (X(I), I=1, 10)
        TERM=X(1)
        DO 10 I = 1, 9
          TERM=1/TERM
          TERM=TERM+X(I+1)
     10 CONTINUE
        PRINT *, TERM
```
(d)
```
        REAL A(50),B(50),C(100)
        READ *, N, A, B
        DO 10 I = 1, N
          C(2*I) = A(I)
          C(2*I-1) = B(I)
     10 CONTINUE
        PRINT *, C
```

6.18 (a)
```
        REAL A(10,10)
        DO 30 I = 1, 10
          DO 30 J = 1, 10
            A(I,J) = I + J
     30 CONTINUE
```
(b)
```
        REAL A(10,10)
        READ *, A
        DO 40 I = 1, 10
          DO 40 J = 1, 10
            IF(A(I,J).LT.0.0)THEN
              A(I,J) = 0.0
            ENDIF
     40   CONTINUE
```

6.19 (a)
```
        REAL A(100,100)
        READ *, A
        PRINT *, 'Row Number?'
        READ *, I
        SUM = 0.0
        DO 10 J = 1, 100
          SUM = SUM + A(I,J)
     10 CONTINUE
        PRINT *, 'Sum of row:', SUM
        END
```
(b)
```
        REAL A(100,100), B(100,100)
        READ *, A, B
        AMAX = A(1,1)
        BMAX = B(1,1)
        DO 20 I = 1, 100
          DO 10 J = 1, 100
            IF(A(I,J) .GT. AMAX) AMAX = A(I,J)
            IF(B(I,J) .GT. BMAX) BMAX = B(I,J)
     10   CONTINUE
     20 CONTINUE
        PRINT *, 'Maximum values of A and B:', AMAX, BMAX
        END
```
(c)
```
        REAL A(100,100), B(100,100)
        READ *, A
        DO 20 I = 1, 100
          DO 10 J = 1, 100
            B(I,J) = A(J,I)
     10   CONTINUE
```

```
     20  CONTINUE
         PRINT *, B
         END
(d)      REAL A(100,100), B(100,100)
         READ *, A, B
         DO 20 I = 1, 100
           DO 10 J = 1, 100
             A(I,J) = A(I,J) - B(I,J)
     10    CONTINUE
     20  CONTINUE
         PRINT *, A
         END
```

6.20 (a) Trace Table:

A:	1.0	4.0	9.0	16.0	25.0	36.0	49.0	64.0	81.0	100.0

I: 1, 2, 3, 4, 5, 6, 7, 8, 9, 10, 11, 2, 4, 6, 8, 10, 12

Output:

4.0   9.0   16.0   25.0   36.0 (on separate lines)

(b) Trace Table:

A:	1.0	−8.0	9.0	−16.0	25.0	−24.0	49.0	−32.0	81.0

I: 1, 3, 5, 7, 9, 11, 2, 4, 6, 8, 10, 1, 2, 3, 4, 5, 6, 7, 8, 9, 10, 11

Step by Step Trace (Summary):

Elements 1, 3, 5, 7, and 9 are assigned values equal to their index squared. Elements 2, 4, 6, and 8 are assigned the value equal to their preceding neighbor, minus their following neighbor. The last element is never assigned a value.

Output:

```
    1   -8
    9   -16
   25   -24
   49   -32
   81   ****  Last value could be anything, but most likely 0.
```

6.21

```
         REAL X(100), MAX
         PRINT *, 'Number of items?'
         READ *, N
         READ *, (X(I), I = 1, N)
         MAX = ABS(X(1))
         DO 10 I = 1, N
           IF(ABS(X(I)) .GT. MAX)MAX = ABS(X(I))
     10  CONTINUE
         PRINT *, 'Maximum value:', MAX
         END
```

6.22

```
       INTEGER A(100), B(100)
       PRINT *, 'Number of items and data values:'
       READ *, N, (A(I), B(I), I = 1, N)
C
C  Start the sorting operation
C
       DO 20 I = 1, N-1
          MIN = A(I)
          INDEX = I
          DO 20 J = I+1, N
             IF(A(J) .LT. MIN) THEN
                MIN = A(J)
                INDEX = J
             END IF
 20    CONTINUE
C
C Switch values in A
C
          SWAP1 = A(I)
          A(I) = A(INDEX)
          A(INDEX) = SWAP1
C
c Now switch values in B
C
          SWAP2 = B(I)
          B(I) = B(INDEX)
          B(INDEX) = SWAP2
 30    CONTINUE
       DO 40 I = 1, N
          PRINT *, A(I), B(I)
 40    CONTINUE
       END
```

6.23

```
       INTEGER COUNT(5)
       REAL ULRANGE(5)
       DATA COUNT/5*0/
       PRINT *, 'Five upper limits:'
       READ *, ULRANGE
       DO WHILE (X .GE. 0 .AND. X .LE. 100)
          READ *, X
          IF(0 .LE. X .AND. X .LT. ULRANGE(1)) THEN
             COUNT(1) = COUNT(1) + 1
             ELSE IF(ULRANGE(1) .LE. X .AND. X .LE. ULRANGE(2)) THEN
             COUNT(2) = COUNT(2) + 1
             ELSE IF(ULRANGE(2) .LE. X .AND. X .LE. ULRANGE(3)) THEN
             COUNT(3) = COUNT(3) + 1
             ELSE IF(ULRANGE(3) .LE. X .AND. X .LE. ULRANGE(4)) THEN
             COUNT(4) = COUNT(4) + 1
          ELSE
             IF(X .GE. 0.0) COUNT(5) = COUNT(5) + 1
          ENDIF
       END DO
```

```
      DO 10 I = 1, 5
            PRINT *, 'Number within range ', I, ' was ', COUNT(I)
  10  CONTINUE
      END
```

6.24
```
      INTEGER PLOT(-20:20, -20:20)
      DATA PLOT/1681*0/
      DATA PI/3.14159/
      DO 10 I = -20, 20
        DO 10 J = -20, 20
          X = PI*J/10.0
          Y = -PI*I/10.0
          Z = COS(SQRT(X**2+Y**2))
          K = NINT((Z+1)/2*9)
          PLOT(I, J) = K
  10  CONTINUE
      DO 20 I = -20, 20
        PRINT 15, (PLOT(I, J), J = -20, 20)
  15    FORMAT(' ', 41I1)
  20  CONTINUE
      END
```

6.25 (a) The array must have four dimensions: age, smoking level, gender, and state.

(b)
```
      INTEGER RESPOND(10:100, 3, 2, 50)
      INTEGER AGE, SMOKE, GEN, STATE
      DATA RESPOND/27300*0/
      PRINT *, 'Number of respondents?'
      READ *, N
      DO 10 I = 1, N
          READ *, AGE, SMOKE, GEN, STATE
          RESPOND(AGE, SMOKE, GEN, STATE) =
     1          RESPOND(AGE, SMOKE, GEN, STATE)+1
  10  CONTINUE
```

(c) If the total number of respondents is not read in, this is the code that would be needed:
```
      NTOTAL = 0
      DO 20 AGE = 10, 100
        DO 20 SMOKE = 1, 3
          DO 20 GEN = 1, 2
            DO 20 STATE = 1, 50
                      NTOTAL = NTOTAL + RESPOND(AGE, SMOKE, GEN, STATE)
  20  CONTINUE
```

(d)
```
      NONSMK = 0
      DO 30 AGE = 10, 100
        DO 30 GEN = 1, 2
          DO 30 STATE = 1, 50
            NONSMK = NONSMK + RESPOND(AGE, 1, GEN, STATE)
  30  CONTINUE
```

(e)
```
      FEMSMK = 0
      MALSMK = 0
      DO 40 AGE = 10, 100
        DO 40 SMOKE = 1, 3
          DO 40 STATE = 1, 50
            FEMSMK = FEMSMK + RESPOND(AGE, SMOKE, 2, STATE)
```

```
                  MALSMK = MALSMK + RESPOND(AGE, SMOKE, 1, STATE)
           40 CONTINUE
              PFEMSMK = FEMSMK/NTOTAL
              PMALSMK = MALSMK/NTOTAL
```

6.26
```
              REAL X(100,100)
              PRINT *, 'Number of rows?'
              READ *, N
              PRINT*, 'Number of columns?'
              READ *, M
              PRINT *, 'Enter data values:'
              READ *, ((X(I, J), J=1, M), I=1, N)
              PRINT *, 'Enter scalar value:'
              READ *, S
              DO 10 I = 1, N
                DO 10 J = 1, M
                  X(I,J) = X(I,J)*S
           10 CONTINUE
              PRINT *, 'Resulting array is:'
              PRINT *, ((X(I, J), J=1, M), I=1,N)
              END
```

6.27 (a) A(1, 1)=1, A(1, 2)=2, A(1, 3)=3, A(2, 1)=1, A(2, 2)=2, A(2, 3)=3, A(3, 1)=1, A(3, 2)=2, A(3, 3)=3

(b) A(1,1)=1, A(1, 2)=2, A(1, 3)=3, A(2, 1)=4, A(2, 2)=5, A(2, 3)=6, A(3, 1)=7, A(3, 2)=8, A(3, 3)=9

(c) A(2, 1, 2)=1, A(1, 1, 2)=2, A(2, 2, 2)=3, A(1, 2, 2)=4, A(2, 1, 1)=5, A(1, 1, 1)=6, A(2, 2, 1)=7, A(1, 2, 1)=8

6.28
```
              DO 10 I = 0, 59
                X = I*2*3.1416/59.0
                Y = SIN(X)
                N = NINT(99/2.0+Y*99/2.0+1)
                PRINT *, ('*', J=1, N)
           10 CONTINUE
```

6.29 (a)
```
              REAL X(100,100)
              PRINT *, 'Enter number or rows, columns:'
              READ *, IMAX, JMAX
              PRINT *, 'Enter data values by rows:'
              READ *, ((X(I,J), J=1,JMAX), I=1,IMAX)
              DO 10 I = 1, IMAX
                DO 10 J = 1, JMAX
                  IF(X(I,J) .GT. 0.0) THEN
                    X(I,J) = ALOG(X(I,J))
                  ELSE
                    X(I,J) = 0.0
                  ENDIF
           10 CONTINUE
```

(b)
```
     INTEGER X(100,100)
     PRINT *, 'Enter number or rows, columns:'
     READ *, IMAX, JMAX
     PRINT *, 'Enter data values by rows:'
     READ *, ((X(I,J), J=1,JMAX), I=1,IMAX)
     DO 10 I = 1, IMAX
       DO 10 J = 1, JMAX
         IF(MOD(X(I,J),2) .EQ. 0) THEN
           X(I,J) = 0
         ELSE
           X(I,J) = 1
         ENDIF
  10 CONTINUE
```

6.30 Trace Table:

Notes: 1)   "*" indicates undefined value

          2)   the following table shows the sequential values for each array element

M	1	4	7	10	*	*	*	*	*	*
	2, 3	5, 9	8, 15	11, 21	*	*	*	*	*	*
	3, 6	6, 15	9, 24	12, 33	*	*	*	*	*	*
	*	*	*	*	*	*	*	*	*	*
	*	*	*	*	*	*	*	*	*	*
	*	*	*	*	*	*	*	*	*	*
	*	*	*	*	*	*	*	*	*	*
	*	*	*	*	*	*	*	*	*	*
	*	*	*	*	*	*	*	*	*	*
	*	*	*	*	*	*	*	*	*	*

I: 1, 2, 3, 1, 2, 3   J: 1, 2, 3, 4, 5, 1, 2, 3, 4, 5

Output:

      1.00000   3.00000   6.00000   4.00000   9.00000   15.00000   7.00000   15.00000
24.00000

Chapter 7

Subprograms

7.1 MODULARITY — THE KEY TO PROGRAMMING SUCCESS

If we ask ten professional programmers the question, "What is the best strategy to write a complex program?" all ten would probably answer "Modularize!" In effect, the professionals are telling us that if we break the complex problem down into several smaller problems (modules), we stand a better chance of being successful. A "divide and conquer" approach is the key to success.

What do we mean by "Modularize"? Most programmers agree that to modularize a task is to break it into individual, well-focused *subtasks*. If you concentrate on solving one small subtask at a time, the overall task is simpler to solve. There is nothing unique about this approach since we do it all the time in our personal lives. How often have you heard "I can only do one thing at a time!" Well, that's what modularization is all about — concentrating on one thing at a time.

In this chapter, we will not learn any new ideas about programming, other than how to package programs differently. We will break long programs into several smaller subprograms, all held together by a main program, whose primary function is to oversee all the subtasks. Each of the subprograms will have only a single task to perform.

The best way for us to introduce the need for modularization is to introduce a simple problem. One type of program that is a candidate for modularization is one that repeats the same type of calculation a number of times. This quite often occurs when you need to use a mathematical operation that is not built into the compiler, so that you are forced to do it yourself. The factorial function $[n! = (n-1)(n-2)...(2)(1)]$ is such an example.

EXAMPLE 7.1

Suppose that a laboratory instructor wants to divide 12 students into two groups with 7 and 5 students. We can show that the number of possible combinations c that can occur is

$$c = \frac{12!}{5!\ 7!} = 792$$

To generalize this to a class of n students and groups of i and $n-i$, we use the formula:

$$c = \frac{n!}{i!\ (n-i)!}$$

A program to calculate c would require <u>three</u> separate loops to calculate $n!$, $i!$, and $(n-i)!$ as shown in the following program and flowchart:

Flowchart

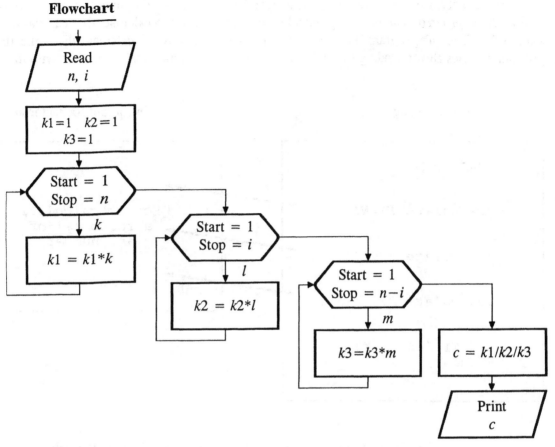

Program

```
        READ * , N , I
        K1 = 1
        DO 10 K = 1 , N              Loop to
            K1 = K1 * K             calculate N!
10      CONTINUE
        K2 = 1
        DO 20 L = 1 , I             Loop to
            K2 = K2 * L             calculate I!
20      CONTINUE
        K3 = 1
        DO 30 M = 1 , N - I         Loop to
            K3 = K3 * M             calculate (N−I)!
30      CONTINUE
        C = K1 / K2 / K3
        PRINT * , C
        END
```

Although this program works, it is an awkward structure since we use the loops for calculating the factorial three times, with only small changes each time. Thus, we needlessly wrote extra code for the factorials. Hopefully, there is a better way so that we won't have to write the same code over and over again.

Fortunately, most programming languages have a way to avoid unnecessary repetition such as this. A *subprogram* can be set up outside the main program to calculate the factorial $n!$ for any value of n. The subprogram worries about the details of how to calculate $n!$, while the main program worries about sending the right values to the subprogram and what to do with the results.

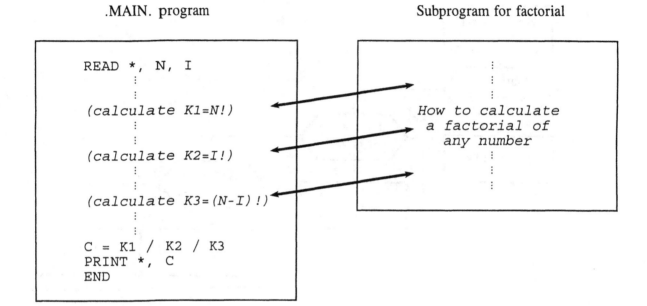

Every time that the main program needs to calculate the factorial, the values of N, I, or $(N-I)$ is sent to the subprogram for the calculation. One advantage of programming this way is that we write the subprogram <u>only once</u>. If set up correctly, the subprogram can calculate the factorial for any number sent to it. Notice that the main program controls what to send and what to do with the results. However, the main program leaves all the details of the calculation to the subprogram.

There are several major advantages to breaking programs into smaller subprograms:

- You can simplify your job by focusing on a small task assigned to the subprogram.
- You can reuse the code in the subprogram as often as needed.
- Subprograms are *portable*, which means that they can be saved in a library and used in other programs or by other programmers. Thus, the factorial subprogram written here can be used in a different program.
- In addition to your own libraries, you can also use libraries created by others. Some of these, such as IMSL®, contain thousands of mathematical functions.
- Subprograms make it easier to debug your programs. A 20-line subprogram is much easier to test than a 200-line program with the same code embedded in it.

As we will see shortly, subprograms contain all the elements that we have already discussed, such as control structures, arrays, and I/O commands. The only new concept that we introduce here is that the subprogram will work in concert with, and under the control of, a main program or another subprogram.

7.2 THE FUNCTION SUBPROGRAM

The simplest type of subprogram is the *function subprogram* whose purpose is to calculate a *single numerical* answer and return the result. You have already seen many examples of functions when you used *intrinsic* or *built-in functions* such as:

```
Y = SQRT(X)
```

The execution of this statement is so automatic that you didn't give it much thought. But it is important that we review the process for using functions and how to transfer the data. The statement Y=SQRT(X) is a *calling* statement, which tells the computer to use the function built into the compiler for calculating the square root. The computer transfers the value of X to the appropriate function and stores the answer $\sqrt{X}$ in the variable Y.

Even though Fortran has many built in functions, there are still many that are missing. The factorial $n!$ is one of these. Therefore, we need a way to construct these missing functions that can be called just like the SQRT function. The principal difference though is that we now need to supply the necessary instructions in the form of a *function subprogram*. These have the syntax

type FUNCTION *name* (*list of variables*)
    subprogram instructions
RETURN
END

The first line of the subprogram states that this is a function and gives it a name, which is the same as the one to be used in the main program calling statement. This name is also used as a variable within the subprogram to which the desired value will be assigned. Because the function name is also a variable inside the function, the type of the variable may need to be declared. That is why there is a typing option at the beginning of the function statement. Following the name is an optional list of variables that the function needs for the calculation.

EXAMPLE 7.2

Since the function name will be used as a variable, we sometimes need to declare the type (real, integer, character, and so forth) at the beginning of the function. This typing is optional though, if implicit typing rules are sufficient. Thus, the following are equivalent:

```
INTEGER FUNCTION IFACT(N)    or    FUNCTION IFACT(N)
```

Since the variable IFACT is implicitly integer, we do not need to redeclare it. In the subsequent examples, we will always assume implicit typing. However, this option is only available with real or integer data. With character, double precision, logical, or complex data, the type declaration is required in the function statement as shown in this example:

```
DOUBLE PRECISION FUNCTION COMPUTE(A, B, C)
```

In this example, we did not have a choice. Since real and integer are the only implicit data types, we had to declare the variable COMPUTE to be double precision.

The function subprogram body is similar to any other program in that it can contain declaration and assignment statements, loops and branches. At the end of the function subprogram are the RETURN and END statements. The computer uses the RETURN statement at execution time to return control back to the module that called it. The END statement indicates the end of the specific module and separates it from the other modules.

EXAMPLE 7.3

Let's return to Example 7.1 to compute the number of possible combinations of groups with size i and $n-i$. But we will replace the code that was repeated three times with a function. Since the factorial function ($i!$) does not exist on most compilers, we must write our own function subprogram:

Flowchart

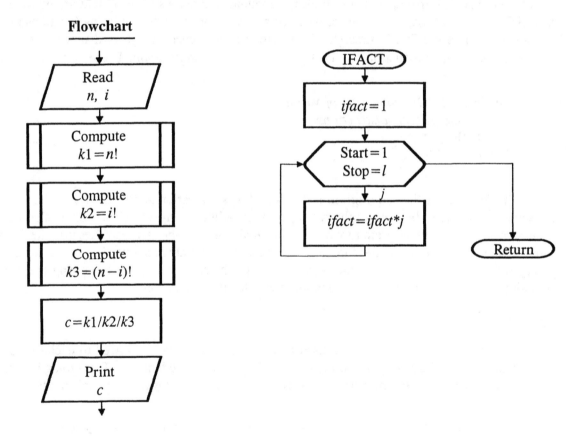

Program

```
C The MAIN program is primarily concerned with control. Details
C of the factorial calculation are handled in the function.
C*******************************************************************
        PRINT *, 'ENTER N & I:'
        READ *, N, I
```

(Program continues on next page)

```
C Three calls to the function to compute N!, I! and (N-I)!
C**********************************************************
       K1 =   IFACT ( N )
       K2 =   IFACT ( I )
       K3 =   IFACT ( N-I )
       C = K1 / K2 / K3
       PRINT *, 'C= ', C
       END
C**********************************************************
C The function is written as a stand alone module.
C**********************************************************
       FUNCTION IFACT ( L )
       IFACT = 1
       DO 10 J = 1 , L
          IFACT = IFACT * J
10     CONTINUE
       RETURN
       END
```

The function follows the end of the main program. The computer will know where the main program ends and the function subprogram begins by their respective END and FUNCTION statements. When the computer comes to the assignment statement in the main program

$$K1 = IFACT(N)$$

it seeks out the function IFACT and transfers the value inside the parentheses (N in this case) to the subprogram where it is matched to the variable L. The function then computes N! and returns its value to the variable K1. When the program comes to the next call

$$K2 = IFACT(I)$$

the same thing will happen, except that the computer now transfers the value of I to the subprogram and returns the result to K2. Finally, the third call to the function subprogram sends (N−I) to the function for computation, and (N−I)! is returned. Note how we use the same function subprogram three times, but with different values transferred each time.

The subprogram IFACT computes the factorial of the value within the parentheses in the calling statement with the aid of a *dummy variable* (L in Example 7.3). The value transferred to L is used locally within the subprogram for the computation of the factorial.

There were two new flowchart symbols that we introduced in this last example. Within the main program, we used a rectangular box with double lines to indicate that an *off-page process* is being used. An off-page process is a standalone unit (such as a function) that contains details about how to perform the required operation. In the example, we used this symbol three times to indicate the number of times we are calling this function. The function itself is indicated by the elliptical flowchart symbol. We place the ellipse at the beginning and place the name of the routine inside. Also, we place an ellipse at the end of the function to indicate its end. Note that the function stands alone, and could have been placed on another piece of paper for convenience: hence its name *off-page* process.

Variables in Fortran are *local*. They exist only in the module in which they explicitly appear. Thus, if we had two variables with the same name within a main program and the function, they would not be the same. In BASIC, where variables are *global*, they would have the same value.

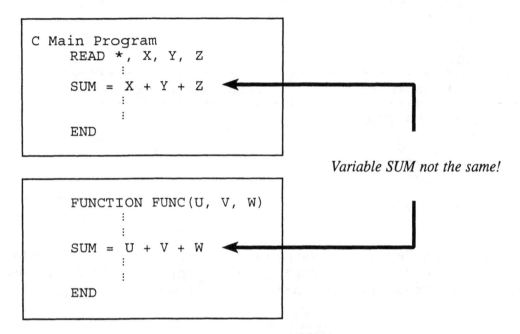

Variable SUM not the same!

The fact that variables in Fortran are <u>local</u> is very important when constructing large programs with many subprograms. Without this feature, you would find it difficult to use subprograms written by others, and you would lose the portability that is so important .

EXAMPLE 7.4

Trace through the following program segment to see what the output of the program will be:

```
        X = 1.2345
        Y = 9.8765
        SUM = X + Y
        PRINT *, SUM
        PRINT *, FUNC(X, Y)
        PRINT *, A, B
        END
C******************************************************************
C The values of X and Y are transferred to the local variables
C A and B. The function computes A+B and returns the result.
C******************************************************************
        FUNCTION FUNC(A, B)
        FUNC = A + B
        RETURN
        END
```

The first PRINT statement in the main program prints out the value of SUM, or 11.11100. When the second PRINT statement executes, it will call the function subprogram FUNC and transfer the values 1.2345 and 9.8765 to A and B, respectively. Inside the function, A and B are added and their sum assigned to the variable FUNC. This value (11.11100) is then returned to the main program and printed. Now, when the computer executes the third print statement (PRINT *, A, B), it will find that A and B have not been assigned values in the main program (only in the function!), so you may receive an error message. In all likelihood though, the computer will print two zeros. The point of this exercise is to show that variables are local to the module in which they are defined and assigned values.

The local feature is very useful because it allows different sets of input data to use the same function repeatedly with a minimum of effort. All you need to do to send down new data is to write another calling statement and include the data within the argument list. The figure below schematically shows the most common way of transferring data to a function.

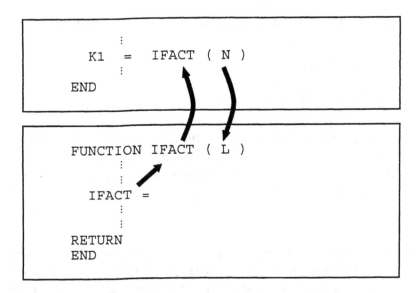

The value of the variable N inside the parentheses in the main program calling statement goes to L in the subprogram, even though the two variables do not have the same name. This feature makes it easy to transfer different values to the subprogram. The result of the calculation returns to the main program through the name of the function (IFACT). Notice first, though, that the subprogram uses the function name as a variable to store the result. Thus the function name IFACT occurs at least three different times:

- In the calling statement in the main program
- In the name of the function subprogram
- As a variable within the subprogram

An important point about subprograms is that the type of the corresponding variables in the main program and the subprogram argument lists must match. Thus, in the above figure, the variables sent to the subprogram are integers, as are the dummy variables set up to receive them. Similarly, IFACT is implicitly integer in both modules. You must pay special attention to the type of the variables since it is easy to create a mismatch. Also, you must be careful that the argument list in the calling statement and the function statement match in the *number* of variables and in their *order*. If you send four variables, you must have four variables to receive them. Finally, there is a one–to–one correspondence between the position of the variables within the two lists. The third variable in one list will be sent to the third variable in the other list, for example.

EXAMPLE 7.5

Assume that we wish to send three variables to a function called ADD. The first two variables, X and Y, are real, but the third, J, is an integer:

$$\begin{array}{ccc} real & real & integer \\ \updownarrow & \updownarrow & \updownarrow \end{array}$$
$$Y = ADD\ (\ X,\quad Y,\quad J\ )$$

The corresponding function statement variables must match in number, order and type:

$$\begin{array}{ccc} real & real & integer \\ \updownarrow & \updownarrow & \updownarrow \end{array}$$
$$FUNCTION\ ADD\ (\ A\ ,\ X\ ,\ I\ )$$

Note that X from the main will be assigned to A in the function, not to X in the function, even though they have the same variable name. Position within the list determines the assignment, not similarity of variable names! This confusion often creeps in when you are using subprograms written by someone else.

EXAMPLE 7.6

If necessary, you may have to explicitly declare some variables in the function subprogram to satisfy the requirement that variables must match in type. For example, if we had used W instead of the variable I in Example 7.5, we would need to redeclare one of the variables. Note that W is an intrinsic real, while I is an intrinsic integer. So one of them must be changed by use of the explicit declaration statement.

```
C**********************************************************************
C The variable J is implicitly integer in the main program
C**********************************************************************
            ⋮
      Y = ADD ( X, Y, J )
            ⋮
      END
C**********************************************************************
C The variable W must be declared as integer to match data sent
C**********************************************************************
      FUNCTION ADD ( A , B, W )
      INTEGER W
            ⋮
      RETURN
      END
```

Under normal circumstances (using implicit typing), the variable W would be real. But the data item being sent (stored in J) is an integer, so there will be a type mismatch unless we change the variable type. That is the reason for the declaration statement inside the function.

Function subprograms are easy to use. You may use them in assignment statements, as part of mathematical expressions, or inside print statements. In other words, treat them like any other variable. For this reason, they are the preferred method to calculate mathematical functions. But there are other times when we need more complex operations. For these we will need another type of subprogram, which is described in the next section.

7.3 SUBROUTINES

The second type of subprogram is the *subroutine*. Like the function, it stands outside the main program and uses local variables. The difference is that the subroutine can do more sophisticated things than the simple function. Whereas the function can give only single numerical answers such as the square root of a number, subroutines can return more than a single numerical answer. For example, we can use the subroutine to sort an entire array or to carry out a curve fitting procedure on a large data set. There is no limit to the amount of data that the subroutine can return. Therefore, it is a more powerful tool than the function.

As with functions, the use of a subroutine requires a three-step process to

- call the subroutine from the main program
- pass data to the subroutine
- set up the subroutine to receive the passed data, process it, and return the results

The procedure for calling a subroutine is a little different from that for a function because of the larger amount of data returned. We used functions when a single numerical answer was sufficient. But with subroutines, we can return any amount of data. Therefore, the subroutine is more versatile. With subroutines, we pass data to and from the subroutine with the calling statement:

CALL *subroutinename* (*variable1* , *variable2* , . . . , *variableN*)

where *subroutinename* is the name of the specific subroutine that you want to use and *variable1* ... *variableN* is a list of variables passing back and forth between the main and the subroutine. These variables are *two-way* variables. They may pass data to the subroutine or they may receive results, depending upon the context. The corresponding statements which set up the subroutine are:

SUBROUTINE *subroutinename* (*variable1* , *variable2* , . . . , *variableN*)
　　⋮
　　⋮
RETURN
END

The identifier *subroutinename* must be identical with the one in the calling statement and must follow the standard rules for any variable name. The argument list in the calling statement and in the subroutine statement must have the same number of variables, and each must agree in type with its counterpart. They need not have the same variable names. Thus:

```
         ⋮
CALL ADD ( X , Y , Z , I , SUM )
         ⋮




SUBROUTINE ADD ( A , B , C , L ,TOT  )
         ⋮
RETURN
END
```

In this example, the first variable in the subroutine argument list A receives the value of the first variable in the calling argument list X. Similarly, B receives the value of Y, C receives the value of Z, and so forth. Also, the variables sending and receiving the data must match in type. Thus, if X is real, A must be real, and if I is an integer, then L must also be an integer.

The variables in the argument lists can either send or receive data. Usually, this will be obvious from the context of the problem. In the example given, X, Y, Z, and I are sending data to the subroutine, while SUM is the variable where the returned answer is stored. But each variable is also a two-way variable. Thus, we may use X to send data down, but if the subprogram modifies the corresponding variable A, then X will change also.

EXAMPLE 7.7

The following main program calls the subroutine ADD, transfers the values of X, Y, Z, and I, and assigns them to their corresponding variables in the subroutine, A, B, C, and L:

```
             ⋮
DATA X, Y, Z, I/2.0, 3.0, 4.0, 3/
CALL ADD ( X , Y , Z , I , SUM )
PRINT *, SUM
             ⋮
```

```
   SUBROUTINE ADD(A , B , C , L ,TOTAL )
   DO 10   K = 1 , L
      TOTAL = TOTAL  + A / B
10 CONTINUE
   A = TOTAL/C
   RETURN
   END
```

The values in the main program are X=2.000000 Y=3.00000, Z=4.00000, and I=3. These are transferred to the variables A, B, C, and L, respectively, in the subroutine. There, a value of TOTAL=2.00000 is computed, returned to the variable SUM in the main program, and printed.   Also note that the subroutine changes the value of A with the statement A=TOTAL/C. Since A is equivalent to X in the main program, X will change also.

The subroutine must physically follow the last line of the main program. If there are several subroutines and functions, they may go in any order:

.MAIN.   or   .MAIN.
SUBROUTINE .TWO.   FUNCTION .ONE.
FUNCTION .ONE.   SUBROUTINE .ONE.
SUBROUTINE .ONE.   SUBROUTINE .TWO.

The order in which you list the various subprograms is unimportant, since the computer will seek them out by name when it needs them. It may help in debugging, though, if you list them in a logical order — for instance, the order in which you call them.

7.4 ARRAYS AND SUBPROGRAMS

Our discussion so far has focused on passing single-valued variables to subprograms. But we can pass arrays also if we declare the arrays in both modules. While this sounds like a duplication of effort, recall that subprograms are standalone modules. Thus, if we are going to use an array in the module we must declare it in the main and subprogram modules where they are used.

EXAMPLE 7.8

When we pass the entire array A to the subroutine SUM, we have to declare the array twice:

```
REAL A(100)
     ⋮
CALL SUM ( A, TOT )
     ⋮
END
```

```
SUBROUTINE SUM( X , TOTAL )
REAL X(100)
     ⋮
RETURN
END
```

The array A is declared in the main program as a one-dimensional array with 100 elements. When we pass the array to the subroutine, all we need do is give the array name in the calling statement. Since we have already declared A as an array, the computer understands that the calling statement sends all 100 array elements. Finally, note that the variable receiving the array in the subroutine is X. Since we are sending down an array with 100 elements, X must also be a real array with 100 elements.

One of the most important results of the ability to pass arrays is the possibility of using a subprogram with variable-sized arrays. Recall that in a main program we had to specify explicitly the maximum size of an array in the declaration statement. Fortran does not permit variable size arrays in main programs. Inside subprograms, though, variable-sized arrays are allowed.

EXAMPLE 7.9

Assume that we have two arrays declared as A(100) and B(10). We wish to send A to a subroutine for processing first, followed by a second call with B. First, we send the array A with its size of 100. Then we send B with its size of 10. We set up the subroutine so that the local array X has a variable size M. When the computer receives the value of M (either 100 or 10) it will set up the required amount of memory space.

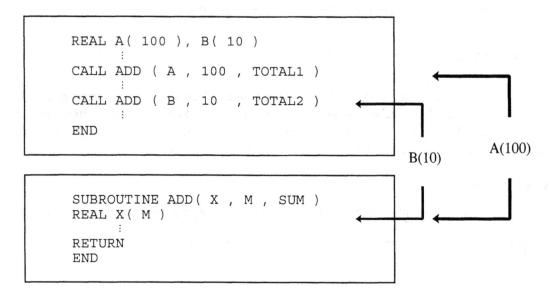

A key point to observe is that the array in the subroutine is a *variable*-sized array. Only when a value is transferred to M will the computer set up the array X with the requested number of elements. With the first calling statement in the main program, we are sending the A array with M = 100; the second time M = 10, so the array X is set up with 10 elements.

Besides sending entire arrays, it is also possible to transfer individual elements. But, of course, the data types must match.

EXAMPLE 7.10

In the program below, array A is declared in the main program to have 25 elements, but we are sending only two of the elements, A(1) and A(2), to the subroutine. Since each array element is a single value, the variables receiving the data must be single-valued variables.

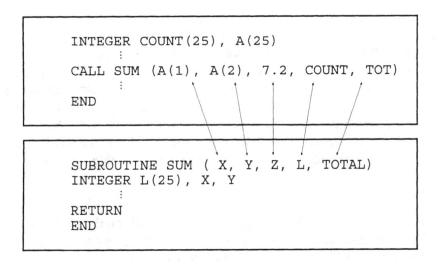

A(1) and A(2) are individual elements of the array A. These elements are assigned to the single-valued variables X and Y in the subroutine. Also, we have sent down a constant 7.2 to the variable Z, and the whole array COUNT to the array L. Note in this case that COUNT and L are declared as the same type (integer) and size (25 elements).

7.5 CREATING GLOBAL DATA — THE COMMON STATEMENT

We have stressed several times that Fortran uses variables which are local; these local variables exist only in the modules in which you explicitly use them. Thus, the variable X in the main is different from the variable X in a subprogram. This is a very important feature since it allows us to reuse subprograms with few changes. Still, there are times when you may wish to have *global variables*, or variables that exist in several modules simultaneously. Fortran has such a feature, called the *common block*, that allows you to declare selected variables as global.

Before we show you how to use the common block, we want to show you why the need exists. Suppose that you have a lengthy program that makes many calls to subroutines and that each call transfers many items in the argument list:

```
CALL DUMMY(A, B, I, J, C, D, E, F, U)
CALL DUMMY(A, B, I, J, C, D, E, F, V)
CALL DUMMY(A, B, I, J, C, D, E, F, W)
```

In all three call statements, we have sent many of the same variables. The only difference in the three calling statements was in the last item in the list, U, V, or W. The first eight variables were all the same and resulted in extra typing that could easily result in errors if you were not careful. If we could turn these eight into *global* variables there would be no need to explicitly transfer them to the subroutine — they would already be there.

The common block structure allows us to declare a list of variables to be global in several modules. The syntax of the statement is:

COMMON *variable1, variable2, . . ., variableN*

The COMMON statement contains a list of variables to be stored in common memory for use by each module given access to it. If a module will need these variables, then the COMMON statement must be included. If the subprogram will not use the common data, then you do not need the COMMON statement and may omit it. When the COMMON statement appears in the subprogram, the variable names need not be the same as the ones in the main program. Instead, the data are transferred by the <u>location</u> in the variable list. For example, the first variable listed inside the parentheses of the main program COMMON statement is assigned to the first variable in the subprogram COMMON statement, regardless of its name. Similarly, the second variable in the main program COMMON statement is matched with the second variable, and so forth.

EXAMPLE 7.11

To demonstrate how to use the COMMON statement, let's work on the program where we have three CALL statements, each with the same eight variables plus one different variable. We will put the eight variables into the COMMON statement and send down only the variable that is not common.

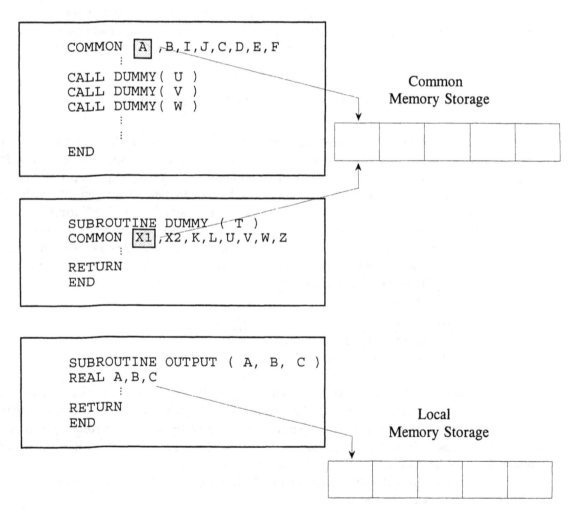

The variables A (in the main) and X1 (in the first subroutine) share the same memory block because of the COMMON statement. Therefore, they will always have the same value. Note that in the second subroutine (OUTPUT), which does not have a COMMON statement, there are only local variables. Thus, the variable A in subroutine OUTPUT is different from A in the main.

This example shows that you can have a mixture of local and global variables. By default, variables are local. So if you want global variables, you must set up a common block and specify it in each subprogram that will use it. We must warn you, though, that global variables can cause many problems if you are not careful. Overuse of common blocks will greatly increase the difficulty of debugging programs containing them.

There is a second type of common block called the *named common block*. We can give each common block a name, which will allow us to break all the shared data into smaller packages. This will allow us to share some data with one subprogram and other data with another subprogram. The syntax of the named common block is:

COMMON /*name* / *variable1, variable2, . . ., variableN*

We give the block a name by specifying it inside the slash marks, and we list the variables to be associated with that block. To transfer this block of variables to the subroutine, all we need do is to specify the same block name in the subroutine.

Suppose we wanted to share variables A, B, C, and D with one group of subroutines, and E, F, G, and H with a second set of subroutines. We would do it as shown below.

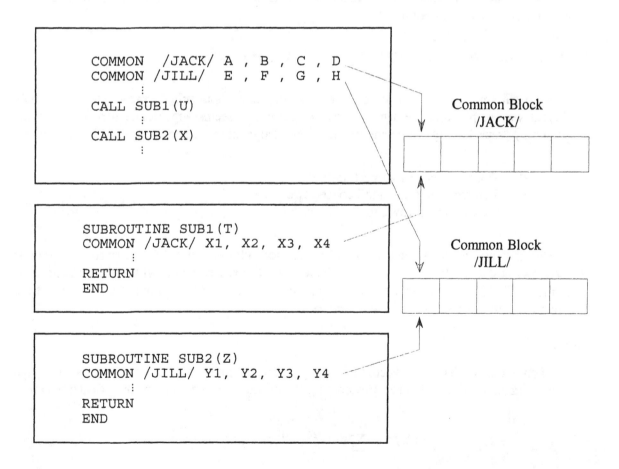

The named common block /JACK/ shares the variables A, B, C, and D with the SUBROUTINE SUB1 variables X1, X2, X3, and X4. The second named common block /JILL/ shares only the variables, E, F, G, and H with the variables Y1, Y2, Y3, and Y4 in SUBROUTINE SUB2.

One requirement of the named common block (but not unnamed blocks) is that it must be the same length (4, 5 or however many variables) in every module in which it appears. Even if you will not use all the variables in the block, you must provide a variable to receive the data. For example, in SUBROUTINE SUB2, you may not need the variables Y2 and Y4 for any calculations. Yet, you must provide these two variables. Finally, variables listed in the common blocks cannot be initialized with the DATA statement. Each variable must be explicitly assigned a value with either a READ statement or a direct assignment.

One problem with common blocks is that you may pass character data in either a named or unnamed common block. But if you do so, you cannot pass other types of data such as reals, integers, and so forth. You must use a separate named common block for these. In these blocks, though, you can mix different types, provided that there is no character data.

In spite of its apparent usefulness, we strongly recommend that you avoid common blocks if possible. Sometimes, they can be used to good effect, as we will show in the section on debugging. In general, though, they compromise the safety of the individual modules. We go to great lengths to set up subprograms that are independent of each other to ensure that there is no "crosstalk." Common blocks directly attack this structure and may produce errors that are very difficult to locate and then eliminate.

7.6 ENGINEERING AND SCIENCE APPLICATIONS

We began this chapter by stating there is nothing new about subprograms. They are simply a different way of packing the same goods. Therefore, it seems appropriate here to begin the discussion by "repackaging" three engineering related algorithms as subprograms. These include:

- Dot product of two vectors
- Determining the angle between two vectors
- Vector transformation

The first two can be implemented with a function subprogram only. The third will be done with subroutines. Sometimes, you can implement the desired program with either functions or subroutines. This is certainly true in these examples. So, as an additional exercise, you may want to convert functions to subroutines and vice versa.

EXAMPLE 7.12

Assume that we have two vectors, f^1 and f^2. The *dot product* of the two vectors (indicated by the symbol $\odot$) is defined by summing the products of the components of each vector:

$$f^1 \odot f^2 = \sum_{i=1}^{i=3} f_i^1 f_i^2 = f_1^1 f_1^2 + f_2^1 f_2^2 + f_3^1 f_3^2$$

This equation tells us to multiply the two x components of the vectors together, the two y components together, and the two z components together. The sum of all these products is the dot product. For example, if f^1 has components (3, 4, 7) and f^2 has components (0, 1, 3), then the dot product is given by $(3 \cdot 0 + 4 \cdot 1 + 7 \cdot 3) = 4 + 21 = 25$. The result of this calculation is a *scalar* quantity, which means that it has only a magnitude and lacks direction. The vectors themselves, on the other hand, have both magnitude and direction. Below this procedure is shown in the form of a flowchart for a main program.

Flowchart

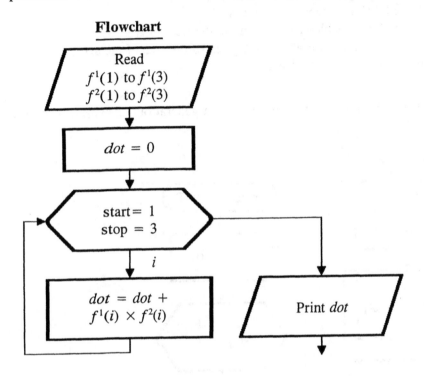

Program

```
c Declare the two vectors in the MAIN program as one-dimensional
C arrays and then read them in.
C*********************************************************************
      REAL F1(3), F2(3)
      READ *, (F1(I), I=1,3), (F2(J), J=1,3)
C*********************************************************************
C Now compute the dot product by summing the product of
C the individual components of the two vectors.
C*********************************************************************
      DOT = 0.0
      DO 10 I=1,3
         DOT = DOT + F1(I)*F2(I)
10    CONTINUE
C*********************************************************************
C Print the results. Note that DOT is a scalar quantity.
C*********************************************************************
      PRINT *, DOT
      END
```

In this version of the dot product, we have written it as a main program. We will now convert the dot product into a function subprogram called DOT. We could also convert it into a subroutine but as you will see shortly the function is more convenient.

We can convert this into a function subprogram almost directly. There are only a few changes and additions that we need to make:

- Create a main program to call the function
- Move the READ statement to the main
- Make the arrays variable size to improve the flexibility
- Make the loop control variable correspond to the size of the arrays
- Give the name DOT to the function

Once we make these changes, the function will be a general one that we can reuse without modifications.

Flowchart

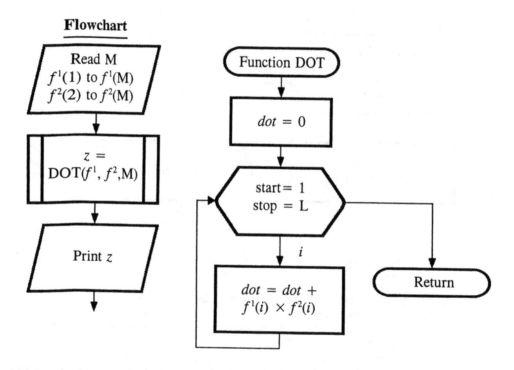

Program

```
C******************************************************************
C Main program reads in A and B vectors and calls function DOT
C to compute the dot product of A and B
C******************************************************************
      REAL A(100), B(100)
      PRINT *, 'Enter number of components, and A & B vectors:'
      READ *, M, (A(I), I = 1, M), (B(I), I = 1, M)
      Z = DOT(A, B, M)
      PRINT *, 'DOT PRODUCT = ', Z
      END
```

```
C************************************************************
C Function subprogram to calculate the dot product of two vectors
C of arbitrary size (L)
C************************************************************
        FUNCTION DOT(F1, F2, L)
        REAL F1(L), F2(L)
        DOT = 0.0
        DO 10 I = 1, L
           DOT = DOT + F1(I)*F2(I)
10      CONTINUE
        RETURN
        END
```

The main program sets up the two arrays and reads in their values. Notice that the declaration statements there must specify an actual size for the arrays. Therefore, we usually set them arbitrarily high so that it is unlikely that we will exceed the reserved memory space. In this case, we set each vector to have 100 elements. Then we read in M, which is the actual number of elements in the array, which is usually 3 for real space vectors. Once the program reads in the arrays their values transfer to the function, along with the value of M. The function then uses the value of M to set up the arrays and to control the loop that computes the dot product. Finally, the function name DOT is a variable within the function and contains the desired scalar result.

This is the first time that we have used variable-sized arrays in a subprogram. Note carefully how the main program must send down an integer value to the local variable L that can be used to size the arrays. Study this example carefully since you will use it frequently.

A key point about setting up a subprogram is that you should make an effort to have the subprogram as flexible as possible so that you will not have to edit it each time you want to use it. For instance, we could use this function for dotting two vectors with 3, 10, 100, or any number of elements. The critical step is to set up the arrays as *variable* arrays. Also, you must set up any associated DO loops to run with variable limits. Finally, notice that we took the I/O statements out of the subprogram.

EXAMPLE 7.13

Consider two vectors, F^1 and F^2, where we wish to know the angle between them:

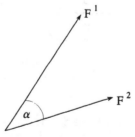

We can find the angle α between the two vectors, F^1 and F^2, with the formula:

$$\cos(\alpha) = \frac{F^1 \odot F^2}{|F^1|\,|F^2|}$$

where $F^1 \odot F^2$ = the dot product of the two vectors, and $|F^1|$ and $|F^2|$ are the lengths of the vectors respectively. The length can be computed by

$$|F| = [(F_1)^2 + (F_2)^2 + (F_3)^2]^{1/2}$$

For example, if we had two vectors, $F^1 = (12, 5, 6)$ and $F^2 = (3, 2, 0)$, we calculate the angle as follows:

$$
\begin{aligned}
F^1 \odot F^2 &= 12 \times 3 + 5 \times 2 + 6 \times 0 &= 46 \\
|F^1| &= \sqrt{12^2 + 5^2 + 6^2} &= \sqrt{205} \\
|F^2| &= \sqrt{3^2 + 2^2 + 0^2} &= \sqrt{13} \\
\cos(\alpha) &= 46 / \sqrt{205 \times 13} &= 0.891065 \\
\alpha &= \cos^{-1}(0.891065) &= 26.992770°
\end{aligned}
$$

We will convert this calculation to a function called ANGLE that receives the two vectors and returns the single numerical value that is α. Keep in mind that when a computer does trigonometric calculations, all answers appear in radians, not degrees! So we will have to convert the answer before printing any results.

Flowchart

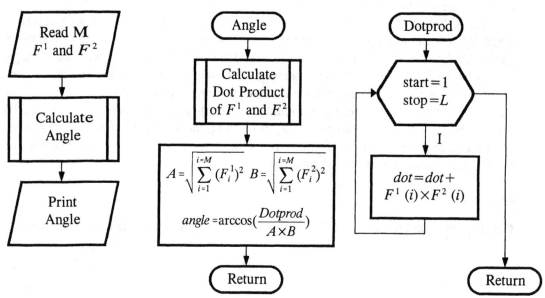

Program

```
C In the main program, we read in the vectors and call the
C appropriate functions. We use the main program to control the
C sequence of operations and leave the details to the functions.
C******************************************************************
      REAL F1(100), F2(100)
      PRINT *, 'Enter number of elements and F1 and F2:'
```

(Program continues on next page)

```
      READ *, M, (F1(I), I=1,M), (F2(I), I=1,M)
      ANS = ANGLE(F1, F2, M)
      PRINT *, 'Angle = ', ANS * 57.296
      END
C*************************************************************
C Function Angle to compute the angle between two vectors. This
C function calls another function (DOT) to compute the dot
C product that is needed for the computation of the angle.
C*************************************************************
      FUNCTION ANGLE(F1, F2, M)
      REAL F1(M), F2(M)
      A = 0.0
      B = 0.0
      DO 10 I = 1, M
          A = A + F1(I)**2
          B = B + F2(I)**2
10    CONTINUE
      DOTPROD = DOT(F1, F2, M)
      ANGLE = ACOS(DOTPROD/SQRT(A*B))
      RETURN
      END
C*************************************************************
C Function to compute the dot product of two vectors
C of arbitrary size (L)
C*************************************************************
      FUNCTION DOT(F1, F2, L)
      REAL F1(L), F2(L)
      DOT = 0.0
      DO 10 I = 1, L
         DOT = DOT + F1(I)*F2(I)
10    CONTINUE
      RETURN
      END
```

The main program first transfers the arrays F1 and F2 to FUNCTION ANGLE. The way that we have set this up, though, requires this function to call another function (DOT) before completing its calculations. Thus, the sequence of transfer is as follows:

- Main program sends F1, F2, and M to ANGLE
  - ANGLE sends F1, F2, and M to DOT to compute F1 $\odot$ F2
  - DOT calculates the dot product and return the answer with the variable DOT
  - ANGLE then uses DOT to compute the angle, which is sent back to the MAIN
- MAIN program prints out the value of the angle

A function may call another function or any other subprogram. The only restriction is that it may not call itself. Any function that calls itself is termed a *recursive* function, which the current version of Fortran does not allow. Future editions (Fortran 90) though will allow recursion, and some Fortran 77 compilers may also allow it, so check with your instructor.

Before we leave this example, you should note that we could have incorporated the function DOT into the function ANGLE, thus minimizing the number of transfers. But then we could not use the function subprogram DOT, which we have already written and debugged. The goal of the modular approach to programming is to break the problem into smaller, more manageable parts. This is exactly what we have done here. Yes, we could have written the entire program as a main program, without any calls to subprograms, but then we would have to reinvent the algorithms.

EXAMPLE 7.14

If we have a vector F in the X-Y-Z coordinate system, it is sometimes easier to work in a different coordinate system such as X'-Y'-Z' shown below (Z and Z' axes not shown for clarity). The new, transformed coordinate system might be more desirable due to the fact that the mathematics might be simpler. The simplest transformation is a rotation about one axis:

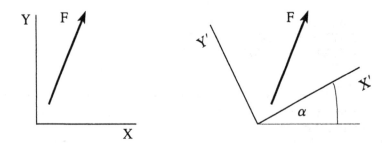

In this transformation, we have taken a rotation through an angle α about the axis perpendicular to the page. Notice that the vector has not changed position, nor has its length changed. But the *components* in the new X'-Y'-Z' coordinate system have changed. If the vector coordinates in the old X-Y-Z system were $F = (F_1, F_2, F_3)$, then we can calculate the components of the new vector as (F'_1, F'_2, F'_3) with the aid of the equation:

$$\begin{bmatrix} F'_1 \\ F'_2 \\ F'_3 \end{bmatrix} = \begin{bmatrix} \cos(\alpha) & -\sin(\alpha) & 0 \\ \sin(\alpha) & \cos(\alpha) & 0 \\ 0 & 0 & 1 \end{bmatrix} \begin{bmatrix} F_1 \\ F_2 \\ F_3 \end{bmatrix}$$

As an example, if we rotate the vector $F = (2, 4, -1)$ by 30°, we have:

$$\begin{bmatrix} F'_1 \\ F'_2 \\ F'_3 \end{bmatrix} = \begin{bmatrix} \cos(30) = 0.866 & -\sin(30) = -0.500 & 0 \\ \sin(30) = 0.500 & \cos(30) = 0.866 & 0 \\ 0 & 0 & 1 \end{bmatrix} \begin{bmatrix} 2.0 \\ 4.0 \\ -1.0 \end{bmatrix}$$

Following the rules for multiplication of two matrices from the previous chapter, we obtain $F' = (-0.268, 4.464, -1.0)$. The Z component has not changed but the other two components have. To carry out the desired coordinate transformation, we need to multiply the original vector by a square matrix containing the values of the trigonometric functions. This problem is somewhat different from the previous algorithm, where we considered the multiplication of a L × M by a M × N matrix to produce a L × N matrix. In this example, the vector is a L × 1 matrix, or a matrix with only one row. Therefore, we can simplify the algorithm for matrix multiplication for this special case.

In the flowchart below, notice that the subroutine for the matrix multiplication has eliminated one loop from the algorithm shown in Example 6.14. We leave it as an exercise for you to show that this is correct for multiplication of a vector by a square matrix.

Flowchart

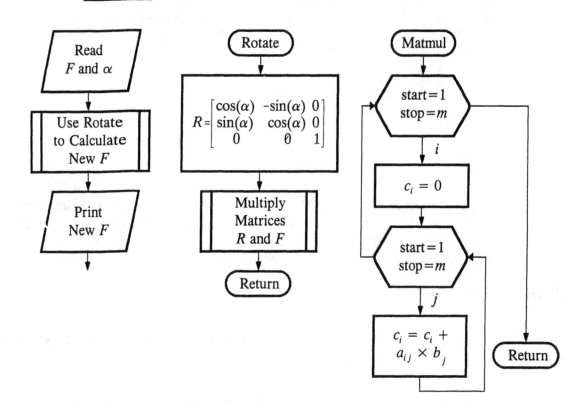

Program

```
C Main program reads in F and angle alpha, then calls the
C subroutine Rotate to perform the transformation.
C***********************************************************
      REAL F(3), F2(3)
      PRINT *, 'ENTER THE VECTOR AND THE ROTATION ANGLE:'
      READ *, (F(I), I = 1, 3), ANGLE
      CALL ROTATE (F, ANGLE, F2)
      END
C***********************************************************
C  Subroutine rotate for a simple rotation about the Z axis
C***********************************************************
      SUBROUTINE ROTATE (F, ANGLE, F2)
      REAL F(3), F2(3), R(3,3)
      ANGLE=ANGLE/57.2958
      R(1,1) = COS(ANGLE)
      R(1,2) = -SIN(ANGLE)
      R(2,1) = SIN(ANGLE)
```

(Program continues on next page)

```
      R(2,2) = COS(ANGLE)
      R(3,3) = 1.0
      CALL MATMUL( R, F, F2, 3, 3)
      RETURN
      END
C*********************************************************************
C Subroutine MATMUL performs multiplication of two matrices
C (A and B) and storing the result in array C.
C*********************************************************************
      SUBROUTINE MATMUL( A, B, C, M, N)
      REAL A(M,N), B(N), C(M)
      DO 10 I = 1, M
         C(I) = 0.0
         DO 10 J = 1, N
            C(I) = C(I) + A(I,J)*B(J)
10    CONTINUE
      RETURN
      END
```

The main program takes the value of F and ANGLE and sends them to the first subroutine. There the rotation matrix R is prepared, after which F is sent along with R to MATMUL for matrix mutliplication. Note in the calling statement of MATMUL that we list F twice — once as the input, and a second time as the variable to receive the transformed matrix.

7.7 DEBUGGING TIPS

Subprograms are one of the most useful and desirable features of any programming language. They allow programmers to:

- Modularize their code to take advantage of repetitive occurrence of operations
- Break the problem down into several smaller, more manageable steps
- Allow the creation of libraries of commonly used operations and functions

By creating libraries of subprograms that you will use frequently, you indirectly test and debug the subprograms repetitively, resulting in high-quality code. You have probably heard the saying, "Don't reinvent the wheel." By using subprograms in the fashion just outlined, you avoid reinventing the wheel as intended, and in addition, you take out the flat spots over time.

Now, we must talk about the downside of modular programming. By modularizing the code to this extent, it can become difficult to determine where an error originates. Since we must transfer data between a main program and one or more subprograms, there may be conflicts in how the data are defined in each (real in one but integer in the other, for example). Also, there is sometimes difficulty in locating logic errors because of the many transfers of control to one of the subprograms. This poses a unique problem. For example, if your program calls a function 10 times in the main program, and 4 times in a subprogram, how do you know which of the 14 calls produces the error? Also, we tend to nest subprograms (as with the example of a subroutine calling a function). After several levels of nesting, you need a road map to keep track of what's happening.

There are two types of errors that are unique to subprograms. These are:

- Incorrect data transfers between the calling statement and the subprogram
- Difficulty in following the multiple transfers between the main program and the subprogram(s).

Of course, other types of problems, such as syntax errors, will occur. But these will be the same as those discussed in previous chapters, and the strategies to remove them are the same. For example, an improperly declared array may produce the same message whether the error occurs in the main program or the subprogram. So we will not discuss these errors any further. What we are more concerned with here are those errors unique to subprograms. Unfortunately, your compiler will not give you much help in locating these types of errors. Therefore, we must develop our own strategies.

Incorrect Data Transfers

One common problem that occurs with subprograms is that the variables being sent to a subprogram are mismatched with the variables in the argument list of the subprogram. You may inadvertently send down too many or too few variables, the types may mismatch, or one variable is an array while the receiving variable is not. The best way to detect these types of errors is to use a PRINT statement before the transfer to the subprogram and after it is received.

EXAMPLE 7.15

If the type of the variables being sent through a calling statement does not match with the variables in the subprogram argument list, a run-time error will result. We will add PRINT statements at key points to detect these types of errors.

```
C*****************************************************************
C The variables X and Y in the main program will be real. But
C the variable I will be an integer. We will then send all
C three to the subroutine, which is expecting three real
C variables.
C*****************************************************************
      X = 2.0
      Y = 3.0
      I = 4
      PRINT *,'In main program, X,Y,I=', X, Y, I
      CALL COMPUTE ( X, Y, I)
      END
C*****************************************************************
C The subroutine is expecting three real variables, but it is
C being sent two reals and one integer. Thus, there is a type
C mismatch.
C*****************************************************************
      SUBROUTINE COMPUTE ( A, B, C)
      PRINT A, B, C
         ⋮
      RETURN
      END
```

When you run this program, the values in the main program are 1.000000, 2.000000, and 4. But after transfer to the subprogram, they become 1.000000, 2.000000, and 0.000000. The integer value in the main program is "lost" when we transfer it to a different type (a real variable) in the subprogram.

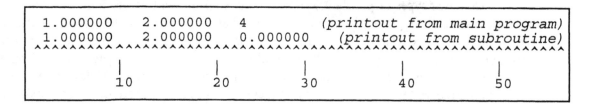

```
1.000000    2.000000    4              (printout from main program)
1.000000    2.000000    0.000000       (printout from subroutine)
^^^^^^^^^^^^^^^^^^^^^^^^^^^^^^^^^^^^^^^^^^^^^^^^^^^^^^^^^^^^^^^^^^^^

       |              |            |            |            |
       10             20           30           40           50
```

Notice that the program compiles and runs, but that it produces the wrong answer. Therefore, these types of errors can easily creep into your programs if you are not careful. As we show in this example, we print out the data from the module (the main program) that calls the subprogram, and then we print them out a second time from within the subprogram to make sure that data are transferred correctly. In the printout shown, it would then be obvious that there is a problem. So use the PRINT statement liberally throughout your programs when debugging.

Tracing Transfers Between Subprograms

Tracing through a series of calls to subprograms can become confusing, because control is transferred many times and it is sometimes difficult to determine where the call came from. As a result, it may not be clear that the subprograms are being executed in the proper order. One way to handle this is to use PRINT statements that produce a path of all transfers. The messages to add to your subprograms should indicate when you enter or leave a particular module, and its name.

EXAMPLE 7.16

The following program contains three subroutines, some of which call each other. Thus, it may be difficult to follow all the transfers. But, by adding PRINT statements at the beginning and end of each of the subroutines, the computer will construct a complete record of all the transfers.

```
        PRINT *,' Starting the Main program'
        CALL A
        CALL B
        END
C**************************************************************
C First subroutine
C**************************************************************
        SUBROUTINE A
        PRINT *,' Entering Subroutine A'
            :
        PRINT *,' Leaving Subroutine A'
        RETURN
        END
```

(Program continues on next page)

```
C****************************************************************
C Second Subroutine
C****************************************************************
      SUBROUTINE B
      PRINT *,' Entering Subroutine B'
            :
      CALL  C
      PRINT *,' Leaving Subroutine B'
      RETURN
      END
C****************************************************************
C Third Subroutine
C****************************************************************
      SUBROUTINE C
      PRINT *,' Entering Subroutine C'
            :
      PRINT *,' Leaving Subroutine C'
      RETURN
      END
```

When you run this program, the following output will appear on the screen:

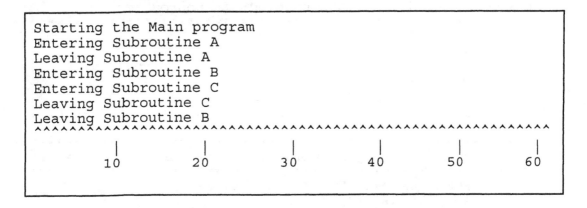

This output is useful for two reasons. First, it identifies the exact path the computer followed in executing the program. By comparing it to your algorithm or flowchart, you can determine if the transfer logic is correct. The second important feature of this type of output is that it can help identify where run-time errors are occurring. For example, suppose we had the following printout for the same program:

```
Starting the Main program
Entering Subroutine A
Leaving Subroutine A
Entering Subroutine B
^^^^^^^^^^^^^^^^^^^^^^^^^^^^^^^^^^^^^^^^^^^^^^^^^^^^^^^^^^^^^^^^
        |         |         |         |         |         |
       10        20        30        40        50        60
```

Since subroutine B never transferred to C, we can conclude that there was a run-time error in subroutine **B**. Without the path trace shown here, we would not know exactly where the error occurred. Consequently, it is important to isolate each of the subprograms and try to determine which of them is faulty by using PRINT statements.

Tracing Subprograms

When tracing subprograms, you need to perform two additional steps beyond those used when tracing a program without subprograms. First, the data in the argument list must be transferred to the appropriate variables in the subprogram at the beginning of the trace. Then, the second step is to trace the subprogram like any other program. After completing the trace, data returns to the appropriate variables in the calling program. To do this, the only additional information that you need are the names of the variables being passed from the calling program.

EXAMPLE 7.17

Consider the following program that uses both a function subprogram and a subroutine. You must execute three separate traces, one each for the .MAIN., the function, and the subroutine.

```
C Program to demonstrate tracing of subprograms
C***********************************************************************
      INTEGER A, B, C, D
      READ *, A, B, C, D
      PRINT *, 'Maximum value entered is', MAXI(A, B, C, D)
      CALL SWAP(A, B)
      CALL SWAP(C, D)
      PRINT *, 'A,B,C, and D now have values ' , A, B, C, D
      END
C***********************************************************************
C Determine the largest value in a list of four variables
C***********************************************************************
      FUNCTION MAXI(X1, X2, X3, X4)
      INTEGER X1, X2, X3, X4
      MAXI = X1
      IF (X2 .GT. MAXI) MAXI = X2
      IF (X3 .GT. MAXI) MAXI = X3
      IF (X4 .GT. MAXI) MAXI = X4
      RETURN
      END
C***********************************************************************
C Swap the values of the variables X and Y
C***********************************************************************
      SUBROUTINE SWAP(X, Y)
      INTEGER X, Y, TEMP
      TEMP = X
      X = Y
      Y = TEMP
      RETURN
      END
```

Assume that we have 2, 1, 4, 3, as the initial input. The trace table will then consist of three separate columns, one for each of the modules:

.MAIN.		Function .MAXI.		Subroutine .SWAP.			
A	2, 2, 1	MAXI	2, 4	X↔A	2, 1	X↔C	4, 3
B	1, 1, 2	X1↔A	2	Y↔B	1, 2	Y↔D	3, 4
C	4, 4, 3	X2↔B	1	TEMP	2	TEMP	4
D	3, 3, 4	X3↔C	4				
MAXI	4	X4↔D	3				

We have introduced a new notation in tracing the function and the subroutine. Since variables are <u>local</u> to the subprogram, we show these variables with the corresponding variables from the calling routine, which may have a different name. Thus, in the function MAXI, the computer associates the local variable X1 with the variable A from the main program. Similarly, the program calls the subroutine SWAP twice. Thus, we show the local variable X with A for the first transfer, and with C for the second transfer. Follow this example closely to make sure that you understand how we traced this simple program. To help you, we show below the trace documentation:

<u>Program Trace:</u>

.MAIN. Trace
　　　READ values for A, B, C, D
　　　Call function MAXI(A, B, C, D)

.MAXI. Trace
　　　Transfer variable names and values to dummy variables
　　　Assign X1 to MAXI
　　　X2 > MAXI? 1 > 2? false
　　　X3 > MAXI? 4 > 2? true, then MAXI = 4
　　　X4 > MAXI? 3 > 4? false
　　　Return MAXI to MAIN
　　　Return argument values to MAIN
　　　A = 2, B = 1, C = 4, D = 3

.MAIN. Trace
　　　Print MAXI value
　　　Call subroutine SWAP(A, B)

.SWAP. Trace
    Transfer variable names and values to dummy variables
    Assign TEMP value of X
    Assign X value of Y
    Assign Y value of TEMP
    Return argument values to MAIN
    A=1, B=2

.MAIN. Trace
    Call SWAP(C, D)

.SWAP. Trace
    Transfer variable names and values to dummy variables
    Assign TEMP value of X
    Assign X value of Y
    Assign Y value of TEMP
    Return argument values to MAIN
    C=3, D=4

.MAIN. Trace
    Print A, B, C, D

Output: The maximum value entered was 4
            A, B, C, D have values 1   2   3   4

We should point out a few things about this trace. First, each program module requires its own variable table. Second, when tracing a function, the function name is also a variable that you must consider. Finally, you must be careful that when the dummy variable in the subprogram changes its corresponding variable in the calling routine also changes.

In summary, our advice for tracing subroutines is:

- Create a variable table for each program module.
- When tracing a function also include its name as a variable.
- Show dummy arguments and the names of the corresponding calling variables together.

As we found in previous chapters, there is no substitute for tracing a program to detect logic errors. Although tracing a program with subroutines and functions is more involved than tracing programs without subprograms, it is still a good idea to trace. Some of the ideas presented here should make that job a little bit easier.

Some commercial compilers offer a debugger included with the compiler. Many of these debuggers offer features such as automated tracking of each variable and recording control transfers between modules. If you have such a debugger available on your system, you can reproduce many of the features shown here.

Solved Problems

7.1 Locate syntax errors in each of the following program segments.

(a)
```
INTEGER I,J
    :
CALL MULT(I,J,K)
    :
END
SUBROUTINE MULT(A,B,C)
    :
END
```

(b)
```
REAL A(10)
    :
CALL SUB1(A(10))
    :
END
SUBROUTINE SUB1(A(10))
REAL A
    :
END
```

(c)
```
REAL A, B
    :
ANS = 2.0*SUB3(A,B,1)
    :
END
REAL FUNCTION SUB3(X,Y,1)
REAL X, Y
    :
END
```

(d)
```
REAL IFACT
I = 5
PRINT *, IFACT(I)
END
REAL FUNCTION IFACT(I)
IF(I .LE. 1) THEN
    IFACT = 1
ELSE
    IFACT = I*IFACT(I-1)
ENDIF
END
```

(e)
```
READ *, X
CALL SUBROUTINE SUB(X, ANS)
PRINT *, ANS
END
SUBROUTINE SUB(X, ANS)
ANS = SQRT(SIN(X)**2)
RETURN
END
```

(f)
```
REAL A(5), B(5)
CALL SUB4(A,B,5)
END
SUBROUTINE SUB4(A,B,I)
REAL A(I), B(I), C(I)
    :
END
```

(a) Type mismatch since I, J, and K are integers, but A, B, and C are real (this may only produce a warning on some compilers).

(b) The array A in the subroutine is not properly declared .

(c) Attempt to transfer a constant (1) to another constant (1).

(d) The function attempts to call itself. Recursion in Fortran is not allowed.

(e) Calling statement in the main program should be CALL SUB(X, ANS).

(f) RETURN statement missing in subroutine (some compilers may only issue a warning).

7.2 Program segments generally must have unique names. Some compilers, though, will allow a subroutine, a built-in function, or a user-defined function to share the same name. Run the following to see how your compiler responds.

```
X = 0.145
PRINT *, SIN(X)
CALL SIN(X)
END
```

```
SUBROUTINE SIN(X)
PRINT *, X
RETURN
END
```

7.3   The storage of double precision data is not standardized. On the compiler used on one computer, for example, the standard default compiler option is the /D_FLOAT which produces a different storage from the /G_FLOAT option. The latter option produces greater precision and also a greater range for the exponent. You may need some help from your instructor about the exact compiler options for your machine. Once you find the different options, run the following program different ways to see what effect the storage precision has on subroutines:

```
DOUBLE PRECISION JACK(1), JILL(1)
JACK(1) = 1437.342E21
JILL(1) = -4343.32E-23
CALL SUB(JACK, JILL)
END
SUBROUTINE SUB(JACK, JILL)
DOUBLE PRECISION JACK(2), JILL(2)
PRINT *, JACK(1), JACK(2), JILL(1), JILL(2)
RETURN
END
```

7.4   Write program segments to accomplish the following using either built-in functions or user-defined functions:

(a) Read in a number at execution time and determine the square root. Keep in mind that the number may be negative. (Use ABS function to handle such problems.)

(b) Read in five numbers and determine which is the largest.

(c) Examine the first two elements of the 100-element array A at a time and determine which is larger. Then repeat this process for all the remaining pairs of array elements.

(d) Read in an array with 100 elements and determine the sum of all elements in the array. Print out the results in the main program.

(e) Repeat exercise (d) but for an arbitrary size array.

(a)
```
C*********************************************************
C We can use the SQRT built in function, either in an
C assignment statement or in a print statement.
C*********************************************************
      PRINT *, 'Enter a number:'
      READ *, X
      PRINT *, 'Square root of X is:', SQRT(ABS(X))
      END
```

(b)
```
C*********************************************************
c The MAX function can take any number of variables in the
C argument list.
C*********************************************************
```

```
            PRINT *, 'Enter five numbers:'
            READ *, A, B, C, D, E
            PRINT *, 'Largest value is:', MAX(A, B, C, D, E)
```
(c)
```
      C We can also send individual elements of an array
      C to the MAX built in function.
      C*********************************************************
            REAL A(100)
            PRINT *, 'Enter A:'
            READ *, (A(I), I=1, 100)
            DO 10 I=1, 99, 2
                PRINT *, MAX(A(I), A(I+1)), 'is larger'
      10    CONTINUE
```
(d)
```
      C*********************************************************
      C There is no built in function to add a list of numbers, so
      C we must build our own. The main program reads in the list
      C and then calls the function SUM to add the numbers.
      C*********************************************************
            REAL A(100)
            PRINT *, 'Enter A:'
            READ *, (A(I), I = 1, 100)
            PRINT *, SUM(A)
            END
      C*********************************************************
      C Function SUM to add together all elements in the array X
      C*********************************************************
            REAL FUNCTION SUM (X)
            REAL X(100)
            SUM = 0.0
            DO 10 I = 1, 100
                SUM = SUM + X(I)
      10    CONTINUE
            RETURN
            END
```
(e)
```
      C*********************************************************
      C In the previous example, we knew in advance how many
      C array elements there were. In this example, we use a
      C variable sized array to handle the situation where we
      C read in the number of elements at execution time.
      C*********************************************************
            REAL A(1000)
            PRINT *, 'Number of elements (less than 1,000)?'
            READ *, N
            PRINT *, 'Enter A:'
            READ *, (A(I), I = 1, N)
            PRINT *, SUM(A, N)
            END
      C*********************************************************
      C Note that we must send the value of N in order to
      C set up the variable size array, and to control the loop.
      C*********************************************************
            REAL FUNCTION SUM (X, M)
            REAL X(M)
            SUM = 0.0
            DO 10 I = 1, M
                SUM = SUM + X(I)
```

```
10        CONTINUE
          RETURN
          END
```

7.5 Write a main program to read in a value x. Then create a function subprogram to compute the number x raised to the nth power. Then using this function, write another function that computes the repeated fraction:

$$\cfrac{1}{x^5 + \cfrac{1}{x^4 + \cfrac{1}{x^3 + \cfrac{1}{x^2 + \cfrac{1}{x^1}}}}}$$

In this example, compute the approximation for only five terms, as shown above.

```
          PRINT *, 'Enter X:'
          READ *, X
          PRINT *, APPROX(X)
          END
C*****************************************************************
C After each term in the series is computed, we take the
C reciprocal of that term and add it to X**I to compute the
C next term.
C*****************************************************************
          REAL FUNCTION APPROX(X)
          APPROX = 0.0
          DO 10 I = 1, 5
             APPROX=1.0/(APPROX + POWER(X,I))
10        CONTINUE
          RETURN
          END
C*****************************************************************
C Function to compute X**N, where X is sent from the calling
C statement in the function APPROX. Notice that N receives its
C value from I in the main program.
C*****************************************************************
          REAL FUNCTION POWER(X, N)
          POWER = X**N
          RETURN
          END
```

7.6 Write program segments to accomplish the following, using subroutines.

(a) Transfer the one-dimensional array A to a subroutine that computes a new B array such that B(I) = A(I) when I is odd, but B(I) = 2A(I) when I is even.

(b) Transfer the two one-dimensional arrays A and B to a subroutine that performs matrix addition according to the formula C(I) = A(I) + B(I) and transfers C back..

(c) Transfer a one-dimensional array A to a subroutine where each element of the array is multiplied by a constant K, defined by $K = 1.0/A(1)$ and stores the result back into A.

(d) Transfer a one-dimensional array to a subroutine that determines the maximum value in the array and then divides all elements of the array by that value.

(a)
```
C*******************************************************************
C We assume arrays A and B have 100 elements each. After
C reading in A, we summon CREATE where B is created.
C*******************************************************************
      REAL A(100), B(100)                    (Assuming 100 elements)
      PRINT *, 'Enter array:'
      READ *, (A(I), I = 1, 100)
      CALL CREATE(A, B)
      PRINT *, 'The B array is:'
      PRINT *, (B(I), I = 1, 100)
      END
C*******************************************************************
C One easy way to handle the even/odd decision is to set up
C a loop with a step count of two.
C*******************************************************************.
      SUBROUTINE CREATE(A, B)
      REAL A(100), B(100)
      DO 10 I = 1, 99, 2
         B(I) = A(I)
         B(I+1) = 2.0*A(I)
 10   CONTINUE
      RETURN
      END
```

(b)
```
C*******************************************************************
C We read in A and B in the main program and send them
C to the subroutine where C is created.
C*******************************************************************
      REAL A(100), B(100), C(100)            (Assuming 100 elements)
      PRINT *, 'Enter A and B values:'
      READ *, (A(I), I = 1, 100), (B(I), I = 1, 100)
      CALL CREATEC(A, B, C)
      PRINT *, 'C array is:'
      PRINT *, (C(I), I = 1, 100)
      END
C*******************************************************************
C Note that all the arrays have to be declared in the
C subroutines also. We use a loop to create the array C
C by adding the corresponding elements of A and B.
C*******************************************************************
      SUBROUTINE CREATEC(A, B, C)
      REAL A(100), B(100), C(100)
      DO 10 I = 1, 100
         C(I) = A(I) + B(I)
 10   CONTINUE
      RETURN
      END
```

(c)
```
C*******************************************************************
C The main program is concerned with I/O of the array A and
C leaves all the details to the subroutine.
C*******************************************************************
```

```
      REAL A(100)                           (Assuming 100 elements)
      PRINT *, 'Enter array A:'
      READ *, (A(I), I = 1, 100)
      DENOM=A(1)
      CALL DIVIDE(A, DENOM)
      PRINT *, 'Normalized array is:'
      PRINT *, (A(I), I = 1, 100)
      END
C**********************************************************
C This subroutine divides all elements of A by DENOM=A(1).
C**********************************************************
      SUBROUTINE DIVIDE(A, DENOM)
      REAL A(100)
      DO 10 I = 1, 100
10       A(I) = A(I)/DENOM
      RETURN
      END
```

(d)
```
C**********************************************************
C The main is primarily concerned with I/O of the array A.
C**********************************************************
      REAL A(100)                           (Assuming 100 elements)
      PRINT *,'Enter A array:'
      READ *, (A(I), I = 1, 100)
      CALL NORMAL(A)
      PRINT *, 'A array after normalization is:'
      PRINT *, (A(I), I = 1, 100)
      END
C**********************************************************
C The DO 10 loop determines the maximum value within the
C array A. Once this is determined, each element of A is
C divided (or normalized) by the maximum value.
C**********************************************************
      SUBROUTINE NORMAL(A)
      REAL A(100), MAX
      MAX = A(1)
      DO 10 I = 2, 100
         IF(A(I) .GT. MAX) MAX = A(I)
10    CONTINUE
      DO 20 I = 1, 100
         A(I) = A(I)/MAX
20    CONTINUE
      RETURN
      END
```

7.7   Find the errors in the following code designed to print the sum of the elements in array A and the sum of the elements in array B.

```
      REAL A(10), B(10), SUM
      PRINT *, 'Enter A and B:'
      READ *, (A(I), I = 1, 10), (B(I), I = 1, 10)
      PRINT *, SUM(A), SUM(B)
      END
      REAL FUNCTION SUM(MAT)
      REAL MAT(N)
```

```
       DO 10 I = 1, N
           SUM = SUM + MAT(I)
   10  CONTINUE
       RETURN
       END
```

Solution: We start by tracing the program. Let's assign values for A and B such as:

A	1	2	3	4	5	6	7	8	9	10
B	2	4	6	7	8	9	2	6	7	9

Program Trace:

.MAIN. Trace:
   READ in the ten values of the arrays A and B
   Transfer values of A to function SUM

.SUM. Trace:
   The array A is assigned to the local array MAT

At this point, one of the errors has occurred. Notice that we cannot set up the array MAT in the function since the value of N is unknown. So, let's change N to 10 and restart the trace.

.MAIN. Trace:
   READ in the ten values of the arrays A and B
   Transfer values of A to function SUM

.SUM. Trace:
   The array A is assigned to the local array MAT
   Begin the loop
   I=1, SUM = 0 + A(1)=1
   I=2, SUM = 1 + A(2)=3
       ⋮
   I=10, SUM = 45 + A(10)=55
   Return value of 55 to .MAIN.

.MAIN. Trace:
   Print out value of SUM(A), which is 55
   Transfer values of B to function SUM

.SUM Trace:
   The array B is assigned to the local array MAT
   Begin the loop
   I=1, SUM+SUM+B(1)=55+2=57

When we go to compute the sum of the second array B, an error occurs in the function.

Note that when we add the first element of MAT(1), which is equivalent to B(1), the old value of SUM is not reset. Thus, the value of SUM=55 was left over from the first use of the function for the array A. To solve this problem, we should add an initialization statement, SUM=0.0, before the DO 10 loop.

7.8 Trace through the following program segments and predict their output:

(a)
```
      REAL F
      Y =   2
      PRINT*,  F(F(F(Y)))
      STOP
      END
      FUNCTION F(X)
      F = X**2
      RETURN
      END
```

(b)
```
      DATA A/1.0/
      DATA B/2.0/
      CALL SUB(A, B, C)
      PRINT*, A, B, C
      STOP
      END
      SUBROUTINE SUB(X, Y, Z)
      X = 2.0*X*Y
      Y = -Y
      Z = X/Y
      RETURN
      END
```

(a) Program Trace:

.MAIN. Trace:
  Y = 2
  Compute F(2)

.F. Trace:
  X = 2
  F = X**2 = 4
  Return value of 4 to MAIN

.MAIN. Trace:
  Compute F(4)

.F. Trace:
  X = 4
  F = X**2 = 16
  Return value of 16 to MAIN

.MAIN. Trace:
  Compute F(16)

.F. Trace:
  X = 16
  F = X**2 = 256
  Return value of 256 to MAIN

Output:
  256.0000

(b) Program Trace:

.MAIN. Trace:
  DATA: A=1.0, B=2.0
  Print values of A, B, C
  Transfer to SUB

.SUB. trace:
  X = 2.0*X*Y = 4.0
  Y = -Y = -2.0
  Z = X/Y = -2.0
  Return to .MAIN.

.MAIN. Trace:
  Print values of A, B, C

Variable Listing:
  .MAIN.
    A: 1.0, 4.0
    B: 2.0, −2.0
    C: −2.0

  .SUB.
    A⇔X: 1.0, 4.0
    B⇔Y: 2.0, −2.0
    C⇔Z: −2.0

Output:
  4.00000 −2.00000 −2.00000

7.9 One of the most important reasons that we write subprograms is that we can store them in libraries of common mathematical operations. Once we have created these libraries, we can then extract any of the subprograms stored there and use them in other programs, thereby greatly reducing our programming efforts. But to be effective, each of the subprograms should execute a single task. Therefore, libraries tend to be large, with several hundred common functions. To help you begin creating your own personalized library, write subprograms to perform the following simple mathematical tasks:

(a) FACT   computes the factorial ($n! = n(n-1)$. . .$(2)(1)$) for any positive integer.
(b) SUMLIS   computes the sum of all elements in a list of arbitrary size.
(c) SUMCOL   computes the sum of all elements in column I of a table with m rows and n columns.
(d) MAXSRC   searches for the maximum value in a list of arbitrary size.
(e) DERIV   calculates a numerical approximation to the derivative of a function $f(x)$ at a point x. One approximation (known as the central difference method) is given by the formula:

$$DERIV \approx \frac{f(x + \Delta x) - f(x - \Delta x)}{2\,\Delta x}$$

where x is the point of evaluation of the derivative, Δx is a small number, and $f(x)$ is the function at point x. The accuracy of the approximation improves as Δx becomes smaller.
(f) SWITCH   switches two numbers.
(g) MATADD   adds two matrices element by element.
(h) BUBBLE   sorts a one-dimensional array in ascending order.

(a)
```
C****************************************************************
C The factorial of N<0 is not defined, so we must check for
C this special case first. The STOP 'ERROR' command will
C terminate execution and print an error message. To compute
C the factorial of N, we first set FACT=1.0 and then multiply
C FACT by all integers between 2 and N.
C****************************************************************
      REAL FUNCTION FACT(N)
      IF(N .LT. 0) STOP 'ERROR'
      FACT = 1.0
      DO 10 I = 2, N
         FACT = FACT * I
   10 CONTINUE
      RETURN
      END
```
(b)
```
C****************************************************************
C We transfer the list through the array X. We also must send
C N, which is the number of items. N sets up the variable
C size array and also controls the loop to add the items in
C the list. The result is returned in the variable SUMLIST.
C****************************************************************
```

```
      REAL FUNCTION SUMLIS(X, N)
      REAL X(N)
      SUMLIS = 0.0
      DO 10 I = 1, N
          SUMLIS = SUMLIS + X(I)
   10 CONTINUE
      RETURN
      END
```

(c)
```
C***************************************************************
C The function assumes a table with M rows and N columns.
C The variable I is the column that we wish to sum. The
C sum of that column is returned via SUMCOL.
C***************************************************************
      REAL FUNCTION SUMCOL(X, I, M, N)
      REAL X(M, N)
      SUMCOL = 0.0
      DO 10 L = 1, N
          SUMCOL = SUMCOL + X(L, I)
   10 CONTINUE
      RETURN
      END
```

(d)
```
C***************************************************************
C The list to be searched, X, has N elements. We assume
C that the first element is the largest and then check each
C element to see if it is larger. If it is, then that element
C becomes the temporary largest value.
C***************************************************************
      REAL FUNCTION MAXSRC(X, N)
      REAL X(N)
      MAXSRC = X(1)
      DO 10 I = 2, N
          IF(X(I) .GT. MAXSRC) MAXSRC = X(I)
   10 CONTINUE
      RETURN
      END
```

(e)
```
C***************************************************************
C We send X and DELTAX to the function to compute the
C derivative at X. DELTAX should be a very small value.
C We must also supply a function for F(X).
C***************************************************************
      REAL FUNCTION DERIV(X, DELTAX)
      DERIV = (F(X+DELTAX)-F(X-DELTAX))/(2.0*DELTAX)
      RETURN
      END
C***************************************************************
C You must also fill in the function for the equation F(X).
C***************************************************************
      REAL FUNCTION F(X)
      F = . . . . . . .          (Reader fills in the function to be evaluated here)
      RETURN
      END
```

(f)
```
C***************************************************************
C To switch two numbers, we must set up a dummy variable
C TEMP. Once we store A in TEMP, we free up A to receive
C the value of B. Then B is free to receive the value in TEMP
```

```
      SUBROUTINE SWITCH(A, B)
      TEMP = A
      A = B
      B = TEMP
      RETURN
      END
```

(g)
```
C*******************************************************************
C All three arrays must be declared with the same size: M
C rows and N columns. Both M and N are sent down at execution
C time. C is then generated by adding A and B.
C*******************************************************************
      SUBROUTINE MATADD(A, B, C, M, N)
      REAL A(M, N), B(M, N), C(M, N)
      DO 10 I = 1, M
         DO 10 J = 1, N
            C(I, J) = A(I, J) + B(I, J)
   10 CONTINUE
      RETURN
      END
```

(h)
```
C*******************************************************************
C See Example 6.7 for a discussion of a popular sorting
C method. We have modified that main program by converting
C the array into a variable sized array. Also, we perform the
C switching by calling the subroutine SWITCH from (g) above.
C*******************************************************************
      SUBROUTINE SORT(X, N)
      REAL X(N)
      DO 10 L = 1, N-1
         BIG = X(L)
         DO 10 I = L, N
            IF(X(I) .GT. BIG) THEN
               CALL SWITCH(X(I), X(L))
               BIG=X(L)
            ENDIF
   10 CONTINUE
      RETURN
      END
```

7.10 Write a function subprogram that computes the average *avg*, the variance *var*, and the standard deviation *std* of a list of numbers using the following formulas:

$$avg = \bar{x} = \frac{\sum_{i=1}^{i=n} x_i}{n}$$

$$var = \sigma^2 = \frac{\sum_{i=1}^{i=n} (avg - x_i)^2}{(n-1)}$$

$$std = \sigma = \sqrt{\sigma^2}$$

Use a main program to read in the data, and the subprogram to perform the computations.

```
C Main program to read in all X values
C****************************************************************
      REAL X(1000)
      PRINT *, 'How many data points?'
      READ *, N
      PRINT *, 'Enter data points:'
      READ *, (X(I), I = 1, N)
      CALL STAT(X, N, AVG, VAR, STD)
      PRINT *, 'Average= ', AVG, 'Variance= ', VAR,
     1         'Standard Deviation= ', STD
      END
C****************************************************************
C Subroutine STAT to compute statistics of a group of data.
C We calculate the average first, because we need it to compute
C the variance. Then we compute the standard deviation.
C****************************************************************
      SUBROUTINE STAT(X, N, AVG, VAR, STD)
      REAL X(N)
      SUM = 0.0
      DO 10 I = 1, N
         SUM = SUM + X(I)
   10 CONTINUE
      AVG = SUM/N
C****************************************************************
C Once the AVG is known, we can use it to compute the variance
C****************************************************************
      TOT = 0.0
      DO 20 I = 1, N
         TOT = TOT + (AVG - X(I))**2
   20 CONTINUE
      VAR = TOT/(N-1)
C****************************************************************
C The standard deviation is just the square root of the variance
C****************************************************************
      STD = SQRT(VAR)
      RETURN
      END
```

7.11 The *determinant of a matrix A*, indicated by $|A|$, is a frequent calculation needed in engineering and science. For a 3×3 matrix, the determinant is given by:

$$\begin{vmatrix} a_{11} & a_{12} & a_{13} \\ a_{21} & a_{22} & a_{23} \\ a_{31} & a_{32} & a_{33} \end{vmatrix} = a_{11}(a_{22}a_{33} - a_{23}a_{32}) - a_{12}(a_{21}a_{33} - a_{23}a_{31}) + a_{13}(a_{21}a_{32} - a_{22}a_{31})$$

Write a function subprogram to calculate the determinant of a 3×3 matrix.

```
C We set up the array as a fixed, not a variable size.
C****************************************************************
```

```
      REAL A(3, 3)
      PRINT *, 'Enter the array A by rows:'
      READ *, ((A(I,J), J=1,3), I=1,3)
      PRINT *, 'Determinant of A is: ', DET(A)
      END
C************************************************************
C The determinant of a 3 x 3 matrix is rather simple, so we can
C evaluate it in a single assignment statement. Note that the
C array size is fixed, and that the |A| is returned via DET.
C************************************************************
      REAL FUNCTION DET(A)
      REAL A(3,3)
      DET = A(1,1)*(A(2,2)*A(3,3)-A(2,3)*A(3,2))-
     1      A(1,2)*(A(2,1)*A(3,3)-A(2,3)*A(3,1))+
     1      A(1,3)*(A(2,1)*A(3,2)-A(2,2)*A(3,1))
      RETURN
      END
```

7.12   One of the best-known methods for solving a system of simultaneous equations (called Cramer's rule) uses the determinant. Assume that we have the following series of equations:

$$a_{11}x_1 + a_{12}x_2 + a_{13}x_3 = b_1$$
$$a_{21}x_1 + a_{22}x_2 + a_{23}x_3 = b_2$$
$$a_{31}x_1 + a_{32}x_2 + a_{33}x_3 = b_3$$

where the a_{ij} and b_i are constants, and x_i are the unknowns. An example of such a system of equations would be

$$7x_1 + 2x_2 + 3x_3 = 45$$
$$-1x_1 + 4x_2 + 8x_3 = 44$$
$$2x_1 - 3x_2 + 2x_3 = 28$$

with a solution $x_1=4$, $x_2=-2$, and $x_3=7$. We can solve these equations by using determinants as defined in the previous solved problem (7.11).

$$x_1 = \frac{\begin{vmatrix} b_1 & a_{12} & a_{13} \\ b_2 & a_{22} & a_{23} \\ b_3 & a_{32} & a_{33} \end{vmatrix}}{\begin{vmatrix} a_{11} & a_{12} & a_{13} \\ a_{21} & a_{22} & a_{23} \\ a_{31} & a_{32} & a_{33} \end{vmatrix}} \qquad x_2 = \frac{\begin{vmatrix} a_{11} & b_1 & a_{13} \\ a_{21} & b_2 & a_{23} \\ a_{31} & b_3 & a_{33} \end{vmatrix}}{\begin{vmatrix} a_{11} & a_{12} & a_{13} \\ a_{21} & a_{22} & a_{23} \\ a_{31} & a_{32} & a_{33} \end{vmatrix}} \qquad x_3 = \frac{\begin{vmatrix} a_{11} & a_{12} & b_1 \\ a_{21} & a_{22} & b_2 \\ a_{31} & a_{32} & b_3 \end{vmatrix}}{\begin{vmatrix} a_{11} & a_{12} & a_{13} \\ a_{21} & a_{22} & a_{23} \\ a_{31} & a_{32} & a_{33} \end{vmatrix}}$$

Notice that the denominator in all three cases is the same (determinant of A or $|A|$), where

A is the square matrix formed by the coefficients of the unknowns. The numerators consist of $|A'|$, where the matrix A' is formed by replacing one of the columns of A by the vector B, which is the constants in the equations to be solved.

Write a main program that reads in the coefficient matrix A and the constant vector B to form the matrices A'. Then use the function DET from solved problem 7.11 to solve for the three unknowns.

```
C Main program to read in the coefficients and the equation
C constants into A and B respectively
C*******************************************************************
      REAL A(3, 3), X(3), B(3)
      DO 10 I = 1, 3
         PRINT *,'Enter coefficients and constant for eq',I
  10     READ *, A(I, J), J = 1, 3), B(I)
      CALL CRAMER(A, X, B)
      PRINT *, 'The unknowns are:', (X(I), I = 1,3)
      END
C*******************************************************************
C Cramer forms the matrices A' by successively substituting the
C vector B into the first, second, and third column of A. The
C function DET is then used to compute the determinant of each
C of these matrices to solve for the unknowns.
C*******************************************************************
      SUBROUTINE CRAMER(A, X, B)
      REAL A(3,3), X(3), B(3), A1(3,3), A2(3,3), A3(3,3)
C*******************************************************************
C Since the denominator is the same, calculate that first
C*******************************************************************
      DENOM = DET(A)
C*******************************************************************
C Loop computes the matrices A1, A2, and A3 in which the B
C vector substitutes into 1st, 2nd, and 3rd column of A.
C*******************************************************************
      DO 10 I = 1, 3
         DO 10 J = 1, 3
            A1(I, J) = A(I, J)
            A2(I, J) = A(I, J)
            A3(I, J) = A(I, J)
  10  CONTINUE
      DO 20 I = 1, 3
         A1(I, 1) = B(I)
         A2(I, 2) = B(I)
         A3(I, 3) = B(I)
  20  CONTINUE
C*******************************************************************
C Once A1, A2, and A3 are formed, we take the determinant of
C each and divide by DET(A) to obtain the unknowns - X(1), X(2),
C and X(3). The determinant function is given in solved
C problem 7.11 and must be included.
C*******************************************************************
      X(1) = DET(A1)/DENOM
      X(2) = DET(A2)/DENOM
      X(3) = DET(A3)/DENOM
      RETURN
      END
```

7.13 Mesh analysis is often used for solving complex resistor networks to calculate the currents flowing in different legs of an electrical circuit. Consider the following network with a single voltage source and eight resistors arranged as shown:

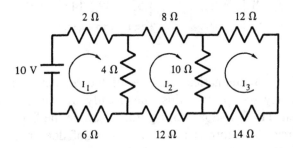

Because the voltage drop around each loop must be zero, it can be shown that the following set of simultaneous equations describes the current flow in each leg:

$$12I_1 \ - \ 4I_2 \qquad\qquad = 10$$
$$-4I_1 \ + \ 34I_2 \ - \ 10I_3 \ = 0$$
$$\qquad\qquad - \ 10I_2 \ + \ 36I_3 \ = 0$$

Use the subprogram for Cramer's method from the previous problem to solve for the current I_j in each of the three legs of the circuit.

Solution: The coefficient matrix A and the constant vector B are given by:

$$A = \begin{bmatrix} 12 & -4 & 0 \\ -4 & 34 & -10 \\ 0 & -10 & 36 \end{bmatrix} \qquad B = \begin{bmatrix} 10 \\ 0 \\ 0 \end{bmatrix}$$

When you run the program given in the previous problem (7.12), enter the values for A by rows (12, −4, 0, etc.) along with the values for B (10, 0, 0). The results should be approximately I(1) = 0.8705, I(2) = 0.1115, and I(3) = 0.03097.

7.14 One of the most famous series in mathematics is named in honor of Leonardo Fibonacci (b.1175). This series seems to describe many different phenomena in nature and has fascinated scientists for almost 800 years. The series is a simple one:

$$1 \quad 1 \quad 2 \quad 3 \quad 5 \quad 8 \quad 13 \quad 21 \quad 34 \quad 55 \ ...$$

Notice that any term in the series is simply the sum of the two previous terms, or $T_n = T_{n-1} + T_{n-2}$. An interesting feature of this series is that the determinant of a matrix made from consecutive terms in this series is always zero. For example, look at the determinant of the matrix made from the first nine terms, or the determinant of the matrix made from nine terms later in the series; the result is always the same:

$$\begin{vmatrix} 1 & 1 & 2 \\ 3 & 5 & 8 \\ 13 & 21 & 34 \end{vmatrix} = 0 \qquad \begin{vmatrix} 13 & 21 & 34 \\ 55 & 89 & 144 \\ 233 & 377 & 610 \end{vmatrix} = 0$$

This can be proven by a mathematical analysis of the sequence of terms. But it is also instructive for you to try to "prove" this numerically by substituting the numbers and calculating the determinant. This does not rigorously prove the hypothesis but it does help to support it. Sometimes, a rigorous mathematical proof does not exist for a particular problem, and you will have to try this numerical approach.

In this problem you are to examine the first ten matrices formed in this way and then evaluate the determinant. Here is the approach that you should use:

(a) Generate the first 50 terms in the Fibonacci series and store them in an array.
(b) Create a matrix of terms in the series using the first through the ninth terms.
(c) Calculate the determinant of the matrix thus formed.
(d) Repeat (b) and (c) nine additional times, but each time form the matrix with the second through the tenth terms in the series, then the third through the eleventh, and so forth.
(e) If any of the determinants are not zero, print out an appropriate message.
(f) Take special care that the determinant may not be *exactly* equal to zero because of round-off errors associated with real numbers. It is better to use real numbers for this problem because real numbers allow you to store larger values.

```
C*****************************************************************
C Create the first 50 terms in the series and store in the one-
C dimensional array FIB
C*****************************************************************
        REAL FIB(50), A(3,3)
        FIB(1) = 1.0
        FIB(2) = 1.0
        DO 10 I = 3, 50
           FIB(I) = FIB(I-1) + FIB(I-2)
  10    CONTINUE
C*****************************************************************
C The outer loop executes 10 times, each time setting the value
C of INDEX and performing the following instructions:
C      1) form the matrix starting with the INDEX'th term
C      2) calculate the determinant of the matrix formed
C      3) if the determinant is less than 0.001, then the
C         program concludes that the identity holds.
C*****************************************************************
        DO 30 INDEX = 1, 10
           DO 20 I = 1, 3
              DO 20 J = 1, 3
                 A(I, J) = FIB(J+(I-1)*3+INDEX-1)
  20       CONTINUE
           IF(ABS(DET(A)) .LT. 0.001) THEN
```

```
                    PRINT *, 'Test #', INDEX, 'OK'
              ELSE
                    PRINT *, 'Test #', INDEX, 'Invalid'
              ENDIF
       30     CONTINUE
              END
C****************************************************************
C See solved problem 7.11 for the DET function
C****************************************************************
```

7.15 We presented a program for calculating the components of a vector after a rotation about the z axis. There are many times, however, where we need to apply more complex rotations. Therefore, in this problem, you are to rewrite the subprogram given in Example 7.14 to allow a rotation about *any* axis. The equations for the rotation matrix are (r_x, r_y, r_z = matrix for rotation about the x, y, and z axes, respectively):

$$r_x = \begin{bmatrix} 1 & 0 & 0 \\ \cos(\alpha) & -\sin(\alpha) & 0 \\ \sin(\alpha) & \cos(\alpha) & 1 \end{bmatrix} \quad r_y = \begin{bmatrix} \cos(\alpha) & 0 & \sin(\alpha) \\ 0 & 1 & 0 \\ -\sin(\alpha) & 0 & \cos(\alpha) \end{bmatrix} \quad r_z = \begin{bmatrix} \cos(\alpha) & -\sin(\alpha) & 0 \\ \sin(\alpha) & \cos(\alpha) & 0 \\ 0 & 0 & 1 \end{bmatrix}$$

Rewrite the program and subprogram from Example 7.14 so that you may take three rotations about each of the axes in succession. Use an initial vector of (2.5, 3.0, 0.0) and rotate it 25° about X, −45° about Y, and 90° about Z. To double check your program, take the new vector that you get from these calculations and put it back into the program. This time, however, rotate the vector in the reverse direction (−90° about z, 45° about y, and −25° about x). Did you get the original vector back?

```
C****************************************************************
C We define three rotation matrices, RX, RY, and RZ, for each
C rotation desired. Then we will send the vector A to the
C subroutine MATMUL along with RX for the first transformation
C (answer stored back into A). Then we will send the vector A
C down to MATMUL a second time with RY to compute the effect of
C the second rotation. Finally, we send A down to MATMUL with
C RZ for the third transformation. The rotation matrices are
C evaluated in the subroutine ROTATE, which we will use twice
C — once for the forward transformations, once for the reverse
C transformations.
C****************************************************************
       REAL A(3),A2(3),A3(3),A4(3),RX(3,3),RY(3,3),RZ(3,3)
       DATA RAD/57.295827/
       PRINT *, 'Enter vector components'
       READ *, (A(I), I = 1,3)
       PRINT *, 'Enter rotations about x, y, z axes:'
       READ *, ANGLEX, ANGLEY, ANGLEZ
       ANGLEX=ANGLEX/RAD
       ANGLEY=ANGLEY/RAD
       ANGLEZ=ANGLEZ/RAD
```

```
C******* *********************************************************
C Once the rotation angles have been read in, compute the
C components of the three rotation matrices.
C******* *********************************************************
      CALL ROTATE(RX, RY, RZ, ANGLEX, ANGLEY, ANGLEZ)
C******* *********************************************************
C Send A down to MATMUL with RX for the first transformation.
C Then send the modified A to MATMUL with RY for the
C second transformation. Finally, send the twice modified A
C down to MATMUL with RZ for the third transformation.
C******* *********************************************************
      CALL MATMUL(RX, A, A2, 3, 3)
      CALL MATMUL(RY, A2, A3, 3, 3)
      CALL MATMUL(RZ, A3, A4, 3, 3)
      PRINT *, 'After 3 rotations, the vector is:'
      PRINT *, (A4(I), I = 1, 3)
C******* *********************************************************
C Now, reverse the directions and repeat the calculations
C******* *********************************************************
      CALL ROTATE(RX, RY, RZ, -ANGLEX, -ANGLEY, -ANGLEZ)
      CALL MATMUL(RZ, A4, A3, 3, 3)
      CALL MATMUL(RY, A3, A2, 3, 3)
      CALL MATMUL(RX, A2, A, 3, 3)
      PRINT *, 'After reversing, the vector is:'
      PRINT *, (A(I), I = 1, 3)
      END
C******* *********************************************************
C Subroutine to compute the rotation matrices
C******* *********************************************************
      SUBROUTINE ROTATE(RX, RY, RZ, ANGLEX, ANGLEY, ANGLEZ)
      REAL RX(3, 3), RY(3, 3), RZ(3, 3)
      RX(1,1) = 1.0
      RX(2,1) = COS(ANGLEX)
      RX(2,2) = -SIN(ANGLEX)
      RX(3,1) = SIN(ANGLEX)
      RX(3,2) = COS(ANGLEX)
      RX(3,3) = 1.0
      RY(1,1) = COS(ANGLEY)
      RY(1,3) = SIN(ANGLEY)
      RY(2,2) = 1.0
      RY(3,1) = -SIN(ANGLEY)
      RY(3,3) = COS(ANGLEY)
      RZ(1,1) = COS(ANGLEZ)
      RZ(1,2) = -SIN(ANGLEZ)
      RZ(2,1) = SIN(ANGLEZ)
      RZ(2,2) = COS(ANGLEZ)
      RZ(3,3) = 1.0
      RETURN
      END
```

Supplementary Problems

7.16 Locate syntax and run-time errors in each of the following program segments:

(a)
```
READ *, A
CALL SUB(A)
    ⋮
END
REAL SUBROUTINE SUB(A)
PRINT *, A
RETURN
END
```

(b)
```
CALL JACK(A, B)
END
REAL FUNCTION JACK(A, B)
JACK = A*B
RETURN
END
```

(c)
```
COMMON Y
X = 4.0
CALL SUB(X)
END
SUBROUTINE SUB(X)
COMMON X
PRINT *, X
RETURN
END
```

(d)
```
REAL F, X, Y, Z
READ X, Y, Z, I
    ⋮
PRINT *, F(X, Y, Z, I)
END
REAL FUNCTION F(X, Y, I)
F = SIN(X)*EXP(-Z*Y)**I
RETURN
END
```

(e)
```
DOUBLE PRECISION A, B
CALL SUB3(A, B)
    ⋮
END
SUBROUTINE SUB3(A, B)
    ⋮
RETURN
END
```

(f)
```
INTEGER DOT, A(3), B(3)
DATA A/1,2,3/, B/1,2,6/
C=DOT(A,B)
    ⋮
END
FUNCTION DOT(A, B)
INTEGER A(3), B(3)
DOT = ...
RETURN
END
```

7.17 Variable dimensioning of arrays in a subprogram is really a misnomer. The storage location has been set up in the calling module and this can't change, no matter what you use to dimension the array in the subprogram. Run these two examples to see how your compiler handles variable-sized arrays.

```
REAL A(1)
A(1) = 100
CALL SUB1(A,1)
END
SUBROUTINE SUB1(A,I)
REAL A(I)
PRINT *, A
RETURN
END
```

```
       REAL A(100)
       DO 10 I = 1, 100
           A(I) = I
10     CALL SUB1(A,1)
       END
       SUBROUTINE SUB1 (A, I)
       REAL A(I)
       PRINT *, (A(J), J=1,100)
       RETURN
       END
```

7.18 Write program segments to accomplish the following, using either built-in functions or user-defined functions.

(a) Read in a two-dimensional array of size N × M and compute the sum of all elements.

(b) Read in a two-dimensional array of size N × M and compute the sum of any row I.

(c) Read in an M × N two-dimensional array, compute the sum of each row, and print the results.

(d) Read in a one-dimensional array A of size N, a two-dimensional array Y of size M × N, and compute the elements of the new array Z defined by $Z(I)=A(I)/Y(M-N,I)$

7.19 Write a function that computes the factorial ($i!$) of a number i. Then use that function in a second subprogram to compute the series shown below.

$$\sum_{i=1}^{i=n} (-1)^{(i+1)} \frac{1}{i!}$$

The main program should read in the value of n, then compute the series for the appropriate number of terms, and print out the sum of the series terms. All computations should be done in the function subprograms.

7.20 Write program segments to accomplish the following using subroutines.

(a) Read in a one-dimensional array of arbitrary size (up to 1000 elements) and send it to a subroutine that searches for the largest number and reports how many elements are larger than 0.5 times the maximum value.

(b) Compute the average $xavg$ of an array X and then determine the deviation d of each element of X from the average according to the formula $d_i = X_i - xavg$.

(c) The dot product ($\odot$) of two vectors a and b (each containing three elements) is defined by $a \odot b = a_1 b_1 + a_2 b_2 + a_3 b_3$. Write a function to implement the dot product. Then write a subroutine to compute the magnitude of $(a \odot b)(b \odot d)(b \odot c)$.

(d) The cross product ($\otimes$) of two vectors a and b (each containing three elements) is defined by $c = a \otimes b = [(a_2 b_3 - a_3 b_2), (a_3 b_1 - a_1 b_3), (a_1 b_2 - a_2 b_1)]$. Note that c is a vector whose components are given by the terms in the parentheses. Write a subroutine to compute the cross product of two vectors a and b.

(e) Use the function for the dot product and the subroutine for the cross product to prove the identity $(a \otimes b) \odot (c \otimes d) = (a \odot b)(b \odot d)(b \odot c)$.

7.21 The following program was supposed to print out the elements of an array in a sequential manner (*viz.* A(1), A(2), A(3), . . ., A(10)). What went wrong?

```
REAL A(10)
PRINT *, 'Enter the array A:'
READ *, (A(I), I = 1, 10)
DO 10 INDEX = 1, 10
    CALL TEST(A)
10 CONTINUE
END
```

```
SUBROUTINE TEST(A)
DATA I/1/
PRINT *, A(I)
I=I+1
RETURN
END
```

7.22   One of the most important reasons that we write subprograms is that we can create libraries
of common mathematical operations. Once we have created these libraries, we can then use
any of the subprograms stored there in other programs and greatly reduce our programming
efforts. But to be effective, each of the subprograms should execute only a single task or
a few very closely related tasks. Therefore, libraries tend to be large, with several hundred
common functions. To help you begin creating your own personalized library, write
subprograms to perform the following simple mathematical tasks:

(a) TABSRC   searches a table for the maximum value
(b) ROWSUM   sums all elements in the ith row in a table
(c) TABSUM   sums all elements in a table
(d) VECADD   adds two vectors
(e) MATMUL   multiplies two matrices
(f) TRANSP   generates the transpose of a matrix. A transpose is generated by
             substituting A(I, J) into B(J, I)
(g) VECLEN   calculates the length of a vector (see Example 7.13 for definitions)

7.23   Write a program to approximate the value of the infinite series for $R(x)$ given by

$$R(x) = J_0(x) + \frac{J_0(x^2)}{2!} + \frac{J_0(x^3)}{3!} + \ldots$$

where J_0 is known as the zero-order Bessel function defined by

$$J_0(x) = 1 - \frac{x^2}{2^2} + \frac{x^4}{2^2\,4^2} - \frac{x^6}{2^2\,4^2\,6^2} + \ldots$$

When computing the Bessel function, terminate the series when the absolute value of any
new term changes the approximation by no more than 0.1%. In a similar way, terminate the
approximation for $R(x)$ when the absolute value of any new term adds no more than 0.1%
to the series total.

7.24   The functions presented in this chapter for finding the maximum value (Solved Problems
7.9d and Supplementary Problem 7.22a) are only useful for examining a list or table of
discrete data values. They cannot be used to find the maximum value of a continuous
function. For such a function, we must use a different approach. Write a program that
utilizes the following algorithm:

(a) Read in a starting point x, a step size Δx, and an allowable error ϵ
(b) Start the search by calculating $f(x)$ and $f(x+\Delta x)$
(c) If $f(x) < f(x+\Delta x)$, then increase x by Δx and repeat step (b)
(d) Otherwise, reduce the step size Δx by half and repeat step (b)
(e) Repeat until $|f(x) - f(x+\Delta x)| < \epsilon$.
(f) Report $(x+x+\Delta x)/2$ as the position of the maximum value of the function.

Apply the above algorithm to the function $y(x) = \sin(x)e^{-x}$. Start your search at $x=0.7$ with an initial $\Delta x=0.1$ with ϵ to 0.001.

Answers to Selected Supplementary Problems

7.16 (a) Typing (REAL) is not used with subroutines.
(b) Calling statements are used with subroutines, not functions.
(c) The variable X is sent to the subroutine via both the COMMON statement and the argument list. This is not allowed.
(d) There is a mismatch in the number of arguments in the calling statement and the FUNCTION statement.
(e) A and B must be declared in the subroutine as double precision.
(f) DOT is declared as an integer in the main program. Therefore, the function should be declared as an integer also.

7.18 (a)
```
C******************************************************************
C Use the main program to read in the two dimensional array
C and the number of rows (N) and columns (M).
C******************************************************************
      REAL A(100, 100)
      PRINT *, 'Enter size of array (less than 100 x 100):'
      READ *, N, M
      PRINT *, 'Enter the array by rows:'
      READ *, ((A(I, J), J = 1, M), I = 1, N)
      PRINT *, SUM(A, N, M)
      END
C******************************************************************
C To sum the table, we add each element to the variable
C SUM. Note that we use a variable size array with I and J
C sent down at execution time.
C******************************************************************
      REAL FUNCTION SUM(X, I, J)
      REAL X(I, J)
      SUM = 0.0
      DO 10 K = 1, I
         DO 10 L = 1, J
            SUM = SUM + X(K, L)
   10 CONTINUE
```

```
          RETURN
          END
```

(b)
```
C******************************************************************
C We enter a specific row for summing through the variable
C I. We send this to the subroutine along with the table, the
C number of rows (N), and the number of columns (M).
C******************************************************************
          REAL A(100, 100)
          PRINT *, 'Enter size of array (less than 100 x 100):'
          READ *, N, M
          PRINT *, 'Enter the array by rows:'
          READ *, ((A(I, J), J = 1, M), I = 1, N)
          PRINT *, 'Which row is to be summed?'
          READ *, I
          PRINT *, SUM(A, N, M, I)
          END
C******************************************************************
C Inside the DO loop, we sum all the elements in the Lth
C row. Note that only the column subscript changes inside the
C loop.
C******************************************************************
          REAL FUNCTION SUM(X, I, J, L)
          REAL X(I, J)
          SUM = 0.0
          DO 10 K = 1, I
             SUM = SUM + X(L, K)
   10 CONTINUE
          RETURN
          END
```

(c)
```
C******************************************************************
C We will use the function from problem (b) above. But this
C time, the variable that fixes the row for summing will be
C cycled by the main program.
C******************************************************************
          REAL A(100, 100)
          PRINT *, 'Enter size of array (less than 100 x 100):'
          READ *, N, M
          PRINT *, 'Enter the array by rows:'
          READ *, ((A(I, J), J = 1, M), I = 1, N)
          DO 10 I = 1, N
             PRINT *,'Sum of row', I, 'is', SUM(A, N, M, I)
   10 CONTINUE
          END
C******************************************************************
C The main program will send down a different value of L
C each time the function is called. But for the duration
C of the calculation, L is fixed until all elements in
C that row are added.
C******************************************************************
          REAL FUNCTION SUM(X, I, J, L)
          REAL X(I, J)
          SUM = 0.0
          DO 10 K = 1, I
             SUM = SUM + X(L, K)
   10 CONTINUE
```

```
      RETURN
      END
```

(d)
```
C************************************************************
C Use the main program to read in the data. But leave the
C computation to the subprogram.
C************************************************************
      REAL A(100), Y(100,100), Z(100)
      PRINT *, 'Enter size of A (less than 100):'
      READ *, N
      PRINT *, 'Enter number of rows in Y:'
      READ *, M
      PRINT *, 'Enter A:'
      READ *, (A(I), I = 1, N)
      PRINT *, 'Enter Y by rows:'
      READ *, ((Y(I,J), J = 1, N), I = 1, M)
      DO 10 I = 1, N
         Z(I) = COMPUTE(A, Y, N, M, I)
   10 CONTINUE
      PRINT *, 'Z values:', (Z(I), I = 1, N)
      END
C************************************************************
C The computation is a single assignment statement. The main
C program controls which element is being computed.
C************************************************************
      REAL FUNCTION COMPUTE(X, Y, N, M, I)
      REAL X(N), Y(M, N)
      COMPUTE = X(I)/Y(M-N,I)
      RETURN
      END
```

7.19
```
      PRINT *, 'Enter number of terms in the series:'
      READ *, N
      PRINT *, 'Series total = ', SERIES(N)
      END
C************************************************************
C The DO 10 loop computes one term in the series at a time
C and adds it to the running total. The sign of each term
C alternates. One way to do this is with (-1)**(I + 1)
C where I is the loop control variable. The denominator is
C computed by the factorial function.
C************************************************************
      REAL FUNCTION SERIES(N)
      SERIES = 0.0
      DO 10 I = 1, N
         SERIES = SERIES + (-1.0)**(I + 1)/IFACT(I)
   10 CONTINUE
      RETURN
      END
C************************************************************
C The factorial function from Example 7.3
C************************************************************
      INTEGER FUNCTION IFACT(I)
      FACT = 1
      DO 10 K = 2, I
```

```
                     FACT = FACT * K
          10 CONTINUE
             RETURN
             END
```

7.20   **(a)**
```
             REAL A(1000)
             PRINT *, 'Enter Number of items:'
             READ *, N
             PRINT *, 'Enter Data:'
             READ *, (A(I), I = 1, N)
             CALL MEDIAN(A, N, J)
             PRINT *, J, 'data points were above 0.5(max value)'
             END
C***********************************************************
C The array A is searched element by element to find the
C largest value.
C***********************************************************
             SUBROUTINE MEDIAN(A, N, J)
             REAL A(N)
             BIG = A(1)
             DO 10 I = 2, N
                IF(A(I) .GT. BIG) BIG = A(I)
          10 CONTINUE
C***********************************************************
C The variable J is the number of elements that exceed
C BIG/2. We examine each element in the DO loop to see if
C it exceeds BIG/2. If it does, J is increased by 1.
C***********************************************************
             J = 0
             DO 20 I = 1, N
                IF(A(I) .GT. BIG/2.0) J = J + 1
          20 CONTINUE
             RETURN
             END
```

  (b)
```
             REAL X(1000), D(1000)
             PRINT *, 'Enter number of items:'
             READ *, N
             PRINT *, 'Enter data:'
             READ *, (X(I), I = 1, N)
             CALL DEV(X, D, N)
             PRINT *,'Input data and Deviations:'
             PRINT *, (X(I), D(I), I = 1, N)
             END
C***********************************************************
C DEV computes the average error between each data point and
C average.
C***********************************************************
             SUBROUTINE DEV(X, D, N)
             REAL X(N), D(N)
             SUM = 0.0
             DO 10 I = 1, N
                SUM = SUM + X(I)
          10 CONTINUE
             AVG = SUM/N
```

```
C*****************************************************************
C Once the average has been determined, it is subtracted
C from each of the elements to determine the D array.
C*****************************************************************
      DO 20 I = 1, N
         D(I) = X(I) - AVG
 20   CONTINUE
      RETURN
      END
```

(c)
```
      REAL A(3), B(3), C(3), D(3), MAG
      PRINT *, 'Enter A, B, C, and D vectors:'
      READ *,(A(I), I = 1, 3), (B(I), I = 1, 3),
     1       (C(I), I = 1,3), (D(I), I = 1, 3)
      CALL COMPUTE(A, B, C, D, MAG)
      PRINT *, 'Triple scalar product = ', MAG
      END
C*****************************************************************
C DOT(A,B) is a scalar quantity. So when we compute the
C three dot products, we can multiply them directly to
C obtain the value of MAG
C*****************************************************************
      SUBROUTINE COMPUTE(A, B, C, D, MAG)
      REAL A(3), B(3), C(3), D(3), MAG
      MAG = DOT(A, B)*DOT(B, D)*DOT(B, C)
      RETURN
      END
C*****************************************************************
C DOT function from Example 7.12
C*****************************************************************
      REAL FUNCTION DOT(X, Y)
      REAL X(3), Y(3)
      DOT = 0.0
      DO 10 I = 1, 3
         DOT = DOT + X(I)*Y(I)
 10   CONTINUE
      RETURN
      END
```

(d)
```
      REAL A(3), B(3), C(3)
      PRINT *, 'Enter A and B vectors:'
      READ *, (A(I), I = 1, 3), (B(I), I = 1, 3)
      CALL CROSS(A, B, C)
      PRINT *, 'Cross product ='
      PRINT *, (C(I), I = 1, 3)
      END
C*****************************************************************
C The cross product of two vectors is itself a vector.
C Therefore, we must calculate the components individually.
C*****************************************************************
      SUBROUTINE CROSS(A, B, C)
      REAL A(3), B(3), C(3)
      C(1) = A(2)*B(3)-A(3)*B(2)
      C(2) = A(3)*B(1)-A(1)*B(3)
      C(3) = A(1)*B(2)-A(2)*B(1)
      RETURN
      END
```

```
(e)       REAL A(3), B(3), C(3), D(3), E(3), F(3)
          PRINT *, 'Enter A, B, C, and D vectors'
          READ *, (A(I), I = 1, 3), (B(I), I = 1, 3),
         1         (C(I), I = 1, 3), (D(I), I = 1, 3)
C*****************************************************************
C Take the cross product of A and B and store in E. Then
C take the cross product of C and D and store in F. This
C enables us to evaluate the right-hand side (RHS) of the
C identity by taking the dot product of E and F. The left
C hand side (LHS) is evaluated by a series of dot products.
C*****************************************************************
          CALL CROSS(A, B, E)
          CALL CROSS(C, D, F)
          RHS = DOT(E, F)
          LHS = DOT(A, B)*DOT(B, D)*DOT(B, C)
C*****************************************************************
C The RHS may not be exactly equal to the LHS because of
C round off errors. So we allow for a small residual.
C*****************************************************************
          IF(ABS(LHS-RHS) .LT. .00001) THEN
             PRINT *, 'Identity valid'
          ELSE
             PRINT *, 'Identity not valid'
          ENDIF
          END
          REAL FUNCTION DOT(X, Y)
          REAL X(3), Y(3)
          DOT = 0.0
          DO 10 I = 1, 3
             DOT = DOT + X(I)*Y(I)
   10     CONTINUE
          RETURN
          END
          SUBROUTINE CROSS(A, B, C)
          REAL A(3), B(3), C(3)
          C(1) = A(2)*B(3)-A(3)*B(2)
          C(2) = A(3)*B(1)-A(1)*B(3)
          C(3) = A(1)*B(2)-A(2)*B(1)
          RETURN
          END
```

7.21 Trace through the program. Assume that, A(1) = 10, A(2) = 20, . . . A(3) = 100.

Program Trace:
.MAIN. Trace:
    READ in values into the array A
    Begin Loop, INDEX=1
    Send array A to the subroutine TEST

.TEST. Trace:
    Execute the DATA statement. I = 1
    PRINT value of A(1) → error, since A is not declared as an array in the subroutine.

We must declare A as an array in the subroutine by adding a statement REAL A(10) before the DATA statement. Note that once this is done, the program will work correctly. The DATA statement will provide only <u>initial</u> values to the indicated variables. Thus, I will be assigned a value of 1 during the first call to the function. But subsequent calls will ignore the DATA statement and will use the updated values of I through the I=I+1 statement.

7.22 (a)
```
C*******************************************************************
C We assume that X(1,1) is the largest value and then
C compare each of the remaining elements to the maximum
C value. When a larger value is found, this becomes the
C new max value.
C*******************************************************************
      REAL FUNCTION TABSRC(X, M, N)
      REAL X(M, N)
      TABSRC = X(1, 1)
      DO 10 I = 1, M
         DO 10 J = 1, N
            IF(X(I, J) .GT. TABSRC) TABSRC = X(I, J)
   10 CONTINUE
      RETURN
      END
```
(b)
```
C*******************************************************************
C The table is set up as a variable-sized array. The row
C to be summed is stored in the variable I. Each element
C in that row is then added to the variable ROWSUM.
C*******************************************************************
      REAL FUNCTION ROWSUM(X, M, N, I)
      REAL X(M, N)
      ROWSUM = 0.0
      DO 10 L = 1, N
         ROWSUM = ROWSUM + X(I, L)
   10 CONTINUE
      RETURN
      END
```
(c)
```
C*******************************************************************
C Add every element in the array from row 1 to M and column
C 1 to N.
C*******************************************************************
      REAL FUNCTION TABSUM(X, M, N)
      REAL X(M, N)
      TABSUM = 0.0
      DO 10 I = 1, M
         DO 10 J = 1, N
            TABSUM = TABSUM + X(I, J)
   10 CONTINUE
      RETURN
      END
```
(d)
```
C*******************************************************************
C To add two vectors, you add the corresponding elements of
C each vector and store the results in a new vector RESULT.
C*******************************************************************
      REAL FUNCTION VECADD(X, Y, RESULT, N)
      REAL X(N), Y(N), RESULT(N)
```

```
      DO 10 I = 1, N
         RESULT(I) = X(I) + Y(I)
10 CONTINUE
      RETURN
      END
```

(e)
```
C*******************************************************************
C To multiply, you take the row of one matrix and multiply it
C by the corresponding column of the other matrix. The sum
C of the products is a single element of C. See Example 6.14
C for an in-depth discussion.
C*******************************************************************
      SUBROUTINE MATMUL(A, B, C, M, N)
      REAL A(M, N), B(N, M), C(M, M)
      DO 10 I = 1, M
         DO 10 J = 1, M
            C(I, J) = 0.0
            DO 10 K = 1, N
               C(I, J) = C(I, J) + A(I, K)* B(K, J)
10 CONTINUE
      RETURN
      END
```

(f)
```
C*******************************************************************
C The transpose of a matrix is generated by switching the
C indices. A(I,J) becomes B(J,I) for example.
C*******************************************************************
      SUBROUTINE TRANSP(A, B, M, N)
      REAL A(M, N), B(N, M)
      DO 10 I = 1, M
         DO 10 J = 1, N
            B(I, J) = A(J, I)
10 CONTINUE
      RETURN
      END
```

(g)
```
C*******************************************************************
C The length of a vector is a scalar quantity and is the
C square root of the sum of the square of all the elements of
C that vector.
C*******************************************************************
      REAL FUNCTION VECLEN(X, N)
      REAL X(N)
      VECLEN = 0.0
      DO 10 I = 1, N
         VECLEN = VECLEN + X(I)**2
10 CONTINUE
      VECLEN = SQRT(VECLEN)
      RETURN
      END
```

7.23
```
C*******************************************************************
C Enter the key parameters, X, JLIMIT, and RLIMIT. X is the
C value at which the function is to be evaluated, while JLIMIT
C is the acceptable limit for terminating the Bessel function
C computation; it is passed to the function via a COMMON
C statement. RLIMIT is the corresponding value for terminating
```

```
C the computation of R(x).
C***********************************************************************
      REAL J0, JLIMIT
      COMMON JLIMIT
      PRINT *, 'Enter X, JLIMIT, RLIMIT'
      READ *, X, JLIMIT, RLIMIT
C***********************************************************************
C Initialize the approximation to the series R to JO(X). We must
C also keep track of the number of the term since we must use
C it to compute the argument for J. We initialize N (the term
C counter to 2 and increment it by 1 each time through the loop.
C***********************************************************************
      R = J0(X)
      N = 2
C***********************************************************************
C Use a DO while loop to compute the series approximation for
C R. Whenever any ABS(TERM)/R becomes less than RLIMIT, we stop.
C***********************************************************************
      TERM = R
      DO WHILE (ABS(TERM)/R .GT. RLIMIT)
         TERM = J0(X**N)/IFACT(N)
         R = R + TERM
         N = N + 1
      END DO
      PRINT *, 'Series Approximation = ', R
      END
C***********************************************************************
C Function to approximate the Bessel function. The limit to
C decide when to terminate the approximation is passed
C through a COMMON statement.
C***********************************************************************
      REAL FUNCTION J0(X)
      REAL JLIMIT
      COMMON JLIMIT
C***********************************************************************
C Variables: TERM = individual power term (X**2N) in the series
C            N    = number of the term
C            SIGN = +1 or -1
C            DENO = denominator (2**2, (2**2*4**2), etc.)
C***********************************************************************
      J0 = 1.0
      TERM = 1.0
      N = 0
      SIGN = 1
      DENO = 1
C***********************************************************************
C Continue the series evaluation until any term contributes
C so little that there is no sense continuing the computation.
C This is done by noting whether ABS(TERM)/JO < JLIMIT.
C***********************************************************************
      DO WHILE (ABS(TERM)/JO .GT. JLIMIT)
         SIGN = -SIGN
         N = N+2
         DEN = DEN*N**2
         TERM = X**N/DEN
         JO = JO + SIGN*TERM
```

```
      END DO
      RETURN
      END
C********************************************************************
C Use the function subprogram for the factorial from Example 7.3
C and must be included.
C********************************************************************
```


7.24
```
C********************************************************************
C In the main program, we read in X, DX, and EPS and then call
C the function before printing out the results.
C********************************************************************
      PRINT *, 'Enter starting value, step size, and error:'
      READ *, X, DX, EPS
      PRINT *,'Maximum Value of function:', FMAX(X, DX, EPS)
      PRINT *,'Maximum Value is at:', (2*X+DX)/2.0
      RETURN
      END
C********************************************************************
C Function to conduct search for maximum value in a function.
C********************************************************************
      REAL FUNCTION FMAX(X, DX, EPS)
      CHECK = F(X+DX)-F(X)
      IF(CHECK .LT. 0) STOP 'Bad start point'
      DO WHILE (CHECK .GT. EPS)
         IF(F(X) .LT. F(X+DX)) THEN
            X = X + DX
         ELSE
            DX = DX/2
         ENDIF
         CHECK = ABS(F(X) - F(X + DX))
      END DO
      FMAX=(X+DX)/2.0
      RETURN
      END
C********************************************************************
C Function to be evaluated which will vary for each problem.
C********************************************************************
      REAL FUNCTION F(X)
      F = SIN(X) * EXP(-X)
      RETURN
      END
```

Chapter 8

Character and Logical Data

8.1 OVERVIEW

Most engineering and scientific applications deal with the processing of numerical data, but there are occasions when character data (text) is also an important consideration. In previous chapters, we presented only limited examples of character data. This chapter will take a closer look at character data and some applications that require its use.

The topics to be covered in this chapter include:

- The need for character data
- Declarations and assignment statements
- Character manipulations
- Formatted and unformatted input/output
- Internal files
- Character-based library functions
- Logical data
- Debugging tips.

8.2 THE NEED FOR CHARACTER DATA

There are many reasons for creating programs. One important reason is to save time through increased productivity. By computerizing the solution to a commonly encountered problem, the time it takes to solve that problem can be dramatically reduced. With computerization comes an even bigger advantage: consistency. Once a program is written to solve a problem, the computer will faithfully execute the same procedure every time (as long as the program isn't changed). This means that, right or wrong, the answer will always be the same given the same input. Assuming the program has been properly validated, the only cause of an error would be improper input.

One way to help prevent improper I/O, or a misunderstanding about what your data mean is through the use of character data, which is the subject of this chapter. For example, you may want to include identifying information with your input. This might include sample identification, processing history, testing date, and identification of testing personnel that is to be kept with the numerical data used for analysis. With proper use of nonnumeric data, your programs will become easier to use, both by yourself and others. While this is a simple matter, it is an important one.

Character data can be used to add a level of versatility to your programs. Up to this point the programs presented have been mostly procedural. This means that you run a particular program to perform a particular task. Some programs, however, require a dialog and are designed to be more general. For example, you may present in your program a list of options that trigger a series of calculations. The program may be required to interpret the user responses, store some of them,

274

and direct the operation of the program based on these inputs. Sometimes, the input data will consist of a mixture of numeric and nonnumeric data, and your program may have to sift through these data to extract the essential information needed to begin execution.

While most engineering problems focus on the manipulation of numerical data, there is a vast area of applications that requires textual data instead. Consider the problems of sorting a list of names in alphabetical order, or counting the number of words in a passage. When looking up information in data tables, it is convenient to construct tables such that the row and column headings mean something significant. For example, assume that a table of material properties exists and can be accessed through a function named PROPRTY. To retrieve the modulus of elasticity E (a measure of the material's stiffness) for a common stainless steel (SA-240-304) the necessary line of code might look like this:

```
ESTEEL = PROPRTY('SA-240-304', 'E')
```

By using strings such as 'SA-240-304' or 'E', it is much easier to understand what actions are taking place. In the following sections, we will discuss the mechanics of setting up and using character or string data and illustrate how they can be useful in engineering and science applications.

8.3 DECLARATIONS AND ASSIGNMENT STATEMENTS

A group of alphanumeric symbols is known as a *character*. A character or string variable is declared to be of type CHARACTER. A character variable has a property known as length, which is the number of characters that can be stored in the character variable. The following example illustrates the declaration of a character variable.

EXAMPLE 8.1

This is how to declare the variable NAME to store nonnumeric data that can be up to 20 characters long:

```
CHARACTER NAME*20
```

You may also declare several variables with the same declaration statement.

```
CHARACTER NAME*20, ADDRES*20, PHONE*20
```

If all the variables are to be the same length, you may use an alternate form of the declaration statement:

```
CHARACTER*20 NAME, ADDRES, PHONE
```

If the variables are of different length, however, you may not use the alternate form and must explicitly state the length of each.

As with any other Fortran data type, an array of character data can be constructed. For a character array, all of the elements must have the same length. Thus, you must specify the number of elements and the length of each.

EXAMPLE 8.2

The following declaration statement creates an array called TABLE of 5 rows and 2 columns with character elements of length 7. Thus, each element in the table can be as large as 7 characters long.

```
CHARACTER *7, TABLE(5, 2)
```

You refer to each element in the table just as before. Thus, TABLE(3,2) refers to the element in row 3, column 2, that is 7 characters long or less. As we will see shortly, if fewer than 7 characters are used, the compiler will substitute blank spaces as needed.

One application of character arrays is generating printer graphics. If your compiler or monitor system does not have graphics capabilities, you can create low-resolution graphics by using a character array.

EXAMPLE 8.3

Most terminal screens measure 80 columns by 20 rows. We will use a character array of this size on which to plot the function $y = \sin(x)$. The process involves plotting 80 points from $-$pi to pi and scaling these points to fit within the array bounds.

```
C Use of character data to graphically display data
C The character array SCREEN will fit onto a conventional
C screen of 80 columns by 20 rows. Each element is
C one character long (either a '*' or ' ').
C*******************************************************************
      PARAMETER(COLS=80, ROWS=20, PI=3.1416)
      INTEGER COLS, ROWS
      CHARACTER*1 SCREEN(ROWS, COLS)
C*******************************************************************
C Initialize all elements of SCREEN to blank spaces.
C*******************************************************************
      DATA SCREEN / 1600*' '/
C*******************************************************************
C From the column value calculate X. From the Y value calculate
C the row number in which to place a '*'.
C*******************************************************************
      DO 30 JX = 1, 80
         X = (-PI + (JX-1)*(PI))/(80-1)
         Y = SIN(X)
         IY = 1 + NINT((Y-1.0)/(-2.0)*(ROWS-1))
         SCREEN(IY, JX) = '*'
30    CONTINUE
```

```
C********************************************************************
C Now print the results by rows to the screen.
C********************************************************************
        DO 40 I = 1, ROWS
            PRINT *, (SCREEN(I,J), J = 1, COLS)
  40    CONTINUE
        END
```

The two assignment statements that define X and IY inside the DO 30 loop normalize these values so that X ranges between $-\pi$ and 0, while IY ranges between 1 and 20, corresponding to the number of rows in the output graph. The purpose of these statements is to determine into which element of the character array SCREEN the star '*' symbol will be placed. The output from this program will look like this:

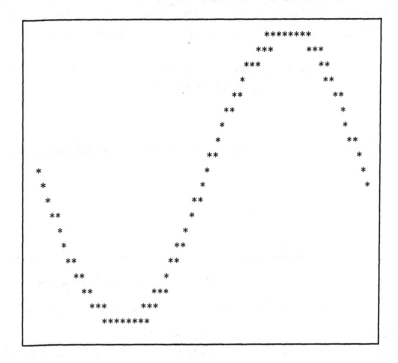

Note: If you find that your computer tries to "wrap" the text rather than print 80 characters on a line, you may need to use formatting to make the program work properly. This crude type of "plotting" is necessary only if your compiler and monitor do not support graphics. Fortunately, most compilers now support higher resolution graphics, so you won't have to resort to crude methods such as this.

8.4 CHARACTER MANIPULATION

In Fortran a number of operations are available for manipulating character data. These include assigning values to variables, extracting a portion of a string value, assigning a portion of a string value, appending strings together, and relational operations with strings. All these are described in the following sections.

The process of assigning a value to a character variable is similar to that used for numeric variables. The only change is that the assigned value must be enclosed between single quotation marks. Here are the rules and simple examples illustrating assignment statements:

Rule 1:   character must be enclosed between single quotation marks (X = 'string value')

Rule 2:   if the string value has a shorter length than the variable, blanks will be added at the end of the string to fill out the missing characters. This is known as padding. (Example: If Y has length 5, then Y = 'ABC' results in Y = 'ABC ' with two blanks added.)

Rule 3:   if the string value being assigned is longer than the length of the receiving variable, then the overflowing characters are not stored. (Example: If Z has length 3, then Z='abcde' results in Z='abc'. Note that 'de' is dropped.)

Rule 4:   to include an apostrophe in the string, you must type it twice. (Example: X='It''s an example' results in the value — It's an example.)

EXAMPLE 8.4

In the table below are examples of character assignment statements using the declaration statement:

```
CHARACTER X*5, Y*7, Z*10
```

Statement	Result , Rule, and Comments
X = '123AB'	123AB *(Rule 1)*
Y = '123AB'	123AB *(Rule 2 - 2 blank spaces at end)*
X = 'she''s'	she's *(Rule 4 and result is of length 5)*
Y = "she's"	*(Illegal since Fortran 77 uses single quote marks)*
Z = 'X has length 5'	X has leng *(Rule 3)*

Fortran 77 also allows for the concept of a *substring*, where a substring is a consecutive sequence of characters from within a string. Substrings allow us to remove desired characters from a longer string and perform various operations on them.

EXAMPLE 8.5

Consider the string 'Help'. We can form various length substrings from the characters that make up the total string. Consider the following examples:

Length 1 substrings:	'H', 'e', 'l', 'p'
Length 2 substrings:	'He', 'el', 'lp'
Length 3 substrings:	'Hel', 'elp'
Length 4 substrings:	'Help'

Notice that we could only form substrings from consecutive characters. For example, we could not form a substring of 'Hep' because we would have to skip a letter.

Fortran supports a simple notation which allows you to extract substrings from a string. The concept of a character variable having many elements is much like a one-dimensional array. Each character resides in its own element. Substrings allow you to extract or replace a list of characters stored in a string variable. The general form to reference a substring of a variable is as follows:

String variable(I: J)

where $1 \leq I \leq J \leq$ length of the string variable. If I is omitted, then the default value of 1 is assumed. If J is omitted, then the default value of the variable string length is assumed. The colon (:) must be included.

EXAMPLE 8.6

Assume that the variable ALPHA is a character variable and is declared to have length 26 with the value 'ABCDEFGHIJKLMNOPQRSTUVWXYZ'

Substring	Value and Comments
ALPHA(1:3)	ABC
ALPHA(24:26)	XYZ
ALPHA(:3)	ABC *(Assumed starting index = 1)*
ALPHA(24:)	XYZ *(Assumed ending index = 26)*
ALPHA(2:2)	B *(Single character substring)*
ALPHA(:)	ABCDEFGHIJKLMNOPQRSTUVWXYZ

Substrings can be used in assignment statements. When placed on the right side of the equals sign, the substring is assigned to the receiving string variable. When placed on the left side of the equals symbol, the substring receives the assigned value. This allows you to modify a portion of a string. The rules for padding (adding blanks) and truncation apply.

EXAMPLE 8.7

Assume that the character variable A has length 3, B has length 5, ALPHA has length 26 with the value 'ABCDEFGHIJKLMNOPQRSTUVWXYZ', and BETA has length 10 with the value '1234567890'. Here are several assignment statements based on these values:

Assignment Statement	Result and Comment
A = ALPHA(1:3)	A has value — ABC
B = BETA(1:3)	B has value — 123 *(2 blanks added at the end)*
A = BETA(5:10)	A has value — 567 *(890 was dropped)*
BETA(1:3) = ALPHA(1:3)	BETA has value — ABC4567890
BETA(1:4) = ALPHA(24:26)	BETA has value — XYZ 567890 *(Blank added)*

One operation that we commonly perform with strings and substrings is *concatenation*, which is the process of appending one string or substring to another. You can think of this operation as being a string "addition," and it is indicated by //. The strings to be "added" are placed on either side of the // symbol.

EXAMPLE 8.8

In this example, we will read in a person's first name and last name and then form a character variable FULLNAME by use of the concatenation operation.

```
C****************************************************************
C The first and last names will be stored in FIRST and LAST
C respectively. The full name will be created by joining
C these two names.
C****************************************************************
      CHARACTER*20 FIRST, LAST
      CHARACTER*45 FULLNAME
      PRINT *, 'Enter your first name within apostrophes'
      READ *, FIRST
      PRINT *, 'Enter your last name within apostrophes'
      READ *, LAST
C****************************************************************
C Create FULLNAME by joining the first and last names
C (separated by a comma) by using two concatenation operations
C****************************************************************
      FULLNAME = LAST//', '//FIRST
      PRINT *, FULLNAME
      END
```

The above program will print your last name and a comma followed by your first name. Note that concatenation is order dependent. LAST//FIRST and FIRST//LAST will not produce the same strings.

We have seen in previous chapters the use of relational operations on numerical data. These same operations can be applied to character data. To understand what the outcome of a relational operation will be, it will be necessary to understand the character set's *collating sequence*. The collating sequence is the order in which the characters are arranged from a minimum to a maximum value. For example 'A' is "less" than 'B', 'B' is "less" than 'C', and so on. For the alphabetic symbols, the collating sequence is equivalent to alphabetical order. But how do characters like '!', '*', and even uppercase versus lowercase letters appear in the collating sequence? This will depend on the character set adopted by the computer and the compiler.

It was stated earlier that two common character sets are encountered as the default character sets. They are ASCII and EBCDIC. The collating sequences for each of these character sets are different and are illustrated as follows:

ASCII collating sequence for printable characters:
　　　Blank ! " # $ % & ' ( ) * + , - . /
　　　0 1 2 3 4 5 6 7 8 9 : ; < = > ? @
　　　A B C D E F G H I J K L M N O P Q R S T U V W X Y Z { } ^ _ `
　　　a b c d e f g h i j k l m n o p q r s t u v w x y z { | } ~

EBCDIC collating sequence for printable characters:
　　　Blank] . < (+ ! & [$ *) ; ^ - / , % _ > ? : # @ ' = "
　　　a b c d e f g h i j k l m n o p q r s t u v w x y z
　　　A B C D E F G H I J K L M N O P Q R S T U V W X Y Z
　　　0 1 2 3 4 5 6 7 8 9

The six relational operations (.LT., .LE., .EQ., .NE., .GT., and .GE.) can be applied to character data. The equals and not equals operations are easily understood in the context of character data — either strings match or they don't. But, the issue is not so clear for the < and > operations, which require knowledge of the collating sequence. When comparing single character strings, the order is determined by the position within the collating sequence. For strings of more than one character, the comparison starts with the first character of each string. If those characters are the same, the comparison moves to the second character, and so on. This is the same procedure used when alphabetizing a list. The following example shows the use of relational operations:

EXAMPLE 8.9

Character Set	Expression	Result and Comments
ASCII	'A' .LT. 'a'	True
EBCDIC	'A' .LT. 'a'	False
ASCII	'AAA' .LT. 'B'	True
ASCII	'AAA' .LT. 'AA'	False *(Blank is less than any character)*
ASCII	'<' .LT. '='	True
EBCDIC	'<' .LT. '='	True
ASCII	'>' .GT. '='	True
EBCDIC	'>' .GT. '='	False

Because of the collating sequence, procedures to sort a list of numbers can be utilized to sort a list of names. This is the most common way to alphabetize a list of names.

EXAMPLE 8.10

The following example puts a list of names into alphabetical order. The names are stored in an array with 100 elements, and we will swap two names just as we did with numbers.

```
C*****************************************************************
C The array LIST stores the 100 names. We search the list for
C the minimum value within the list, where the minimum
C value is decided by the collating sequence. Once found,
C we will switch this value with the one in the target
C position.
C*****************************************************************
        CHARACTER*20 LIST(100), LISTMIN, SWAP
        PRINT *, 'Number of names in the list (100 max.)?'
        READ *, N
        DO 10 I = 1, N
            PRINT *,'Enter name', N,' between apostrophes'
            READ *, LIST(I)
10      CONTINUE
C*****************************************************************
C Start the sorting operation
C*****************************************************************
        DO 30 I = 1, N-1
            LISTMIN = LIST(I)
            INDEX = I
            DO 20 J = I+1, N
                IF(LIST(J) .LT. LISTMIN) THEN
                    LISTMIN = LIST(J)
                    INDEX = J
                END IF
20          CONTINUE
            SWAP = LIST(I)
            LIST(I) = LIST(INDEX)
            LIST(INDEX) = SWAP
30      CONTINUE
        DO 40 I = 1, N
            PRINT *, LIST(I)
40      CONTINUE
        END
```

Dealing with string variables in subprograms is similar to working with any other variable type. You are required to declare all input and output variables to match their declaration in the calling program. This is especially problematic with character data, since we must declare string length which varies considerably from variable to variable. Fortunately, Fortran allows for automatic string length assignment, which means that you are not required to know the declared length of a string variable. This feature not only makes it easier for you by avoiding errors in declaration statements, but also adds versatility to your subprograms. Since the called subprogram will automatically match the input/output variables, different variables of different lengths can be utilized by the same subprogram.

To have the string length automatically assigned in a subprogram, replace the length parameter with a star enclosed within parentheses (*). This will force the length of the variable to be the same as the argument being passed. With the convenience of automatic string length assignment comes the need to interrogate a variable to determine how long a string it can hold. The LEN function is used for this purpose.

EXAMPLE 8.11

This example illustrates how to determine the length of a string by using the LEN built-in function. In this example, we will search a string until a blank space is found. From that point on in the string, we will add a series of dollar signs ($) to fill out the variable.

```
C********************************************************************
C The character variable INPUT will contain a string which
C will have trailing blank spaces. We will send this to the
C subroutine ADDSTAR, which will replace these blanks by stars
C********************************************************************
      CHARACTER*40 INPUT,OUTPUT
         PRINT *,'Enter text string enclosed between apostrophes'
      READ *, INPUT
      CALL ADDSTAR(INPUT,OUTPUT)
         PRINT *,'The string with $s replacing trailing blanks'
      PRINT *, OUTPUT
      END
C********************************************************************
C Variables IN and OUT are declared with the *(*) statement.
C This will allow the subroutine to accept any size string.
C We start by copying IN into the output variable OUT in line
C 3. In line 4 we use the LEN function to determine the length
C of the character variable. The DO loop then starts at the end
C and works backward to replace the blanks with dollar signs.
C When the first non-blank character is found, the loop ends.
C********************************************************************
      SUBROUTINE ADDSTAR(IN,OUT)
      CHARACTER*(*) IN, OUT
      OUT = IN
      I = LEN(OUT)
      DO WHILE(OUT(I:I) .EQ. ' ')
         OUT(I:I) = '$'
         I = I-1
      END DO
      RETURN
      END
```

8.5 FREE-FORMATTED AND FORMATTED I/O OF CHARACTER DATA

We have already seen examples of free-formatted input and output (I/O) of character strings in Example 2.14. Recall that free-formatting, also known as list-directed formatting, leaves the formatting up to the compiler and is used when the appearance of the output data is generally unimportant. Free-formatted I/O is accomplished by placing a "*" after the READ or PRINT statement. In this context, strings are printed out by including them inside single quote marks in the PRINT statement. But, if you want to print out a character variable, all you need do is list the variable in the free-formatted output statement.

EXAMPLE 8.12

Below is a program to read in a name and then echo it to the screen:

```
C********************************************************
C The variable NAME is declared to be 40 characters long. After
C entering the name, it will be printed back via free-formatted
C I/O statements.
C********************************************************
        CHARACTER*40 NAME
        PRINT *, 'Enter your name inside single quote marks:'
        READ *, NAME
        PRINT *,'Name entered was: ', NAME
        END
```

In this example, we have printed out both a string ('Name entered was: ') and the contents of a character variable with free-formatting I/O. The only problem that you might encounter is that you need to enter the input data inside single quote marks. If you forget to include the quotes, the computer is likely to report a run-time error.

Formatting is used to give you control over the appearance of your output. By using formatting in an input statement, you can eliminate the restrictions of special characters, spaces, and so on that are present when using free-formatting. By using formatting in an output statement, you can combine numbers and strings in a fashion that is completely under your control.

Strings are formatted using the "A" edit descriptor within the FORMAT statement. The letter 'A' stands for <u>a</u>lphanumeric. The general form for the A descriptor is as follows:

> n A len

where n =a repeat specifier and len =the length of the string. A simple example would be 3A5, where the instruction A5 is to be repeated three times.

The repeat factor is the same as with all format specifiers. The len is used to indicate how many characters are in the string. If you omit a value for len, then the length of the string variable being referenced is used. But, if len is less than the length of the variable being printed, trailing characters will be truncated. On the other hand, if len is greater than the length of the variable, extra blanks are placed at the front of the string.

EXAMPLE 8.13

For the following examples, assume that the character variable STR1 has length 10 and the value 'ABCDEFGHIJ', and that STR2 has length 5 and the value '12345':

```
        CHARACTER STR1*10, STR2*5
```

Statement	Output	Comments
PRINT 1, STR1 1 FORMAT(1X, A10)	ABCDEFGHIJ	*(Formatting matches exactly)*
PRINT 2, STR1 2 FORMAT(1X, A)	ABCDEFGHIJ	*(Automatic use of variable length)*
PRINT 3, STR1 3 FORMAT(1X, A3)	ABC	*(Only 3 characters can be stored)*
PRINT 4, STR1, STR2 4 FORMAT(1X, A11, A5)	~ABCDEFGHIJ12345	*(Padding with blank (~) at beginning of string)*

8.6 INTERNAL FILES

There are some instances when the form of the output or input will not be known. For example, you might have an application where you will be reading in 1, 2, or 3 numbers, but you do not know in advance how many are present. In such applications *internal files* can be used.

Internal files allow you to convert one data type to another. Consider the problem in which you are asked to read in an integer of up to 6 digits, multiply the number by 2, and then return the result in reverse order. For example, 123 multiplied by 2 yields 246; but we want to return the result as 642. Multiplication can be easily performed on a number, but swapping digits can be more easily performed on character data. Therefore, it makes sense to do the initial phase of the processing on the numerical data and then convert them to character data for the reversal process. We will use the following procedure:

- Multiply the desired number and store the result as a file in the computer memory (as opposed to a file stored on a hard or floppy disk)
- Reread the result as a string
- Manipulate the string to reverse the digits then write it back into memory
- Finally, reread the file as an integer

By reading and writing to the computer memory, we have created an internal file, which is stored only as long as the program that created it is running. We will discuss the other, more permanent type of file (external files), in the next chapter. With internal files, it is possible to interpret the data in any format you wish.

To obtain data from an internal file, we need to use a string variable within the READ statement. To send data to an internal file, we use the WRITE statement

READ(*string, format*) *I/O list*   or   WRITE(*string, format*) *I/O list* where *string* is a character variable indicating the name of the storage location of the internal file, and *format* is the statement label indicating where formatting instructions are to be found.

EXAMPLE 8.14

The following program takes an integer, multiplies it by 2, and then returns the result with the digits reversed as an integer. It does so by storing the integer (after multiplication) in an internal file called 'STRING'. The READ statement then reads in the data from that file as a character array, and prints them back to the file in reverse order. Finally, the third READ statement retrieves this reversed number.

```
C*********************************************************************
C The original integer value is stored in INPUT.
C*********************************************************************
        CHARACTER*1 FWD(16)
        CHARACTER*16 STRING
        PRINT *,'Enter an Integer'
        READ *,INPUT
        INPUT = INPUT*2
C*********************************************************************
C Now, write INPUT to the internal file
C*********************************************************************
        WRITE(STRING, 1) INPUT
   1    FORMAT(I16)
C*********************************************************************
C Reread the internal file as a character string array
C*********************************************************************
        READ(STRING, 2) (FWD(I), I = 1, 16)
   2    FORMAT(16A1)
C*********************************************************************
C Reverse the string by writing it into the file backwards
C*********************************************************************
        WRITE(STRING, 2) (FWD(I), I = 16, 1, -1)
C*********************************************************************
C Read the file as an integer value
C*********************************************************************
        READ(STRING, 1) IOUT
        PRINT *, 'Output is: ', IOUT
        END
```

Internal files work well in situations where you do not know in advance what the input is going to be. They also provide an easy way to convert character data into integer or real data, and vice versa.

8.7 CHARACTER BASED LIBRARY FUNCTIONS

There are several built-in functions that operate on or produce character data, and these functions are summarized below. For the following functions, I represents an integer, C is a single character string, STRING is a multicharacter string, and SUB is a substring. Anything enclosed in [ ] brackets is optional.

CHAR(I)

Returns a single character that is the character at position I of the processor's collating sequence. (Example: If the processor uses the ASCII sequence, then CHAR(65) will produce the character in the 65th location in that sequence, which is the letter 'A'.)

ICHAR(C)

Returns the position in the collating sequence of the desired character. (Example: If the processor uses the ASCII collating sequence, then ICHAR('A') will produce the location in the collating sequence where the letter 'A' is found, in this case 65.)

INDEX(STRING, SUB)

Determines the location of the substring within the larger string. (Example: If STRING is 'ABCDEFGHIJ', and SUB is 'DEF', then INDEX(STRING,SUB) returns a value of 4.)

LEN(STRING)

Returns the length of a string. (Example: If STRING is 'ABCDEFGHIJ', then LEN(STRING) returns the value 10.)

LGE(A, B)

Compares the character strings or variables A and B, and determines whether A is lexically greater than or equal to B. (Example: if A='a' and B='B', then LGE(A, B) is .TRUE.)

LGT(A, B)

Compares the character strings or variables A and B, and determines whether A is lexically greater than B. (Example: if A='a' and B='B', then LGT(A,B) is .TRUE.)

LLE(A, B)

Compares the character strings or variables A and B, and determines whether A is lexically less than or equal to B. (Example: if A='a' and B='B', then LLE(B,A) is .FALSE.)

LLT(A, B)

Compares the character strings or variables A and B, and determines whether A is lexically less than B. (Example: if A='a' and B='B', then LGT(B,A) is .FALSE.)

ADJUSTL(STRING)

Returns a string of the same length as STRING in which all leading blanks are removed and then added to the end (left justification). (Example: ADJUSTL('   abc') produces 'abc   '.)

ADJUSTR(STRING)

Returns a string of the same length as STRING in which all trailing blanks are removed and then added to the beginning (right justification). (Example: ADJUSTR('abc   ') produces '   abc'.)

EXAMPLE 8.15

The following program converts all lowercase characters to uppercase assuming that the ASCII collating sequence is being used. This can be done by noting that lowercase letters are between 097 and 122 in the ASCII collating sequence, while the uppercase letters are between 065 and 090. In the program, we will determine the position of each letter in the ACSII collating sequence. If the position falls between 097 and 122, we will subtract 32 from it to convert the letter to an uppercase letter. As an example, note that in the ASCII collating sequence, lower case 'a' is in position 97 while upper case 'A' is in position 65.

```
C******* ****************************************************
C Program to convert all lowercase letters into uppercase.
C Read in the message as a character array.
C******* ****************************************************
      CHARACTER*1 MESSAG(128)
      PRINT *,'Enter a string'
      READ 1, (MESSAG(I), I = 1, 128)
   1  FORMAT(128A1)
C******* ****************************************************
C Determine location in ASCII sequence and examine each
C whether the character is between the 097 and 122 positions
C inclusively. If it is, subtract 32.
C******* ****************************************************
      DO 10 I = 1, 128
         J = ICHAR(MESSAG(I))
         IF(J .GE. 97 .AND. J .LE. 122) THEN
            J = J-32
            MESSAG(I) = CHAR(J)
         ENDIF
  10  CONTINUE
      PRINT 1, (MESSAG(I), I = 1, 128)
      END
```

The above program can easily be modified to code a message. Consider the process of reversing the order of the characters. If the characters abc. . .ABC. . . were mapped to zyx. . .ZYX. . . a coded message would result. Rerunning the result through the program a second time would decipher the message. Of course, much more complicated coding algorithms can be constructed (see Supplementary Problem 8.23).

8.8 LOGICAL DATA

The final data type that we will examine is logical data that is often used for decision making processes. Since Fortran allows only two possible values (.TRUE. and .FALSE.), we will use logical data where we need to repeatedly use the result of a logical expression. Without logical data, we would have to repeat the logical expression as many times as required. But by setting up a logical variable we only need to perform the logical comparison once.

EXAMPLE 8.16

We can store the results of a logical comparison and use that result as many times as necessary. In this example, we will write a program with and without logical data.

Original program without logical data:

```
        PRINT *,'Enter X'
        READ *,X
        IF(X .LT. 0) THEN
            A = 1.0
        ELSE
            A = 2.0
        ENDIF
        T = X + A
        U = 2 * X
        IF(X .LT. 0) THEN
            B = 10.0
        ELSE
            B = 0.0
        ENDIF
        W = T + U + A + B
        PRINT *,'T, U, W=',T, U, W
        END
```

Improved program utilizing logical variable:

```
        LOGICAL TEST
        PRINT *,'Enter X'
        READ *, X
C***************************************************************
C Once the logical variable is declared with the LOGICAL
C statement, we can assign a value (true or false) with
C an assignment statement, or a logical operator as in this
C line
C***************************************************************
        TEST = X .LT. 0
        IF (TEST) THEN
            A = 1.0
        ELSE
            A = 2.0
        ENDIF
        T = X + A
        U = 2 * X
        IF (TEST) THEN
            B = 10.0
        ELSE
            B = 0.0
        ENDIF
        W = T + U + A + B
        PRINT *,'T, U, W=', T, U, W
        END
```

The second version has two advantages. The first advantage is that the logical expression is executed only once, saving a little bit of computer run time. For the above example, the savings would be trivial. But, when writing programs that loop through a section of code thousands of times, such savings can become significant. In real engineering problems, it is not uncommon to have loops that execute millions of times. And if decisions within those loops are based on logical tests such as those above, the use of logical variables improve the overall program speed.

The second advantage is that the conditional expression appears only in one place. If you had to modify the conditional expression in the first program, you would have to make two editing changes. The second program, on the other hand, requires a change in only one expression.

8.9 DEBUGGING TIPS

When you write a program it is always a good idea to program defensively. Try to anticipate errors, and take advantage of as many simplifications as the language allows you to take. Here are a few suggestions along these lines:

- Whenever it's possible to allow the computer to automatically assign properties for you, use that feature. It save on errors and adds to the versatility of the program. An example is the "(*)" option when declaring a string variable in a subprogram. Another example is the "A" edit descriptor without a specified length.
- Consolidate programming segments wherever possible. Use a logical variable so that logical expressions need not be repeated. PARAMETER statements are another example of this philosophy. Consolidation usually speeds up a program's execution and usually makes the software more maintainable.

Even with the best defensive programming, errors are going to happen in spite of your best efforts. As we have seen in other chapters, debugging consists of removing syntax, run time, and logic errors. Usually, the compiler will give you diagnostic messages about the syntax errors, and these messages can be used to remove the simplest errors. But as with debugging problems with the other data types, errors with character and logical data will still require you to trace the program in order to locate the problem. So once again, tracing becomes an important tool.

When debugging programs containing character strings and variables, treat them as one-dimensional arrays and do the following:

- Create a table for each character variable. Each table should have as many columns as characters in the variable. For example, if the character string will have 10 characters, make a table with 10 columns. As you read in (or generate) the variable, place each character into its own column within the table. This will make substring manipulation particularly easy.
- Each time the character variable changes, enter a new row in the table. The last row represents the current value of the string variable.

EXAMPLE 8.17

Trace through the following program. Use ' ~ ' to indicate spaces for clarity.

```
CHARACTER*10 STRING
DATA STRING/'SONG.BIRD'/
STRING(1:1) = STRING(4:4)
STRING(4:4) = STRING(9:9)
STRING = STRING(1:2)//STRING(2:2)//STRING(4:4)
PRINT *, STRING
END
```

Program Trace:

Set up character variable STRING with the characters SONG.BIRD ~
Move the 4th character to the first position → STRING becomes GONG.BIRD.
Move the 9th character to the 4th position → STRING becomes GOND.BIRD
Concatenate the first two letters of STRING with the 2nd letter and the 4th letter
     of STRING, resulting in 'GO'//'O'//'D' = 'GOOD'
Print out the contents of STRING

Variables:

STRING	1	2	3	4	5	6	7	8	9	10
	S	O	N	G	.	B	I	R	D	~
	G	O	N	G	.	B	I	R	D	~
	G	O	N	D	.	B	I	R	D	~
	G	O	O	D	~	~	~	~	~	~

Output:

GOOD

Solved Problems

8.1 Indicate which of the following assignment statements are valid or invalid. For the valid examples, determine the value assigned to the variable. Assume that the character variable X has length 20, Y has length 30, and Z has length 40.

(a) X='This is a test"
(b) X=a string
(c) Y='and he said, ''this is a test'''
(d) X='what''s that?'
(e) Z="I don't know!"

(a) Invalid — Mismatched delimiters (both must be ').

(b) Valid if a string is a variable (space ignored).

(c) Valid — The internal quote marks (' ') are printed intact.

(d) Valid — The double quote marks ('') are interpreted as a single apostrophe.

(e) Invalid — The quote marks (" ") are not the legal way to indicate a character string.

8.2 Write a program to determine your computer's default character set (ASCII or EBCDIC) by utilizing the difference in the ASCII and EBCDIC collating sequences.

```
C******************************************************************
C In the ASCII character set, the capital letters come before
C the lowercase letters, while the reverse is true for EBCDIC
C******************************************************************
      IF ('A' .LT. 'a') THEN
          PRINT *,'ASCII collating sequence used.'
      ELSE
          PRINT *,'EBCDIC collating sequence used.'
      ENDIF
      END
```

8.3 Determine all of the possible substrings constructed from the following strings.

(a) 'a'   (b) 'He'

(c) 'string'   (d) 'a test'

(a) a & null (blank space)   (b) H, e, He & null

(c) s, t, r, i, n, g, st, tr, ri, in, ng, str, tri, rin, ing, stri, trin, ring, string & null

(d) a, [space], t, e, s, t, a[space], [space]t, te, es, st, a[space]t, [space]te, tes, est, a[space]tes, [space]test, a[space]test, & null

8.4 Determine the values of the indicated substrings. Assume that ALPHA has the value 'abcdefghij1234567890' with length 20.

(a) ALPHA(1:1)   (b) ALPHA(3:5)

(c) ALPHA(11:)   (d) ALPHA(:)

(a) 'a'   (b) 'cde'   (c) '1234567890'   (d) 'abcdefghij1234567890'

8.5 For the relational expressions given below, determine the resulting logical value. Use the ASCII collating sequence.

(a) ('John' .LT. 'Jim')   (b) ('Pat' .GE. 'Alex')

(c) ('John' .LT. 'jim')   (d) ('Sue' .GT. 'bob')

(e) ('This' .LT. 'That')   (f) ('12' .GT. '2')

(g) ('Long string' .LT. 'LONGER STRING')   (h) ('Helene' .LE. 'helene')

(a) False — 'o' does not come before 'i'

(b) True — 'P' comes after 'A'

(c) True — 'J' comes before 'j'

(d) False — 'S' does not come after 'b'

(e) False — 'i' does not come before 'a'

(f) False — '1' does not come after '2'

(g) True — 'o' comes after 'O'

(h) True — 'H' comes before 'h'

8.6　Write a program which reads in a list of names (last, first) and phone numbers as a single string, and returns the list in alphabetical order.

```
      CHARACTER*50 LIST(100), LISTMIN, SWAP
      PRINT *,'Number of names in the list (100 max.)?'
      READ *, N
      DO 10 I = 1, N
         PRINT *, 'Enter Last Name, First Name,
     1                  and phone number'
         READ *, LIST(I)
 10      CONTINUE
C***********************************************************
C Start the sorting operation using the bubble sort process
C***********************************************************
      DO 30 I = 1, N-1
         LISTMIN = LIST(I)
         INDEX = I
         DO 20 J = I+1, N
            IF (LIST(J) .LT. LISTMIN) THEN
               LISTMIN = LIST(J)
               INDEX = J
            END IF
 20         CONTINUE
         SWAP = LIST(I)
         LIST(I) = LIST(INDEX)
         LIST(INDEX) = SWAP
 30      CONTINUE
C***********************************************************
C After sorting, print out the sorted list
C***********************************************************
      DO 40 I = 1, N
         PRINT *, LIST(I)
 40      CONTINUE
      END
```

8.7　Write a subprogram that performs the same function as ADJUSTR.

```
C***********************************************************
C Variable listing:
C    IN = string to be adjusted
C    OUT = string after adjustment
C    NUMCHR = number of characters in the string
C    NBEG = position where blanks begin to appear at the end
C           of the string.
C***********************************************************
```

```
      SUBROUTINE ADJUSTC(IN,OUT)
      CHARACTER*(*) IN, OUT
      OUT = IN
C*********************************************************************
C First, determine the length of the string IN
C*********************************************************************
      NUMCHR=LEN(IN)
C*********************************************************************
C Determine where the extra blank spaces begin
C*********************************************************************
      I = 1
      DO WHILE (IN(I:I) .NE. ' ' .OR. I .LE. NUMCHR)
         I = I + 1
      END DO
      NBEG = I-1
      NBLANK = NBEG
C*********************************************************************
C If there are no blank spaces, do nothing and return
C*********************************************************************
      IF (NBEG .EQ. NUMCHR) RETURN
C*********************************************************************
C Move all the characters one space to the right
C*********************************************************************
      DO 20 I= NUMCHR-NBLANK, 1, -1
         OUT(I:I) = IN(I-1:I-1)
   20 CONTINUE
      RETURN
      END
```

8.8   Write a program that prints a border of "*"s around a text string such as

```
                * * * * * * * * * * * * * *
                *This is a test*
                * * * * * * * * * * * * * *
```

```
C*********************************************************************
C Determine the length of the string. Then add one '*' to the
C beginning, and one '*' to the end of the string. Finally,
C print out one line of stars of length LEN(STRING)+2.
C*********************************************************************
      CHARACTER INPUT*50, NEWIN*52, LINE*52
      PRINT *, 'Enter the string'
      READ 1, INPUT
    1 FORMAT(A50)
C*********************************************************************
C Determine the length of the string
C*********************************************************************
      NCHAR = LEN(INPUT)
C*********************************************************************
C Add stars to the beginning and end of the string
C*********************************************************************
      NEWIN = '*'//INPUT//'*'
```

```
C**************************************************************
C Now print out the new string preceeded and followed by a
C series of stars of length NCHAR+2
C**************************************************************
          DO 10 I = 1, NCHAR + 2
             LINE(I:I) = '*'
   10     CONTINUE
          PRINT *, LINE
          PRINT *, NEWIN
          PRINT *, LINE
          END
```

8.9   Modify Example 8.3 so that the beginning and ending regions can be read in at run time. Currently, the program is set to plot from −pi to pi.

```
          PARAMETER(COLS=80, ROWS=20, PI=3.1416)
          INTEGER COLS, ROWS
          CHARACTER*(1) SCREEN(ROWS, COLS)
          DATA SCREEN/1600*' '/
C**************************************************************
C New section to read in XMIN and XMAX
C**************************************************************
          PRINT *,'Enter starting and ending X values:'
          READ *, XMIN, XMAX
C**************************************************************
C Calculate the star position in the plot. The functions for X
C and Y have been modified to take into account XMIN and XMAX.
C**************************************************************
          DO 30 JX = 1, COLS
             X = XMIN + (JX-1)*(XMAX-XMIN)/(COLS-1)
             Y = SIN(X)
             IY = 1 + NINT((Y-1.0)/(-2.0)*(ROWS-1))
             SCREEN(IY,JX) = '*'
   30     CONTINUE
C**************************************************************
C Output section is unchanged
C**************************************************************
          DO 40 I = 1, ROWS
             PRINT *, (SCREEN(I,J), J = 1,COLS)
   40     CONTINUE
          END
```

8.10   Predict the output of the PRINT statements below if X = '12345678901234567890'.

(a)   PRINT *, X   (b)   PRINT 1, X
                                        1   FORMAT (' ', 1A5)

(c)   PRINT 2, X(1:3), X(1:3)   (d)   PRINT 3, X, X
      2   FORMAT(' ', 2A)   3   FORMAT(' ', A5)

(a)   12345678901234567890   *(Simple list directed output)*
(b)   12345   *(Truncation after 5 characters)*

(c) 123123   *(Repeat factor with auto length)*
(d) 12345   *(When insufficient number of edit descriptors, the*
     12345   *formatting reuses the edit descriptors)*

8.11 Rewrite the alphabetical sorting example (8.10) to utilize the character lexical comparison functions (.LLT., .LLE., .LGT., or .LGE.). This would effectively force sorting based on the ASCII collating sequence even if your machine uses the ECBDIC collating sequence.

```
      CHARACTER*20 LIST(100), LISTMIN, SWAP
      PRINT *, 'Number of names in the list (100 max.)?'
      READ *, N
      DO 10 I = 1, N
          PRINT *,'Enter name', N,' between apostrophes'
10        READ *, LIST(I)
C********************************************************************
C Start the sorting operation
C********************************************************************
      DO 30 I = 1, N-1
          LISTMIN = LIST(I)
          INDEX = I
C********************************************************************
C Change the conditional test to use LLT
C********************************************************************
          DO 20 J = I+1, N
              IF (LLT(LIST(J),LISTMIN)) THEN
                  LISTMIN = LIST(J)
                  INDEX = J
              END IF
20        CONTINUE
          SWAP = LIST(I)
          LIST(I) = LIST(INDEX)
30        LIST(INDEX) = SWAP
      DO 40 I = 1, N
40        PRINT *, LIST(I)
      END
```

8.12 Trace through the following program and predict the output. Assume that the input is 'This is a test' and that the number of times, $n=1$.

```
      CHARACTER LINE*15, DUMMY*1
      PRINT *,'Enter the message string (15 char max.)'
      READ 1, LINE
1     FORMAT (A)
      PRINT *,'Enter the number of times to run'
      READ *, N
      DO 10 I = 1, LEN(LINE)*N
          DUMMY=LINE(1:1)
          LINE = LINE(2:)//DUMMY
          WRITE (*,2) LINE
2         FORMAT(' ', A)
10    CONTINUE
      END
```

Variable Listing:

N: 1   I: 1, 2, 3, 4, 5, 6, 7, 8, 9, 10, 11, 12, 13, 14, 15, 16

LIST	1	2	3	4	5	6	7	8	9	10	11	12	13	14	15
	T	h	i	s	~	i	s	~	a	~	t	e	s	t	~
	h	i	s	~	i	s	~	a	~	t	e	s	t	~	T
	i	s	~	i	s	~	a	~	t	e	s	t	~	T	h
	s	~	i	s	~	a	~	t	e	s	t	~	T	h	i
	~	i	s	~	a	~	t	e	s	t	~	T	h	i	s
	i	s	~	a	~	t	e	s	t	~	T	h	i	s	~
	s	~	a	~	t	e	s	t	~	T	h	i	s	~	i
	~	a	~	t	e	s	t	~	T	h	i	s	~	i	s
	a	~	t	e	s	t	~	T	h	i	s	~	i	s	~
	~	t	e	s	t	~	T	h	i	s	~	i	s	~	a
	t	e	s	t	~	T	h	i	s	~	i	s	~	a	~
	e	s	t	~	T	h	i	s	~	i	s	~	a	~	t
	s	t	~	T	h	i	s	~	i	s	~	a	~	t	e
	t	~	T	h	i	s	~	i	s	~	a	~	t	e	s
	~	T	h	i	s	~	i	s	~	a	~	t	e	s	t
	T	h	i	s	~	i	s	~	a	~	t	e	s	t	~

Output:
   If the system responds to carriage control characters such as '+', the effect would be
to have the message scroll to the left repeating N times.

Supplementary Problems

8.13 Indicate the validity of the following assignment statements. For the valid examples
determine the value assigned to the variable, assuming that X is declared as a character
variable of length 20, Y of length 30, and Z of length 40.

(a) Y=a_string
(b) X='what's this?'
(c) Z='he said,"she said, 'they did. . .'"'
(d) Y='That''s all.'

8.14 Write a program to print out your computer's character set utilizing the necessary function outlined in this chapter. Have the program determine if the ASCII or EBCDIC character sets is used. The ASCII character set has 128 characters with the collating number ranging from 0 to 127. The EBCDIC character set has 256 characters (0 to 255). Note that some characters in these sets will not print.

8.15 Determine all of the substrings that are possible from the following strings:

(a) 'z'   (b) 'She'
(c) 'range'   (d) 'values'

8.16 Determine the values of the indicated substrings. Assume that the character variable ALPHA has the value 'abcdefghij1234567890' with length 20.

(a) ALPHA(:1)   (b) ALPHA(5:9)
(c) ALPHA(21:)   (d) ALPHA(4:3)

8.17 For the following relational expressions, determine the resulting logical values. Use the EBCDIC collating sequence.

(a) 'John' < 'Jim'   (b) 'Pat' > = 'Alex'
(c) 'John' < 'jim'   (d) 'Sue' > 'bob'
(e) 'Long' > 'LONGER'   (f) 'This' < 'That'

8.18 Write a program which reads in a TITLE string (30 characters max) and a NAME string (30 characters max). Then print a string of 80 characters with TITLE left justified (starts the string with no preceding blanks) and NAME right justified (ends the string with no trailing blanks). Any intermediate characters should be filled with "."s. (For example: TITLE='Student', NAME='John Jones' results in: Student....................John Jones)

8.19 Write a subroutine that performs the ADJUSTR function without using the built-in function.

8.20 Modify Example 8.3 so that the beginning and ending domain and range can be read in at run time. Currently the program plots a domain from −pi to pi with a range of values from −1 to 1. If a value is generated beyond the array index domain, ignore that data point.

8.21 Predict the output of the following PRINT statements. X is a character variable of length 20 with the value '12345678901234567890'.

(a)   PRINT 1, X
   1   FORMAT(' ', A)

(b)   PRINT 2, X(1:5)
   2   FORMAT(' ', A10)

(c)   PRINT 3, X(1:3)//X(1:3)
   3   FORMAT(' ', 2A)

(d)   PRINT 4, X
   4   FORMAT(' ', 'X=', A)

8.22 Modify Example 8.15 to code a message by swapping the characters abc. . .ABC. . . with zyx. . .ZYX. . . Verify that the program works by entering a coded message back into the program to see if it is correctly deciphered.

8.23 Trace through the following program and predict its output.

```
CHARACTER LINE*25, DUMMY*4
DATA LINE/'all that is forever keep'/
LINE(5:10) = LINE(5:8)//''''//LINE(11:)
DUMMY=LINE(4:4)//LINE(1:3)
LINE(1:10) = LINE(5:10)//DUMMY
LINE(11:) = LINE(12:)
LINE(14:) = LINE(2:2)//LINE(20:20)//LINE(10:10)
LINE(14:14) = LINE(16:16)
LINE(16:16) = LINE(6:6)
PRINT *,LINE
END
```

Answers to Selected Supplementary Problems

8.13 (a) Invalid since _ is not a legal character
    (b) Invalid since the internal quote ('s) needs to be entered twice (''s)
    (c) Invalid since inner set of double quote marks (") is illegal
    (d) Valid

8.14

```
        IF ('A'.LT.'a') THEN
            PRINT *,'ASCII collating sequence used.'
            LIMIT=127
        ELSE
            PRINT *,'EBCDIC collating sequence used.'
            LIMIT=255
        ENDIF
        DO 10 I = 0, LIMIT
  10        PRINT *,'Character ',I,' is |',CHAR(I),'|'
        END
```

8.15 (a) z and null   (b) S, h, e, Sh, he, She & null

(c) r, a, n, g, e, ra, an, ng, ge, ran, ang, nge, rang, ange, range & null

(d) v, a, l, u, e, s, va, al, lu, ue, es, val, alu, lue, ues, valu, alue, lues, value, alues, values, & null

8.16 (a) 'a'   (b) 'efghi'   (c) Invalid index out of range   (d) null string

8.17 (a) False — 'o' does not come before 'i'

(b) True — 'P' comes after 'A'

(c) False — 'J' does not come before 'j'

(d) True — 'S' comes after 'b'

(e) False — 'o' comes before 'O'

(f) False — 'i' comes after 'a'

8.18
```
          CHARACTER*30 TITLE,NAME
          CHARACTER*80 LINE
C**********************************************************************
C Load decimal points into all positions of LINE
C**********************************************************************
          DO 10 I = 1, 80
              LINE = LINE//'.'
   10     CONTINUE
          PRINT *,'Enter the TITLE'
          READ '(A)',TITLE
          PRINT *,'Enter the NAME'
          READ '(A)',NAME
C**********************************************************************
C Left justify the title with ADJUSTL and right justify the name
C with ADJUSTR functions
C**********************************************************************
          TITLE=ADJUSTL(TITLE)
          NAME=ADJUSTR(NAME)
C**********************************************************************
C Now add periods to any blank spaces in TITLE and NAME
C**********************************************************************
          DO I=30,1,-1
              IF (TITLE(I:I).EQ.' ') THEN
                 TITLE(I:I)='.'
              ELSE
                 EXIT
              ENDIF
          END DO
          DO I=1,30
              IF (NAME(I:I).EQ.' ') THEN
                 NAME(I:I)='.'
              ELSE
                 EXIT
              ENDIF
          END DO
```

```
C*************************************************************
C Now copy TITLE into the first 30 positions of LINE and NAME
C into the last 30 positions
C*************************************************************
        LINE(1:30)=TITLE
        LINE(51:80)=NAME
        PRINT *,LINE
        END
```

8.19
```
        SUBROUTINE ADJUSTR(IN,OUT)
        CHARACTER*(*) IN,OUT
        OUT=IN
C*************************************************************
C First, determine the length of the character variable
C*************************************************************
        NUMCHR=LEN(IN)
C*************************************************************
C Next, determine the position of the first blank space
C*************************************************************
        DO 10 I=1,NUMCHR
            IF(IN(I:I).NE.' ') EXIT
   10   CONTINUE
        NBEG=I-1
C*************************************************************
C Determine the number of blanks needed. If none, then stop
C*************************************************************
        NBLANK=NBEG
        IF (NBEG.EQ.NUMCHR) RETURN
C*************************************************************
C Copy the IN variable into the OUT variable with NBLANK
C spaces at the beginning, and the input data at the end.
C*************************************************************
        DO 20 I=NUMCHR,1,-1
            IF(IN(I:I).NE.' ') EXIT
   20       NBLANK=NBLANK+1
        OUT=' '
        OUT(NBLANK+1:)=IN(NBEG+1:)
        RETURN
        END
```

8.20
```
        INTEGER COLS,ROWS,IY,JX
        REAL PI,X,Y
        PARAMETER(COLS=80,ROWS=20,PI=3.1416)
        CHARACTER*(1) SCREEN(ROWS,COLS)
        PRINT *,'Enter starting and ending X values:'
        READ *,XMIN,XMAX
        PRINT *,'Enter minimum and maximum range values:'
        READ *,YMIN,YMAX
        DO 30 JX=1,COLS
C*************************************************************
C From column value calculate X. From Y value calculate row C
C number.
C*************************************************************
```

```
      X=XMIN+(JX-1)*(XMAX-XMIN)/(COLS-1)
      Y=SIN(X)
      IY=ROWS-NINT((Y-YMIN)/(YMAX-YMIN)*(ROWS-1))
      IF (1.LE.IY.AND.IY.LE.ROWS) SCREEN(IY,JX)='*'
30    CONTINUE
      DO 40 I=1,ROWS
      PRINT *,(SCREEN(I,J),J=1,COLS)
40    CONTINUE
      END
```

8.21 (a) 12345678901234567890   *(Automatic length assignment)*

    (b) 12345   *(Formatted larger than required, which causes padding with blanks)*

    (c) 123123   *(Not all of the edit descriptor is used)*

    (d) X = 12345678901234567890   *(Formatting with a constant string in the format statement)*

8.22
```
      CHARACTER*53 OUTALPHA, INALPHA
      CHARACTER*50 INPUT
      INALPHA = ' abcdefghijklmnopqrstuvwxyz
     1 ABCDEFGHIJKLMNOPQRSTUVWXYZ'
      OUTALPHA = 'zyxwvutsrqponmlkjihgfedcba
     1 ZYXWVUTSRQPONMLKJIHGFEDCBA '
      PRINT *,'Enter a string'
      READ *,INPUT
      DO K=1, 50
         I=INDEX(INALPHA, INPUT(K:K))
         IF (I .EQ. 0) EXIT
         INPUT(K:K)=OUTALPHA(I:I)
      END DO
      PRINT *,'Coded message:',INPUT
      END
```

8.23 <u>Program Trace:</u>

    Assign 'all that is forever keep' to character variable LINE

Concat:	LINE(5 to 10) becomes LINE(5 to 8)//''''//LINE(11 to 25), or
	LINE(5 to 10) becomes 'tha'//''//~ forever ~ keep, or
	LINE(5 to 10) becomes 'tha''
Concat:	LINE(1 to 10) becomes LINE(5 to 10)//LINE(4)//LINE(1 to end), or
	LINE(1 to 10) becomes 'that''// ~ //'all ~ ', or
	LINE(1 to 10) becomes 'all ~ that's'
Replace:	LINE(11 to end) becomes LINE(12 to end)
	LINE(11 to end) becomes 'forever ~ keep ~ ~ '
Concat:	LINE(14 to end) becomes LINE(2)//LINE(20)//LINE(10)
	LINE(14) becomes LINE(16)
	LINE(14) becomes 's'
Concat:	LINE(16) becomes LINE(6)
	LINE(1 to end) becomes 'that's ~ '//'all ~ '//'folks ~ ~ ~ ~ ~ ~ ~ ~ ~ ~ '

Variable Listing:

LINE:

1	2	3	4	5	6	7	8	9	0	1	2	3	4	5	6	7	8	9	0	1	2	3	4	5
a	l	l	~	t	h	a	t	~	i	s	~	f	o	r	e	v	e	r	~	k	e	e	p	~
a	l	l	~	t	h	a	t	'	s	s	~	f	o	r	e	v	e	r	~	k	e	e	p	~
t	h	a	t	'	s	~	a	l	l	s	~	f	o	r	e	v	e	r	~	k	e	e	p	~
t	h	a	t	'	s	~	a	l	l	~	f	o	h	k	l	~	~	~	~	~	~	~	~	~
t	h	a	t	'	s	~	a	l	l	~	f	o	l	k	s	~	~	~	~	~	~	~	~	~

Output:

that's all folks

Chapter 9

Data Files

9.1 INTRODUCTION

Up to now, you have done all input and output through the keyboard and the terminal screen (CRT). When your program encountered a READ * command, you typed in the data, one item at a time. Similarly, when a PRINT * statement occurred, the computer sent output to the screen. While this is convenient, there is no permanent record of the program results. As soon as the CRT screen is cleared, all output is lost. There are many times, however, when it would be desirable to send data to a file. Once this is done, another program or user could access this information later. Figures 9-1 and 9-2 illustrate some of the many different ways of storing data.

It is sometimes desirable to be able to read data from a file rather than to enter them from the keyboard. A good example is when you are writing a program that requires a large amount of input data. Let's assume that your program requires 100 data points and that you have set it up without the use of an input file. Whenever you rerun the program, you must re-enter the data by hand. So if you needed to edit the program 10 times before you removed all the bugs, you would have entered a total of 1000 data points by hand! If instead, the data had been read from a data file, you would have entered the data only once. An even better scheme has the computer itself generate the data (perhaps through a computer-controlled data acquisition system) and enter it into a file for you. This way, you don't need to enter the data even once!

Data files are really no different from other types of files, such as the one in which you store your program. These files may be manipulated with commands from the operating system. For example, you can type them onto your CRT screen, send them onto the system printer(s), or make duplicate copies of the data on another disk. One of the biggest advantages of data files is that you can access them from within your program. Thus, you can send your output to an alternate output device instead of the CRT. Mostly, the data will be sent to a data file. Other options might be a printer, floppy or hard disks, FAX modems, plotters, CD disks, and so forth.

In this chapter, we will focus on the technique for diverting I/O from within a program to a device other than the CRT. To do this, there are three things that you must add to your program:

- Instructions to open a file
- Instructions to communicate with the designated file
- Instructions to close the file when finished

In previous chapters, when we had the simple task of printing directly to the CRT, there was no need to worry about these things. All we had to do was enter the command for I/O to send the data directly to the proper device. Unless told otherwise, the computer will communicate exclusively through the CRT and its keyboard, which are termed the *default I/O devices*.

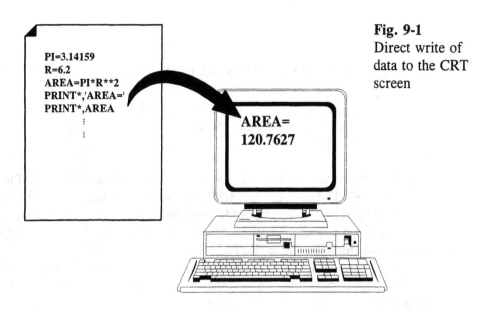

Fig. 9-1
Direct write of data to the CRT screen

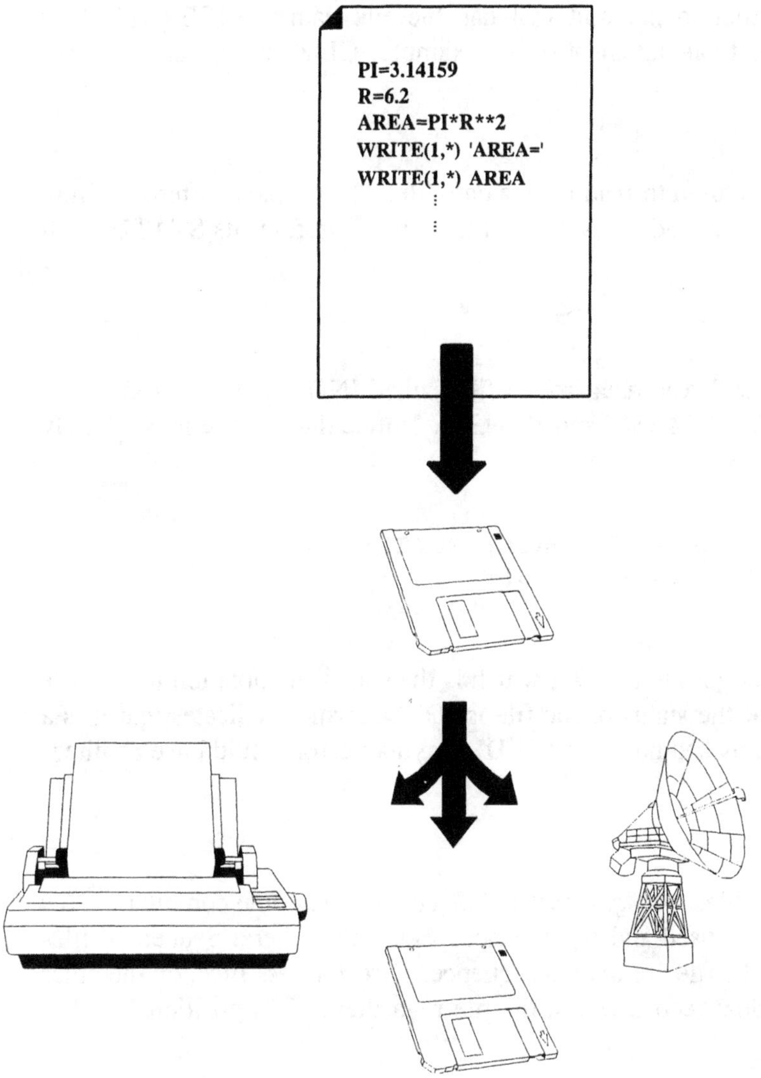

```
PI=3.14159
R=6.2
AREA=PI*R**2
PRINT*,'AREA='
PRINT*,AREA
    ⋮
    ⋮
```

AREA=
120.7627

Fig. 9-2
Writing to a data file.

```
PI=3.14159
R=6.2
AREA=PI*R**2
WRITE(1,*) 'AREA='
WRITE(1,*) AREA
    ⋮
```

305

EXAMPLE 9.1

Here is a simple example of how to write to a data file named EXPER.DAT:

```
OPEN(UNIT=8, FILE='EXPER.DAT', STATUS='NEW')
WRITE(8,*) DIST, TIME, VELOC
CLOSE(8)
```

The first statement, OPEN(...), contains all the information needed to set up the file with the name 'EXPER.DAT'. We will call this for simplicity the UNIT. This unit number comes in handy since it is easier to type the single number (8) than to use the full file name in every I/O statement. Thus, in subsequent statements when we refer to 8, we are referring to its equivalent file name 'EXPER.DAT'. The final listing in the OPEN statement shows the *status* of the file. As we will see shortly, it will be either 'NEW', 'OLD', 'SCRATCH', or 'UNKNOWN' indicating whether the file needs to be created, already exists, is only temporary, or unknown respectively.

   The second statement, WRITE(8,*) *list* , is used to direct the output to the desired file. Remember that we have given the file the short name of 8. Thus, the WRITE statement tells the computer to send the output to the unit that has the file name 'EXPER.DAT'and associated with UNIT=8. The final statement of the example, CLOSE(...), simply closes the file after we finish with it.

A similar set of statements can be used to read from a data file. The primary difference from the output statement is that the file must already exist to read from it. Therefore, its STATUS will be 'OLD'.

EXAMPLE 9.2

In the following example, we will read data from a file named 'NOBEL.DAT' and assign the data to the variables WEIGHT, MASS, and DENSIT. Notice that the file must already exist in order to read from it.

```
OPEN(UNIT=3, FILE='NOBEL.DAT', STATUS='OLD')
READ(3,*) WEIGHT, MASS, DENSIT
CLOSE(3)
```

Notice that the READ statement goes to unit #3, which is the shorthand notation for the file 'NOBEL.DAT'. Also note that the status of the file is 'OLD', which indicates that it is a valid file for reading. If the status had not been 'OLD', a syntax error would have resulted.

9.2 TYPES OF FILES

Fortran recognizes two types of files — *sequential* and *direct access*. Some compilers allow other types of files, but these are rarely used and we will not discuss them here. Sequential files are those in which the records within the file are read in sequence. Direct access files, on the other hand, allow you to access any individual record within the file regardless of its position.

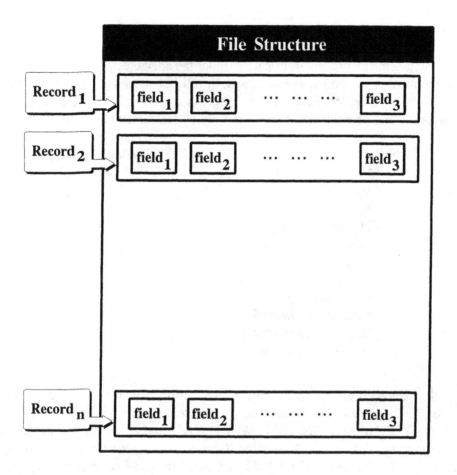

Fig. 9–3

To help you understand the terminology in this chapter, refer to Fig. 9–3. A file is a block of memory that is given a name determined by the user. For permanent storage, a file is placed in nonvolatile memory such as a hard or floppy disk, while for temporary storage, files are placed into the computer's volatile memory. The file consists of a series of *records*. A record is a convenient-sized block of data that you establish to store *fields* of data. Individual data values are stored within the fields, and each type of data has a different field size. Recall that alphanumeric character data can occupy any size field, while numeric data occupy fixed field widths. The computer reads (or writes) one record at a time. Thus it is possible that some of the fields within a record may not be read at all, depending on the structure of the I/O statements. For example, if your READ statement contains only one variable, but the record contains three numbers, the last two numbers in the record will be unread and therefore lost.

Sequential files must read the records in the order that they were written into the file. Direct access files, on the other hand, can move to any record and read (or write) that one only. When data are written to a file, the two types of files behave very differently. When you write to a sequential file, the data values can only be written at the end of the file. If you write the data to any other position, all subsequent entries are erased. Direct access files, on the other hand, allow you to write to any record in the file without disturbing any other records. Engineers and scientists tend to rely almost exclusively on sequential files, so we will focus on them. Direct access files are used less frequently in the sciences, but are used very frequently when dealing with large data files — census data, tax returns, or bank records, for example.

9.3 OPENING A SEQUENTIAL FILE

The OPEN statement contains information about the attributes of the file to be used for I/O. There are a large number of options available with the OPEN statement, only a few of which were shown in the first two examples. In the general form of the OPEN statement shown below, only the first two items in the parentheses are required, while the remaining items are optional:

```
OPEN ([UNIT=] integer expression, [FILE=] string,
        [ACCESS=string,]
        [ACTION=string,]
        [BLANK=string,]
        [DELIM=string,]
        [ERR=statement label n,]
        [FORM=string,]
        [IOSTAT=integer variable,]
        [PAD=string,]
        [POSITION=string,]
        [RECL=integer expression,]
        [STATUS=string,])
```

Only a few of the options listed above are part of the Fortran standard. However, since almost all commercial compilers have all or most of these options, we present them all here. As an example, the attributes POSITION, ACTION, DELIM, and PAD are not available in the Fortran 77 standard, so be careful when using them since this may make your programs less portable. As stated earlier, only the UNIT and FILENAME attributes are required. But use of the others may make it easier for you to handle many of the problems that occur.

The attribute UNIT is required and specifies the identifying number of the file to be accessed. The statement "UNIT=" may be omitted, but an integer constant or variable must appear.

EXAMPLE 9.3

The following statements are equivalent and open a file that we will refer to as unit #3:

```
        OPEN(UNIT=3,...)            or            OPEN(3, ...)
        READ (3,*) X, Y                          READ (3,*) X, Y
```

You may also use an integer variable or expression to specify the unit number, but this is rarely used.

Be careful when selecting unit numbers, since most systems reserve a few unit numbers for their own use. For example, on many computer systems, UNIT=5 is reserved for the CRT screen. Apart from these few reserved unit numbers (set by the computer administrators), the only other restriction is that the number must be between 1 and 99.

The attribute FILE specifies the name of the file connected to the specified unit number. You may use either a character string or a character variable that can be read in at execution time. The statement FILE= may be omitted if this file name comes second. The allowed name of the file will vary from computer to computer, so be careful to check the file naming conventions on your system.

EXAMPLE 9.4

The following statements are equivalent and indicate that the file to be opened has the name 'VOLTS.DAT':

```
OPEN(UNIT=3,FILE='VOLTS.DAT',...)
READ (3,*) X, Y
```

or

```
OPEN(3,'VOLTS.DAT',...)
READ (3,*) X, Y
```

EXAMPLE 9.5

You may specify the file name to be a variable that is read in at execution time, provided that you have properly set up the name as a character variable. In the following example, we use the character string stored in NAME to create the desired file entered by the user:

```
CHARACTER*10 NAME
PRINT *, 'Enter output file name:'
READ *, NAME
     :
OPEN(UNIT=16, FILE=NAME,...)
WRITE (16,*) X, Y
     :
```

When you declare the character variable, be sure to set up the variable with sufficient characters for the machine that you are using. For example, 10 characters is the customary limit on a file name on desktop computers. But some larger computers allow more characters, typically in the range of 13 to 20. Finally, note in this example that the input of the file name is interactive and is entered at the time that the program is run.

The attribute ACCESS specifies whether the file is *sequential* or *random access*. In a sequential file, all preceding items in the file must be read to get to the one that you are interested in. Direct access files, on the other hand, permit you to go directly to the position of the data item.

EXAMPLE 9.6

The following example opens a sequential file 'OUT.DAT' and reads ten data points into the array X:

```
REAL X(10)
OPEN(UNIT=9, FILE='OUT.DAT', ACCESS='SEQUENTIAL',...)
READ (9,*) (X(I), I=1,10)
```

If you omit the ACCESS attribute, then 'SEQUENTIAL' is assumed. Thus, the following is equivalent to the previous three statements.

```
REAL X(10)
OPEN(UNIT=9, FILE='OUT.DAT', ...)
READ (9,*) (X(I), I=1,10)
          ⋮
```

Most applications in engineering and science require sequential access, so this latter form is more common.

EXAMPLE 9.7

Some compilers have an optional ACCESS='APPEND' instruction available for sequential files. When this is included, any new data being written to the file will be written at the end of the file, immediately after the last data point. Previous data will not be disturbed.

```
        ⋮
17.9                          Data file before new data is appended
21.6
<end of file>
```

When the following program executes, the new data values will be added to the end of the file, and the end of the file indication will move down the required number of lines.

```
X=4.1
OPEN(UNIT=9, FILE='OUT.DAT', ACCESS='APPEND', ...)
WRITE (9,*) X
```

```
        ⋮
17.9                          Data file after new item is appended
21.6
4.1
<end of file>
```

The ACTION attribute allows you to provide a degree of protection for your files. The allowed commands are 'READ', 'WRITE', and 'READ/WRITE', which limit you to read only, write only, or both reading and writing only from the specified file, respectively. Thus, if you specify ACTION='READ', you will not be allowed to write to that file. This prevents you from losing data by accidentally overwriting them.

EXAMPLE 9.8

The following example opens a sequential file 'SALES.DAT' for reading in the data and, at the same time, protects the file from having anything written to it:

```
REAL SALES(10)
OPEN(UNIT=11, FILE='SALES.DAT', ACTION='READ', ...)
READ (11,*) (SALES(I), I=1,10)
```

Once the ACTION='READ' is included as an attribute of the file 'SALES.DAT', that file will be protected against accidental erasure. Some compilers also offer additional options with the ACTION attribute to allow you to safely share files between multiple READ or WRITE statements, so check your manual for further details.

The attribute BLANK has only two values — 'NULL' or 'ZERO', which will determine how blanks at the beginning of a number are to be interpreted. If 'NULL' is used, the computer will ignore blanks, but choosing 'ZERO' will cause the leading blanks to be interpreted as zeros.

EXAMPLE 9.9

Assume that we have the following data file named 'NULLZERO.DAT' (Note: blank = ~)

```
~ ~ ~ ~4.2
~ ~2.3~ ~
1.7~ ~ ~ ~
<end of file>
```
Data file: 'NULLZERO.DAT'

If we read the file with the following program segment, the leading blank spaces (indicated by ~) are converted to zeros, but the trailing blank spaces are ignored.

```
OPEN(UNIT=10, FILE='NULLZERO.DAT', BLANK='ZERO', ...)
READ (10,*) A, B, C
```

will produce:

```
A=00004.2
B=002.3
C=1.7.
```

The attribute DELIM selects the character that will be used to mark the beginning or end of character strings in a data file. The three possible values are 'APOSTROPHE', 'QUOTE', and 'NONE'. If 'APOSTROPHE' or 'QUOTE' is used, that character will be used to identify the character string, and any internal apostrophe or quote marks will be doubled. If, however, 'NONE' is specified, then any internal apostrophes or quotes will be unaffected.

EXAMPLE 9.10

Assume that we have the following data file named 'DELIM.DAT' that contains a series of character strings:

```
'this is''nt a test'
"this is''nt a test"
< end of file >
```
Data file: 'DELIM.DAT'

If we specify quote marks as the delimiter, the data will be read as follows:

```
CHARACTER*20 TEST1, TEST2
OPEN(UNIT=10, FILE='DELIM.DAT', DELIM='QUOTE', ...)
READ (10,*) TEST1, TEST2
```

This will result in the following assignments:

TEST1 ← this isn't a test   TEST2 ← this is''nt a test

When reading the first line of the data file, the computer treats the internal quotes as a single quote, based upon the leading delimiter ('). But in the second line of the data file, the leading delimiter is the double quote ("), so the internal quote is treated as a double quote.

The ERR command is useful because it allows you to *trap errors*. If an error occurs while attempting to communicate with a file, control transfers to the statement specified by *sl* in the ERR=*sl* statement. This gives you a chance to try again or to undertake another procedure.

EXAMPLE 9.11

Assume that we have the following data file named 'OUT.DAT':

```
9.654
1.256
3.450
< end of file >
```
Data file: 'OUT.DAT'

If we attempt to run the following program segment, an error will occur because we will reach the end of the file (EOF) before we have read in all the specified data:

```
REAL X(5)
OPEN(UNIT=4, FILE='OUT.DAT', ...)
READ (4,*) (X(I), I=1,5)
```

We can use the ERR attribute to handle such errors, as shown below:

```
      REAL X(5)
      OPEN(UNIT=4, FILE='OUT.DAT', ERR=10, ...)
      READ (4,*) (X(I), I=1,5)
         ⋮
10    STOP 'ERROR IN DATA FILE'
```

There is an alternate way to do the same thing, in which we embed the error handling within the READ command. This is done by adding ERR=*sl1* or END=*sl2* clauses:

READ(*unit, format*, ERR=*sl1*, END=*sl2*)

If the end of the file is reached before all the data values are read, control will transfer to statement label 2 (*sl2*), while any other error will cause control to transfer to statement label 1 (*sl1*).

The FORM attribute has only two possible options, FORMATTED or UNFORMATTED. The formatted option permits the program to read data in a converted form, while the unformatted option will read in data from a file as binary strings. Almost all of your files will be of the formatted type. Some files, however, are stored as binary files because they are smaller and because they can be read and written more quickly than formatted files.

EXAMPLE 9.12

If you wish to store data in a binary file, you can do this simply by adding the statement FORM='UNFORMATTED' to the OPEN statement.

```
REAL X(5)
OPEN(UNIT=4, FILE='TEST.DAT', FORM='UNFORMATTED', . . .)
WRITE (4,*) (X(I), I=1,5)
```

This will write all the data in binary form to the indicated file. Once this is done, the only way we can read the data within this file would be to use a corresponding READ statement that was opened with the FORM='UNFORMATTED' statement.

The IOSTAT attribute allows you to receive information from the computer about the type of error that has occurred. This instruction is different from the others in that you are receiving rather than sending data. If no error occurs, the integer variable in the IOSTAT=*integer variable* is set to zero. But if an error does occur, then the variable is set to a nonzero value. You can use this value to do something. Perhaps you want to retry reading the file, or read another file, or print an error message. The point is that you now have some control over handling errors. The exact value of the variable returned is compiler dependent, but the following are typical values:

integer variable	$<$	0	*(end of file error)*
integer variable	$=$	0	*(no errors)*
integer variable	$>$	0	*(other types of errors)*

EXAMPLE 9.13

In the following program segment, a message will be printed whether the file 'IOSTAT.DAT' was read correctly or not:

```
REAL X(5)
OPEN(UNIT=8, FILE='IOSTAT.DAT', IOSTAT=ITEST,...)
READ (8,*) (X(I), I=1,5)
SELECT CASE (ITEST)
    CASE(:-1)
        PRINT *, 'End of file error'
    CASE(0)
        PRINT *, 'No problems'
    CASE(1:)
        PRINT *, 'Other type of error'
END Select
```

After the file is read, an integer value will be assigned by the computer to the variable ITEST. In the case select structure, we examine the value of ITEST. If it is negative, the error message "End of file error" is printed. If ITEST is zero, the message "No problem" is printed, and if ITEST is positive, "Other type of error" is printed.

Once you find what the other error codes are for your compiler, you can add these to an expanded case select block. These error codes will be machine dependent, so it may affect the portability of your program. Therefore, we recommend that you stay with this simple segment.

The PAD option, if selected, will deliberately add extra blank spaces when a list of input variables requires more data than the record (line) in the data file contains. There are only two values allowed, 'YES' and 'NO'.

EXAMPLE 9.14

In the following program segment, data will be read into a character variable DUMMY which requires 20 characters to fill it, but the data file contains a smaller number of characters (8 in this case):

```
CHARACTER*20 DUMMY
OPEN(UNIT=8, FILE='PAD.DAT', PAD='YES',...)
READ (8,*) DUMMY
```

If we use this program to read the following data file:

```
ABCDEFGH
<end of file>
```
            Data file: 'PAD.DAT'

the value assigned to DUMMY will be padded with an extra 12 blank spaces to fill out the 20 spaces reserved for the variable:

$$DUMMY = 'ABCDEFGH \sim \sim \sim \sim \sim \sim \sim \sim \sim \sim \sim \sim'$$

The PAD clause can only be used with input statements. If you attempt to use it with an output statement, a compiler error will occur. If the instruction is omitted, the compiler assumes a value of 'YES'.

The POSITION option changes the position of a hypothetical pointer within a sequential file. After communicating with a file, this pointer "points" to the next position in the file. The POSITION command will change that position to one of three possibilities — 'ASIS', 'REWIND', or 'APPEND'. The 'ASIS' option leaves the file unaffected, while the 'APPEND' option moves to the end of the file. The 'REWIND' option moves the pointer to the beginning of the file.

EXAMPLE 9.15

In the following program segment, the hypothetical pointer will be reset to the beginning of the file before it reads the first data point:

```
OPEN(UNIT=2, FILE='POINTER.DAT', POINTER='REWIND',...)
READ (2,*) N
```

The STATUS attribute is used to indicate the type of file that is being accessed. The possible values are 'NEW', 'OLD', 'UNKNOWN', or 'SCRATCH'. If the STATUS attribute is omitted, a value of 'UNKNOWN' is assumed. The value of STATUS indicates whether the file has already been created ('OLD'), should be created ('NEW'), is temporary ('SCRATCH'), or has a status of unknown ('UNKNOWN'). The use of STATUS should be intuitive, since you cannot read data from a file that does not exist.

EXAMPLE 9.16

In the following program segment, we will open the file STATUS.DAT and read data from it. We will then create a second file and then send the data (in reverse order) that we have just read to the new file 'TEST.DAT'.

```
OPEN(UNIT=1, FILE='STATUS.DAT', STATUS='OLD')
OPEN(UNIT=2, FILE='TEST.DAT', STATUS='NEW')
READ (1,*) (X(I), I=1,10)
WRITE (2,*) (X(I), I=10, 1, -1)
```

The first OPEN statement tells the computer to go to file 'STATUS.DAT' and associate it with unit 1. The READ statement will then open that file and read the data. Notice that the OPEN statement tells the computer that the file should already exist, hence its STATUS='OLD'. Once the data have been read, they are then sent to the newly created file 'TEST.DAT', which is associated with unit 2 and STATUS='NEW'.

Most of the data file work that you will need to do requires only the UNIT, FILE, and STATUS attributes in the OPEN statement. The additional specifiers are rarely required except for error trapping purposes. So most OPEN statements that you will see will be of the form:

```
OPEN(UNIT=4, FILE='MINE.DAT', STATUS='OLD')
```

9.4 CLOSING A SEQUENTIAL FILE

You close files in your program with the CLOSE statement whose general form is:

CLOSE ([UNIT=] *integer expression,*
        [ERR=*statement label n,*]
        [IOSTAT=*integer variable,*]
        [STATUS=*string,*])

Any attribute in brackets ([...]) is optional and can be left out. The UNIT= *integer expression* has the same meaning as in the OPEN statement. It is the only attribute that is required with the CLOSE statement. All other attributes (ERR, IOSTAT, STATUS) are optional.

EXAMPLE 9.17

The following program segment opens a file 'TESTCLOSE.DAT', writes a value to that file, and then closes it after the data have been written to the file:

```
OPEN(UNIT=3, FILE='CLOSE.DAT', STATUS='NEW')
WRITE (3,*) X, Y
CLOSE(UNIT=3)
```

Just as with the OPEN statement, the unit number must always be included, but the UNIT= clause is optional. Thus, an equivalent way of writing the program segment is:

```
OPEN(3, 'CLOSE.DAT', STATUS='NEW')
WRITE(3,*) X, Y
CLOSE(3)
```

Actually, the entire CLOSE statement may be omitted since the computer closes all files when the program terminates. But it is not a good idea to leave files open since you may inadvertently write to the file in another part of the program.

The STATUS attribute associated with the CLOSE statement is different from the one used with the OPEN statement. The only allowable values of STATUS are 'KEEP' and 'DELETE'. If 'KEEP' is selected, the file is made permanent for future use, but if 'DELETE' is chosen, the file is deleted immediately. If the file status is not specified, 'KEEP' is assumed.

If the file in the OPEN statement has STATUS='SCRATCH', then the computer will <u>always</u> delete the file after you finish. Even if you use STATUS='KEEP' in the CLOSE statement, the machine will delete the file. Once you declare a file to be a scratch file, you cannot save it.

The two other attributes (IOSTAT and ERR) used in the CLOSE statement are both optional and have the same meaning as that described earlier with the OPEN command. Therefore we will not repeat them here.

9.5 SEQUENTIAL FILE POSITIONING STATEMENTS

There are a few additional commands used with files that you may find useful. These allow you to move around within a file and to mark the end of the file. The first of these commands allows you to rewind the file to the beginning. Its general form is

REWIND ([UNIT=] *integer expression,*
          [IOSTAT=*integer variable,*]
          [ERR=*statement label n,*])

where all of the attributes have the same meaning as before. The only required attribute is the file number with or without the optional clause UNIT=. The error-trapping attributes are optional.

EXAMPLE 9.18

Some computer systems may require you to rewind a file before you attempt to read it. So even though it is not required, it may be a good idea to rewind before reading to improve the portability of your programs. The following program segment rewinds the file 'REWIND.DAT' before attempting to read it:

```
OPEN(UNIT=3, FILE='REWIND.DAT', STATUS='OLD')
REWIND (UNIT=3, ERR=10)
READ (3,*) X, Y
CLOSE(UNIT=3)
    ⋮
10 STOP 'FILE REWIND ERROR'
```

In this example, we first opened the file and attempted to rewind it. If an error occurs, control will transfer to the STOP statement and print out the error message. If the rewind is successful, the program proceeds to read the required data and then closes the unit. Notice that you can only rewind a file after it has been opened.

The second positioning statement allows you to backspace one record within the file. Whereas the REWIND command goes to the beginning of the file, the BACKSPACE command moves back only one record. Its general form is

BACKSPACE ([UNIT=] *integer expression,*
            [IOSTAT= *integer variable,*]
            [ERR= *statement label n*])

All of the attributes have their usual meaning. The only required attribute is the file number with or without the optional UNIT= clause. The error-trapping attributes are optional. This statement is useful when you need to reread data because of a reading error.

EXAMPLE 9.19

In the following program segment, we will read a value of X from a data file. If an error occurs during reading, we will backspace and try again.

```
        OPEN(UNIT=7, FILE='BACK.DAT', STATUS='OLD')
        READ (7,*, ERR=3) X
          ⋮
3       BACKSPACE (7)
        READ (7,*) X
          ⋮
        CLOSE(UNIT=7)
```

We have added an error-trapping option to the READ statement in this example. If a read error occurs, control transfers to statement label 3, where the computer is instructed to backspace one record and reread the data. This is about the only use of the BACKSPACE command.

The third statement is used to place an end-of-file indication into a file. Its general form is:

ENDFILE ([UNIT=] *integer expression,*
         [IOSTAT= *integer variable,*]
         [ERR= *statement label n*])

All of the attributes have their usual meaning. The only required attribute is the file number with or without the optional UNIT = clause. The error trapping attributes are optional.

EXAMPLE 9.20

In the following program segment, we read values from a data file until an end-of-file is encountered. At this point, we write a message to the screen. We can then begin to do other work. For example, we could begin computations on the numbers just entered.

```
        REAL X(100), Y(100)
        OPEN(UNIT=11, FILE='EOF.DAT', STATUS='OLD')
        OPEN(UNIT=12,'FILE='CONTINUE.DAT', STATUS='NEW')
        READ (11,*, END=9) (X(I), I=1, 100)
          ⋮
9       WRITE (12, *) (Y(I), I=1,100)
        ENDFILE (12)
          ⋮
        CLOSE(UNIT=12)
```

Once again, we have added an END option to the I/O statement. When the computer comes to the original EOF mark, control will transfer to statement label 9 where the new data will be written. When finished writing, the program places an EOF mark at the new end.

The EOF command is generally not needed since this is automatically added to the end of a file when it is closed. So the use for this statement is very limited.

9.6 DIRECT ACCESS FILES

The second type of file is the direct access file. Recall that the distinguishing feature of this type of file is that we can communicate with a single record within the file without having to go through all the other records. But in order to do this, we need to specify a *record number* that points to the specific record. We will do this in the READ or WRITE statement. Also, the OPEN statement is slightly different with direct access files. The record length must be the same for all records in the direct access file. This is done with the RECL attribute in the OPEN statement:

```
OPEN ([UNIT=] integer expression, [FILE=] string,
      [ACCESS=string,]
      [ACTION=string,]
      [BLANK=string,]
      [DELIM=string,]
      [ERR=statement label n,]
      [FORM=string,]
      [IOSTAT=integer variable,]
      [PAD=string,]
      [POSITION=string,]
      [RECL=integer expression,]
      [STATUS=string,])
```

The RECL clause indicates the length (in number of columns) of each record within the file. You can determine the length of the record by simply counting the number of columns that the data occupy. In many ways, this is similar to the way that we set up the output fields in formatting. All the other attributes have the same meaning as those discussed previously.

EXAMPLE 9.21

In the following program segment, we will open the direct access file 'RECL.DAT' in which the data within the file have a record length of 23:

```
      OPEN(UNIT=3, FILE='RECL.DAT', ACCESS='DIRECT',
     1             FORM='FORMATTED', RECL=23, STATUS='NEW')
      WRITE (3, 5, REC=34) 'Value of N is:', N
    5 FORMAT(A14, I9)
```

We used the ACCESS='DIRECT' clause to create a direct access file. When the file is formatted, the RECL is determined by the number of columns that the data occupy. Thus, in this example, we had 14 characters and 9 digits, for a total of 23. This number appears in the clause RECL=23.

The new clause (REC=34) within the READ statement indicates that the data in the I/O list are to be written to the 34th record. Any previous data in that location will be lost, but no other data will be disturbed.

The attributes UNIT, FILE, and RECL are required with direct access files, while FORM and STATUS are optional. If FORM is omitted, the computer assumes 'FORMATTED' for sequential files and 'UNFORMATTED' for direct access files. So, in the previous example if we had left out the FORM attribute, the file would have been different from the RECL=23 that we used. This is due to the fact that unformatted files are stored in bytes and are machine dependent. In most cases, it is better to stay with formatted files, because the storage method for unformatted files will vary.

9.7 DEBUGGING

There are several problems that you might run into when using data files. The things to watch out for are:

- You attempt to write to a file before it is opened or you try to read from a file after it is closed.
- You attribute the wrong status to a file that results in a conflict with the I/O command that follows.
- You mix attributes designed for sequential and direct files.
- Any attempt to replace a record in a sequential file will result in the remainder of the file being erased.

Once you have diagnosed which type of error has occurred, it is usually a simple matter to correct the problem. Each of these problems is illustrated in the examples below.

EXAMPLE 9.22

If you attempt to access a file before it has been opened (or after it has been closed), you will receive a run-time error.

```
OPEN(UNIT=3, FILE='MINE.DAT', STATUS='NEW')
WRITE(3,*) DIST, TIME, VELOC
CLOSE(3)
READ(3,*)  X , Y , Z
```

Once you close a file, you cannot access it again unless you use another OPEN statement. Thus, in the example above, the third line has closed the file. After that point, you cannot try to read from or print to the file.

EXAMPLE 9.23

If you attempt to read from a file, the proper status attribute in the OPEN statement must be STATUS='OLD'. Otherwise, you will be attempting to read from a file that doesn't exist yet, and you will receive a run-time error.

```
OPEN (UNIT=4, FILE='MINE.DAT', STATUS='NEW')
READ (4,*) DIST, TIME, VELOC
CLOSE (4)
```

The OPEN statement has specified the file 'MINE.DAT' will be created as a new file. Yet, we attempt to read from the file not yet been created. Therefore, a run-time error occurs.

EXAMPLE 9.24

If you mix attributes designed for sequential and direct files, an error will occur.

```
    OPEN (UNIT=5, FILE='TEST.DAT', ACCESS='SEQUENTIAL',
1        RECL=32, STATUS='NEW')
    WRITE (5,*, REC=14) DIST, TIME, VELOC
    CLOSE (5)
```

The file TEST.DAT was declared to be a sequential file, yet a record length was specified, and the WRITE statement included a REC= command. Both of these options are used for direct access files, not sequential files. Therefore, an error message will result.

EXAMPLE 9.25

If you attempt to write to a sequential file at any position other than the end of the file, all the remaining data will be lost. Assume for example that we had the following data file:

```
12.34
14.57
43.56
13.687
13.56
2.78
−0.45
<end of file>
```

Data file before reading

If we now read a value, and attempt to replace it with a revised value, then everything after that point will be lost. For example, assume we read the first three values, backspace one position, and then rewrite a new value in the third record of the file:

```
OPEN (UNIT=6, FILE='REPLACE.DAT', STATUS='OLD')
READ (6,*) X, Y, Z
    ⋮
(Compute new value of Z)
    ⋮
BACKSPACE (6)
WRITE (6,*) Z
CLOSE (6)
```

This will result in the following change to the data file:

```
12.34
14.57
new value of Z
erased
erased
erased
erased
< end of file >
```
Data file after updating information

The revised file would not have the four blank lines indicated in the file. Instead, the end-of-file record would appear immediately after the new value of Z. We showed the erased records to reinforce the fact that everything after a new entry to a sequential file will be erased. To do what we wanted to do in this example, we would need to use a direct access file.

EXAMPLE 9.26

There is one final area where an unexpected error may occur. This is in the use of carriage control characters with data files. Generally, you only use a carriage control character (CCC) when the output is going to be sent to a printer or a CRT. The CCCs are not needed when the data are being sent to a data file. The problem occurs when you attempt to send the data file to a printer at a later date. In this case, the CCCs would be needed, but they are not included in the file. Therefore, some of the data may be truncated. Consider the following data file:

```
9.3425
6.234
6.324
< end of file >
```
Data file

If you now type this file on a printer, the following output will result:

```
.3425
.234
.324
```

If the CCC is omitted, the computer will use the first character in the record to reset the printer. In the case shown, this corresponds to the first digit of each number being lost. In fact, you may not even be aware of the problem, since the loss of a single digit is not obvious. The solution to this problem is to use CCCs when using formatted output to a data file.

Solved Problems

9.1　Locate the syntax and run-time errors in the following program statements:

    (a) `OPEN(UNIT=114, FILE='TEST.DAT')`
    (b) `OPEN(20, 'TEST.DAT', ACCESS=SEQUENTIAL)`
    (c) `CLOSE(UNIT=7, FILE='TEST.DAT', STATUS='SCRATCH')`
    (d) `OPEN(3, 'SCRATCH')`
    (e) `OPEN(9, FILE='IO.DAT', ACCESS='DIRECT')`
       `READ(9,*,RECL=7) X`
    (f) `OPEN(11, FILE='THERMAL.DAT', ACCESS='DIRECT', RECL=14)`
       `WRITE(11,*,REC=13) A, B, C`

    (a) The unit number may not exceed 99 on many computers.
    (b) Sequential should be inside apostrophes ('SEQUENTIAL').
    (c) A CLOSE statement does not use the "FILE=" attribute.
    (d) No errors, but the file name will be 'Scratch'. This does not refer to the status.
    (e) Direct access files require a record length (RECL) attribute in the OPEN statement.
    (f) The variables A, B, and C, will occupy approximately 24 columns (assuming a maximum of 8 columns each). Therefore, the RECL clause is inadequate.

9.2　Write OPEN statements to accomplish the following:

    (a) Create a sequential file called 'WEIGHTS.DAT'
    (b) Connect to a file called 'INPUT' as an old file on unit 6.
    (c) Open a file called 'RESULTS' as a new file on unit 5.
    (d) Open a scratch file on unit 7.
    (e) Open a file 'DATA.DAT' whose status is uncertain on unit 4.

    (a) `OPEN(UNIT=1, FILE='WEIGHTS.DAT', STATUS='NEW')`
    (b) `OPEN(UNIT=6, FILE='INPUT', STATUS='OLD')`
    (c) `OPEN(UNIT=5, FILE='RESULTS', STATUS='NEW')`
    (d) `OPEN(UNIT=7, STATUS='SCRATCH')`
    (e) `OPEN(UNIT=4, FILE='DATA.DAT', STATUS='UNKNOWN')`

9.3　The following exercises are designed so that you can find out the limitations or extensions of your Fortran compiler. Run small programs to find out if the following suggestions work. You may also need to consult the documentation for your system.

    (a) What is the UNIT number for CRT output and keyboard input on your system? If there are two such numbers such as 5 or 6, is there any difference in the way that each behaves?
    (b) What is the set of valid unit numbers on your system? Do any other unit numbers have any special significance, such as tape drives, floppy disks, optical scanners, or plotters? (You need to ask the system administrators to answer these questions.)

(c) Some compilers will allow the use of * for unit directed I/O. If that's the case, the following are equivalent. Does your system support this feature?

```
PRINT *, X         is equivalent to         WRITE(*,*) X
```

9.4   Assume that we have a file that contains the following data:

```
1, 2, 3
4
5
6, 7
<end of file>
```

Data file 'INPUT'

What are the values of the variables if the file is read with the following program segments? (Assume the file has the attributes UNIT=7, FILE='INPUT', STATUS='OLD')

```
(a) READ(7,*)  A, B, C
(b) READ(7,*)  A, B, C, I, J
(c) READ(7,*)  A
    READ(7,*)  B
    READ(7,*)  C, I
(d) READ(7,*)  (X(I), I=1, 7)
```

(a) Each READ statement reads one record. So the first numeric field is assigned to A, the second to B, and the third to C. This results in the assignments: A=1.000000, B=2.000000, and C=3.000000.

(b) The READ statement requires five numeric values to assign to the variables. But the first record contains only three values, so additional records are read until all the variables have values. The result is A=1.000000, B=2.000000, C=3.000000, I=4, and J=5.

(c) The first READ statement needs only one value for assignment. Therefore, it uses only the first field within the first record. The second and third values are ignored. The second READ statement then begins input with the second record, and the third READ begins with the third record. The result is: A=1.000000, B=4.000000, C=5.000000, and I=6. Notice that the values 2 and 3 from the first record are never read.

(d) The single READ statement requires seven values to fill the X array. This can only be achieved by reading beyond the first record until all values are assigned. The result is $X_1=1.000000$, $X_2=2.000000$, $X_3=3.000000$, $X_4=4.000000$, $X_5=5.000000$, $X_6=6.000000$, $X_7=7.000000$.

9.5   In all of the previous examples, we knew in advance what the name of the input or output file would be. But many times we will not have this information. Therefore, it is desirable to enter the desired file name at execution time and proceed to open the desired file. Write a program segment which will accomplish this task.

```
C******************************************************************
C We will declare FILENAME to be a character variable and use
C this to hold the desired file name.
C******************************************************************
      CHARACTER*20 FILENAME
      PRINT *, 'Enter desired file name:'
      READ *, FILENAME
C******************************************************************
C Now that the file name has been entered, use it to create
C the file. Notice that we do not include single quote marks
C around the file name since it is a character variable.
C******************************************************************
      OPEN(UNIT=1, FILE=FILENAME, STATUS='NEW')
      WRITE(1,*) ...
         :
      END
```

9.6 Write a program to read a file CONCENTR.DAT whose records contain concentrations of various species, [a], [b], and [c] in a chemical reaction. Assume that the data are written to the file with the format specifier (3F10.6). Read in one record at a time, and for each set of concentrations compute the rate constant defined by

$$k = \frac{[\,a\,]\,[\,b\,]}{[\,c\,]}$$

Print the results ([a], [b], [c], and k) to the screen. If an error occurs during the read operation, print the message "Input Error!" When the end-of-file occurs, terminate the program and print the message "Calculations Complete."

```
C******************************************************************
C Open the file and then read one set of [a], [b], and [c]
C values at a time. Use these to compute k and print the
C results. Include in the READ statement the options ERR=
C and END=. These will detect read errors and end-of-file
C respectively.
C******************************************************************
      REAL K
      OPEN(UNIT=1, FILE='CONCENTR.DAT', STATUS='OLD')
      DO WHILE( .TRUE.)
         READ(1,10, ERR=20, END=30) A, B, C
10       FORMAT(3F10.6)
         K=A*B/C
         PRINT *, A, B, C, K
      END DO
20    STOP 'Input Error!'
30    STOP 'Calculations Complete'
      END
```

9.7 Assume that data from a bacteria-growth experiment are stored in two files 'GROWTH.DAT' and 'POTENCY.DAT' with the following formats

'GROWTH.DAT'		'POTENCY.DAT'

10/12/93	23:47	1234568
10/13/93	11:47	1458450
10/14/93	06:34	1534389
10/15/93	09:23	1637238
<end of file>		

10/12/93	23:47	147.345
10/13/93	11:47	146.234
10/14/93	06:34	148.346
10/15/93	09:23	147.225
<end of file>		

The first two columns in each file represents the date and time, respectively, at which the data were taken. The third column represents the number of cells (in 'GROWTH.DAT') and their potency (in 'POTENCY.DAT'). Write a program that opens both files and merges them into a new file 'BACTERIA.DAT' with the following format:

10/12/93	23:47	1234568	147.345
10/13/93	11:47	1458450	146.234
10/14/93	06:34	1534389	148.346
10/15/93	09:23	1637238	147.225
<end of file>			

```
C***************************************************************
C Open all three files at the same time, but give each a
C different unit number.
C***************************************************************
      CHARACTER DATE*12, TIME*7
      REAL NUMCEL
      OPEN(UNIT=1, FILE='GROWTH.DAT', STATUS='OLD')
      OPEN(UNIT=2, FILE='POTENCY.DAT', STATUS='OLD')
      OPEN(UNIT=3, FILE='BACTERIA.DAT', STATUS='NEW')
C***************************************************************
C Set up a loop to read the data from GROWTH.DAT and POTENCY.DAT
C and merge them. Be sure to remove redundant information before
C writing it to the new file. If an end-of-file specification
C is encountered, stop.
C***************************************************************
      DO WHILE (.TRUE.)
         READ(1,*, END=10) DATE, TIME, NUMCEL
         READ(2,*, END=10) DATE, TIME, POTENC
         WRITE(3,*) DATE, TIME, NUMCEL, POTENC
      END DO
  10  STOP 'End of Input Data'
      END
```

9.8   Write a program to read the file 'CIRCUIT.DAT' and count the number of records n in the file. Assume that each record was written with the format (X, 2(F10.2, 2X)). The first field within each record represents the voltage V_j, and the second field represents the current I_j. After reading in the data, compute the power P dissipated by the circuit and the average current I_{avg} given by

$$P = \sum_{i=1}^{i=n} V_j I_j$$

$$I_{avg} = \sum_{i=1}^{i=n} \frac{I_j}{n}$$

```
C************************************************************
C Open the file and read the data using the same format that
C was used to save it.
C************************************************************
      REAL V(1000), I(1000), IAVG
      OPEN(UNIT=1, FILE='CIRCUIT.DAT', STATUS='OLD')
      N=1
      DO WHILE(.TRUE.)
          READ(1,10,END=20) V(N), I(N)
   10     FORMAT(1X, 2(F10.2, 2X))
          N=N+1
      END DO
   20 PRINT *, N, 'Data records read'
C************************************************************
C Now that all the data have been entered, use N to compute the
C required values of P and IAVG.
C************************************************************
      P=0.0
      ISUM=0.0
      DO 30 K=1, N
          P=P+V(K)*I(K)
          ISUM=ISUM+I(K)
   30 CONTINUE
      IAVG=ISUM/N
      PRINT *, 'Power Dissipated= ', P
      PRINT *, 'Average Current= ', IAVG
      END
```

9.9 Assume that you are hired as a technician to conduct a lengthy series of chemical experiments. The project is set up so that each experiment takes one day to complete. At the end of each day, the data that you have collected are stored in a data file called 'DATA.DAT' in the following format:

Date	Tester's Name	Temperature	Humidity	Concentration	Activity

Also, at the top of the file in the first record is the number of experimental entries (N). Write two programs to accomplish the following:

- Enter the data into the file at the end of a day
- Read any specified record within the file when needed to make corrections

```
C***********************************************************
C The best way to handle this problem is with a direct access
C file which will allow us to go to a specific record within
C the file without having to read all the data. Also, the
C direct access file will allow us to correct any one of the
C records without losing any of the others.
C      We will store the total number or records to date in the
C first record. This will allow us to interrogate this value
C at the end of each day so that we know where to store the
C newest results. Once we have this number, then we will store
C the daily results in N+1. Also, we will have to update the
C first record.
C***********************************************************
      CHARACTER DATE*8, NAME*20
      REAL TEMP, HUMID, CONCEN, ACTIV
      PRINT *, 'Enter today''s date (d/m/y):'
      READ *, DATE
      PRINT *, 'Enter your name:'
      READ *, NAME
      PRINT *, 'Enter temperature and humidity:'
      READ *, TEMP, HUMID
      PRINT *, 'Enter concentration and activity:'
      READ *, CONCEN, ACTIV
C***********************************************************
C Open the file, extract the first data value, and assign to N
C***********************************************************
      OPEN(UNIT=1, FILE='DATA.DAT', ACCESS='DIRECT', RECL=77)
      READ(1,REC=1) N
C***********************************************************
C Write the new data to REC=N+1, and update the first record
C***********************************************************
      WRITE(1,REC=N+1) N+1, DATE, NAME, TEMP, HUMID,
     1                CONCEN, ACTIV
      WRITE(1,REC=1) N+1
      CLOSE(1)
      END
C***********************************************************
C Second program to correct faulty data. The program asks the
C user to enter the record number for the correction. Then the
C data currently stored there are retrieved and displayed for
C examination. The user then enters the correct data.
C***********************************************************
      CHARACTER DATE*8, NAME*20, DUMMY*84
      REAL TEMP, HUMID, CONCEN, ACTIV
      PRINT *, 'Enter record number of faulty entry:'
      READ *, NREC
      OPEN(UNIT=1,FILE='DATA.DAT',ACCESS='DIRECT',RECL=77)
      READ(1,REC=NREC) N, DATE, NAME, TEMP, HUMID,
     1                CONCEN, ACTIV
      PRINT *, 'Enter correct date (d/m/y):'
      READ *, DATE
      PRINT *, 'Enter correct name:'
      READ *, NAME
      PRINT *, 'Enter correct temperature and humidity:'
      READ *, TEMP, HUMID
      PRINT *, 'Enter correct concentration and activity:'
```

```
          READ *, CONCEN, ACTIV
C*****************************************************************
C Write the corrected data to REC=NREC.
C*****************************************************************
          WRITE(1,REC=NREC) N, DATE, NAME, TEMP, HUMID,
     1                      CONCEN, ACTIV
          CLOSE(1)
          END
```

9.10 Write a program that interactively reads in students performance in a course and creates a file 'GRADES' in which each record consists of the following data:

ID Number	*Name*	*Midterm Exam*	*Final Exam*	*Homework*	*Quizzes*

Then create a second program to read this file and compute the student's term grade based on a weighting of 40% final exam / 30% midterm exam / 15% homework / 15% quizzes. When the final grades have been computed, create a new file 'AVG' in which only the ID number and the term grade appear.

```
C*****************************************************************
C Read in all the data and send it to the file GRADES.
C*****************************************************************
          CHARACTER*20 NAME(1000)
          REAL MID(1000), FINAL(1000), HOME(1000), QUIZ(1000)
          PRINT *, 'How many students?'
          READ *, N
          DO 10 I=1, N
              PRINT *, 'Enter student''s name:'
              READ *, NAME(I)
              PRINT *, 'Midterm, final, homework, quiz scores?'
              READ *, MID(I), FINAL(I), HOME(I), QUIZ(I)
   10     CONTINUE
C*****************************************************************
C Now put the data into a sequential file.
C*****************************************************************
          OPEN(UNIT=9, FILE='GRADES', STATUS='NEW')
          DO 20 I=1, N
              WRITE(9,*) NAME(I),MID(I),FINAL(I),HOME(I),QUIZ(I)
   20     CONTINUE
          CLOSE(9)
          END
C*****************************************************************
C The second program will open the file and perform the required
C computations.
C*****************************************************************
          CHARACTER*20 NAME(1000)
          REAL MID(1000), FINAL(1000), HOME(1000), QUIZ(1000)
          REAL AVG(1000)
          OPEN(UNIT=9, FILE='GRADES', STATUS='NEW')
          N=1
          DO WHILE(.TRUE.)
              READ(9,*,END=20) NAME(N), MID(N), FINAL(N),
     1                         HOME(N), QUIZ(N)
```

```
            N = N + 1
         END DO
C******************************************************************
C We will compute the weighted average of the exam scores and
C store the result for each student in the array AVG.
C******************************************************************
   20    DO 30 I=1,N
                     AVG(I)=0.4*FINAL(I)+0.3*MID(I)+0.15*(HOME(I)+QUIZ(I))
   30    CONTINUE
C******************************************************************
C Create the new file, but send only the ID number and the
C average.
C******************************************************************
         OPEN(UNIT=4, FILE='AVG', STATUS='NEW')
         DO 40 I=1,N
           WRITE(4,*) I, AVG(I)
   40    CONTINUE
         CLOSE(4)
         CLOSE(9)
         END
```

Supplementary Problems

9.11 Locate the syntax and run-time errors in the following program statements:

(a) OPEN(61, 'TEST.DAT', STATUS=NEW)
(b) OPEN(11)
(c) OPEN(4, FILE='STRESS.DAT')
    CLOSE(4, STATUS='SCRATCH')
(d) OPEN(31, 'STRAIN.DAT', STATUS='NEW')
    READ(31,*) (STRAIN(I), I=1,100)
    CLOSE(31)
(e) OPEN(19, FILE='TEMP.DAT', ACCESS='DIRECT', RECL=40)
    WRITE(19,*) X, Y, Z
(f) OPEN(21, FILE='MATERIAL.DAT')
    READ(21, *, REC=4) X

9.12 Write OPEN statements to accomplish the following:

(a) Open an existing file named 'TEST1' on unit 10
(b) Open a file that previously did not exist. Name it 'TEST2' and use unit 9.
(c) Check to see if the file 'TEST3' has already been opened. If not, then open it as a new file.
(d) Open two files, one named 'BINARY' to store data in binary format and one named 'DATA' to contain the same data in conventional notation.

9.13 The following exercises are designed so that you can find out the limitations or extensions of your Fortran compiler. Run small programs to find out if the following suggestions work. You may also need to consult the documentation for your system.

    (a) Will your system allow you to drop the CLOSE statement? On some compilers, either of the following will work:

```
          OPEN(UNIT=3, FILE='XXXXX', STATUS='NEW')
          WRITE(3,52)
    52    FORMAT(' THIS IS A TEST ')
          CLOSE(3)
or
          OPEN(UNIT=3,FILE='XXXXX',STATUS='NEW')
          WRITE(3,52)
    52    FORMAT(' THIS IS A TEST ')
```

    (b) Some compilers will also allow you to drop the OPEN statement and will give the file a name based on the unit number. For example, if you choose UNIT=11, the compiler will name the file 'FOR011.DAT'. Try running this program segment to see if this option is available.

    (c) What happens on your system if you forget to CLOSE a file? Write a program that reads data from a file, prints the data to the CRT screen, but does not close the file. Now try running the program a second time.

    (d) Does your system allow you to close files manually (through the operating system)?

9.14 Assume that we have a file that contains the following data:

```
11
22
33                    Data file 'INPUT'
44
55
66
<end of file>
```

What are the values of the variables if the file is read with the following program segments? (Assume the file has the attributes UNIT=5, FILE='INPUT', STATUS='OLD'.)

```
(a) READ(5,*)  A,  B,  C
(b) READ(5,*)  A,  B,  C
    REWIND(5)
    READ(5,*)  I,  J
(c) READ(5,*)  A
    READ(5,*)  B
    BACKSPACE(5)
    READ(5,*)  C,  I
```

9.15 Run the following program on your computer to find out how it handles carriage-control characters (or lack of them) in data files. Here is a small program to read the file 'CCC.DAT'.

```
C************************************************************
C Program to see how your computer handles lack of carriage
C control characters in a data file.
C************************************************************
      OPEN(3,FILE='CCC.DAT', STATUS='OLD')
      READ(3,*) X, Y, Z
      CLOSE(3)
      PRINT *, X, Y, Z
```

```
Column 1
↓              'CCC.DAT'

123.456
789.012        947.012
<end of file>
```

9.16 Write a program that will read in at execution time the unit number and the file name of a file to be opened. Then open that file and read in X values until all the data have been read. The file has one numeric value per record with an unknown number of records.

9.17 Write a program that reads values of X from a data file 'COUNTS' and computes the average value, the largest and smallest values, and their positions within the list. Write these values into a new data file STAT.

9.18 Assume that there is a file 'ORDERED' in which the real data are organized in ascending order. Write a program that will read in a new value from the keyboard and insert it into the proper position within the file.

9.19 A data file 'HEART' lists personal data of several thousand people taking part in a medical experiment on heart disease. Each record is organized as follows:

ID Number   Name   Date of Birth   Weight   Height   Cholesterol Level

Write a program that will search the file to match a given name and if the name is found will display all the information in that record. The user is then prompted to enter corrected data.

9.20 Assume that there is a direct access data file 'INVENTORY' which lists the following information about each of the items for sale in a large store:

Stock Number   Description   Unit Price   Number on Hand   Sales This Year

Write a program that will read in all the items and compute the total value of the inventory and the amount of sales for the year.

Answers to Selected Supplementary Problems

9.11 (a) NEW should be inside single quotes (STATUS='NEW').
    (b) No file name is specified. Some compilers may accept this, though.
    (c) A scratch file is not given a name since it is not saved.
    (d) Attempt to read from a file before any data have been written to it causing a run-time error.
    (e) Direct access files require the WRITE command to contain the "REC=" clause.
    (f) If the ACCESS attribute is not specified, Fortran assumes a sequential file. Therefore, the "REC=" clause inside the READ statement is improper since this is used only with direct access files.

9.12 (a) OPEN(UNIT=10, FILE='TEST1', STATUS='OLD')
    (b) OPEN(UNIT=9, FILE='TEST2', STATUS='NEW')
    (c) OPEN(UNIT=2, FILE='TEST3', STATUS='UNKNOWN')
    (d) OPEN(UNIT=1, FILE='BINARY', FORM='UNFORMATTED', STATUS='NEW')
       OPEN(UNIT=2, FILE='DATA', STATUS='NEW')

9.14 (a) Each READ statement reads one record. So the first numeric field (11) is assigned to A, but there are no more fields in that record. Therefore, the next value will come from the next record and will be assigned to B. Similarly, the third value comes from the third line. This results in the assignments: A=11.00000, B=22.00000, and C=33.00000.
    (b) The READ statement assigns the first three values to A, B, and C. Then the file is rewound to the beginning. So when the next READ statement is executed, it will begin with the first two values and assign them to I and J. The result is A=11.00000, B=22.00000, C=33.00000, I=11, and J=22.
    (c) The first READ assigns the first value (11) to A. The second READ assigns the second value (22) to B. The BACKSPACE command will move the pointer from the third record (the next in line) back one record. The next two values (22 and 33) are then assigned to C and I. The result is: A=11.0000, B=22.0000, C=22.0000, and I=33.

9.16
```
C******************************************************************
C Read in the unit number as an integer and the file name as a
C character string. Then open this file and assign the values
C to the array X. We use a conditional loop with an END=
C option in the read statement.
C******************************************************************
```

```
        CHARACTER*20 FILENAME
        REAL X(1000)
        PRINT *, 'Enter file name:'
        READ *, FILENAME
        PRINT *, 'Enter unit number:'
        READ *, IUNIT
        OPEN(UNIT=IUNIT, FILE=FILENAME, STATUS='OLD')
        I=1
        DO WHILE(.TRUE.)
           READ(IUNIT,*,END=20) X(I)
           I=I+1
        END DO
   20   PRINT *, I,' Records were found'
        END
```

9.17
```
C*****************************************************************
C First, open the file and read the values into the array
C X. Note that we may not know in advance the number of records
C in the file, so we need to look for the end-of-file record.
C*****************************************************************
        REAL X(1000), LARGE
        INTEGER POSMAL, POLARG
        OPEN(UNIT=1, FILE='COUNTS', STATUS='OLD')
        N=1
        DO WHILE(.TRUE.)
           READ(1,*,END=20) X(N)
           N=N+1
        END DO
        CLOSE(1)
   20   PRINT *, N,' Records were found'
C*****************************************************************
C Now compute the average of the numbers in the list
C*****************************************************************
        SUM=0.0
        DO 30 I=1, N
           SUM=SUM+X(I)
   30   CONTINUE
        AVG=SUM/N
C*****************************************************************
C Now look for the largest and smallest values and their
C positions.
C*****************************************************************
        SMALL=X(1)
        LARGE=X(1)
        POSMAL=1
        POLARG=1
        DO 40 I=2, N
           IF(X(I) .LT. SMALL) THEN
              SMALL=X(I)
              POSMAL=I
           ENDIF
           IF(X(I) .GT. LARGE) THEN
              LARGE=X(I)
              POLARG=I
           ENDIF
```

```
   40    CONTINUE
C*****************************************************************
C Print out the results (LARGE = the largest value, SMALL = the
C smallest value, POSMAL = position of the smallest value,
C POLARG = position of the largest value).
C*****************************************************************
         OPEN(UNIT=2, FILE='STAT', STATUS='NEW')
                WRITE(2,*) 'Largest value and position=', LARGE, POLARG
                WRITE(2,*) 'Smallest value and position=', SMALL, POSMAL
         CLOSE(2)
         END
```

9.18
```
C*****************************************************************
C Read in the new value from the keyboard.
C*****************************************************************
         REAL Y(1000), Z(1000)
         PRINT *, 'Enter new value for storage in the file:'
         READ *, X
C*****************************************************************
C Open the file and read all the values into the array Y. Then
C find the appropriate position to store the new value. We will
C prepare a new array Z that contains the old values of Y and
C the new value of X.
C*****************************************************************
         OPEN(UNIT=1, FILE='ORDERED', STATUS='OLD')
         N=1
         DO WHILE(.TRUE.)
            READ(1, *, END=20) Y(N)
            N=N+1
         END DO
   20    PRINT *, N,'Records found'
C*****************************************************************
C Find the position for the new value.
C*****************************************************************
         DO 30 I=1, N
            IF(Y(I) .GT. X) THEN
               EXIT
            ELSE
               POS=I
            ENDIF
   30    CONTINUE
C*****************************************************************
C Load Y(1) to Y(POS-1) into Z(1) to Z(POS-1). Load X into
C Z(POS). Finally, load Y(POS) to Y(N) into Z(POS+1) to Z(N+1).
C*****************************************************************
         DO 40 I=1, POS-1
            Z(I)=Y(I)
   40    CONTINUE
         Z(POS)=X
         DO 50 I=POS+1, N+1
   50       Z(I)=Y(I-1)
C*****************************************************************
C Now write the array Z into the old file. Notice that when we
C overwrite a file, the old values are destroyed.
C*****************************************************************
```

```
            DO  60  I=1, N+1
                WRITE(1,*)  Z(I)
    60      CONTINUE
            CLOSE(1)
            END
```

9.19
```
C**********************************************************
C The file must be a direct access file to permit updating. So,
C we will read in the name, open the file, read one record at
C a time, and compare the name to the desired entry. If it
C matches, we stop the search and display the full record. (We
C assume a record length = 63 for convenience.)
C**********************************************************
            CHARACTER NAME*20, PERSON*20, BIRTH*8
            PRINT *, 'Enter the Patient''s Name:'
            READ *, PERSON
            OPEN(UNIT=1, FILE='HEART', ACCESS='DIRECT', RECL=63)
            I=1
            DO WHILE(.TRUE.)
                READ(1,END=20,REC=I) ID,NAME,BIRTH,WEIGHT,HGT,COL
                I=I+1
                IF(NAME .EQ. PERSON) EXIT
            END DO
C**********************************************************
C The patient's record has been found. Print it out.
C**********************************************************
            PRINT *, ID, NAME, BIRTH, WEIGHT, HGT, COL
            PRINT *, 'Enter corrected data:'
            READ *, ID, NAME, BIRTH, WEIGHT, HGT, COL
C**********************************************************
C Now write the corrected data to the file at REC=ID.
C**********************************************************
            WRITE(1,REC=ID) ID, NAME, BIRTH, WEIGHT, HGT, COL
            CLOSE(1)
            STOP 'Changes Made'
    20      STOP 'Patient Entered not in the File'
            END
```

9.20
```
C**********************************************************
C This application works best with a sequential file. Open it
C and read each record one at a time. Multiply the unit price
C by the number on hand and add it to the running total INVEN.
C While we have the record, we will also accumulate the unit
C price times the sales this year value and store it in YRSALE.
C**********************************************************
            CHARACTER DESCRB*20
            INTEGER SALES
            REAL INVEN
            OPEN(UNIT=7, FILE='INVENT', STATUS='OLD')
            INVEN=0.0
            YRSALE=0.0
```

```
       DO WHILE(.TRUE.)
           READ(7,*,END=20) ID, DESCRB, UNIT, NUM, SALES
           INVEN=INVEN+UNIT*NUM
           YRSALE=YRSALE+UNIT*SALES
       END DO
       CLOSE(7)
   20  PRINT *, 'Total Value of Inventory :', INVEN
       PRINT *, 'Total Sales Year-to-date:', YRSALE
       END
```

Index

ABS function, 55
ACCESS= clause, 308, 309–310, 319–320
ACOS function, 55
ACTION= clause, 308, 310–311, 319
A edit descriptor, 71, 79–80, 284
algorithms, 1–2
   (see also examples)
algorithm development, 1–16
ALOG function, 55
ALOG10 function, 55
alternate form of DO loop, 137–138
AMAX function, 55
AMIN function, 55
.AND. operator, 105–107
argument list, 215, 221–222
arguments to a function, 55
arrays
   assignment statements with, 166
   character array, 274–303
   declaration statement, 167–168
   formatting of array output, 187–188
   higher-order arrays, 178–183
   implied DO loops and, 184–187
   in DATA statements, 190–191
   index, 165–167
   in subprograms, 223–225
   limits, 167–168
   lists of data, 168
   manipulating arrays, 168–178
   merging arrays, 202–206
   multidimensional arrays, 178–183
   one-dimensional arrays, 166
   subscript, 165
   subscripted variables, 165–211
ASCII collating sequence, 281
ASIN function, 55
assignment statement, 38, 48–50

ATAN function, 55

BACKSPACE statement, 317–318
BLANK= clause, 308, 311, 319
block IF structure, 107–112
binary search, 176–178
built-in function, 55–56, 215, 286–288
branching operations:
   basic, 7–10
   nesting of, 9
   select construct, 9–10
building blocks of programming:
   sequential executions, 2
   branching operations, 2
   loops, 2

calling statement, 215
carriage control character (CCC), 70–71
case value, 10
character-based library functions, 286–288
character:
   ASCII data set, 281
   data, 274–303
   data set, 42
   data types, 39, 42–43
   EBCDIC data set, 281
   length, 275
character data manipulation, 277–283
CHARACTER statement, 46
closing a file, 304, 316–317
coding, 1–2
collating sequence, 280–282
comments:
   in a flowchart, 19–20
   in programs, 38

9 780070 411555